# Toward a Common Destiny

Willis D. Hawley
Anthony W. Jackson
Editors

# Toward a
# Common
# Destiny

### Improving Race
### and Ethnic Relations
### in America

Jossey-Bass Publishers • San Francisco

Substantial discounts on bulk quantities of Jossey-Bass books are available to corporations, professional associations, and other organizations. For details and discount information, contact the special sales department at Jossey-Bass Inc., Publishers. (415) 433-1740; Fax (415) 433-0499.

For sales outside the United States, please contact your local Paramount Publishing International Office.

Manufactured in the United States of America on Lyons Falls Pathfinder Tradebook. This paper is acid-free and 100 percent totally chlorine-free.

**Library of Congress Cataloging-in-Publication Data**

Toward a common destiny : improving race and ethnic relations in America / Willis D. Hawley and Anthony W. Jackson, editors. — 1st ed.
        p.        cm.
Includes bibliographical references and index.
ISBN 0-7879-0097-4 (alk. paper)
1. United States—Ethnic relations. 2. United States—Race relations.   I. Hawley, Willis D.    II. Jackson, Anthony (Anthony Wells)
E184.A1T68      1995
305.8'00973—dc20                                                                    94-48172

*HB Printing*    10 9 8 7 6 5 4 3 2 1                              FIRST EDITION

# Contents

**Part Three: Effective Strategies for Improving
Race and Ethnic Relations**

# Introduction

# Our Unfinished Task

## Willis D. Hawley

This book seeks to summarize what is known about the sources of racial and ethnic prejudice in the United States and to identify some ways that individuals and organizations can act to reduce intolerance and discrimination and thus render a person's race and ethnicity irrelevant to the determination of his or her chances to live the good life and contribute to the welfare of others. The urgency of this goal is asserted eloquently by Cornel West (1993, p. 4): "There is no escape from our interracial interdependence, yet enforced racial hierarchy dooms us as a nation to collective paranoia and hysteria—the unmasking of any democratic society."

The notion that the people of the United States share a common destiny goes beyond the moral responsibility we have to eliminate discrimination and ensure equal opportunity. The current status of race relations in America weakens the social fabric, undermines the nation's economy, poisons its politics, and denies the opportunity to learn from the richness of its racial and ethnic diversity.

## Where Do We Stand?

After more than a decade during which the issue of race relations has been swept under the rug by governments and virtually ignored by political, religious, educational, and civic leaders, the early 1990s saw a renewal of interest in news magazines, on public television, and among a small number of influential intellectuals. For a brief moment in late 1992, the need to "bring us together" even entered the rhetoric of the presidential campaign.

Almost without exception, the theme of recent reports and commentary on the status of interracial and interethnic relations has been that prejudice and discrimination are widespread and much worse than might have been expected some forty years after the civil rights movement began. Consider, for example, West's assessment: "The paradox of race in America is that our common destiny is more pronounced and more imperiled precisely when our divisions are deeper . . . And, our divisions are growing deeper" (1993, p. 4). Consider, as well, the title of Andrew Hacker's best-selling 1992 book, which succinctly and powerfully summarizes his analysis of a considerable amount of survey and demographic data— *Two Nations: Black and White, Separate, Hostile, and Unequal.* In addition, a report of a nationwide study of college campuses conducted by the People for the American Way (1991) is called *Hate in the Ivory Tower.*

There is no one convincing description of the status of race relations in America. To a large extent, the way an individual assesses race relations depends on where that person lives and on the color of his or her skin. But it seems important to put the question of where we are and where we seem to be going in historical perspective. If we were to conclude that we have been going downhill or even standing still, we would also have to conclude that what has been done to ensure civil rights and improve intergroup relations has had little impact, and that prejudice is so much a part of our society that little can be done. To reach such conclusions is to argue for either inaction or revolution. And to argue thus is to be wrong.

With respect to almost any indicator of racial tolerance among whites, the proportion of adults expressing positive beliefs about persons of color, rejecting traditional stereotypes, and disapproving of discrimination has increased over the last several years. In 1989 the National Academy of Sciences published an extensive report that, among other things, identified positive trends in public opinion related to race relations (Jaynes and Williams, 1989). Studies of the opinions of college students also show increasing opposition to discrimination as well as increasing support for aggressive action by government to end injustices and to promote integration. For example, a clear and growing majority of college freshmen express support for school desegregation and for busing as a strategy for implementing it (Astin and others, 1990).

Opinion surveys are not the only evidence of declining prejudice. Whether the statistics focus on employment in relatively well-paying jobs, on election to public offices, or residential integration, the story they tell is one of progress. Yet many people of color see the progress being made as inadequate, whereas many whites see it as work completed, believing that racial and ethnic discrimination is largely under control.

What about the attitudes and behavior of nonwhites toward whites—are there any discernible trends? Most studies of racial acceptance focus on whites' attitudes and actions toward nonwhites and show that nonwhites are less prejudiced than whites and want more rapid progress. But they also reveal that blacks are more negative than other people of color in their assessment of the progress being made in ending racial and ethnic discrimination in the United States, and that blacks appear to be increasingly skeptical of the willingness of whites to make further progress.

To be sure, the United States has a long way to go in ending racial and ethnic prejudice. But it would be wrong to conclude from this appropriately dire warning about the problems we face that we have made little progress and that the task before us is impossible to accomplish.

## About This Book

This book had its origins in a 1993 meeting held under the auspices of the Common Destiny Alliance (CODA) and with the support of the Carnegie Corporation. (For further information about the CODA and the Carnegie Corporation, see the Appendix). The papers prepared for that meeting were revised as a result of the discussions held then. Subsequently, three additional papers were commissioned. The scholars whose contributions appear in this volume are among the leading behavioral and social scientists doing research related to the improvement of intergroup relations.

Racial and ethnic prejudice and discrimination are rooted deeply in the fact that people of color are disproportionately poor. And poverty, of course, is itself a product of prejudice and discrimination. There is no question that the nation's ability and willingness to end racism are undermined by social and economic inequalities. This book, however, does not address issues related to the creation of jobs, the development of more equitable and effective health and welfare policies, or the redistribution of resources available to schools and local governments that serve large proportions of the nation's poor. Rather, its objective is to reveal the social and developmental influences on beliefs and behavior, and to identify and assess alternative strategies for improving intergroup relations that are within the grasp of individuals, organizations, and institutions.

The book has four parts. Part One deals with the historical and social contexts of race and ethnic relations in the United States and includes a chapter on the status of ethnic conflict in European countries. Part Two examines the developmental processes and social conditions that influence the way individuals come to understand their own racial and ethnic identity and how this understanding, in turn, affects their dispositions toward and interactions with persons whose race or ethnicity is different from their own. Part Three focuses on a variety of strategies for improving intergroup relations and reviews what we know and do not know about their effectiveness. Finally, Part Four consists of two chapters. The first one draws on several previous chapters in order to identify a number of principles that can be used to guide the design and implementation of strategies for reducing prejudice and discrimination by changing policies, practices, and behavior. The last chapter identifies a number of important issues about which further research should be a high priority for those concerned with improving intergroup relations.

## A Five-Part Plan for Action to Reduce Racial and Ethnic Prejudice

If the quality of intergroup relations is a major problem for the nation, why has so little been done to solve it? Perhaps it is because this problem seems so entangled with the concentration of poverty among blacks, Latinos, and many immigrant groups. Or maybe our inaction is a consequence of our frustration over the apparent staying power of racial and ethnic prejudice. Then again, our collective reticence may derive from a belief that we just do not know how to make a difference.

The authors of this book have sought to be rigorously analytical and as accurate as possible in order to facilitate understanding. But the project that has brought them together seeks more than comprehension; it strives, as well, to motivate and direct action. What follows, accordingly, is an overview of the actions that can be taken by individuals and groups to effectively pursue our common destiny.

First, among those with whom we associate, we can work to create an understanding that positive race relations are important and worth working for—specifically, by asserting such beliefs, countering contrary views, and "walking the talk." Similarly, we can tell our leaders that they are doing the right thing when they speak out about eliminating prejudice and discrimination, and that taking this stance earns them our support and the support of those we can influence.

Second, we can learn more about the values and behaviors of people from different races and ethnic groups so that we can correct myths, better interpret one another's actions, and avoid stereotyping people on the basis of their skin color or their ethnicity. We can also learn that significant differences are masked by classifications such as African American, Hispanic, Asian, Native American, or white.

Third, we can recognize and act upon the fact that the most effective way to improve race relations is to provide people with opportunities to learn and work together as equals. Toward this end, we need more neighborhoods, workplaces, religious groups, and schools that reflect the racial and ethnic diversity of our society. Moreover, within each of these situations, interracial and interethnic interactions must be carefully planned and actively encouraged.

Fourth, we can acknowledge that communication and effective interpersonal behavior across racial and ethnic lines require knowledge and skills that many of us do not have. In short, most of us need to learn to behave more productively in intergroup situations. Many race relations programs emphasize appreciation of diversity, sensitivity to differences, and other attitude-formation activities; but such efforts, in themselves, are often ineffective and may even reinforce stereotypes.

Fifth, we need to give one another some slack. Trust among persons of different races, especially when problems surface, is usually in short supply. Not every awkward or painful interracial interaction can be explained in terms of "racial reasoning." Frustration, tension, and feelings of vulnerability often lead us to test others' commitment to and interest in positive intergroup relations. Such tests invariably push us apart rather than bring us together.

## A Common Destiny

Traveling the miles we have yet to go and keeping the promises already made will not be easy. As the nation becomes more diverse racially and ethnically, it is increasingly imperative that we stop agonizing about the evils of racism and intergroup misunderstanding and make it our business to end discrimination and prejudice based on race or ethnicity. As John E. Wideman (1992) has observed, "If we choose to act as though race, class, and gender do not matter, [to] act as if we have not created separate, hostile and warring nations within a nation, we won't survive." Each of us has to choose; no one will do our work for us.

# References

Dey, E. L., Astin, A. W., and Korn, W. E. (1991). *The American Freshman: 25 Year Trends 1966–1990*. Los Angeles, Calif.: Higher Education Research Institute, University of California.

Hacker, A. (1992). *Two Nations: Black and White, Separate, Hostile, and Unequal*. New York: Ballantine Books.

Jaynes, G. D., and Williams, R. M. (1989). *A Common Destiny*. Washington, D.C.: National Academy of Sciences.

People for the American Way. (1991). *Hate in the Ivory Tower*. Washington, D.C.: People for the American Way.

West, C. (1993). *Race Matters*. Boston: Beacon Press.

Wideman, J. E. (1992). "Dead Black Men." *Esquire, 118* (Sept.), 151.

# Acknowledgments

This book would not have been possible without the generous philanthropic support of the Carnegie Corporation. We are also indebted to the many scholars and educators who helped us select the authors who contributed their expertise and insight to this book throughout. In addition, the Lilly Endowment supported the work of a Common Destiny Alliance "consensus panel" whose efforts are reflected in the chapter on design principles for effective intergroup relations strategies. Deborah Curry contributed to the work of the CODA panel. Alma Clayton-Pedersen of the Vanderbilt University's Institute for Public Policy Studies and Connie Braxton of the Carnegie Corporation helped us organize the working conference during which most of the chapters were reviewed and critiqued; they also handled the administrative aspects of this project. Finally, Bonnie Moore and Julia Weinstein provided valuable editorial assistance in preparing the final manuscript for submission to the publisher. All of these folks made this a better book.

February 1995

Willis D. Hawley
College Park, Maryland

Anthony W. Jackson
New York, New York

# Toward a Common Destiny

# Part One

# *The Changing Policy Context*

*Chapter One*

# Schooling and Social Diversity: Historical Reflections

## David Tyack

Issues of social diversity have polarized the politics of education throughout this last generation. The media have focused on a wide gamut of contentious issues, including desegregation, bilingual instruction, prayer in the schools, multicultural curricula, gender policies and practices, separatist Afrocentric academies, common civic and cultural literacy, and the surge of new immigrants coming mostly from Asia and Latin America. But the persistence of an urban "underclass" composed mostly of impoverished people of color makes it clear that the quest for racial justice has fallen far short of its goal. The United States has never been so diverse, it seems, and the challenges facing the schools appear unprecedented.[1]

Policy debate about questions of social diversity has taken some new turns in recent years, but that debate is *not* unprecedented. It draws on a long history of social and political constructions of differences in American society and public schools. Cultural beliefs and educational policies have indeed changed over time, partly in

This chapter is adapted from David B. Tyack "Constructing Differences: Historical Perspectives on Schooling and Social Diversity." *Teachers College Record*, 95 (Fall 1993): 8–34. Used by permission.

response to transformations in society. They have been employed to protect privilege, to mobilize groups to fight subordination, to define and advance group welfare, and to mold what Thomas Bender calls "the public culture."[2]

Political theorist Hannah Arendt has argued that, in the United States, education has played a "different and, politically, incomparably more important role" than elsewhere, in part because of "the role that continuous immigration plays in the country's political consciousness and frame of mind." Attempts to preserve white supremacy and to achieve racial justice have fueled the politics of education for more than a century. The nation declared on its national seal the aim of becoming "The New Order of the Ages" and "One from Many." But how was this to come about? The mottoes expressed an aspiration more than an achievement. Conceptions of race and ethnicity that once were taken for granted as part of the "natural" order in society have become increasingly problematic; indeed, they need to be placed in a comparative and historical framework in order to be fully understood.[3]

It is easier to devise fashionable slogans about diversity in education than to develop coherent and just policies. The First Amendment lays down a rough principle to follow with respect to church and state in public schools. In practice, however, the establishment clause—that the government shall not establish religion or prohibit its free exercise—has proven difficult to interpret. Because of a long history of explicit racial discrimination, the courts have come to regard race as a "suspect category" in distinguishing among people in public schools (though this principle, too, has become blurred in practice). On other issues of social diversity in education the Constitution and its interpreters are either silent or ambiguous. There is no explicit separation of ethnic group and state, no special court of ethnic appeals, no guarantee of proportionate representation of social groups in school politics. One of the most important forms of social difference, economic class, has been blurred by the myth that the United States is a "classless" society; as Benjamin DeMott argues, this "myth of social sameness" has disguised the reality of vast economic inequality and thus perpetuated social wrongs.[4]

Leaders have often based policies concerning social diversity in education on either-or polemics and patchwork solutions designed to satisfy changing coalitions of power among contending groups. There is no more important question in educational policy than how to deal with social diversity, but discourse on this subject has all too frequently resembled photographs that are not so much underdeveloped as overexposed.[5]

As Paula Fass says, "The shape of American education in the twentieth century . . . is crucially related to the problems associated with American diversity." The historical conflicts, compromises, retreats, advances, and contradictions evident in the schools' encounters with social differences and similarities persist into the present and pose an intellectual as well as a practical challenge to those who seek social justice today: Amid the welter of programs for dealing with social diversity today, how is school reform to be grounded in sound policy? How might educational goals and practices do justice, in John Higham's formulation, to "individualistic rights and group solidarity"?[6]

One way to clarify such issues is to probe not only the comparative histories of social constructions of "race" and "ethnicity" but also the educational policies linked to these conceptions of diversity. Comparison can illuminate the degree to which boundaries between different kinds of groups are porous and can suggest ways in which individuals may experience multiple identities in different social settings. Studying cultural constructions of difference over time shows how they have varied in response to shifting alignments of political power and changing climates of opinion.[7]

## Social Constructions of Diversity

Conceptions of social differences often spin complex meanings from supposedly natural distinctions among people. "The problem with this language of difference," Michael Katz observes, "is both philo-

sophic and practical. We assume that verbal distinctions reflect natural or inherent qualities of people. . . . For reasons of convenience,
power, or moral judgment, we select from among a myriad of traits
and then sort people, objects, and situations into categories which
we then treat as real." Invidious distinctions often infuse the categories that divide people into groups. And such divisiveness creates
a dilemma, notes Martha Minow: "How to overcome the past hostilities and degradations of people on the basis of group differences
without employing . . . those very differences." We may deplore and
dismiss, for example, the notion that some "races" are inferior, but
in order to correct the educational injustices buttressed by that concept, we must pay attention to the way racism has structured opportunity and exploitation.[8]

The scientifically invalid impulse to classify humans into different "races" has been part of a changing discourse and practice of
power and subordination. However arbitrary such distinctions may
be—as in the notion that "Negroes" and "whites" are essentially
different—notions of "race" come to seem real and thus shape
behavior. Like white women, black men earn only about three-fifths
of the income of white men. Concepts of racial inferiority form
what Horace Mann Bond called "a crazy-quilt world of unreality"
in a society that proclaimed equality, opportunity, and democracy
as goals while it "brutalized, degraded, and dehumanized" African
Americans "by every instrument of the culture." During World War
II, for example, the racial caste system of the South made it seem
natural that white Nazi prisoners of war on their way to a prison
camp in the South should be allowed inside a "whites only" dining
room in a railroad station, but that their black guards should not.[9]

Notions of "ethnicity" as applied to European immigrants have
likewise changed over time and served the interests of different
groups. Ardent "Americanizers" defined newcomers as strangers, as
potentially dangerous "aliens" who must become "naturalized" and
accept the values and leadership of whites born in this country—
the so-called "native-born." Some defined "ethnic" difference as
genetic; others, as cultural. By contrast, some defenders of cultural

pluralism urged the retention of "old-world traits" intact as if these were unchanging heirlooms instead of constantly changing cultural practices. But neither perspective captured the constant cultural interaction that occurred in a society of permeable boundaries in which cultural influences moved in every direction. This interaction altered both the newcomers, who discovered their "otherness" in the process of immigration and in the self-consciousness of becoming "American," and the American-born who lived in a culture of kaleidoscopic variety.[10]

In a society so socially diverse as the United States, it is not surprising that major controversies have erupted in public education over the twin themes of unity and diversity. Bender argues that continuing contests of diverse groups for "legitimacy and justice" have created this public culture and established "our common life as a people and as a nation." It is essential to understand what has been excluded from as well as included in this public culture. We need to ask "Why have some groups and some values been so much—or so little—represented in public life and in mainstream culture and schooling at any given moment in our history?" "Understanding our peoplehood," Bender insists, "demands not an assumption of sameness but, rather, a relational sense of the differences that mark and make our society."[11]

The "Americanization" of European immigrants illustrates this complex interaction. Some educators used draconian measures to assimilate the newcomers, while others, believing that coercion was counterproductive, tried to graft the branches of many cultures onto the trunk of Anglo-American society. Meanwhile, different groups of immigrants reacted to "Americanization" in a variety of ways. Some resisted it as a threat to their core values and institutions. Some welcomed it as a doorway into opportunity. Many "hyphenated Americans" saw no inconsistency between being earnest patriots and retaining strong immigrant loyalties; they formed, for example, ethnic chapters of veterans' groups such as the American Legion. "Europeans" were hardly a homogeneous group; they may have had "whiteness" in common, but they were typically quite conscious of ethnic splits and of their different political allegiances and economic status. Only by looking at groups in reciprocal relation to one another can we avoid either the exaggerations of imposition and victimization or the romantic view of ethnic self-preservation.[12]

An approach that looks at reciprocal relations between groups avoids two oversimplifications in educational history: that elites have successfully imposed their will on subordinate groups or, conversely, that socially diverse groups have managed to preserve autonomy as cultural islands in a particularistic society. Not only were the cultural boundaries between groups usually porous, but also any one person—say, an African American, middle-class, Baptist woman teacher—had a mixture of identities that were salient in different ways in different contexts. The groups composing American society have shaped one another as they interacted, but in influencing educational policies for dealing with diversity they did not compete on a level playing field.

## Educators' Policies for Dealing with Diversity

Most of the prominent policy makers in public education and most administrators of public school systems have been born in the United States white, prosperous, male, and Protestant. As "mainstream" leaders, they have generally taken their own beliefs about social diversity for granted, at least until these cultural constructions were challenged politically. They did not think of themselves simply as one group among many—nonbrown, nonfemale, nonimmigrant, nonpoor—but instead regarded their own values and interests as the standard. The "others," however—immigrants, African Americans, Catholics, Jews, females, Asians, and similar groups—have hardly been content to exist as the wax on which leaders stamped their educational imprint.[13]

Differences of ethnicity and race have always been present, though not equally salient, as public issues during different periods in our educational history. In the nineteenth century, for example, ethnic conflicts over schooling—usually mixed with religion—tore communities apart. In the Progressive Era, northern policy makers mostly ignored African Americans but agonized over the assimilation of European immigrants of the working class. Issues of race agitated the politics of schooling in the generation following the *Brown* decision in 1954. Although class conflict often permeated these controversies, the debates were rarely formulated openly in class terms.[14]

Over the years, educators have proposed a wide array of solutions to cope with—or ignore—social diversity. Eight verbs capture the nature of these strategies:

- *Discriminate*. The classic examples of discrimination are the deliberate relegation of blacks to separate and grossly unequal schools and the denial of schooling to "Mongolians" (Chinese and Japanese immigrant children) in California.

- *Separate*. In its effects the strategy of separation is similar to that of discrimination except that it may proceed from benign intent, as when boys and girls are separated into vocational classes supposedly tailored to their needs. "Special education," in the form of classes for physically or mentally handicapped children, has largely meant separate schooling, as its name implies.

- *Assimilate*. The effort to eradicate ethnic differences, to shape pupils from European immigrant families to a common "American" mold, has been a deliberate state policy for more than a century. Today, fear of a polyglot and alien population inspires attacks on bilingual classes and certain forms of multicultural curriculum.

- *Desegregate*. In the past, African Americans, Asians, American Indians, and other people of color were frequently not thought to be assimilable. They were either entirely banned from schools or segregated. Desegregation may thus be understood as an attempt to secure full citizenship and educational rights for these excluded groups. The initiative to secure these rights usually proceeded from the excluded "races" themselves, as in the civil rights and protest movements that have emerged since the *Brown* decision in 1954.

- *Ignore* differences. This strategy was, and still is, a commonly expressed value of those who believe that schools should be color-blind, class-blind, gender-blind, and neutral with respect to ethnoreligious differences. In practice, however, such neutrality is difficult if not impossible to achieve, for schooling is intrinsically value-laden and there are vast differences in power, wealth, and income between groups.

- *Compensate*. In order to make up for some real or presumed "lack" or need, educators have often given special help to certain groups. For example, early in the century New York offered "steamer classes" to recent immigrant children who needed a crash course in English. And in the 1960s much of compensatory education was based on a theory that schools should correct the faulty socialization that poor children supposedly received at home.

- *Celebrate*. Advocates of "intercultural education" and similar forms of ethnic pluralism have proposed that schools teach all students to appreciate the contributions of all social groups to the forming of the nation, in the belief that America is a nation enriched by the contribution of many peoples. This strategy, based on social psychology, sought to lessen prejudice and to give marginalized groups a sense of belonging to the larger society.

- *Preserve*. Advocates of this position believe that public schools should actively seek to maintain differences between groups. Thus some proponents of bilingual/bicultural education argue that schools should preserve ethnic differences, others want an Afrocentric curriculum and separate schooling for blacks, and still others want instruction that will perpetuate distinctions between female and male. This version of the "revolution of rights"—in which *groups* as well as individuals have rights—would seek to use the state (in the form of public schools) to preserve, not attempt to break down, boundaries between groups.

These strategies for dealing with group differences have often overlapped and are rarely so crisp as the verbs might suggest. In formulating or carrying out policies on social diversity, educators have been both reactive and proactive. They were not free agents, for they had to operate within a public zone of consent; but they also sought professional consensus about how to deal with differences. Law and influential public opinion constrained decisions. State legislation as the legal arm of powerful racial caste system of the South, for example, decreed that schools be racially segregated, while the Supreme Court in 1954 ordained racial desegregation and the powerful civil rights movement pressed to enforce that decision. For most of the twentieth century, politicians and the native-born middle class have expected the schools to assimilate immigrants (though professional leeway increasingly characterized the methods by which that purpose was accomplished).

Whether choosing to ignore differences or to compensate for them—the two most common liberal policies in the 1950s—educators worked within a powerful ideology of individualism that, at base, diminished the lasting significance of group membership. Policy makers in public education were working within an institution that had a distinctive character and set of traditions. They were dealing with children and youth who were thought to be uniquely malleable. They inherited a conception of the common school as an agency for preparing the young equitably for the contests of later life. They wanted schools to be "above politics." Both the Protestant-republican ideology of the nineteenth century and the educational science of the twentieth tended to stress *individual* differences as more important than *group* differences. Hence the leaders of public education often resisted thinking about differences of power and culture between social groups when they devised educational programs and policies. To the degree that they were aware of inequalities, liberal educators tended to focus on the prejudice of the individual as an attribute to be changed by appropriate instruction, rather than seeing discrimination as a form of group subordination and supremacy.[15]

Psychology, the academic discipline most influential in the field of education, has reflected and reinforced individualism by using the person as the chief unit of analysis. With this way of seeing, which boasts the label "scientific," educators have often portrayed differences between students—in "intelligence," interests, temperament, or likely social destiny, for example—as characteristics of individuals rather than as products of class or culture. They have considered it their duty to differentiate the curriculum to match the presumed needs of individuals with different abilities, interests, and likely vocations. This apparent individualization, however, has blurred the actual group impact of education. Though theoretically they have adapted schooling to individuals, in practice educators have also created tracks and niches in schools that have tended to segregate pupils by class, gender, and racial or ethnic background.[16]

Despite some important exceptions, educators have rarely sought to preserve islands of cultural difference or to match instruction to the cultures that students brought to their classrooms. As Michael Olneck has argued, even when school officials sympathetically recognized group differences and pursued apparently pluralistic strategies—as in intercultural or multicultural curricula—they usually wanted the final product to be the autonomous, prejudice-free individual, the citizen of what Higham calls the "Great Community," the modernized free agent who escaped from, and chose not to employ politically, a sense of collective group identity.[17]

Although educational leaders have endorsed this ideal of the autonomous individual, they have actually dealt differently with various groups. For example, educators were eager to sweep the children of European immigrants into public schools and to teach them, as the New York superintendent of schools put it in 1918, "an appreciation of the institutions of this country [and] absolute forgetfulness of all obligations or connections with other countries because of descent or birth." By contrast, educational leaders rarely protested when blacks were consigned to segregated and grossly underfunded schools. To explore how constructions of social diversity affected different groups I now turn to two categories of diversity: white ethnic groups and race.[18]

## White Ethnic Groups

In 1891 leaders in the National Education Association (NEA) declared that all children should be compelled to attend schools taught in English. They feared that "foreign influence has begun a system of colonization with a purpose of preserving foreign languages and traditions and proportionately of destroying distinctive Americanism." Demanding compulsory Americanization, one educator asserted that "when the people established this government they had a certain standard of intelligence and morality"; at an earlier time, Americans could assume "that an intelligent and moral people will conform to the requirements of good citizenship." By the 1890s, he warned, this outlook could no longer be taken for granted: "People have come here who are not entitled to freedom in the same sense as those who established this government." It was unthinkable "to lower this idea of intelligence and morality to the standard" of the newcomers.[19]

The NEA leaders spoke during a transitional time when elites were seeking to draw sharp contrasts between the "old" immigrants from northwestern Europe, who presumably were easily assimilated to an "American" mold, and the "new" from southeastern Europe, who presumably did not fit the native pattern of citizenship. By then the immigrants pouring into American cities were chiefly Italians, Poles, and Russians. Most of them were Catholic or Jewish. Already apparent in the NEA discussion were certain central themes in the nativist construction of ethnic difference that would dominate much public discourse about immigrant education for the next thirty years: that "foreign colonies" were forming; that the newcomers were inferior in intelligence and morality to those who preceded them; and that their children must be compelled to attend school, learn English, and be deliberately inculcated with American political and cultural values.

In the 1890s a patriotic colonel in New York City invented the Pledge of Allegiance to inculcate a common loyalty through what would become a familiar school ritual. Social scientists were beginning to classify European "races" (what today would be called nationality groups) and to rank them on a scale of inferiority and superiority. And some politicians and pundits were starting to insist that the nation could be saved only by excluding, or severely limiting, immigration from the offending nations. They began a campaign that would result in federal immigration-restriction laws in 1921 and 1924.[20]

By 1909, 58 percent of students in the thirty-seven largest American cities had foreign-born parents. No longer, thought reformers, could schools go about business as usual. It was necessary to pass effective compulsory-attendance laws and to catch all the newcomer children in the net. The child was coming to belong more to the state and less to the parents, leading educator Ellwood P. Cubberley believed, and the state's interest and duty was to educate the child to be an American. Although a separation of church and state existed at least in theory, there was to be no separation of ethnicity and state, no bill of rights for social diversity. Underlying most attempts at "Americanization," as Michael Olneck has pointed out, was a "symbolic delegitimation of collective ethnic identity"—and this delegitimation became deliberate state policy.[21]

Reformers disagreed not so much about the goal of assimilation as about the best means of accomplishing it. Some urged a sharp-edged intervention: In order to assimilate such a motley collection of humanity, schools should drive a wedge between students and their parental culture and language, thereby assimilating the second generation. Humanitarian reformers who knew immigrant families firsthand—for example, settlement house workers and child labor inspectors—recognized the pain this confrontational strategy could bring. They wanted to give children health care, free lunches, and counseling, and they sought to better match schools to the cultural backgrounds of immigrants so that assimilation could be transitional rather than abrupt.[22]

The outbreak of World War I brought to a boil nativist anxiety about "foreign colonies" and a potential fifth column of unassimilated aliens within the nation. "By 1916," writes John McClymer, "cultural diversity had come to be defined as a national crisis." The Red Scare and nativist organizations kept paranoia alive well into the 1920s. Employers, churches, federal and state bureaus, patriotic associations, and many other organizations joined forces with public schools to eradicate "hyphenism" among foreign-born adults and to ensure that their children were super-patriots. John Dewey attacked this frenzy for conformity in 1916 when he said that "such terms as Irish American or Hebrew American or German American are false terms because they seem to assume something which is already in existence called American, to which the other factory may be externally hitcht [sic] on. The fact is, the genuine American, the typical American, is himself a hyphenated character."[23]

Groups like the American Legion, the American Bar Association, and the Daughters of the American Revolution pressured dozens of states to pass laws prescribing the teaching of American history and the Constitution. Although only one state required the teaching of "citizenship" in 1903, by 1923 thirty-nine did so. The National Security League lobbied to ban the teaching of German and to prescribe super-patriotic instruction. Thanks in part to its efforts, thirty-three states mandated that all teachers pass a test on the Constitution in order to be certified. By 1923 thirty-five states had enacted legislation that made English the only language of instruction in public schools. In Oregon a year earlier, the Ku Klux Klan, which had made the little red schoolhouse a symbol of Americanism, lobbied successfully for a law mandating that all children attend public schools.[24]

Anything foreign was suspect. In New York City, schoolchildren who went into the tenements to sell bonds during World War I were instructed to report adults whose loyalty was dubious. The campaign to define "American" in a narrow conservative mold and to enforce conformity of thought and deed among immigrants outraged many ethnic leaders, much of the ethnic press, and a number of U.S.-born liberals. Despite threats and coercion, only a small minority of adult immigrants enrolled in Americanization classes, and those who did rarely completed the course.[25]

In reaction to the hard-edged Americanizers, a few writers called for ethnic self-preservation. In 1924, for example, Horace M. Kallen proposed "a democracy of nationalities" in which all groups would enhance "the selfhood which is inalienable in them, and for the realization of which they require 'inalienable' liberty." Kallen believed that culture was "ancestrally determined" rather than an interactive and constantly changing set of practices: "Men may change their clothes, their politics, their wives, their religion, their philosophies, to a greater or lesser extent; they cannot change their grandparents." Public schools, he thought, should attempt not to stamp out but, rather, to preserve ethnic "self-realization through the perfection of men according to their kind."[26]

The policies of total ethnic preservation or total assimilation bore little relation to the everyday lives of immigrant families, whose cultural practices blended the old and the new in kaleidoscopic ways. The newcomers were extremely heterogeneous in economic class, formal schooling, religion, economic skills, political experience, and cultural and familial patterns. No stereotype of "the immigrant" could capture such diversity. Some immigrants saw the public school as a gateway into economic opportunity. Others played down education and instead wanted their children to work to contribute to the family's collective long climb out of poverty. Ethnic and religious communities built their own institutions—churches, clubs, mutual benefit societies, and political organizations—as mediating structures that eased adaptation to American life while preserving valued traditions. The children of immigrants

often learned American ways most powerfully not from teachers but
from peers intolerant of cultural differences. Aspirations and alienation criss-crossed the lives of immigrant families—people only
dimly understood by many of the educators who sought to assimilate them.[27]

The frenzy of nativism during World War I and its aftermath
turned "Americanization" into yet another pedagogical specialty,
particularly for adult educators and writers of civics texts. Public
schools became accountable for producing patriots. A good proportion of the experts in "Americanization," however, deplored para-
noid ideology and harsh methods. After laws in 1921 and 1924
restricted immigration, educators could go about assimilating the
second generation at a less frenetic pace. Social scientists began to
portray assimilation as a long-term and complex intergenerational
process. "In the eyes of many liberals," Nicholas V. Montalto writes,
"the Americanization movement epitomized all that was wrong in
the American attitude and policy toward the immigrant: the bank-
ruptcy of racism and chauvinism, the tendency to blame the immigrant for domestic social problems, and the failure of coercion."[28]

These liberal professionals, many of whom were second-generation immigrants themselves, believed that attacks solidified ethnic
groups rather than dissolving them. Denigrating the language and
cultures of students' parents, they argued, split apart families and created an alienated second generation that was neither foreign nor
American. Increasingly, they argued that a more tolerant, slow-paced
approach would produce better results than high-pressure assimilation. They still thought that the public schools should "Americanize"
pupils, but they wanted transitional programs that taught tolerance
for diversity and preached the doctrine that the United States was a
composite of the contributions of many nations.[29]

Many schools and other organizations serving immigrants staged
pageants, dances, plays, and ethnic feasts that stressed the "gifts"
given by immigrants to American society. They celebrated differences while ultimately working toward assimilation—a strategy of
gradual transition rather than forced Americanization. In the 1920s

and 1930s, some progressive educators experimented with forms of cross-cultural learning. Polish pupils in Toledo, Ohio, for example, studied their parents' history and culture; students in Neptune, New Jersey, created ethnic family trees and learned the history of their ancestors; in Santa Barbara, California, pupils prepared exhibits on Chinese art, Scandinavian crafts, and Pacific cultures; and Mexican children in Phoenix, Arizona, attended a class, taught in Spanish, on Mexican history and culture.[30]

The best-articulated version of this early form of pluralism in education appeared in the 1930s in the "intercultural education movement" led by Rachel Davis Dubois, a Quaker and former teacher. In 1924 she inaugurated, in Woodbury High School in southern New Jersey, a series of student assemblies on the achievements of different ethnic groups, pioneering a practice that was to become a hallmark of her career. As she expanded her work, she enlisted powerful allies: progressive educators at Teachers College, Columbia, leaders of ethnic organizations, and social scientists concerned with intergroup relations.[31]

Although this was a disparate coalition, most of the activists in the intercultural education movement agreed on some basic goals. They wanted to dispel prejudices and stereotypes that might trigger a new burst of nativism and intergroup violence during the hard times of the Great Depression and, later, the turmoil of World War II. They were concerned about what Louis Adamic called "Thirty Million New Americans," the youthful second generation suspended between two worlds, described by sociologist Robert Park as "footloose, prowling and predacious." They believed that an appreciation for the traditions of the parents would bridge the family gap and help this second generation find a productive adjustment to American society. And they concurred that all Americans, those "on the hill" as well as those "across the tracks," needed better knowledge of each other in order to establish social harmony. By "cultural democracy" they meant fair play for all groups, self-respect, and appreciation for diversity.[32]

Dubois and key supporters of the intercultural education movement disagreed about an important strategy, however, as Montalto has documented. She thought that ethnic groups should be studied in separate units rather than be mixed together. Only in this manner, she thought, would children of immigrants and minorities be able to acquire a positive self-conception and thereby cure "the alienation, rootlessness, and emotional disorders afflicting the second generation." Psychic strength, she believed, would result from strong positive identification with one's ethnic group.[33]

Influential colleagues in the movement dissented, especially members of the Progressive Education Association and many of the social scientists associated with intercultural education. One critic dismissed Dubois's argument about self-esteem as "compensatory idealized tradition," and many were worried that the separate approach would increase, not diminish, group conflict and thereby solidify ethnic islands. On the eve of World War II, a time of heightened concern about national unity, two superintendents said that Dubois's curriculum would "arouse in the thinking of so-called minority groups an undesirable emphasis upon their own importance and a determination to insist upon their own rights." What they wanted was an intercultural strategy that would use psychological methods to preserve civic peace, not mobilize dissidents to secure their rights.[34]

Olneck has observed that most educators—the hard-line Americanizers and the interculturalists alike—distrusted collective ethnic identities. In civics texts and the writings of the interculturalists, he has identified an underlying ideology of individualism and an ideal of including all people, as individuals, in a greater unity called American society. The cure for group conflict was understanding and appreciation; over time the result would be the inclusion of members of all groups in the mainstream of society as autonomous individuals. Oppression became reduced to stereotyping, and separate ethnic identity was to be dissolved as painlessly as possible.[35]

Professional educators founded and led the intercultural education movement. Although it enjoyed some support from various ethnic organizations and individuals, it did not emerge from the immigrant grass roots. By contrast, much of the energy behind "multicultural education" in recent times stems from the demands of African Americans, Hispanics, and other subordinated groups. Some activists saw that curricular change could go well beyond the inclusion of a few "contributions"; knowledge of how the group was victimized and a better understanding of its internal history could mobilize people in groups, not as individuals, to overcome subordination. Other activists saw ethnic studies and bilingual/bicultural education as a way of preserving the distinctive cultures of groups, rather than as a step toward cultural assimilation.[36]

Thus a competing construction of pluralism began to emerge, one that suggested a goal of equality of groups as opposed to equality of individuals. It demanded a new definition of the public culture that did not simply celebrate cultural differences and then go on to prize a core of common values based on middle-class American individualism. The new version of pluralism was explicitly political; it challenged not just the traditional academic canon but also the entrenched interests that had sustained racism. Not surprisingly, this strategy has aroused far more controversy than did earlier forms of intercultural education.[37]

### Race

There are sharp contrasts between the history of the education of white immigrants and that of people of color—groups such as African Americans, Japanese, and Chinese—who were categorized as members of "inferior races." Although some policy makers wanted to exclude European immigrants from this category, most believed them to be assimilable, insisting that it was the duty of educators to turn them as soon as possible into American citizens who shared similar rights and cultural characteristics. Relatively few educators, however, followed the lead of intercultural reformers like Rachel Dubois, who demanded a frontal assault on racism in both school and society.

People of color often had to fight simply to gain access to public education and frequently had to build and staff their own schools. In the South after the Civil War, for example, African Americans mobilized to educate their people. When whites gained control of public schools in the South, partly by disenfranchising blacks, they designed an educational system calculated to subordinate African Americans, to cramp them under a rigid job ceiling, and to deny them the rights of citizens.[38]

Exclusion and segregation also characterized whites' treatment of "Mongolians." Congress banned Chinese immigrants, and some states, such as California, deprived Chinese and Japanese of many of the rights of citizenship, including the opportunity to send their children to public schools. Quintessential "strangers," these Asians were, like blacks, defined by their descent and identified by their physical characteristics. Whites feared them as competitors for jobs, stereotyped them in vicious ways, and thought them incapable of ever becoming "Americans." When Asian groups formed their own supportive institutions and clustered in enclaves, they were thought to be clannish. Isolated and feared as a domestic fifth column, Japanese Americans were herded into detention centers during World War II at the very time when interculturalists were insisting that racial and ethnic discrimination was un-American.[39]

Another group that faced severe discrimination on grounds of color, but not only for that reason, comprised the children of Mexican immigrants. They occupied an ambiguous "racial" status in a nation that had drawn sharp lines between "whites" and "Negroes." In Texas, as a consequence of the 1930 *Salvatierra* decision, persons of Mexican descent were declared members of the "white race" (as distinct from African Americans, who were totally segregated from whites in that state), while in California that year the attorney general declared them to be "Indians" and hence subject to school segregation. But even where they were legally "white," legal decrees and the conventional wisdom of educators justified separate or different schooling on the grounds that they had distinctive "needs" and "traits." They were poor and often migratory; they spoke Spanish, not English; and they scored low on tests oriented to middle-class Anglos.[40]

Families of Mexican descent, usually impoverished and with little political power, were used as cheap labor when needed and deported when they were not. Denied political power, they had little influence over the schooling of their children. In Texas in 1928, about 40 percent of Mexican children did not attend school, and of those who did, almost half were in the first grade. Educators frequently segregated them, assumed that they needed only a minimal education, and devoted few resources to their instruction. A Texas superintendent explained why:

> Most of our Mexicans are of the lower class. They transplant onions, harvest them, etc. The less they know about everything else, the better contented they are. . . . If a man has very much sense or education either, he is not going to stick to this kind of work. So you see it is up to the white population to keep the Mexican on his knees in the onion patch.[41]

In fact, if not in law, Mexicans were often treated in schools as a separate "race."

The cultural construction of "ethnic" difference was fundamentally different from that of "race." The racial ideology of white supremacy defined people of color as non-assimilable, ineradicably different, and not, therefore, full citizens. An elaborate set of racist beliefs justified segregation, political subordination, hostile and demeaning stereotypes, and economic exploitation of people of color. To be born white was to have powerful advantages in the political and economic system and to dominate the public culture.[42]

How did white educational leaders respond to "the Negro problem"? This question is hard to answer, in part because of widespread silence on the issue. Educators talked a lot about assimilation of immigrants but little about the systematic discrimination against blacks. In addition, strategies for educating blacks differed by region, by time, by individual. In the South it was only the rare and coura-

geous white educator who challenged the caste system in education, so embedded was white supremacy within society. Fearful of
alienating its southern members, the National Educational Association did not desegregate most of its southern branches until the
1960s (though the organization had long endorsed better "intergroup relations").[43]

In the North, African Americans often faced less blatant but
still powerful prejudice and institutional racism. The "science" of
education, on which many educators relied in making decisions
about students, was riddled with racist assumptions. Culturally
biased IQ tests, whose defects were magnified by racist interpretations, seemed to prove the mental inferiority of African Americans
and to justify relegating them to nonacademic tracks. "Realistic"
views of the job market impelled counselors to steer blacks into
manual work. And social differences that were the product of discrimination and poverty became validated as the way things "naturally" were. It is thus not surprising that when Cubberley classified
library books on Negroes, he put them on the shelf next to those
on the "education of special classes," a category that encompassed
the blind, "retarded," and "crippled."[44]

Some individual educators and organizations did attack racism
in education. The Intercultural Education Bureau, for example,
sought to bring about greater understanding between blacks and
whites. The favored approach was the educational strategy of changing prejudicial attitudes rather than mounting political and legal
attacks on the institutional structures that held African Americans
down. But it is probable that only a small minority of white educational leaders from 1890 to 1954 openly confronted the racism
embedded in American society and its system of public education.[45]

Blacks themselves, allied with this small minority of white educators and activists in other fields, took the lead in fighting the educational discrimination that was buttressed by the cultural construction of the "Negro race." Voteless in the South and pushed to
the periphery in the North, blacks faced a cruel dilemma: to accept
segregation was to ratify their status as noncitizens and to send their

children to schools that were grossly unequal; but to enroll their children in desegregated white-dominated schools often meant denying teaching jobs to blacks, exposing their children to prejudiced whites, and failing to instill the self-respect that came from studying their own history and culture. W.E.B. Du Bois, the brilliant spokesman for social justice for African Americans, argued at various times for both strategies.[46]

Horace Mann Bond recalled that, in 1934, "racial segregation appeared to be an immutable feature of the American social order." Twenty years later, however, came the *Brown* decision of the U.S. Supreme Court banning de jure segregation. Support on the part of whites, meanwhile, came primarily not from educators but from what then would have seemed unlikely quarters, the federal government and the U.S. Army. Fass argues that "the New Deal's educational programs exposed and were attentive to the educational needs of black Americans in a wholly unprecedented way." Likewise, the results of draft tests during World War II revealed gross inequities in black education, particularly in the South.[47]

The New Deal did not have a coherent educational or racial policy, and black schools in the South remained impoverished and segregated in the 1930s. But some activist New Dealers did find ways to assist African Americans educationally through programs of employment and relief such as the National Youth Administration (NYA), the Works Progress Administration, and the Civilian Conservation Corps (even though such programs were frequently segregated). These experiments later served as precedents for 1960s programs in the War on Poverty (Lyndon B. Johnson had been a star NYA administrator in Texas during the depression).[48]

When World War II arrived and acute manpower shortages occurred, the legacy of neglect of black education became apparent. About twice as many blacks as whites were rejected for the military, almost always because they failed "to meet minimum educational requirements." As a consequence, proportionally more whites were drafted than blacks. In response, the Army mounted a massive remedial literacy program to counteract the starvation diet of schooling that had beset southern blacks for decades.[49]

By 1946 the National Association for the Advancement of Colored People (NAACP) had attracted nearly 450,000 members and was pressing the series of educational desegregation cases that culminated in the *Brown* decision of 1954. Even before *Brown*, African Americans had glimpsed an opportunity to use schooling as a way to become integrated as full citizens in a polity that had excluded them. But the dilemma of segregation persisted, as W.E.B. Du Bois declared shortly after the court spoke: blacks knew "what their children must suffer [in desegregated schools] for years from southern white teachers, from white hoodlums who sit beside them and under school authorities from janitors to superintendents who despise them." African Americans, he wrote, could lose the opportunity to study their own history of resistance and achievement and "eventually surrender race solidarity and the idea of American Negro culture to the concept of world humanity, above race and nation. This is the price of liberty. This is the cost of oppression."[50]

At first, blacks bore the major burden of enforcing their own constitutional rights. Through sit-ins, demonstrations, boycotts, and strikes in countless local communities, they challenged the old racial order. The battles brought slow progress: a decade after *Brown*, 91 percent of southern African American children were still attending all-black schools. Progress in desegregation picked up momentum in the South in the late 1960s as courts and the Civil Rights Act of 1965 increasingly put the weight of the federal government against de jure segregation and as blacks successfully pressed for the vote.[51]

Desegregation almost always meant opening white schools to blacks, not the reverse. One result in the South was the wholesale firing of black principals and the loss of black schools as a center of African American solidarity, as Du Bois had predicted. The overwhelming majority of African Americans indicated in polls that they favored desegregation, in part because it was so tied to their rights as citizens, especially in the South. They also knew that black schools had far fewer resources than white schools; perhaps if white children—as hostages—studied alongside black children, the latter might finally receive a similar education. But in northern cities many African Americans, dissatisfied with the glacial pace of desegregation, decided to push for their own community-controlled schools in which black staff would predominate and their children could study black culture. If they were going to continue to be defined by their "racial" status, then they, and not whites, should be in charge of their children's education.[52]

On the surface, this stance conflicted with the color-blind ideology of *Brown* and of those white and black liberals who supported racial integration. Underneath both the desegregation and community control strategies, however, was a common aim of African Americans, despite the diversity among them: to achieve greater power over the education of their children and thus over their future in a society where institutional racism, though not the older version of a legalized system of caste, was still a powerful force.[53]

In the last generation, when black activists pushed for an Afrocentric curriculum, they often departed from the psychological model of white professional educators who wanted to promote social harmony by showing the "contributions" of all groups to a common society, thereby lessening prejudice. Many African American school reformers have used a political model instead. They have wanted a black-centered curriculum that could mobilize their people to change the circumstances of their lives by understanding how they had been victimized and by setting their own group goals. As we have seen, W.E.B. Du Bois had thought in 1954 that blacks might "eventually surrender race solidarity and the idea of American Negro culture to the concept of world humanity, above race and nation." The persistence of racism, however, continued to make this seem a distant and ambiguous goal.[54]

## Reflections on Education and Social Diversity

Underneath the surface of much discourse on social diversity in education lie two contrasting points of view. One assumes a basic similarity among individuals regardless of group affiliation (a variant of this approach holds that people may be initially quite different but are capable of becoming the same if properly instructed). The other stresses basic differences between groups. Each contains germs of truth but also displays serious flaws both in its description of social reality and in its prescription of social policy.

The common-school reformers of the nineteenth century believed that the right kind of education could render heterogeneous people alike. The same idea shaped the crusade to instruct American Indians in "civilized" ways. It persisted in the campaign to Americanize the children of immigrants during the Progressive Era. In the 1950s it undergirded the ideology of educators who sought to be race-blind, gender-blind, and class-blind. It inspired those in the 1960s who believed that compensatory instruction could overcome the handicaps imposed by poverty. And it underlay the faith of those integrationists who believed that blacks and whites differed chiefly in the color of their skins.

Policy makers who believed in the potential similarity of all individuals shared an optimistic and often generous faith—as well as tunnel vision. Too often their concept of the "common good" was a "mainstream culture" masquerading as universalism. Confident in their own values, they failed to understand the power of ethnic loyalties or the benefits that dominant groups gained from discrimination. Assimilation was at best only partial, and gross inequalities persisted. Indians remained Indians, ethnic loyalties and cultures did not disappear, race continued to divide society, and the poor were still at a severe disadvantage. Diversity and inequality of groups did not—could not—vanish at the wave of a pedagogical wand.

People who believe that groups are basically different have varied in their ideologies and social location. Some have used concepts of difference to subordinate other people, while others have used group identity as an instrument of liberation from subordination. For example, under the southern caste system, whites defined African Americans as a distinct and inferior group and hence segregated them by law. Blacks resisted such degradation and forced segregation, but even when they won the opportunity to attend schools with whites, many African Americans argued that they needed separate schools. With blacks in charge, their children could escape white racists, learn their own heritage, gain a sense of racial pride, and mobilize to achieve political and economic goals.

In the past, when educators talked about "intercultural education" or "pluralism," they generally believed that individuals of different ethnic groups would eventually become assimilated. Celebrating diverse cultures would make that process less divisive and painful. In recent years, some educators have advocated policies designed to preserve group identities. Individuals, they believe, can best realize themselves through such group membership. The power of the state should be employed not to eradicate ethnic differences but to strengthen them.

People who stress group solidarity as a way to achieve greater social justice tend to exaggerate the fixity of group boundaries and to blur the great variety of opinion within groups. Even within ethnic or racial groups, members often debate about the policies that should inform the education of their children. For example, many Mexican Americans want their children to learn English but may not be of one mind about the role of the school in maintaining their language and culture; and many blacks argue about what priority to give to desegregation. In addition, there is considerable overlap of values among groups. Individuals also have multiple identities that shift in salience according to social context (as in the case, for example, of a feminist who is also a Latina).[55]

Ideologies that stress only similarity or difference do not adequately capture the way social diversity actually operates in American society and public education. By ignoring the interactive nature of cultural exchange and by posing bipolar choices, they also offer questionable guidance about what might be a better approach to social diversity. The public culture is the product of changing relationships among cultural groups that continuously influence one another.[56]

At present, the radically constricted nature of elite discourse about the purposes of schooling further complicates the search for wise policy. From the influential federal report *A Nation at Risk* (1983) onward, policy makers have stressed instrumental values and competition. Bad schooling is to blame for the poor economy, they say. To ensure national and individual competitiveness, students must meet high academic standards. Test scores are now the calculus of success; the aims of education have become instrumental and narrow; and the collective good is the sum of lots of private goods in the form of academic value added to individuals.

What is missing from this utilitarian concept of schooling is a generous vision of cultural democracy that builds on both difference and similarity in a pluralistic society. How can one go beyond the self-interest either of individuals or of separate groups in a nation where people are very unequal in wealth, power, and prestige and in which racism is still rampant? How can schools become, as in John Dewey's vision, microcosms of a just, future society? The chapters in this book address these questions.[57]

## Notes

1. Lawrence A. Cremin, *Popular Education and Its Discontents* (New York: Harper & Row, 1990), pp. 85–125; Paul Gray, "Whose America?" *Time*, July 8, 1991, pp. 13–17; Karen De Witt, "Rise Is Forecast in Minorities in the Schools," *New York Times*, September 13, 1991, p. A8; Jane Gross, "A City's Determination to Rewrite History Puts Its Classrooms in Chaos," *New York Times*, September 18, 1991, p. B7 (on Oakland, California, see also Gary Yee, "Values in Conflict," unpublished study of ethnic conflict over curriculum, Stanford University, June 10, 1991); and Eleanor Armour-Thomas and William A. Proefriedt, "Cultural Interdependence and 'Learner-Centrism,'" *Education Week*, December 4, 1991, pp. 27, 36.
2. Thomas Bender, "Public Culture: Inclusion and Synthesis in American History," in Paul Gagnon (ed.), *Historical Literacy:*

*The Case for History in American Education* (Boston: Houghton Mifflin, 1989), pp. 201, 188–202.

3. Hannah Arendt, "The Crisis in Education," *Partisan Review, 25* (Fall 1958), 493–513.

4. On constitutional issues, see David L. Kirp and Mark G. Yudof, *Educational Policy and the Law: Cases and Materials* (Berkeley, Calif.: McCutchan, 1974); on obfuscations in dealing with class, see Benjamin DeMott, *The Imperial Middle: Why Americans Can't Think Straight About Class* (New York: William Morrow, 1990), and Richard Rubinson, "Class Formation, Politics, and Institutions: Schooling in the United States," *American Journal of Sociology, 92* (November 1986), 519–548.

5. I borrow the metaphor of the overexposed photograph, used in another context, from Paula Fass, *Outside In: Minorities and the Transformation of American Education* (New York: Oxford University Press, 1989), p. 14.

6. Fass, *Outside In*, p. 3; John Higham, "Integration vs. Pluralism: Another American Dilemma," *Center Magazine, 7* (August 1974), 68, 71.

7. Although I focus here on "race" and "ethnicity," "gender" represents another crucial form of cultural construction of social difference. In different societies and times, people have given a vast array of meanings to the biological differences between the sexes, each seeming natural and real. Consider the cultural interpretations of hermaphrodites. Clifford Geertz reports that in some cultures intersexed people are honored as wise counselors; in others, killed as demons; and in the contemporary United States, regarded as medical anomalies to be fixed by surgeons. However fanciful may be some conceptions of gender, they customarily ensure that men will remain in charge; and the cash value of cultural beliefs is evident in the fact that employed white women have earned on average about three-fifths of the income of white men. See Clifford Geertz, *Local Knowledge* (New York: Basic Books, 1983), pp. 80–84; and Tessie Liu, "Teaching the Differences Among Women from a

Historical Perspective: Rethinking Race and Gender as Social Categories," *Women Studies International Forum*, *14* (No. 4, 1990), 265–276.

8. Michael B. Katz, *The Undeserving Poor: From the War on Poverty to the War on Welfare* (New York: Pantheon Books, 1989), pp. 5–6; Minow, quoted in Katz, *Poor*, p. 167; Renato Rosaldo, "Others of Invention: Ethnicity and Its Discontents," *Village Voice Literary Supplement* (February 1990), No. 82, pp. 27–29.

9. Horace Mann Bond, "Main Currents in the Educational Crisis Affecting Afro-Americans," *Freedomways*, 8 (Fall 1968), 38. And on the Nazi incident, which upset some whites who normally took caste for granted, see Morton Sosna, "Stalag Dixie," *Stanford Humanities Review*, 2 (No. 1, n.d.), 38–64; Barbara Jeanne Fields, "Slavery, Race and Ideology in the United States of America," *New Left Review*, *181* (May–June 1990), 95–119.

10. Renato Rosaldo, "Assimilation Revisited," in *In Times of Challenge: Chicanos and Chicanas in American Society*, Mexican American Studies Monograph Series No. 6 (Houston, Texas: University of Houston, 1988), pp. 43–49; Joel Perlmann, *Ethnic Difference* (Cambridge, England: Cambridge University Press, 1988); Gary Gerstle, *Working-Class Americanism: The Politics of Labor in a Textile City, 1914–1960* (New York: Cambridge University Press, 1989); John Bodnar, *The Transplanted: A History of Immigrants in Urban America* (Bloomington: Indiana University Press, 1985).

11. Bender, "Public Culture," pp. 201, 188–202.

12. Gerstle, *Working-Class Americanism*; Bodnar, *The Transplanted*; Nicholas V. Montalto, *A History of the Intercultural Educational Movement, 1924–1941* (New York: Garland Publishing Company, 1982); Stephan F. Brumberg, *Going to America, Going to School: The Jewish Immigrant Public School Encounter in Turn-of-the-Century New York City* (New York: Praeger, 1986).

13. David Tyack, "Pilgrim's Progress: Toward a Social History of the School Superintendency," *History of Education Quarterly*, *16* (1976), 295–300; Paula Fass, *Outside In*; Paul Peterson, *The*

*Politics of School Reform, 1870–1940* (Chicago: University of Chicago Press, 1985); James D. Anderson, *The Education of Blacks in the South, 1860–1935* (Chapel Hill: University of North Carolina Press, 1988).

14. Carl F. Kaestle, *Pillars of the Republic: Common Schools and American Society* (New York: Hill and Wang, 1983); Ira Katznelson and Margaret Weir, *Schooling for All: Class, Race, and the Decline of the Democratic Ideal* (New York: Basic Books, 1985).

15. David Tyack and Elisabeth Hansot, *Managers of Virtue: Public School Leadership in America, 1820–1980* (New York: Basic Books, 1982).

16. Geraldine Joncich Clifford, *The Sane Positivist: A Biography of Edward T. Thorndike* (Middletown, Conn.: Wesleyan University Press, 1968); Robert L. Church, "Educational Psychology and Social Reform in the Progressive Era," *History of Education Quarterly,* 11 (Winter 1971), 390–405; Clarence J. Karier, Paul Violas, and Joel Spring, *Roots of Crisis: American Education in the Twentieth Century* (Chicago: Rand McNally, 1973).

17. Michael R. Olneck, "The Recurring Dream: Symbolism and Ideology in Intercultural and Multicultural Education," *American Journal of Education,* 99 (February 1990), 147–174; Higham, "Integration vs. Pluralism," p. 68.

18. Superintendent quoted in Milton M. Gordon, *Assimilation in American Life: The Role of Race, Religion, and National Origin* (New York: Oxford University Press, 1964), pp. 100–101.

19. *Addresses and Proceedings of the NEA, 1891,* pp. 395, 398, 393–403.

20. George T. Balch, *Methods of Teaching Patriotism in the Public Schools* (New York: D. Van Nostrand, 1890); John Higham, *Strangers in the Land: Patterns of American Nativism* (New York: Atheneum, 1966; Oscar Handlin, *Race and Nationality in American Life* (Boston: Little, Brown, 1957).

21. U.S. Immigration Commission, *Children of Immigrants in Schools,* Vol. 1 (Washington, D.C.: Government Printing Office, 1911), pp. 14–15; David Tyack and Michael Berkowitz, "The Man

Nobody Liked: Toward a Social History of the Truant Officer, 1840–1940," *American Quarterly*, 26 (Spring, 1977), pp. 321–354; Ellwood P. Cubberley, *Changing Conceptions of Education* (Boston: Houghton Mifflin, 1909), pp. 63–64; Adele Marie Shaw, "The True Character of New York Public Schools," *World's Work*, 7 (December 1903); 4204–4221; Michael R. Olneck, "Americanization and the Education of Immigrants, 1900–1925: An Analysis of Symbolic Action," *American Journal of Education*, 98 (August 1989), 398–423.

22. Helen M. Todd, "Why Children Work: The Children's Answer," *McClure's Magazine*, 40 (April 1913), 68–79; William H. Dooley, *The Education of the Ne'er-Do-Well* (Boston: Houghton Mifflin, 1916); Edward G. Hartmann, *The Movement to Americanize the Immigrant* (New York: Columbia University Press, 1948); Robert A. Carlson, *The Americanization Syndrome: A Quest for Conformity* (London: Croom Helm, 1987); Leonard Covello, "A High School and Its Immigrant Community—A Challenge and an Opportunity," *Journal of Educational Sociology*, 9 (February 1936): 331–346; Peter Roberts, *The Problem of Americanization* (New York: Macmillan, 1920).

23. John F. McClymer, "The Americanization Movement and the Education of the Foreign-Born Adult, 1914–25," in Bernard J. Weiss (ed.), *American Education and the European Immigrant: 1840–1940* (Urbana: University of Illinois Press, 1982), pp. 97, 96–116; John Dewey, "Nationalizing Education," *NEA Addresses and Proceedings, 1916*, pp. 185, 183–189.

24. Jesse K. Flanders, *Legislative Control of the Elementary Curriculum* (New York: Teachers College, 1925), p. 62; David Tyack, Thomas James, and Aaron Benavot, *Law and the Shaping of Public Education, 1785–1954* (Madison: University of Wisconsin Press, 1987), chaps. 6–7.

25. Stephan F. Brumberg, "New York City Schools March Off to War: The Nature and Extent of Participation of the City Schools in the Great War, April 1917–June 1918," *Urban Education*, 24 (January 1990), 440–475; McClymer, "Americanization."

26. See Horace M. Kallen, *Culture and Democracy in the United States: Studies in the Group Psychology of the American Peoples* (New York: Boni and Liveright, 1924), pp. 121–24, 139. And for a critique of Kallen's proposals, including his racist attitudes toward African Americans, see Werner Sollors, "A Critique of Pure Pluralism," in Sacvan Berkovitch (ed.), *Reconstructing American Literary History* (Cambridge, Mass.: Harvard University Press, 1986), pp. 250–279.

27. Todd, "Why Children Work"; Bodnar, *Transplanted*; Timothy L. Smith, "Immigrant Social Aspirations and American Education, 1880–1930," *American Quarterly, 21* (Fall 1969), 523–543; David K. Cohen, "Immigrants and the Schools," *Review of Educational Research, 70* (February 1970), 13–26; Weiss (ed.), *Immigrant*.

28. Nicholas V. Montalto, "The Intercultural Education Movement, 1924–41: The Growth of Tolerance as a Form of Intolerance," in Weiss (ed.), *Immigrant*, pp. 144, 142–160; John Daniels, *America via the Neighborhood* (New York: Harper & Brothers, 1920).

29. Albert Shiels, "Education for Citizenship," *NEA Addresses and Proceedings, 1922*, pp. 934–940; Marcus E. Ravage, "The Immigrant's Burden," *The New Republic, 19* (June 1919), 209–211; Daniel E. Weinberg, "The Ethnic Technician and the Foreign-Born: Another Look at Americanization Ideology and Goals," *Societas, 7* (Summer 1977), 209–227; William C. Smith, *Americans in the Making* (New York: D. Appleton-Century, 1939); Ronald D. Cohen, *Children of the Mill: Schooling and Society in Gary, Indiana, 1906–1960* (Bloomington: Indiana University Press, 1990); Nicholas V. Montalto, *A History of the Intercultural Education Movement, 1924–1941* (New York: Garland, 1982), chaps. 1–2.

30. Department of Supervisors and Directors of Instruction, National Education Association, *Americans All: Studies in Intercultural Education* (Washington, D.C.: National Education Association, 1942).

31. Montalto, "Intercultural Education"; Rachel Davis Dubois, "Our Enemy—The Stereotype," *Progressive Education, 12* (March 1935), 146–150.

32. Louis Adamic, "Thirty Million New Americans," *Harpers Monthly Magazine, 169* (November 1934), 684–694; Park, quoted in Montalto, *Movement*, p. 22.

33. Montalto, "Intercultural Movement," p. 147.

34. Superintendents quoted in Montalto, *Movement*, p. 249. For a critique of the shallowness and patchy character of some "intergroup" curricula, see Theodore Brameld, "Intergroup Education in Certain School Systems," *Harvard Educational Review, 15* (March 1945), 93–98; and Ronald K. Goodenough, "The Progressive Educator, Race and Ethnicity in the Depression Years: An Overview," *History of Education Quarterly, 15* (Winter 1975), 365–394.

35. Olneck, "Symbolism and Ideology," pp. 147–174.

36. See Carol D. Lee, Kofi Lomotey, and Mwalimu Shujaa, "How Shall We Sing Our Sacred Song in a Strange Land? The Dilemma of Double Consciousness and the Complexities of an African-centered Pedagogy," *Journal of Education, 172* (No. 2, 1990), 45–61; Christine E. Sleeter and Carl A. Grant, "An Analysis of Multicultural Education in the United States," *Harvard Educational Review, 57* (November 1987), 421–444; James Banks, *Teaching Strategies for Ethnic Studies* (Boston: Allyn & Bacon, 1991). And for a study of types of multicultural education in Australia, see Fazal Rizvi, *Ethnicity, Class and Multicultural Education* (Deakin, Victoria: Deakin University Press, 1986).

37. Joyce Elaine King and Gloria Ladson-Billings, "Dysconscious Racism and Multicultural Illiteracy: The Distorting of the American Mind," paper presented at the annual meeting of the American Educational Research Association, April 16–20, 1991, Boston; Gross, "Classrooms in Chaos," *New York Times,* September 18, 1991, p. B7; Laurie Olsen, *Crossing the Schoolhouse Border: Immigrant Students and the California Public Schools*

(San Francisco: California Tomorrow, 1988); David L. Kirp, "Textbooks and Tribalism in California," *The Public Interest, 104* (Summer 1991), 20–36; Diane Ravitch, "Diversity and Democracy: Multicultural Education in America," *American Educator, 14* (Spring 1990), 16–20, 46–48.

38. Anderson, *Education of Blacks*; W.E.B. Du Bois, *The Negro Common School* (Atlanta: Atlanta University Press, 1901); Louis R. Harlan, *Separate and Unequal: Public Schools and Racism in the Southern Seaboard States* (New York: Atheneum, 1968).

39. Ronald Takaki, *Strangers from a Different Shore: A History of Asian Americans* (New York: Penguin Books, 1989); Thomas James, *Exiles Within: The Schooling of Japanese Americans, 1942–1945* (Cambridge, Mass.: Harvard University Press, 1987); Elliott Grinnell Mears, *Resident Orientals on the Pacific Coast: Their Legal and Economic Status* (Chicago: University of Chicago Press, 1928).

40. Meyer Weinberg, *A Chance to Learn: A History of Race and Education in the United States* (New York: Cambridge University Press, 1977), pp. 165–166; Guadalupe San Miguel, *'Let Them All Take Heed': Mexican Americans and the Campaign for Educational Equality in Texas, 1910–1981* (Austin: University of Texas Press, 1987); Albert Camarillo, *Chicanos in a Changing Society* (Cambridge, Mass.: Harvard University Press, 1984).

41. Superintendent quoted in Weinberg, *Chance to Learn*, p. 146.

42. Fields, "Race"; Horace Mann Bond, *The Education of the Negro in the American Social Order* (New York: Octagon Books, 1966; reprint of 1934 edition); Richard Wright, *12,000,000 Black Voices* (New York: Viking, 1941); George M. Frederickson, *The Arrogance of Race: Historical Perspectives on Slavery, Racism, and Social Inequality* (Middletown, Conn.: Wesleyan University Press, 1988).

43. Rolland Dewing, "Teacher Organizations and Desegregation," *Phi Delta Kappan, 49* (January 1968): 257–260.

44. See Bond, *Education of Negro*, chaps. 15–16; Doxey A. Wilkerson, "A Determination of the Peculiar Problems of

Negroes in Contemporary American Society," *Journal of Negro Education,* 5 (July 1936): 324–350; Cubberley's Library Classification Scheme, Stanford University; W.E.B. Du Bois, *The Philadelphia Negro* (Philadelphia: University Press, 1899); William L. Buckley, "The Industrial Condition of the Negro in New York City," *Annals of the American Academy of Political and Social Science,* 27 (May 1906): 590–596. For a study of the persistence of black faith in schooling, however, see Timothy Smith, "Native Blacks and Foreign Whites: Varying Responses to Educational Opportunity in America, 1890–1950," *Perspectives in American History* 6 (1972): 309–335.

45. Goodenough, "Progressive Educator"; Fass, *Outside In*, chap. 4.
46. W.E.B. Du Bois, "Pechstein and Pecksniff," *The Crisis,* 36 (September 1929), 313–314; Du Bois, "Does the Negro Need Separate Schools?" *Journal of Negro Education,* 4 (July 1935), 328–335.
47. Horace Mann Bond, *The Education of the Negro in the American Social Order* (New York: Prentice-Hall, 1934; reprinted in New York by Octagon Books, 1966), Preface; Fass, *Outside In*, p. 127.
48. David Tyack, Robert Lowe, and Elisabeth Hansot, *Public Schools in Hard Times: The Great Depression and Recent Years* (Cambridge, Mass.: Harvard University Press, 1984), pp. 122, 125, 126, 182, 196.
49. Fass, *Outside In*, pp. 140–141.
50. W.E.B. Du Bois, "Two Hundred Years of Segregated Schools," in Philip S. Foner (ed.), *W.E.B. DuBois Speaks: Speeches and Addresses, 1920–1963* (New York: Pathfinder Press, 1970), p. 238; Weinberg, *Chance to Learn,* chap. 3; Richard Kluger, *Simple Justice: The History of Brown v. Board of Education and Black America's Struggle for Equality* (New York: Vintage Books, 1977).
51. J. Harvie Wilkerson III, *From Brown to Bakke: The Supreme Court and School Integration, 1954–1978* (New York: Random House, 1979).
52. Weinberg, *Chance to Learn,* pp. 122–124, 131; Dorothy Jones, "The Issues at I.S. 201: A View from the Parents' Committee,"

in Meyer Weinberg (ed.), *Integrated Education: A Reader* (Beverly Hills, Calif.: Glencoe Press, 1968), pp. 155–157; Robert C. Maynard, "Black Nationalism and Community Schools," in Henry Levin (ed.), *Community Control of Schools* (Washington, D.C.: Brookings Institution, 1970), 100–101.

53. Robert Newby and David Tyack, "Victims Without 'Crimes': Some Historical Perspectives on Black Education," *Journal of Negro Education*, 40 (Summer 1971), 192–206.

54. A. Wade Boykin, "The Triple Quandary and the Schooling of Afro-American Children," and John U. Ogbu, "Variability in Minority Responses to Schooling: Nonimmigrants v. Immigrants," in Ulric Neisser (ed.), *The School Achievement of Minority Children* (Hillsdale, N.J.: Erlbaum, 1986), pp. 57–92, 255–278; Joyce Elaine King and Thomasyne Lightfoote Wilson, "Being the Soul-Freeing Substance: A Legacy of Hope in Afro Humanity," *Journal of Education*, 172 (No. 2, 1990), 9–27; Molefi Kete Asante, "The Afrocentric Idea in Education," *Journal of Negro Education*, 60 (Spring 1991), 170–180.

55. Sollars, in "Pluralism," pp. 156–158, notes that ethnic groups are neither static nor homogeneous; and Renato Rosaldo, in "Assimilation," notes that it was not necessary to be culturally assimilated to get ahead economically. See also Tyack and Hansot, *Learning Together,* chaps. 9, conclusion.

56. Higham, "Integration v. Pluralism," p. 72.

57. Renato Rosaldo, "Cultural Democracy," unpublished paper, Stanford University, 1993; John Dewey, *Democracy and Education* (New York: Macmillan, 1916).

## Chapter Two

# Race, Ethnicity, and the Defiance of Categories

Shirley Brice Heath

Step into a summer day in the life of several young people in a major metropolitan area. These youngsters have joined together in a summer theater program, where they go each day to prepare scripts, practice, and ready the series of performances they will give throughout the city at the end of the summer.[1]

The setting is a major housing project, one of the most notorious in the nation for its reported violence, gang activity, and drug trade. It is early morning.

Danny rolls over and sees the first rays of light around the edges of a piece of drape tacked across the window. He scoots gently toward the edge of the bed, trying not to awaken Trino and Jorge, his two younger brothers. Slipping on his pants, he tiptoes down the hall to the bathroom. He hears his mom already in the kitchen, preparing the Puerto Rican foods she will sell to Marcos, the vendor whose cart will take these foods into the commercial Latino district ten blocks away. He looks in the mirror at his bruised face, sees how far he can move his left arm in its cast, and decides to head out early to catch the metro, too early to meet any other Latin Kings this morning. After carefully choosing a shirt of vivid colors and his prized hat with the attached marijuana leaf, he ties his hightops and steps into the kitchen. His mother shoots a quick look at his bruised face, hands him a wrapped parcel of food, and he's off, taking the fire-escape steps and heading out the back way across the lots behind his housing project to the metro. He will reach Liberty Theatre well before any of the other players, and he will have time to play some tapes on Marcia's boom box, while he figures out how he will explain his face and arm. He decides "an auto accident" will do, and Jeremy and Deejay will be buddies enough to shut the girls up before too much questioning. They will know he had to turn down an assignment from the Kings, because he had to be at play practice, and his face reveals the effort involved in easing out of one gang into another—the Liberty Theatre players.

An hour later, after taking the metro and a bus and walking the final three blocks, Danny reaches Liberty Theatre, housed on the second floor of an abandoned school now occupied by the city's Parks and Recreation office. As he runs down the final block, he sees Onyx, Opal, Sula, and Marcia sitting on the concrete steps listening to Marcia's boom box. He charges up to them and mock-battles Marcia for the box; then all of them head upstairs where Jeremy, Deejay, Arturo, and others are gathered around Tanisha, the director of their theater group. Soon the group will begin their full day of practice. Within three weeks, they must be ready to perform several times a day all over the city for youngsters involved in the Parks and Recreation programs. For their work, they are paid the minimum wage through a city youth employment program; to be eligible for this drama program, their families must qualify for public assistance. The youngsters audition, have job interviews, and must agree to the strict terms of the work arrangement: show up on time or be docked in pay, be present every day for the full six weeks, and follow the directions of the artistic director in charge. The group members range in age from fourteen to nineteen years and come from all parts of the city. They have met here for the first time to write, produce, and perform the show they will take all through the city for several weeks of three or four performances daily.

Led by Tanisha, an African American director, the group of

twenty young people includes four who identify as African American and three as Puerto Rican; the remainder resist a single label. Their director, Tanisha, brings to rehearsal each day her four-month-old daughter, whose father is of Northern European descent. She tells the students on their first day together that she is a playwright and actress. She goes on to explain that her background is middle to upper class, and that she will depend on them to tell her about their lives, since her own background in another city a decade earlier probably has little in common with their current lives. Their procedure will be to talk each day about central themes they want included in their play; she will tape-record much of that talk and transcribe portions of it each night, and the next day, they will revoice each other's words, gradually putting together a script in which they can easily slip into and out of each other's roles.

On the third day of practice, Danny, Jeremy, and Arturo are horsing around working on script lines that center on what seems to be the group's current theme of "me-myself-I." The boys begin "doggin' on," or teasing one another.*

> *Jeremy:* Me, myself, I, let me tell you why. My face is beautiful, black, and brilliant.
> *Arturo:* Me, myself, I—let me tell you why. *(in Spanish)* I play baseball, basketball, and soccer—and I like to play them a lot/
> *Danny:* *(in Spanish)* /Yea—you might like to play them, but are you any good?
> *(Laughter from the group)*
> *Jeremy:* Don't do that=
> *Danny:* =do what?
> *Jeremy:* Speak Spanish.

---

*Within the transcript, slashes (/) at the end of one speaker's utterance and at the opening of another's indicate an interruption. Equal signs (=) indicate that the second speaker began talking immediately after the first, latching the second utterance to the first without pause.

*Danny:* Porque?
*Jeremy:* I said don't—
*Onyx:* He just asked why/
*Jeremy:* /Because I can't understand what he is sayin'/
*Danny:* /You could try to learn Spanish.
*Jeremy:* Why? (turns away) Aw, forget it!
*Danny:* (*in Spanish*) I don't know why this is such a big deal=
*Jeremy:* =Oh, so you're talkin' about me now.
*Onyx:* No, he isn't. He just said he doesn't know why this is a problem/
*Jeremy:* /It's a problem because this is America and we speak English/
*Danny:* /well, this *American* speaks Spanish—

Later this segment of actual interaction becomes part of their play, whose title and theme has shifted from "me-myself-I" to "All for one," with considerable discussion of the double meaning of *one* as either a single individual or the group as unified whole.

In the segment just shown, the translator for Danny's Spanish is Onyx, who, though she is phenotypically African American, comes from a family that includes a Dominican stepfather and several younger siblings with whom he speaks Spanish only. Others in the group speak Haitian Creole. Arturo speaks Mexican Spanish, Danny speaks a Puerto Rican variety, and Deejay, who has an African American mother and an El Salvadoran father, speaks yet another dialect of Spanish. Into their play the youth gradually incorporate the general theme of what their cultures hold in common, along with some historical discussion of the ancient linkages of Spain, Africa, and the Middle East, and the later mixings of the Moors in Spain and the Africans in the Caribbean and Brazil. Included in the play is a Cuban-Brazilian dance that all members of the troupe learn to perform under the direction of a Brazilian dance instructor.

Following the first few weeks of sometimes rowdy and tension-filled rehearsals, members of the group begin to talk about what learning to work with so many different people has meant to them. Danny and Jeremy often face off in raps, or pit "black dance" against hip hop, switching styles back and forth, while others look on with shouts of approval for one or the other. Tanisha says at the close of many such occasions, "Danny, you let Jeremy beat you every time!" because Jeremy could switch styles more readily than Danny. Members of the troupe see their theater experience as "real" and point out that the young audiences to whom they play are just as " 'mixed' and proba- bly 'mixed up' as we are!" Their families, like those of their younger counterparts, reflect what anthropologists would term "preferential exogamy," a practice of marrying outside of one's "own" ethnic group. More and more, these kids note that their younger brothers and sisters are of multiple "races" and identities that enable them to move across different groupings as they grow older.

## The "Reason" of Categories

As Bakhtin writes: "It is an unfortunate misunderstanding (a legacy of rationalism) to think that truth can only be the truth that is com- posed of universal moments; that the truth of a situation is precisely that which is repeatable and constant in it" (1993, p. 37). Re- peatable and constant for these young people and many like them across the country is the truth of their multiracial/multicultural lives. The young people of many, though certainly not all, inner cities grow up among differences affecting their families, friendship networks, and communities that tell them the fixing of racial or ethnic labels and identities cannot be universal. In an increasing number of American cities, housing projects and streets of single- or double-family-occupancy homes no longer belong to a single racial or ethnic group. Only some cities, such as Baltimore, Washington, D.C., and most urban areas of the South, retain what in the 1950s came to be termed "solidly black" residential sections. But even these cities include neighborhoods, especially those of the working class, locally called "integrated," "immigrant," or "mixed." Within these areas, as well as in the multiethnic public housing

*[margin note, handwritten: multi- racial & ethnic diffs. about young peop.]*

areas of most major metropolitan regions, the experiences of youth growing up there encourage deflection from a single self-assigned ethnic or racial identity.

As youngsters grow old enough to move in peer groups around town, from shopping mall to popular music performance and moviehouse complexes, and as their schools become more mixed, they choose friends based on situational needs. Danny, Deejay, Onyx, and Sula come from four different kinds of housing projects in four different parts of the city. Danny's project is predominantly Latino, inhabited mostly by second-generation Mexican Americans, Puerto Ricans who formerly lived in New York City, El Salvadorans, and some Guatemalans. Recently, several Hmong families and a couple of African American families also moved in. Deejay comes from a housing project still predominantly African American, but with a rapidly diminishing population. Only two of seven floors in his building are now open. The others are boarded up—the result of years of neglect and vandalism. Onyx lives nearby, in a two-family house in a neighborhood increasingly integrated by "yuppies" seeking to live closer to the city center and attracted to the solidly built older homes of the area. This neighborhood, almost in the shadow of Deejay's housing project, now includes several young Eastern European families, two new Latino families (one with an African American adult male), and several former residents, from the days when the neighborhood was "black only," who have moved back in the hope of preventing the city from taking over the entire area for commercial redevelopment.

Other youngsters at Liberty Theatre give similar descriptions: their projects or neighborhoods are constantly changing, people are highly transient, and most families include members not identifiable by the usual kin ties or racial and ethnic affiliations. Some include three generations; others include friends and their friends who are temporarily down and out of luck. The young people talk also of their schools, both public and parochial, as being both transient and mixed; there, outside of classes, friends (generally "of color)" hang out together in school spaces separated according to neighborhood and language grouping. Having a group to hang with at school depends, in large part, on having a "homey" (male term) or "crib" (female term) affiliation. Youngsters talk about how the samenesses discussed in social studies classes—in terms of either distinct black and white groupings or specific immigrant populations— "sure don't seem like it is for us today—all mixed up and always changin.'" The young complain that at school, in job applications and interviews, and during public encounters, they are constantly faced with the question "What are you?" which calls for their self-assignment into a category, such as African American, Hispanic, or Asian American, that others can comprehend. But these categories have no central self-identity value for those who think of themselves as a *who* and not a *what*.

[Conceptualizing groups and individuals in terms of racial and ethnic membership is an American habit difficult to dislodge.] Am. ideology Linked to this categorizing habit is the resistance of Americans to talk about "mixing" or "intermingling" racial and ethnic groups. The "truths" of behavior assigned to those of particular ethnic or racial membership are only too readily, and relentlessly, extended to actual individuals and situations. stereo-typing

In her acceptance speech for the 1993 Nobel Prize in Literature, Toni Morrison spoke of "word work." The Academy noted in its award to her: "She delves into the language itself, a language she wants to liberate from the fetters of race" (*New York Times*, December 8, 1993, p. B1). She elaborated: "Oppressive language does more than represent violence; it is violence; does more than represent the limits of knowledge; it limits knowledge." The words that build walls by labeling race and ethnicity stand in opposition to those created by Danny and his friends and similar young people elsewhere— words that allow the young to stand aside, narrate, and debate the terms that others assign them. Morrison's warning is an apt one for these youth of mixed culture and mixed race: words should never be used to pin down the lives of speakers, readers, and writers.

But the legacy of language's oppressive and exclusionary force is a powerful one. Legal labels were carried through miscegenation prohibitions and Jim Crow laws; the xenophobic frenzy of the early decades of the twentieth century demanded racial assignment; and the unrest of the 1960s civil rights movement set firm policies that called for desegregation while requiring self-assignment to labels used to determine reassignment (especially in the case of school desegregation in regions with numerous "minority" groups). Ironically, many of the privileging and affirming actions and institutions that followed this decade built higher than before some of the barriers within policy and institutional decisions that set ethnic groups off into separately designated categories (Carter, 1992). Moreover, policies that followed this era substantiated for mainstream institutions an entire discourse around racial and ethnic differences. Newspapers initiated policies about naming the ethnic membership of victims and offenders; scholarship funders raced to develop ways to signal to those "in the know" that members of certain groups would be given priority; and universities and other public service institutions, such as police and fire departments, worried about meeting quotas for "targeted minorities." Those so identified saw themselves as both targets and tokens.[2] Particularly within schools and other federally funded institutions that dispensed public services, one's category by race and ethnicity became a highlighted area for record keeping. While it became less and less acceptable to divide opportunities along racial lines of black and white, the evolving move toward acknowledgment of a "diverse" society stepped up the need to assign ethnic membership for access to education, jobs, and services; for participation in committees of public and civic service; and for local representation of diversity in art shows and performances, annual celebrations, and small-business awards.

Categorical or essentialist assignments in this last decade of the twentieth century surface most frequently in public policies, particularly those related to education and employment, and in media presentations of individuals as members of particular groups. Teachers, reporters, public figures, and lawmakers become schooled in the proper ways to refer to others, and multicultural education emerges as the curricular area through which students learn about

multicultural
education

the diversities and differences that exist within the American melt-ing pot. Multicultural education enables "others" to be studied, through their literatures and histories. Implicit within this lump-ing mechanism lies the understanding that such "others" are out-side the perceived mainstream of American ethnic background (northern Europe and the British Isles) and Caucasian racial lin-eage. Hence multicultural means nonwhite, defined by what its members are *not* rather than by what they are. Perpetuated within current approaches to multicultural education is the view that eth-nic or "cultural" communities are homogeneous across classes, regions, and histories of immigration, when, in fact, they are con-stantly realigning themselves into different "communities" (Heath, forthcoming).[3]

"Other"

## The Perspective of Youth

This chapter looks at resistance to such assignments by youth "of color" in inner-city environments. Alliances of "home boys" and "home girls" in urban areas, in public housing and underground employment affiliations, and in kin (and pseudo-kin) networks defy easy categorization into racial and ethnic divisions. If they refer to themselves using terms other than geographic region or friendship alliance names, young people see themselves as "of color" or "kinda' all ethnic." In private conversations, they also acknowledge that, unlike young people of color in Advanced Placement classes or in the elite student government at school, they live in sections of the city that have the reputation of being "poor." In addition, and again, unlike their Advanced Placement counterparts, they do not so much see themselves as African American (or Mexican, or Polish, or El Salvadoran) per se as they view themselves as simply "ethnic." Such a feeling allows them to be different, and part of this declaration of difference is the refusal to identify with a particular stable ethnicity. The young in these environments point to multi-cultural education in school as just one among many sorts of evi-dence that adults "don't know where it's at for us in terms of who we are." [Youth charge teachers and administrators with seeing more similarities between an African American student in an Advanced Placement class and another in basic math than between two students "of different ethnicities" from the same part of town and in the same general English class.] Young people outside the academic mainstream further charge that multicultural literature seems to "live off" the exploited, "making out as though all poor kids get raped by their daddies, steal for a living, occasionally get their lives turned around and survive by learning to live like the teachers who teach this stuff."

Contrary to general perceptions, within the daily lives of young people in many (not all) inner cities, racial or ethnic identities are always situated and multiple.[4] They move about the city "passing" as something, depending on where they are and on the advantages or safety they can gain by doing so. They grow up in mixed-race families, live in housing units that encompass numerous cultures and languages, and get around in cities marked into zones primarily by social-class boundaries and gang turf lines. At school or in other public places where young people from across the city come together, they find ways to mark themselves as members of different group affiliations that increasingly bear little relationship to race or ethnicity per se. To a great extent, their early socialization in housing projects and low-income neighborhoods has prepared them for such crossings and criss-crossings. Within their repertoire lies knowledge about where in the city race "matters" and where it does not. Because many of the informal public gathering places for youth (playgrounds, corner drugstores, schoolyards, and community baseball fields) no longer exist as safe havens, they create their own place through their groupings. They create a space for themselves by moving in groups that host "regular, voluntary, informal, and happily anticipated gatherings of individuals beyond the realms of home and work" (Oldenburg, 1989, p. 24). The fear that groups of young people generate among adults ensures that certain public corners they claim will be their own. There they continue the socialization begun when they were toddlers in the projects learning to coexist, compete, and claim on the basis of self-efficacy. Common experiences build affiliation.

Public housing policies do not permit assignment of housing on the basis of racial or ethnic membership. Yet some groups, especially new immigrants, strive to achieve such aggregations simply through network recommendations. But fluid mixtures of families within housing projects still persist, because members of such groups move up or down socioeconomically and leave one project for another that they judge to be somewhat better or closer to their job or to relatives. In many cities of the 1990s, areas of town that were previously predominantly "black" or "white" have shifted to achieve the ambiguous labels of "immigrant" or "diverse." Asian, Latino, Caribbean, and African American families live side by side with those from South America, the Middle East, and parts of Africa as well as of the former Soviet Union. When they take note of these situations, policy makers use the term *ethnic recomposition of neighborhoods*, as if to suggest that some sort of shakedown will occur in which one or another ethnic identity will eventually emerge.

Between 1988 and 1990, the Ford Foundation funded a multi-ethnic team of researchers from a variety of disciplines to study residential areas of six U.S. cities: Miami, Chicago, Houston, Philadelphia, Monterey Park, California, and Garden City, Kansas. Reported in Lamphere (1992), their research illustrates repeatedly, from housing projects to neighborhood businesses to youth affiliations, the "divided social worlds" these groups experience by virtue of their separation and social distance from others in their cities. Institutions ranging from school systems to corporations to local governments make it difficult for new immigrants, in particular, to build bridges between their neighborhoods and other segments of society. Often policies and practices close out residents from decisions related, for example, to locations of freeways, condemnation of buildings, or city monitoring of housing project rules. Resistance to these exclusions ironically brings residents closer together in their diversity. Affiliating in order to be heard or to take action into their own hands instills recognition and expectation of the value of pooling local talents while ignoring ethnic, racial, or national backgrounds. In the case of "Big Red," a Chicago housing project, Conquergood (1992) describes the response of local residents when the city cut off their water supply in the midst of a summer heat wave: Ethiopian, Hmong, Mexican, Assyrian, and Puerto Rican families joined together to plan how to dig down to the water main and turn the water back on without city authorization.

Close living circumstances, not just individual attractions, bring people together in intimate as well as public interactions. Multiracial marriages and relationships have increased since the 1967 Supreme Court case of *Loving* v. *Virginia* struck down all anti-miscegenation laws prohibiting the marriage of U.S. citizens from different races. According to the U.S. Census, intermarriages between "blacks" and "whites" more than tripled between 1970 and 1990, with a 30 percent increase between 1980 and 1990. In the past decade, different groups brought together under the general rubric of "ethnic" have called attention to the particular policy implications of these linkages. For example, Afro-based multiracial groups have claimed the greatest attention and exerted the strongest influence. "Project: RACE" is an Atlanta-based national organization dedicated to the goal of changing the U.S. Census to include "multiracial" as a category. Other Afro-based groups have moved through the arts and local cultural activities to announce themselves as the "quintessential U.S. multiracial group" that can afford to celebrate its "unabridged heritages" and to include European heritages. By the mid 1990s, universities and public cultural institutions included study programs and art shows devoted to combinations such as Afro- and Latin American Studies, Pacific and Asian Studies, and Afro-Cuban Studies.

## Demand Sharing and Youth Affiliations

The young people of Liberty Theatre and their counterparts in other cities of the United States find themselves asked almost daily to choose a label of racial or ethnic identity that, in many cases, will exclude other members of their family and friendship network. Such exclusion may apply in particular to younger siblings whose fathers are different from those of their secondary-school siblings, and, given the vagaries of genetic transmission for phenotypical appearances, may reflect a range of features that will lead school personnel to identify fraternal siblings as being of two different "races."

But what enables Danny and his friends, and groups like his in youth organizations throughout American metropolitan areas, to come together "above the racial thing" and sound so sophisticated and mature in their reflections on being "American"? Deejay, Jeremy, Onyx, and Danny can join together across their differences in neighborhood backgrounds to affiliate through Liberty Theatre. Elsewhere, their counterparts reflecting the same variations in racial, ethnic, and linguistic histories come together in gangs—some bearing names that suggest ethnic similarity, such as Latin Kings. Yet within these groups, skin color, extent to which Spanish is spoken, and migration source and history vary greatly; Latin Kings in some cities can include youth from Mexico, El Salvador, and Puerto Rico, as well as from the Latino-based neighborhoods (such as East Harlem) of any other U.S. city.[5] In some metropolitan areas, gangs take on names that announce their intention to recruit across ethnic groups as well as neighborhoods; groups with titles such as DWHs (down-with-the-hood) say they go for "the best" and not "just any home boy." What then explains the attractions of such youth alliances and their rules, habits, and frequent push into violence?

Anthropologists studying pseudo-kin alliances, as well as violence, among young people in urban areas in the past decade offer insights based on the current context of these groups. Unlike earlier gangs in U.S. cities whose members came together to cement bonds of ethnic allegiance, many (though not all) such groups in the 1980s and 1990s formed in the face of dissolution of family structure and the absence of economic opportunities (Vigil, 1993). Explanations for these groups and for the "wanna-be" imitations springing up throughout America's communities extend beyond those given in models that focus on the behaviors of such youth as aberrant or explicable through individual behavioral case histories.

## The Power of Place and Space

Having a sense of place and space empowers. People achieve their *place* through interpersonal relations, initially through family linkages and then through friendships and conjugal ties as well as work-related associations. Belonging within a *space* ensures safety, a zone for being and acting according to rules known and shared by others familiar with this space. Young people in inner cities, subject to the transience of frequent moves and the rapid unpredictabilities of life among alcohol and drug abusers, rarely feel that they have a secure or safe place. Many of their alliances, as exhibited in the streets and in institutions such as schools, depend literally on association with physical geography ("turf") and "home." But they also depend on the creation of "family" that such alliances promote. Many of the rituals and rules the young groups develop, whether in gangs or in strong alliances that go by a host of names (such as "posse," "just friends," and so on), instill allegiance to claim and protect a stated turf. Young people "look out" for each other within these groups and develop methods of declaring their control of these regions that range from "tagging" buildings and public facilities with their graffiti to "hanging" at particular border zones in order to avoid "takeover" of "their" territory.[6]

Within these territories during the late 1980s and early 1990s, new underground economies linked to drugs and gun supplying added to such economic patterns as the peddling of personal services (such as merchant "protection") and discounted goods from unnamed sources, and the selling of information and sexual favors. Distribution of drugs and guns made what had been a strictly rule-governed and fairly predictable system far more unpredictable than other economic or turf-guarding activities. Similarly, the easy access to highly destructive weapons shattered the established hierarchical rule system by which individuals earned their increase in rank through physical and mental prowess.[7] In particular, as ideals of "locoism" (acting crazy) spread throughout young people's alliances, adults and young people outside this cult of craziness found themselves more and more vulnerable to losing not only their personal and household goods but also their personal safety.

Certainly life among the poor in urban housing projects has for decades involved some degree of risk and uncertainty, especially because securing one's goods within a household is never a sure matter. Anthropologists and sociologists have pointed out that under any circumstances—whether among hunters and gatherers or city dwellers—whereby such security is not possible and goods are limited, sharing makes good sense (Peterson, 1993; Schieffelin, 1990; Stack, 1974). But within an urban setting, an individual cannot share with everyone, so strategies as well as hard-and-fast rules are necessary to help determine just who will be shared with and who will not. Adults set such rules and develop tactics within the terms of their kin and nonkin relationships with other adults and also along lines of judgment about the potential of the other to reciprocate. Thus, if someone is known to be always "down and out," handouts from within the community to such an individual will generally be minimal. Similarly, if a woman or man can be counted on for coming into some money or good fortune every once in a while or on a somewhat regular basis, sharing beyond a minimal level is more likely, especially from those who have either a friendly or pseudo-kin ("Don Jaime" or "Mamma Ellis") relationship.

Among the young, relationships both within same-sex groups and across the sexes are in almost constant flux, as individuals maneuver for places within the hierarchy and for recognition according to particular talents or areas of knowledge. Alliances of differing degrees of intensity often result in gang or quasi-gang formations. These groups establish the lines around the groups with whom one shares and makes clear distinctions concerning those with whom one does not share but also those from whom one demands. Whereas adults control demand-sharing through established relationships and reciprocal agreements, the young, inexperienced at such subtleties, depend primarily on space or turf-based groupings that have within them arbitrary rules of obedience and hierarchy. Sharing is thus preestablished by these rules and is not open to at-whim interpersonal negotiations. Those who "stay" (or live) within an objectifiable and visible space are "home boys" or "home girls" and receive names particular to their youth group associates. They are eligible for sharing and are themselves expected to share. Newcomers to these spaces must pass tests of belonging that ensure their commitment to the group and their willingness to take part in all that the group shares, including punishments that are meted out for initiation, the risks of participating in drive-by shootings or raids into "enemy" territories, and, often for young women, sexual favors to gang members. In some cities, they must also participate actively in "writing" their spaces through graffiti wars (Martinez, 1992–1993). Such experiences of sharing symbolize belonging but, even more important, illustrate the giving and taking of the most intimate parts of one's being—severe physical pain, risk of losing freedom or life (if caught in a drive-by), and, for young women, sexual privileges indicative within the larger society of a lifelong commitment. Part of constituting one's place within this space for sharing is taking part in the rites of passage or initiation into the groups. Both the activities themselves and the creation of narratives about them constitute what it takes for full membership and for showing that one can "play along."

## The Play of Emotions

Such allegiance groups also allow the young to replay among themselves the top-down power and dominance relations they observe in the larger society. They know and experience numerous indignities in their dealings with "superiors" of mainstream institutions (primarily social service–related, legal, and educational institutions). Within their own groupings, they find ways to make a statement, a mark, or a claim—all of which are ostensibly linked with turf and the membership identity constructed around this turf.

These statements begin with the choosing of victims, but victims that are not outside the group's own system of rules; members of one alliance attack other groups like them who have sets of rules for continuing their constructed identity. Young people rarely step outside their own group's rule system to act against the police, teachers, or social service workers—those they may see as either bringing them harm or denying them privileges in mainstream institutions. Thus their group rule-boundedness in terms of where, when, and how their violence is directed becomes the inverse of the highly unpredictable, individual-focused violence of aggrievement, slight, and injustice that adults in the mainstream exhibit in both domestic and workplace violence.

Yet the emotions connected with the vulnerability of self and society, as well as those linked with failed, hurtful, or disappointed human relations, abound among these young people. Those who enter youth organizations, especially the ones that emphasize dramatic arts or athletics linked with community service, report that their opportunities to talk, play, and act out their emotions provide a release that their counterparts on the streets do not typically have. They echo in their comments what anthropologists have noted with respect to similar dramatic plays and athletic contests around the world:

> [The kinds] of performances we find in popular culture have become for the people involved more than ever ways to preserve some self-respect in the face of constant humiliation, and to set the wealth of artistic creativity against an environment of utter poverty. All this is not to be dismissed off-hand as escape from reality; it is realistic praxis under the concrete political and economic conditions that reign [Fabian, 1990, p. 19].

In short, the youth see their playing out of these roles as a matter of "trying to control the negativity" and "making the positive more powerful." As one youth put it, "It's the positivity that we oughta listen to." They see themselves converting relationships into displays, and they view their displays—especially within theater—as a means of ordering relationships. They want their theater to give the same positive message about them to others. Danny and all the other members of the new and short-term summer groupings at Liberty Theatre talked out and then acted and reenacted their ways of coming to know each other and their differences. They had no home turf to bind them—only the knowledge that all of them would be contributing to a brief play that had to carry symbolic density within its words, music, and dance. In playing out the "rituals" of fights, of aggression, they joined in the end as "all for one," a title that promoted considerable metacommentary from the group about its double-edged meanings ("all for one goal," all agreeing to stick together to help any one member, and so on). Their director made it clear that the organization had a policy of "no stars" in the shows; thus, in the final version of the script, each person would speak the same number of lines. Asymmetry, so rampant in other parts of their lives, was resolved through the top-down rules of the youth theater.

The writing and other literary acts that occur in connection with youth drama, as well as the many events within youth organizations, further promote the opportunity to experience the play of emotions without negative repercussions. "Writing is my life. . . . It is very therapeutic, and more people should be involved in it," noted one young woman who had kept a secret diary and poetry journal before she joined Liberty Theatre. But within the group, when all members had to keep journals and see their own words as poetry with potential for the play script, she brought her writing into the open. She encouraged others to write and to admit writing as another positive way by which "people are able to express themselves through art."

Anthropologists who study rituals and rites of passage, as well as dramatic performances, in societies around the world have long agreed that the metaphorical qualities of performance are transformative (Turner, 1976, 1982, 1988). They speak of the "human seriousness of play" that allows people to play not only at being worse than they can be in real life but also at being better. Moreover, they can play someone other than they are, entering into the feelings and experiences of another, explored not only in acting but also in research about the origins and history of particular groups within the United States. They move in and out of each other's shoes through revoicing their own daily conversations, which Tanisha types up for them to use when creating their play scripts. Particularly important to these youth is the possibility of creating, for positive reinforcement through their athletics or drama, what may be called the sacred. Separated from others throughout the months of their script creation and practice, they bond and build a strong and broad sense of who they are as individuals. Transformations, turnarounds, public accounts of introspection, rituals of bonding, overt displays of unity, and displays specifically designed to show how the best rise up from the worst mark the sacred in cultures around the world (Grotowski, 1976). Rituals have been especially prominent within the religious traditions most honored in the United States, and yet, since the 1960s, as churches and sacred celebrations have left the inner cities, occasions for talk about or recognition of transformations, introspection, and the like have been rare. The young talk of their youth organizations with passion and often reflect a proselytizing spirit. They speak of "having something to stand for," "to live up to," and to "carry with me" from their participation in such groups. The fact that they can act out, talk about, and reflect jointly on violent emotions, desperate conditions at home, or horrible past experiences removes from them the sense of being alone in their "badness." These experiences bind across the societal boundaries of race and ethnicity.

## Beyond Race and Ethnicity

The views on ethnicity and race held by many young people within inner cities carry little weight with middle-class members of ethnic and racial groups who see pride in one's heritage as central to self-esteem. Such has certainly been the case for many groups since the

1960s. Throughout most of U.S. history, settlement in the United States tended to bring groups that were alike together in residential zones that exhibited common language and religious allegiance, as well as shared background experiences of oppression, whether in slavery, in forced immigration, or in voluntary immigration to escape political upheaval or economic impoverishment in one's home country. By the early 1980s, however, changed economic conditions that scattered the sites of low-income, low-skilled jobs away from the former industrial zones of urban areas brought increasingly rapid shifts in the nature of residential zones. Economic conditions imposed a wider oppression that reached across the boundaries of racial and cultural groups in low-income communities. No longer were neighbors of the same language or background of oppression; shared now was the immediate repression of an economic system that offered little opportunity for those with low skills and limited English-language abilities. Low-skilled wage opportunities were in short supply, as were cultural brokers who could parallel in function the foremen of earlier eras who spoke their own language and could broker warehouse or factory sections where all spoke the same mother tongue.

For middle- and upper-class educated members of former "minorities," sharing a heritage as the basis of a confirmation of self reinforces what they see as their identity, as does promotion of multicultural education within schools. Historical and literary stories in such curricula echo their own experiences of being individuals who could and did rise above their earlier circumstances of impoverishment, exploitation, and disenfranchisement. Multicultural anthologies do not yet include stories of members of such groups pitted against each other in struggles for power or for shares of the relatively small piece of the cake that the larger society offers to "minorities."

Yet for those who continue to promote multicultural education and increased uses of commercial materials prepared for such curricula, what matters is that their central message of pride and future hope comes through to today's young people. The message they want taken from such stories is "you can do it, too," as an alternative to the hopelessness they see in youth. Materials, literary and historical, that promote such messages tend to valorize not only poverty as the first stepping stone on the path to improvement but also a limited number of types of difference such as race and ethnicity. But as the twentieth century closes, both the *it* and the *you* of these assertions are in sharp question. For adults, the *it* is personal individual achievement, economic success, job security, and choices of consumption and leisure. But for young people of the inner city, that *it* is not so clear; moving ahead—or even surviving—becomes a matter of group affiliation rather than of individual accomplishment. Those youth who stand out from the crowd and reject the demand-sharing norms and strategies of inner-city life risk isolation, injury, and death. In the long run, the *it* for the group that now offers security has no precursors, and earlier paths to individual achievement seem far less secure than in earlier decades. Again, no adequate new models seem to exist.

Moreover, for adults who offer the recommendation "you can do it, too," the *you* is a member of a homogeneous group of similar background, struggling against both historical and current evidence of particular kinds of repression brought about by discrimination and racism—evidence usually located within individuals. But for young people of the inner city, the *you* that would identify either them or their oppressors is not so easily identified. Is the *you* now all young people of color? If so, how much color? And to what extent is color affected by national histories before immigration? Moreover, different groups—whether political refugees escaping oppression in Southeast Asia or Central America, or second-generation Mexicans chafing under the unexpectedly keen competition from more recent immigrants from Guatemala and El Salvador—see different histories of oppression and have varying degrees of experience with either literacy or public speaking through which to explore their pasts. The repression and oppression against which the young of inner cities are struggling at the end of the twentieth century now lie far less frequently in identifiable personified enemies than in abstractions of "economic recession and downturns" and institutional policies of "downsizing" and "cutbacks" that the young sometimes see as having been orchestrated to keep them out of work. Individual cases of hatred, exclusion, and denial can much more easily hide behind larger socioeconomic forces than was the case in the 1960s and 1970s, when many of the middle-class "minorities" made their move up and out of the ghetto. This larger, more abstract picture does not deny that individuals are excluded or simply unseen on the basis of their race, class, and gender.[8]

However, the barriers in the lives of the young today lie much more in the general conditions and policies of educational, legal, and governmental institutions. Moreover, as "the crime problem" within the United States comes increasingly to be identified with young people of ethnic groups, they see themselves painted in the media as aggressive, if not violent; as unreasonably demanding and self-willed; and as unwilling to step into jobs that require docile, compliant workers.

The complexities of definition and the contradictions between old fixed categories and new blurred boundaries further complicate the scene for young people. Civil rights legislation, affirmative action policies, and celebrations of multiculturalism and diversity have brought into the public consciousness prohibitions against discrimination on certain grounds. "Proving" discrimination has become more and more difficult, even for those with the best of legal resources. Moreover, the "rights" of people previously excluded along color lines now belong also to those of different nationalities, ages, genders, and, in some locations, sexual orientations. Hence, any interaction between individuals with different levels of power may bring about accusations of denied rights. This wider distribution of the notion of rights has contributed to the reduction in media reports of *race* as the most salient basis of discrimination.

Increasingly, individuals refuse to assign themselves to specific categories of race or ethnicity on official forms. Both ethnic mixing and the fact of more widespread source regions for immigrants coming to the United States in the 1980s and 1990s have made it increasingly difficult for the typical phenotype features of skin color, hair, and eye shape to signal specific origin. Along with the many other societal forces being "globalized," the comfortable sense of "fit" for race and many of its associated characteristics has felt the effect of media portrayals of the global village at the end of the twentieth century. Whether consciously or not, more and more U.S. citizens now have to "know" that not all Africans are dark-skinned, not all Jews are light-skinned, not all Asians are Chinese, and not all Hispanics are Mexican. Boundaries among the old lumped categories have fallen with the immigrations of Ethiopian Jews to Israel and the United States, and with the acknowledgment of "ethnic Chinese" among Vietnamese refugees and of Filipinos with "Hispanic" names. Groups such as the Hmong, Cambodians, and Vietnamese—all Southeast Asians according to some official categories—exhibit vast differences in language, literacy, religious traditions, and familiarity with capitalist endeavors. As these groups spread across the United States to locations such as Minnesota, Montana, and Louisiana, hitherto home primarily to immigrants of northern European background, recognition of diversities within diversity enter the public scene more and more frequently.[9] New stereotypes get shaped, and different levels of competition and rates of success among those identified as being of "minority" groups add confusion to the issue of just what holding people back from opportunities really means.

## Resistant or Resilient?

Along with this dimming and blurring of categories of racial and ethnic membership for the inner-city youth of some major metropolitan areas, there remains the American festishization of race and ethnicity. Perhaps the long-standing quest for "purity" lies behind the urge to put diversity in a box, to categorize citizens. Increasingly, this habit leads to labeling people by what they are *not*, rather than by how they see themselves. Choosing a box on a form or answering the curious question "What are you?" amounts to an admission of being "other" than white. The media provide a quick case study of this ambivalence. In the 1990s newspaper, television, and radio reporters generally use gender-neutral language (saying "police officer" rather than "policeman") and avoid naming the racial membership of suspects in criminal cases. However, for positive achievements, such as running for or holding political office or winning awards, reporters refer freely to the gender and race of individuals. News services and local presses and media stations have created additional rules to ward against careless and possibly offensive use of racial or ethnic labels and have made attempts to ensure that staff behind the cameras and on the beat reflect the diversity of the communities served.

But subtle stereotypes embedded in racial and ethnic differences persist. Stories that celebrate the academic achievements of a young person are much more likely to refer to a light-skinned individual than to one with darker skin.[10] Far more photographs of dark-skinned athletes, male and female, reach the front pages of sports sections than do representations of such individuals in academic achievements. The same is true of films centered on stories of dark-skinned athletes (often working under a white coach). At the same time, however, dark-skinned persons abound in stories of the individual achievements of young people who perform services to others of less good fortune or who depend on sheer grit and the willingness to say "I dare to be different." A particular genre of the latter sort celebrates the exodus from gangs, drugs, or alcohol by individuals of color who give some of their time to visiting schools and advising youngsters against following the "easy path" of the group or gang.

Most frequent in press coverage of individuals of color are stories that present success through escape *from* their past to what is implied to be a mainstream (and often academic success–based) present. Within such presentations lies the strong bias of the media against giving equal coverage in "success" stories to those who are wage-earners as opposed to those who receive salaries. Known in earlier years as a distinction between the "working" and the "middle" class, and assumed to carry an economic distinction along with the difference of working with the hands or the head, this dichotomy is no longer valid. In most states, carpenters, plumbers, electronics repair personnel, and electricians exceed, in terms of hourly wage equivalents, the earnings of salaried school teachers, law clerks, and insurance office workers. Along with this tendency to celebrate as successful those who "resist" their past oppression and "escape" it is the trend toward describing those who remain within oppressive conditions in terms of pathological or disease-based language. Labels such as "blight," "disease," "cancer," "epidemic," and "sickness" abound for inner-city dwellers, especially the young. Created within this metaphor is the perspective that, as youth, they have the power to spread the "infection" of their violence. This notion persists in spite of statistics from every urban area showing that individuals within the inner city kill one another at far higher rates than they harm outsiders. Yet gangs—more often than not identified as being aligned within racial and ethnic allegiances— receive far more media attention and movie representation as "a major cause of urban violence" than does the domestic violence that occurs in every corner of urban areas. The young know that neither the samenesses of race so often used in the media to explain their gang connections nor the extent of their violence match the realities of the world they know.

In the late 1980s and early 1990s, as U.S. policies promised to "clamp down on crime," many young people within inner cities, especially those in youth organizations such as Liberty Theatre and those taking part in regional "gang peace conferences," turned increasingly cynical. Especially after the civil unrest in Los Angeles in 1991, political leaders offered symbolic promises of reform and short-term programs of employment to defuse the potential of future trouble.[11] These amounted to short-term remedies that young people were eager to take advantage of, all the while realizing that long-term changes in either practical or definitional approaches were unlikely. Moreover, the outflow of jobs and economic resources from urban areas continued, as did the exodus of families who might otherwise have voted to support increased school revenues. As one youth put it, "They crazy? Do they think people with kids who don't have to, gonna live in the city? All they gotta do is look around, and they know that ain't so." Young people see the minority/majority split as one of power and not of numbers or color. They point out the many people of color and "especially blacks" who have gained high positions and exited the inner city, forgetting the people who live there. They acknowledge that whites who go into the ghetto to help have come from backgrounds of privilege, whereas for many people of color, to come there would mean "coming back." The majority of volunteers who work with young people of the inner city are white. Hence, some young people who talk of the future note that the changes of earlier eras, especially advances in civil rights, had more potency than any protests they can now offer. Earlier periods had more unity within blackness, more sacredness, and more claims to rights denied than does the current generation of multiple identities, backgrounds, and impoverished economic opportunities, largely stripped of support from sacred institutions. Thus the young cling together across what others see as their differences, because they see themselves as far more similar to each other than to the prior generation, with all its shared values, experiences, and hopes.

In anthropological terms, then, theirs is a liminal or in-between status, one that does not sit within previously agreed-upon categories or problems-and-solutions and one that invites creativity (Turner, 1982, pp. 27–29; Alves, 1993). Their situation problematizes the normativity that Americans generally ascribe to racial and ethnic membership, often assuming such groups are within themselves relatively homogeneous, monolithic, and transparent in their workings. Social scientists in particular have tended to proceed as though members within these assigned groups act to preserve social equilibrium rather than to dislodge it by breaking into groups intent upon developing their own power inequalities. Far more important than the "is-ness" of race and ethnicity is the working nature of youth groupings; what do they do as they interact, and what are the values and ideologies that drive their actions as group members?

Multiple and situated identities for young people make race and ethnicity a dynamic sociocultural process with shifting and overlapping meanings that are often articulated and demonstrated by "crossover culture" entertainment groups, who sing or perform the music of what many see as a single ethnicity not their own (Jones, 1993). They, and those who applaud them, give ample evidence of the extent to which the young destabilize the comfortable either-or distinction that has characterized most perceptions of race in the United States. Their challenge is for the elders from all ethnicities to take up this "category crisis" and to let youth proclaiming "this *American* speaks" be heard. To do so would mean setting aside the racist views that demand certain kinds of performances within one's race and the use of race and ethnicity as the key binding identity and support linkage. This freedom from race could turn attention to what the realities of cultural, social, and aesthetic dissonances might mean in a search for "the truth" of what is "repeatable and constant" in creating and belonging to communities (Bakhtin, 1993, p. 37).

It is curious that, as the twentieth century nears its close, social and economic conditions within some urban areas of the United States are such that the working together across racial and ethnic lines celebrated in theory since the 1960s is in place *in practice*. The young people described herein have a revolution of a sort within their group affiliations that cuts across old lines of division to build secure groupings. Just as the carnivals and popular festivals of the Middle Ages and Renaissance provided alternative social contexts to society's otherwise traditional, closed places and discourses, so groupings such as Liberty Theatre offer such alternatives. Here the young as full participants have "the right to emerge from the routine of life," so as to test and challenge official and habituated hierarchical differences (Bakhtin, 1984, p. 257). To be sure, many such groups now bond as effective perpetrators of violence and crime; but far more such groups bond to meet positive community-building needs. The structural implications of these latter groupings bear consideration for their possible springboard effect, especially as school-to-work programs and charter school efforts across the states allow the possibility of bringing youth organizations into mainstream awareness. It may be that these young people can create a new type of fabric out of which they can tailor group cohesion and collaboration, joint management and worker production, and serious reconsideration of what it could mean to revolutionize the demand performances so long implicit within American society's views of race and ethnicity.

## Notes

1. The data upon which this chapter is based were drawn from inner-city youth organizations of three major metropolitan areas within the United States. A team of young adult and senior ethnographers worked with youth ethnographers from these neighborhoods to document the language and culture of the organizations that young people in the community judged effective for them. Fieldnotes, interviews, audio-recorded language, news clippings, institutional documents, and sessions in which adults and youth joined together to analyze the findings constitute the full database for this project. Entitled "Language, Socialization, and Neighborhood-based Organizations," this project was funded by the Spencer Foundation and headed by Heath and Milbrey W. McLaughlin.

2. A genre very much on the increase in the early 1990s consists of the writings of individuals "privileged by minority status" who point out the fundamental racism behind policy decisions to pressure individuals to identify race or ethnic membership as their key identity or boundary. These authors do not deny the power of the "simple matter of the color of one's skin" (Williams, 1991, p. 256), but they urge attention to the many other boundaries that increase the complexity of roles within mainstream instructional and social life in the United States.

3. See Gray (1993, p. 364) for a discussion of the "return to so-called essentialist ways of constructing and imaging ourselves (as black people)" and the strong assertion of territorial imperatives.

4. Certain cities of the United States stand out as exceptions to the mixed-group features of the inner-city communities described here. Baltimore, Washington, D.C., and large areas of Los Angeles, Miami, and Houston, for example, retain urban communities that are distinctive for their ethnic and social class homogeneity.

5. For example, one such young adult originally from the Southwest, who now identifies himself as a Chicano gang member, tells a typical tale of movement across gang affiliations in his highly transitory life. Born in a traditional family of recent Mexican origin, he was brought up in a predominantly black neighborhood and initially belonged to a gang that identified itself as "black." Later, when he moved to another town, he was courted into another gang, this one active in the sale of crack. He quickly became a recruitment leader and sales manager within this group, which consisted primarily of Native Americans and "Hispanics," who wished to set themselves off from the Chicanos of southern California. Still later, he moved to California and became a member of a mixed group that identified itself primarily as "Chicano."

6. Just as any discussion of other American institutions, such as schools, corporations, or literary clubs, must guard against over-generalization, so must any discussion of youth gangs or alliances. Considerable variation exists among groups in different urban areas and between groups in these regions and similar ones in smaller towns. Specific details of the unique aspects of youth group life in various regions are best drawn from accounts written by gang members themselves (e.g., Rodriguez, 1993) as well as from long-term sociological analyses (Hagedorn, 1988; Moore, 1991) and novels written by insiders (Mowry, 1992, 1993).

7. What high-powered weapons have done to gang structures and to the unpredictability of social relations, the supply of goods, and established relations with institutions of social control (such as the police) has a close parallel in the classic story of the Siriono of Brazil. Into that hunting and gathering society an outsider introduced a gun. Whereas earlier social relations had been strongly tied to feats of hunting dependent on locally made weapons, the gun jettisoned lower-status and marginal individuals into arenas they previously could not enter. Social cohesion among other group members broke down, leading to the destruction of the group (Holmberg, 1969).

8. Conquergood (1992) offers the following familiar example of such situations. Often, he, a Caucasian male who lived in the Big Red housing project, accompanied Mexican and Guatemalan mothers to school offices or police stations to help them negotiate second chances for their children. He recounts that once, "after the high school principal had been persuaded to give one of my young neighbors a second chance, the mother gratefully extended her hand to thank him. But the principal reached right past her to shake my hand. Quite literally, he did not see her. A short, dark-complexioned Mexican woman. . . ." (p. 127).

9. American literature of the late twentieth century has rapidly come to incorporate these "startling" disjunctures in expectations of racial, national, and ethnic categories. See, for example, Butler (1992), who writes about Vietnamese fishermen in contemporary Louisiana. Also see Cliff (1993) for a literary work that raises awareness about the presence of such "unexpected" groups and individuals as wealthy upper-class black entrepreneurs in the nineteenth century.

10. It is not surprising that black students experience considerable ambivalence with regard to such academic success, especially if they are located in public high schools where the majority designated as "low achievers" are students of color. For one case study of such a situation, see Fordham and Ogbu (1986).

# References

Alves, J. (1993). "Transgressions and Transformations: Initiation Rites Among Urban Portuguese Boys." *American Anthropologist, 95,* 894–928.

Bakhtin, M. M. (1984). *Rabelais and His World.* Bloomington: Indiana University Press.

Bakhtin, M. M. (1993). *Toward a Philosophy of the Act.* Austin: University of Texas Press.

Butler, R. O. (1992). *A Good Scent from a Strange Mountain.* New York, Penguin.

Carter, S. (1992). *Reflections of an Affirmative Action Baby.* Cambridge, MA: Harvard University Press.

Cliff, M. (1993). *Free Enterprise.* New York: Dutton.

Conquergood, D. (1992). "Life in Big Red: Struggles and Accommodations in a Chicago Polyethnic Tenement." In L. Lamphere (ed.), *Structuring Diversity: Ethnographic Perspectives on the New Immigration.* Chicago: University of Chicago Press.

Fabian, J. (1990). *Power and Performance: Ethnographic Explorations Through Proverbial Wisdom and Theatre in Shaba, Zaire.* Madison: University of Wisconsin Press.

Fordham, S., and Ogbu, J. (1986). "Black Students' School Success: Coping with the 'Burden of Acting White.'" *Urban Education, 18*(3), 176–206.

Gray, H. (1993). "African-American Political Desire and the Seductions of Contemporary Cultural Politics." *Cultural Studies, 7*(3), 364–373.

Grotowski, J. (1976). "The Theatre's New Testament." In R. Schechner and M. Schuman (eds.), *Ritual, Play, and Performance: Readings in the Social Sciences/ Theatre.* New York: Seabury Press.

Hagedorn, J. M. (1988). *People and Folks: Gangs, Crime, and the Underclass in a Rustbelt City.* Chicago: Lakeview Press.

Haizlip, S. T. (1994). *The Sweeter the Juice: A Family Memoir in Black and White.* New York: Simon and Schuster.

Heath, S. B. (Forthcoming). "Ethnography in Communities: Learning the Everyday Life of America's Subordinated Youth." In J. Banks and C. Banks (eds.), *Handbook of Research on Multicultural Education.* New York: Macmillan.

Heath, S. B., and McLaughlin, M. W. (eds.). (1993). *Identity and Inner-City Youth: Beyond Ethnicity and Gender.* New York: Teachers College Press.

Holmberg, A. R. (1969). *Nomads of the Long Bow: The Siriono of Eastern Bolivia.* Garden City, N.Y.: Natural History Press.

Jones, S. (1993). "Crossover Culture: Popular Music and the Politics of 'Race.'" *Stanford Humanities Review, 3*(2), 103–118.

Lamphere, L. (ed.). (1992). *Structuring Diversity: Ethnographic Perspectives on the New Immigration.* Chicago: University of Chicago Press.

McLaughlin, M. W., Irby, M. A., and Langman, J. (1993). *Urban Sanctuaries.* San Francisco: Jossey-Bass.

Martinez, R. (1992–1993). "Going Up in L.A." *Centro de Estudios Puertorriquenos*, 2 (Spring), 8–17.

Moore, J. W. (1991). *Going Down to the Barrio: Homeboys and Homegirls in Change*. Philadelphia: Temple University Press.

Mowry, J. (1992). *Way Past Cool*. New York: Harper.

Mowry, J. (1993). *Six Out Seven*. New York: Farrar, Strauss & Giroux.

Oldenburg, R. (1989). *The Great Good Place: Cafes, Coffee Shops, Community Centers, Beauty Parlors, General Stores, Bars, Hangouts and How They Get You Through the Day*. New York: Paragon House.

Peterson, N. (1993). "Demand Sharing: Reciprocity and the Pressure for Generosity Among Foragers." *American Anthropologist*, 95, 860–785.

Rodman, M. C. (1992). "Empowering Place: Multilocality and Multivocality." *American Anthropologist*, 94, 640–656.

Rodriguez, L. J. (1993). *Always Running: La Vida Loca: Gang Days in L.A*. East Haven, Conn: Curbstone Press.

Schieffelin, B. (1990). *The Give and Take of Everyday Life*. New York: Cambridge University Press.

Stack, C. E. (1974). *All Our Kin: Strategies for Survival in a Black Community*. New York: Harper & Row.

Steele, S. (1990). *The Content of Our Character: A New Vision of Race in America*. New York: Harper & Row.

Turner, V. (1976). "Social Dramas and Ritual Metaphors." In R. Schechner and M. Schuman (eds.), *Ritual, Play, and Performance: Reading in the Social Sciences/Theatre*. New York: Seabury Press.

Turner, V. (1982). *From Ritual to Theatre: The Human Seriousness of Play*. New York: PAJ Publications.

Turner, V. (1988). *The Anthropology of Performance*. New York: PAJ Publications.

Vigil, D. (1993). "Gangs, Social Control, and Ethnicity: Ways to Redirect." In S. B. Heath and M. W. McLaughlin (eds.), *Identity and Inner-City Youth* (pp. 94–120). New York: Teachers College Press.

West, C. (1993). *Race Matters*. New York: Vintage Books.

Williams, P. (1991). *The Alchemy of Race and Rights*. Cambridge, Mass.: Harvard University Press.

## Chapter Three

# Youth, Interethnic Relations, and Education in Europe

James Lynch

This chapter is concerned with the way in which European societies have responded to cultural diversity both historically and
more recently, how those responses have set a context for interethnic and intercultural friendships and human relations among young
people, and how those relations are apprehended through present
theoretical constructs.[1] It is also concerned with the extent to
which those constructs facilitate or impede such interactions. In
order to set a historical and cultural context for contemporary conditions, the chapter commences with a brief overview of the eti-
ology of ethnic relations in Europe, emphasizing the patchwork
nature of the original settlement and the more integrative pattern
of recent immigration. This historical description is followed by
a consideration of two major paradigms for the cultural diversity
currently observed in Europe: intercultural and multicultural.
Based on these overarching paradigms, and on minor subpara-
digms, the chapter then provides a description of the current state
of interethnic relations in Europe. It ends with a discussion of
implications for the development of policy, practice, and research
in the United States.

# The Historical Setting

Europe's historical heritage forms a context within which young people have to find their own way to reach out to one another. For European youth that context is a major barrier to communication, interaction, and friendship, for although cultural diversity is a relatively recent concern in Europe, its historical development has been long, complex, often embittered, and violent. The very process of being socialized into one culture has prevented the acceptance of the legitimacy of others. Indeed, the major agencies of cultural transmission and secondary socialization, such as educational systems, have themselves contributed to a cultural context that has made interethnic relations among young people more difficult rather than less so.

## The Mosaic of Early Settlement

Even before Roman times, when a large proportion of the Western continent spoke Celtic, there were other cultures and languages that, overlapping in their occupancy of the terrain, competed for its resources and riches and conflicted over the apportionment of these possessions. With the passage of time, a mosaic of settlement resulted. Many nations, defined as having the same language and culture, sometimes also the same religion, settled into designated spaces, but the boundaries were always frayed at the edges; this nucleated pattern of settlement stood in contrast to the much more integrated pattern of European settlement in the United States. But the "apartheid" in Europe, unlike that in the United States, did not break down substantially over time.

## The Separation of Nations

Even in the period called the "age of nationalism" (in the nineteenth century) diversity was seen as a threat to the nation-state, and with the advent of mass state education systems, a new instrument was forged in order to squeeze out any cultural diversity—a process that eventually spread far beyond the confines of Europe (Ramirez and Beli, 1987; Soysal and Strang, 1989). With few exceptions (Switzerland and Luxembourg being perhaps the most notable), newly confident nation-states of the nineteenth and twentieth centuries saw comprehensive unity as their major goal and education in the national language as the anvil upon which that unity would be forged. (Somewhat paradoxically, bilingual education is illegal at present in trilingual Belgium!) Despite a more recent model of successful multilingual education in the form of the European Schools (Housen and Baetens Beardsmore, 1987; Baetens Beardsmore and Kohls, 1988), the aim of the major European nations was, and still is, for all young people to be furnished with identical loyalties to the unitary nation-state. Both dissent from the dominant culture and espousal of minority culture were actively discouraged and, in many instances, were regarded as tantamount to cultural heresy, even to treason against the nation-state.

## Nationalistic Education and Its Consequences

These language policies, in addition to secular nationalism in the form of compulsory religious instruction, were regarded as the handmaidens of national unity, social stability, and political commitment. Such efforts at homogeneity were, however, only partially successful, although the resultant cultural intolerance reached a fever pitch immediately before the First World War. But the inefficiency of the efforts to "ethnically cleanse" minorities from the national scene can be gauged by the fact that, in spite of massive expulsions at the end of both the First and Second World Wars, old established linguistic minorities still exist in every major country in Europe; some are even supported by well-established, legally binding international treaties (Housen and Baetens Beardsmore, 1987; Baetens Beardsmore and Kohls, 1988).[2] Thus, while it is of course unthinkable to seek to justify "apartheid" and "ethnic cleansing," neither is unprecedented among European responses to ethnic diversity.

Insofar as European nations of the early twentieth century attempted to educate the younger generation in the principles of social interrelationships, they resorted largely to old nationalistic clichés and jingoistic symbols: king and country, national interest, linguistic and cultural pride, even purity (sometimes the issue was subliminally economic)—that is, narrow national objectives and expectations more suited to another time and place. Even where such feelings were combined with a commitment to education in democracy, this commitment was inevitably articulated within the confines of the traditions and literature of a single nation-state and only rarely related to a more global context. Such systems clearly acted as cultural and political barriers to keep young people divided rather than united. Linked to this fostering of patriotism were strains of national superiority, even supremicism—the very stuff of international conflict and cultural bigotry. Thus was created a fertile seedbed for stereotypical perceptions; ethnic, linguistic, religious, and national prejudice; cultural and economic conflict; genocide; holocaust; and disastrous war.

## Increasing Cultural Diversity

The earliest components of the original cultural mosaic of Europe were gradually overlain by increasing religious diversity, through the Muslim invasions, the Reformation, and, more recently, the mass migrations that occurred during the postwar economic boom (Lynch, 1983b). For example, as the Turks moved westward in the fifteenth and sixteenth centuries, they imposed a particularly harsh peace characterized by forced conversions and genocide, thus sowing the seeds of conflict. They stayed 150 years in Hungary and 340 years in Serbia and other parts of the Balkans. As late as 1876, Gladstone was protesting Turkish atrocities against the Bulgarians; the Armenian holocaust began in 1915; and mass expulsions of non-Turks from Turkey date back to the early 1920s. Over one million Serbs died in the First World War, and approximately half that number died in the Second. The mass expulsions of populations at the end of the Second World War have been described as the largest movements of people since the time of the *Voelkerwanderungen* (people's migration). In short, ethnic conflict, bigotry, and violence have been endemic to Europe.

To the long-standing historical cultural diversity of Europe an overlay of contemporary cultural diversity has been added. The consequent distinction to be made is between *established* and *new* minority communities.

## Responding to the "New" Cultural Diversity

In the face of this new cultural diversity, the nations of Europe experienced problems rooted in the European psyche. The societies of Western Europe continued to encounter difficulties with this new cultural diversity, as they struggled to adjust, both culturally and socially, to the arrival of large numbers of immigrants in the postwar period. The consequent demographic change has thrust new concepts of cultural pluralism to the fore and forced nations to reexamine their fundamental cultural values and assumptions, not the least being those cultural presuppositions that are embedded in the hegemony of their elites over the institutions of cultural transmission. But the failure of most European nations to initiate their own *perestroika*, including a newer and more inclusive concept of citizenship, has led to major problems of legitimation. For some, this issue has pertained not to ethnicity but to the denial of citizenship rights and human justice for all young people (Gundara, 1992).[3] Until the 1970s, the dominant assumption in Europe was that all young people should acquire identical primary loyalties (that is, loyalties to the nation-state), but the increasing cultural pluralism of the continent remained dissonant from the structural pluralism of the continent (Lynch, 1990).

## Developments in Eastern Europe

Meanwhile, consciousness of cultural diversity has increased in intensity in Eastern Europe, as nations, formerly locked in political bondage, and with their cultural diversity deep-frozen for almost half a century, have thrown off the yoke of political uniformity and enforced cultural monism, and sought to rediscover a more pluralist political and economic order, unknown to a whole generation. Moreover, youth movements that previously served the narrow purpose of one-party political indoctrination have been abolished. Political pluralism has renewed these nations' awareness of their own cultural diversity (*The Economist*, March 13, 1933, p. 23),[4] and of social, cultural, environmental, and territorial conflicts long suppressed. The latter, of course, involved war and genocide. Even (or perhaps especially) the former Soviet Union has found itself unable to deny the heritage of its history—namely, its dynamic of religious, linguistic, and cultural diversity. Its component parts, propelled outward from their former anchor, have at times appeared to be bound by a cultural conflict that, rooted in historical precursors, predates the Soviet state by many hundreds of years.

## The Changing Paradigm

### The Reasons for the Change

Since the Second World War, the response to cultural diversity in Europe has changed. Several factors account for the emergence of pressure to alter the paradigm within the pluralist societies of this continent:

1. With the end of the Second World War, increasing dissonance became apparent between the declared ideals of democratic European societies, now enshrined both in instruments of the Council of Europe, the European Union (EU), and other bodies, and in the treatment of minorities.

2. Western Europe's insatiable demands for labor in the 1960s and 1970s, combined with the improvement of international transportation, facilitated the movement of large numbers of

culturally diverse citizens. In making their homes and liveli-
hoods in Europe, they raised issues of religious and cultural
freedom, citizenship, and the reconciliation of cultural diversity with political unity. Also contributing to the mobility of
labor was the growing internationalization of industry, business, and commerce, as well as the economic interdependence of nations. Multinational companies increasingly
became the order of the day, and industries, rather than
nations, began to compete globally (Porter, 1990).[5]

3. Dismay over the evident failure of national-citizenship education, as in the Weimar Republic, to enforce a commitment to
the rule of law and democracy, combined with awareness that
the citizenship education of children and young people under a
totalitarian regime had become an instrument for the destruction of fundamental human rights and freedoms, alerted
nations to the need for fundamentally different policies.

4. Improvements in transportation and its increasingly cheap
availability facilitated youth, school, and student exchanges,
which in some cases were supported by regional and supranational agencies fostering a more open approach to other
nations, their languages and culture.

5. The rights of citizens began to be defined beyond the framework of the nation-state and against supranational criteria,
thus providing enhanced political security for those rights.
(This process of internationalizing human rights and freedoms, at first through the International Declaration of
Human Rights and the establishment of regional and international courts of justice, made nations, not just their citizens,
accountable for the upholding of basic human rights.)

6. A series of improvements in international communications
made the transmission of ideas about human rights and freedoms across national boundaries much easier and more effective and, at the same time, ensured that the transgressions of
recalcitrant nations would be known to all.

7. Associated with this latter factor was a more vigorous internationalization of educational endeavor than had occurred under the League of Nations and agencies such as the International Labour Office and the International Bureau of Education in Geneva. This educational internationalization occurred partly through the activities of United Nations agencies such as UNESCO and UNICEF, but also through the efforts of the Council of Europe and, increasingly, through the EEC.

### Precursor Changes in Knowledge

But if these factors were contextual to the development of a new debate about cultural diversity, its form, and its apprehension, the aims, content, and particularly the processes of educational and broader social responses were also influenced by closer concerns in the field of education and the social and environmental sciences, including theoretical and practical advances in sociology, anthropology, science, education, and the theory and practice of teaching in general. While the impact has been slight, thus raising the issue of whether indigenous organizations and institutions can deliver for others what they cannot or will not deliver for themselves, there are some signs of movement. Then too, the rise of the feminist movement, the concern in many European countries with "ethnic" studies, and what later came to be called "multicultural education" in most anglophone Western democracies and "intercultural education" in francophone countries were potential placebos to the perceived social ills and educational exigencies arising from mass immigration and the failure of education systems to deal with that challenge.

Contiguous movements with aims similar to those of multicultural and intercultural education also began to have an impact as the search began for palliatives that could appear radical without basically changing things. Global education and world studies began this process separately from but almost coterminously with the rise of multicultural education. Postwar developments in international human rights instruments led to the development of human rights education, now strongly supported by the Council of Europe (Starkey, 1988), of law-related education (Rowe and Thorpe, 1991), of environmental education (National Curriculum Council, 1991), and of peace education (O'Connell, 1992)—all of which, in a number of countries, have undoubtedly spurred a reappraisal of the ways in which societies may foster healthy social interrelationships and participatory citizenship[6] within a context of human rights and social responsibilities.

Gradually, too, the work of Jürgen Habermas and others of the Frankfurt School on emancipatory education, the work of Pierre Bourdieu, Jean-Claude Passeron, and others in the field of social and cultural reproduction in France, and the work of proponents of the "New Sociology of Education" in Britain in the 1970s addressed issues of the construction of meaning, social consciousness, ideology, power, and domination (Young, 1976). The latter advocated engagement with the aims and underlying assumptions of education and the latent meanings and values of teachers, which are the foundations of taken-for-granted professional consciousness, so as to combat a rationality that oppresses teachers into racism, sexism, or elitism. This model has been referred to as the emancipatory model of citizenship education. The new national curriculum in Britain, though not quite so radical, included for the first time a statutory commitment to citizenship education. As envisaged in the English national curriculum, which was progressively instituted from 1989 onward, this form of education was conceptualized as having a cross-curricular theme with four major components: the nature of community; roles and relations in a plural society; work and employment; and leisure and public services (National Curriculum Council, 1990).

***Content of the Changes.*** Building on such instruments as the United Nations Declaration of Human Rights and subsequent international and regional instruments (Selby, 1987), new and more open paradigms began to emerge. These instruments were given added impetus in the 1980s by the commitment of national and regional organizations such as the Council of Europe to human rights education (Starkey, 1988), and an international model emerged thanks to the attention given to human rights education in Canada through the patriation of the Canadian constitution (Lynch, 1986b).[7] Endeavors were also made to articulate the rights of children in the International Convention on the Rights of the Child, which entered into force in September 1990. Such declarations and instruments have increasingly advanced the need to link together the political education of the next generation, skills in intercultural education and competence, and a commitment to international community responsibility (Lynch, Modgil, and Modgil, 1992). Forming the basis for these documents are such basic moral concepts as human dignity and justice, liberty and equality, human-human and human-environmental interdependence, and mutuality in social and international behavior. Indeed, these are the basic values that must be transmitted to young people.

As the Council of Europe (1985) has put it: "The understanding and experience of human rights is an important element of the preparation of all young people for life in a democratic and pluralistic society. It is part of social and political education and it involves intercultural and international understanding."

***Organizational Initiatives.*** In 1971, the Council for Cultural Cooperation launched a program for the training of teachers; later in the decade it also offered experimental in-service programs (Standing Conference of European Ministers of Education, 1979). And in 1972 the Council of Europe began to provide experimental classes to the children of migrant workers, aimed at *integrating* them into school and society. Such initiatives continued throughout the 1970s and into the 1980s. Gradually, they become oriented toward a broader concept of human rights within a context of cultural diversity (Lynch, 1986b). For instance, in 1980 a project was launched to develop an intercultural perspective on the relationships between the school and its social environment, including not only the cultural activities of the school and those of the community but also the education of adults (Porcher, 1983b). More recently, the cause of minority languages has also come to the fore.

Deriving from a recommendation of the Parliamentary Assembly of the Council of Europe (1981), the EEC in 1982 established the Western European Language Bureau, which now devotes upwards of $4 million per annum to the support of minority languages. In November 1992, eleven of the twenty-two countries of the Council of Europe[8] signed an accord to encourage the use of indigenous languages in school and public life. Accordingly, though in a major departure from previous policy, the French government launched a major bilingual program in January 1993.

*Limitations of the Changes.* But even in those European societies where discussion of cultural pluralism and its implications for human relations is the subject of discourse, the debate has not progressed significantly beyond the frontiers of the nation-state. Indeed, in most cases, it has not spread beyond dialogue among academic cognoscenti about whether the issue of equity and cultural diversity can really be one-dimensional, and, if not, how it can best be understood. What, for instance, are the structural implications of such cultural diversity? When the debate addresses the infringement of the human rights of newcomers to those pluralistic countries, schools are silent and educators lose their eloquence. Moreover, the legal status of ethnic minorities, a major determinant of their participation and interrelationships in society, manifests a wide range of security and participation; nevertheless, the norm is one of disenfranchisement (Churchill, 1986).[9]

*Absence of National Charters of Rights and Freedoms.* Yet no European country has established legislation, like that in Canada, aimed at regulating human behavior and addressing the dilemmas of equity and diversity. While the European Convention on Human Rights is a first step approach, it is inaccessible to most Europeans compared with the Canadian Charter of Rights and Freedoms, attached to the constitution when the latter was patriated to Canada. This charter affords all citizens defense and redress against the infringement of their rights by other citizens or the state. Accompanying this in Canada has been the development of a national strategy on multiculturalism that not only embraces race relations but also comprises legislation recognizing multiculturalism as one of the country's basic norm-generating characteristics. This outcome, in turn, has been linked with the further development of human rights legislation, including educational initiatives. Such composite approaches, though they represent a broad social coalition, address many structures in society simultaneously, and build on a broad ideological consensus, cannot be observed in any European country.

*Absence of Minority/Majority Partnership.* No European country has taken minorities into partnership in the design of its social or educational strategies. Nor have any advanced a coordinated, global set of initiatives to achieve systematic and deliberate change toward agreed-upon goals, based on a national covenant of acceptable norms and values drawn against international obligations. Yet such codifications are available in the many international agreements and conventions to which most Western countries are signatory. This stricture applies as much to the "newer" migrant countries as to the older Eurocentric countries, still imprisoned by their perceptions of immigrants as something other than fellow citizens— perceptions that have led to an outdated calibration of human beings and their worth.

*Cultural Mosaic Rather Than Melting Pot.* No European country has adopted a Zangwillian "melting pot" approach to the recent wave of migration, although diversity and the right to greater equity have at times been expressed in peaceful and creative tension, with cultural and social pluralism providing the momentum for social change, the liberation of the human spirit, and greater human justice. At other times, however, the results have been cultural bigotry, repressive hegemony, violent conflict, and even civil war. Such are the consequences when diversity is used to legitimate economic and political conflict.

## The Two Major Approaches

Accompanying this "renaissance" of cultural diversity has been a wealth of differing intellectual perspectives, many of which complement the already extensive literature of the past half-century. There have been many stages in the attempts to legitimate the existence of continued separation of certain ethnic groups from their peers in school and society (Lynch, 1986b). Firstly there was a *linguistic response*, which implied that the only reason such pupils achieved less success than their European peers was that they did not speak the national language, or at least did not speak it as well. Then came the *socioeconomic-disadvantage approach*, which reasoned that the reason for the deficit was largely economic. As differences in educational attainment and progress among various ethnic groups were rarely adequately documented, this approach did not give a clear picture of the situation. It ignored or underplayed gender differences within ethnic groups, and was unable to explain differences between ethnic groups (Plewis, 1988). Next came the *ethnic studies approach*, which asserted the necessity for the representation of the culture of minorities in the school curriculum.

Finally, there came a series of micro-approaches that sought to facilitate the mutual accommodation of the newer and older cultures and to produce a much more inclusive definition of national culture. With one major exception, these micro-approaches can be classified under two major domains: *intercultural education*, which derives from most of the countries of continental Europe; and *multicultural education*, which derives predominantly from Britain. The exception is *antiracist education*, a mid-1980s radical left-wing offshoot of multicultural education, based almost exclusively in Britain.

At their extreme, the two poles of the continuum of policy options available to pluralist societies in response to cultural diversity are social assimilation and cultural mosaic. At any time an individual society may be at one of several different points along that continuum, in one of many different social sectors; and it is not unusual for societies to simultaneously pursue contrasting, incompatible, or divergent policies in the different sectors. Because of their history, European societies have tended toward the assimilationist pole, although both major marshaling ideologies—multiculturalism and interculturalism—have sought to disguise this aim. School systems, as well as school-attached training corps, have aided and abetted the same aim by stubbornly retaining the epistemologies of their curricula.

As indicated above, the majority of countries in Europe, led by the francophone nations and strongly supported by the Council of Europe and its initiatives, adopted an intercultural rather than a multicultural response to educating youth for cultural diversity (Mitter, Doebrich, Kodron, and Lynch, 1982). *Intercultural education* is seen as the fundamental principle underlying all school activity. Its main characteristics are as follows:

1. With a few exceptions, it rests on well-founded traditions of European research and writing in the field of cross-cultural psychology.
2. It emphasizes the interaction of cultures and individuals at the micro-level in both schools and society (Essinger and Ucar, 1948).
3. It attempts to engage with the dynamic of cultural encounter and change, and to deduce the implications for education.
4. If often emphasizes the comparative method in the study of the mutual socialization of communities and the interlearning involved in cultural encounters.
5. It aims for maximum social and economic integration (Leeman, 1982).
6. It possesses strong links to the development of theory and practice in developing countries.

7. Over time it has developed strong links to human rights education (Council of Europe, 1983).

8. It seeks to reinforce the mutuality of cultures and to facilitate interlearning between them (Porcher, 1983a).

9. It is represented in a vigorous and productive international forum—namely, ARIC (The Association for Research in Intercultural Education).

The issues, methods, and approaches adopted by advocates of intercultural education for young people have been vigorously debated over the past two decades (Rey, 1984). And as P. R. Dasen (1992) has pointed out, "intercultural" advocates represent a very broad spectrum of interests and epistemological outlooks, although recent years have seen an accelerating trend toward a more unified field of inquiry and action. This movement toward greater harmonization was strengthened in the late 1980s by the establishment of the francophone international association for intercultural research (ARIC), based in Geneva.

The concept of *multicultural education* developed in a rather haphazard way, perhaps slightly influenced by the ethnic studies movement in the United States, though it does not have that movement's well-defined precursor traditions, disciplines, and literature. Idealistic teachers and left-wing educators became part of the movement, which was gradually taken over by the latter. It also lacked a well-defined conceptual base that would attach it to the existing curricular structure, although a number of attempts by social scientists and others were made to provide one (Lynch, 1983a). These are the major characteristics of multicultural education:

1. Notwithstanding analogue developments in such countries as Australia, it is an essentially parochially anglophone creation.

2. As a consequence its existence in Europe is characterized by a parochial approach, taking little account of developments elsewhere, even within the anglophone world (Lynch, 1991).

3. It has always been an uneasy coalition of both political and academic forces.

4. It lacks a disciplinary base and never achieved more than a thin veneer of academic credibility.

5. It has had little deep or long-term influence on the content or process of the school curriculum.

6. It has been easily "outbid" by more radical demands, such as those for antiracist education (see below).

7. It has never established strong connections with international and comparative educational traditions.

8. It has never succeeded in "coalitioning" with other movements with similar aims, having taken upon itself a curricular exclusivity and imperialism.

Finally, *antiracist education,* which occurred as an even more parochial offshoot of multicultural education in Britain in the mid-1980s, represents a sort of academic last resort. It was a radical, highly politicized approach, based on naive neo-Marxist explanations of capitalist societies' alleged use of structural racism for their own ends. Usually, such analyses drew on static, single-factor models and explanations of cultural inequity, dubious and unrepresentative research studies and reinforcement of false stereotypes, overcategorization and enhancement of social category salience, and gentle reworking of essentially androcentric theories (Nye, 1988)—all of which were unable to reflect the dynamism of cultural diversity, let alone to combat the prejudice and bigotry that inevitably arise as a cultural by-product of that diversity. Moreover, the movement's tendency to villify and label as "racist" any who opposed its extremist message alienated many multicultural advocates who rejected racism as evil and immoral anyway.

These analyses led to simplistic and, in some cases, harmful and counterproductive pedagogical panaceas that allocated a predominantly technicist role to the teacher[10] and saw social-value positions as absolutes rather than as competing ideological perceptions and aspirations. Politically, the effect was a disastrous backlash perpetrated by socially conservative and culturally exclusive dominant groups against the investigation of alternative responses to cultural diversity, leading to a social, cultural, and intellectual "ice age." True, a more cooperative antiracist education emerged in the early 1990s; indeed, it is less illiberal and coercive than the version that has done so much damage to race relations and to the cause of an effective response to cultural diversity in the United Kingdom.

More recent publications have sought, for example, to place antiracist education within the context of a broader civic, moral, and political education, one that "seeks to extend participation in the democratic process by equipping young people with the range of skills and dispositions needed to become decent, fairminded, responsible and informed citizens" (Carrington and Short, 1989).[11] Most recently, there has been a tendency among scholars to bypass both multicultural and antiracist education and to aim at a more global conceptualization based on citizenship education and the preparation of young people for responsible membership in democratic societies through a strengthening of law-related education.

## Cultural Diversity and Young People in Contemporary Europe

In short, young people in Europe have to carry with them a considerable volume of historical impediments in their efforts to develop human relations beyond their immediate cultural groups. In some countries, such difficulties are compounded by educational systems that discriminate on the basis of birth or inherited wealth; in others, problems of language (including dialect register) and religion remain sometimes insuperable barriers to interethnic friendships among young people. If we consider the overlapping dimensions of cultural diversity—dimensions such as race, religion, language, birthplace, ethnicity, gender, age, social class, and, more recently, caste—we cannot avoid the conclusion that Europe's population as a whole manifests a rich diversity of cultural factors. These factors are still resisted in the major loci of socialization: family and community, school, youth groups and organizations, and centers for the vocational training of young people. Nor have elite academic institutions shown more than a lip-serviced willingness to include this pluralism of pluralisms among their epistemic functions. Indeed, they have been painfully slow to embrace such a cultural challenge within their academic and political discourse about diversity in Western critical pedagogy (Ellsworth, 1989).

Moreover, little effort is made by schools, education and training systems, and youth organizations to ensure reduction of prejudice.[12] Thus, both social policy options and human relations among the young are needlessly constrained, political responses to the newfound pluralism of others are needlessly impeded, and social policies and educational practice are needlessly limited by a false perception, one could say an inadequate apprehension, of what cultural pluralism actually means in the daily construction and negotiation of reality in the lives of young people. Some schools and education systems have taken up the challenge, but such efforts are usually spasmodic, inchoate, and random. Differing strategies, approaches, and points of entry are used to engage the issues, from curricula, teaching/learning methods, and training to sometimes naive implementations of contact theory. And evidence indicates that such efforts rarely succeed. For example, research has shown that ethnic friendships, in school, communities, or youth groups, tend to coexist with negative stereotypes of minority groups, unless such stereotypes are actively challenged by curricula and other interventions (Aboud, 1988). The error of this somewhat facile "application of contact theory," as well as its widespread tenure as the basis of underlying youth exchanges and contacts, is detailed in a 1982 report to the French/German Youth Office (Dussine, 1982).

But for all their inadequacies and failings, the momentum of bilateral and multilateral contacts by both nongovernmental and governmental agencies in the postwar period cannot be denied. Youth exchanges, school exchanges, and reciprocal instruction in the languages of contiguous countries (for example, France and Germany) have all been attempted in initiatives supported by the

EEC and the Council of Europe. The objective is to help young people understand one another better, to learn from one another, and to develop bonds of friendship.

Youth exchanges in Europe underwent numerous phases. Among these was the early postwar period, dominated by a formalistic espousal of peace and international understanding within a deep-frozen political context (United Nations Educational, Scientific and Cultural Organization, 1987). Notwithstanding the earlier existence of a UNESCO travel-grants scheme for youth and student leaders, dating from 1951, this period also produced the UNESCO Associated Schools Project (ASPRO) in 1953, aimed at promoting the introduction of special educational programs for international understanding as well as the facilitation of exchanges of students, teachers, information, and teaching materials among affiliated schools. Arising out of Article 50 of the Treaty of Rome, which established the EEC in 1957, the European Economic Community has supported farmers' exchanges since 1964 and young workers' exchanges since 1979, with a permitted duration of three weeks to eighteen months, including the possibility of homestays. A more international dimension was introduced in 1984 under the Third Lome Treaty with African countries.

Not until the Helsinki Act of 1975, which initiated the second phase, did these aims broaden, becoming less politically constrained and more realistically focused on the potential for interlearning from such contacts and exchanges. The Council of Europe established both the European Youth Center and the European Youth Foundation to promote and finance international encounters among young people. Linked with the development of intercultural education, and influenced by the establishment of the Society for Intercultural Education, Training and Research (SIETAR) in North America, intercultural learning emerged in the 1970s as a major and unifying motivator for such contacts and exchanges.

During these first two periods, the major organizational initiatives were the founding of the Central Bureau for Educational Visits and Exchanges in London in 1948, the establishment of the Franco-German Youth Office in 1963, and the convening of the Williamsburg Summit in 1983. The latter launched a common exchange program in France, Germany, Italy, the United Kingdom, Japan, Canada, and the United States. The third, contemporary phase, however, had to await the "fall of the wall" in order to see a more openly dialogical and less doctrinaire context for the objectives of youth exchanges by all parties. It is still too early to determine the directions in which such initiatives will aim, let alone those in which they will succeed. Nonetheless, there are still many legal and administrative barriers to more effective youth exchanges even within the EEC (LaRooy, 1986).

Other initiatives have included the training of teachers in intercultural education, organized over a number of years by the Council of Europe (Rey, 1986). But the major concern of such initiatives has tended to be almost exclusively the newly arrived migrants, of whom total accommodation has been required, rather than the development of supportive and congruent initiatives vis-à-vis the majority communities (Van den Berg-Eldering, 1987). As mentioned above, a very successful network of European schools exists, but it is intended mainly for the international elite. More recently, schemes for the exchange of students at further and higher education levels have been introduced under the evocative title ERASMUS. Indeed, the three European Economic Community programs—ERASMUS, LINGUA, and COMETT—currently involve approximately 100,000 students in higher education. They offer language studies, teacher training, open and distance learning, and mutual recognition of diplomas. Additional programs entitled FORCE, PETRA, and Eurotechnet are aimed at establishing common approaches to training and technology in the twelve member-states.[13]

These latter schemes, however, tend to include only a small minority of the elite of each society and are more than counterbalanced by the prejudice generated by the mass media and by the embedded stereotypes of "outsiders" still dominant in the national media of each state. Moreover, the evidence regarding the effects of favorable intergroup contact is inconclusive, with the possibility of either favorable or unfavorable outcomes depending on circumstances (Ford, 1986). Further, such approaches leave untouched the whole question of what might be a fair and just balance of power and resources between nations and ethnic groups—a question that remains unresolved in Europe, where different nations are educating their youth according to different goals: assimilation or separatism (Davies, 1991).

With the downturn in European economies, an increasing number of young people, disproportionately minorities, are faced with demoralizing and extended unemployment. Their frustration, furthermore, finds an easy target in more newly arrived minorities. As perceived competition for jobs and economic resources has increased, so has the incidence of antiforeigner prejudice and violence in all European countries. In his work on employment and education among minority youth in England, J. Eggleston (1992) makes the point that work experience provides a basic context for the development of healthy personal identities and human relations. Yet this important socializing experience is being denied to many young people from all groups. Moreover, provision for their vocational training is often inadequate in terms of accessibility, appropriateness, quantity, and quality (Bastenier and others, 1986).

The problem for minority youth is compounded by at least two additional factors: they are more heavily hit by unemployment, and their personal identities are more under attack by antipathy, prejudice, and the threat of violence, because these young people are often "visible" minorities. Perceptions of youth unemployment are, in any case, often based on wildly generalized social attitudes (Bryder, 1991). Such perceptions have been accentuated by media representations of minority youth as temporary guest workers or *saisonniers*, rather than as linguistic and cultural minorities (Council for Cultural Cooperation of the Council of Europe, 1987).

The perceived competition for economic opportunity exacerbates interethnic conflict and draws apart those young people who need opportunities to socialize together. Thus the consequences of unemployment are not solely economic. The tragedy is that unemployment often coexists with unfilled vacancies requiring the kinds of skills achievable by young people of all groups, if appropriate training and other strategies are available.

## Lessons from European Experience

Although the United States has made much progress in integrating new citizens into its society and in coping with ever-increasing cultural diversity in the two centuries of its existence, it could learn from the older countries of Europe how to respond to the challenges of cultural pluralism. Of course, the cultural, political, and historical contexts of Europe and North America are fundamentally different. The United States has always been a society of immigration, whereas European nations have never thought of themselves as such. Yet there is a sense in which one can always learn from others, even if it is knowledge of what to avoid. Given that caveat, let us consider the following recommendations, which allow us to take a profitable look at what has (and has not) happened in Europe with respect to cultural diversity and relationships among young people of different backgrounds and nationalities:

1. Schools can and do make a difference; the importance of education in developing a critically more tolerant and equitable society is indisputable.

2. By learning foreign languages, youth not only gain insight into other cultures but also develop a more detached view of their own culture.

3. What we teach and how we teach it can make a difference in the interethnic relations of young people. Thus strategies and the organizational structures of schools should be designed with that fact in mind.

4. The development of national curricula as well as of national assessment and examinations systems affords important opportunities (often misused) to deflect young people away from ethnic bigotry and discrimination.

5. The training of teachers for the facilitation of human relations and the reduction of prejudice is important for both social and economic reasons.

6. Education revolves about the transmission of values; more cooperative modes of education will yield students who are less competitive and can work with, live with, and tolerate others.

7. Extra-scholastic agencies such as religious associations, youth groups, and exchange organizations can have a powerful socializing influence on young people.

8. Unguided and unplanned interethnic contact can actually exacerbate prejudice and bigotry. Thus holistic institutional policies are needed to make such contact purposeful and successful, whether in school or in youth organizations.

9. New developments are moving away from approaches that previously emphasized social-category salience (for example, ethnic studies or multicultural education) and toward broader, more holistic coalitions (such as the education of young people for citizenship, including global citizenship). They are also drawing more strongly on law-related educational initiatives (Lynch, 1992).[14]

10. Current studies of prejudice rest on an assumption of almost 100 percent environmental causation, thus neglecting important research possibilities and methodologies concerning the relative contributions of both genetic and environmental factors (Eysenck, 1992).

11. Any initiative that fails to take into account the media stereotypes of minority youth is unlikely to succeed. Schools are ill-equipped and untrained to match the persuasive power of television!

12. The consequences of unemployment are not entirely economic; they must also be seen in the context of wasted human capital, increased individual and social frustration and aggression, and lost opportunities for youth socialization.

Such socialization could counter prejudice and bigotry, social conflict and violence (Grossarth-Maticek, Eysenck, and Vetter, 1989).[15]

13. The study of unemployment and its consequences is not seen as a priority for economic and human capital investment in most European countries.

14. This field is very immature, and its research findings are partial and imperfect. More attention needs to be given to the dissemination of accomplished work and to the evaluation (including meta-evaluation) of relevant projects.

15. Both macro- and micro-initiatives are needed at the systemic and institutional levels of education if any durable success is to be achieved. Political will and technical expertise are also necessary prerequisites. Yet a consensus for that kind of coalition is still largely lacking in European states.

16. Current conceptual approaches to responding to cultural diversity are too global to permit practical applications at the institutional and instructional levels. On the other hand, micro-research tends to be too specific and nongeneralizable. More powerful middle-range theories are needed to link the macro- and micro-approaches currently being employed.

In sum, while there is much that Europe and North America may learn from each other in the field of cultural diversity, caution must be exercised so as not to overdraw the parallels or to oversimplify the differing cultural factors.

## Notes

1. The author has prepared this chapter in his own personal capacity, and none of his statements, written or oral, should be taken to imply a policy, commitment, or opinion on the part of the World Bank.

2. Examples include the Danish minority in Germany; the Ger-

man minorities in Denmark, Italy, and Belgium; the Hungarians and Slovenes in Austria; and, more recently, the Sorbs and Wends in Germany and the Germans in Poland.

3. Gundara (1992) argues that the issues for the two kinds of minorities (indigenous and immigrant) are fundamentally different.

4. There are large linguistic and cultural minority communities in all the former Eastern Bloc countries.

5. Moreover, it has been argued by economists and sociologists that through their ability to offer rising living standards to their citizens, governments seek to legitimate their rule.

6. The establishment of the Citizenship Foundation in the United Kingdom was a result of a Law in Education project.

7. Some of the human rights legislation in Canada predates the Universal Declaration of Human Rights.

8. The Council of Europe estimates that one in ten of the people of Western and Eastern Europe (excluding the countries of the former Soviet Union) speak a language other than the official language of their country.

9. Swedish legislation has, however, extended voting rights to minorities.

10. In one English Local Education Authority, race advisers, referred to as "race police," were appointed to supervise teachers.

11. The old illiberal rhetoric and revolutionary purity is beginning to be cast aside in favor of cooperation with other movements, sharing similar and in many cases wider hopes for social change.

12. I have argued elsewhere (Lynch, 1987) that schools must deliberately integrate prejudice-reduction interventions into the content and teaching/learning strategies of their curricula and institutional arrangements for the education of young people.

13. Both these sets of programs are to be replaced by two coordinated programs: one for higher education and one for training and technology. From 1 January 1995, the number of states in the European Union increased to fifteen.

14. The Citizenship Foundation, the National Curriculum Council,

and the Law Society in the United Kingdom have recently published detailed curricular materials for eleven- to fourteen-year-olds, and they are currently developing materials for seven-year-olds.

15. One recent large-scale experiment conducted in Europe found a very significant relationship between prejudice and socioeconomic insecurity.

## References

Abdallah-Pretceille, M. (1986). *Vers une pédagogie interculturelle*. Paris: Publications de la Sorbonne.

Aboud, F. (1988). *Children and Prejudice*. Oxford: Basil Blackwell.

Baetens Beardsmore, H., and Kohls, J. (1988). "Immediate Pertinence in the Acquisition of Multilingual Proficiency: The European Schools." *The Canadian Modern Language Review*, 44(4), 680–701.

Bastenier, A., and others. (1986). *The Vocational Training of Young Migrants in Belgium, Denmark, France, Luxembourg and the United Kingdom: Synthesis Report*. Berlin: European Centre for the Development of Vocational Training.

Bryder, T. (1991). "Generalized Social Attitudes and Perceptions of Youth Unemployment Policy-Making: A Cross-Cultural Comparison of Adolescents in Denmark, Finland, Norway and Sweden." *Political Psychology*, 12(3), 431–455.

Carrington, B., and Short, G. (1989). *Race and the Primary School*. Windsor, England: NFER-Nelson.

Churchill, S. (1986). *The Education of Linguistic and Cultural Minorities in the OECD Countries*. Clevedon, England: Multilingual Matters.

Council for Cultural Cooperation of the Council of Europe. (1987). *Migrants and the Media: From "Guest Workers" to Linguistic and Cultural Minorities* (CDCC Project Number 7: The Education and Cultural Development of Migrants). Strasbourg: Council for Cultural Cooperation.

Council of Europe. (1983). *Secretariat Memorandum on the CDCC's Work on Human Rights Education in Schools*. Strasbourg: Council for Cultural Cooperation.

Council of Europe. (1985). *Committee of Ministers, Recommendation No. 85, 7 of the Committee of Ministers to Member States on Teaching and Learning About Human Rights in Schools*. Strasbourg: Council of Europe.

Dasen, P. R. (1992). "Cross-Cultural Psychology and Teacher Training." In J. Lynch, C. Modgil, and S. Modgil (eds.), *Prejudice, Polemic or Progress?* (p. 193). London and Washington, D.C.: Falmer Press.

Davies, C. (1991). *Nationalism, Education and the Individual*. Reading, England. University of Reading.

Dussine, P. (1982). *Etude portant sur les expériences d'éxchange de jeunes realisées en Europe, visant à permettre leur développement au niveau communautaire.* Bonn: Office Franco-Allemande de Jeunesse.

*The Economist,* March 13, 1993. Special Supplement on Eastern Europe, p. 23.

Eggleston, J. (1992). "Employment, Education and Discrimination." In J. Lynch, C. Modgil, and S. Modgil (eds.), *Equity or Excellence? Education and Cultural Reproduction* (pp. 21–29). London and Washington, D.C.: Falmer Press.

Ellsworth, E. (1989). "Why Doesn't This Feel Empowering? Working Through the Repressive Myths of Critical Pedagogy." *Harvard Educational Review,* 59(3), 297–324.

Essinger, H., and Ucar, A. (1984). *Interkulturelle Erziehung in Theorie und Praxis.* Sulzberg, Germany: Paedagogischer Verlag Schneider.

Eysenck, H. J. (1992). "Roots of Prejudice: Genetic or Environmental?" In J. Lynch, C. Modgil, and S. Modgil (eds.), *Prejudice, Polemic or Progress?* (pp. 21–41). London and Washington, D.C.: Falmer Press.

Ford, W. S. (1986). "Favorable Intergroup Contact May Not Reduce Prejudice-Inconclusive Journal Evidence, 1960–1984." *Sociology and Social Research,* 70, 256–258.

Grossarth-Maticek, R., Eysenck, H. J., and Vetter, H. (1989). "The Causes and Cures of Prejudice: An Empirical Study of the Frustration-Aggression Hypothesis." *Personality and Individual Differences,* 10, 547–558.

Gundara, J. (1992). "The Dominant Nation: Subordinated Nations and Racial Inequalities." In J. Lynch, C. Modgil, and S. Modgil (eds.), *Equity or Excellence? Education and Cultural Reproduction* (pp. 67–78). London and Washington, D.C.: Falmer Press.

Hewstone, M., and Brown, R. (eds.). (1986). *Contact and Conflict in Intergroup Encounters.* Oxford: Basil Blackwell.

Housen, A., and Baetens Beardsmore, H. (1987). "Curricular and Extra-Curricular Factors in Multilingual Education." *Studies in Second Language Acquisition,* 9(1), 83–102.

La Rooy, A. (1986). *Legal and Administrative Barriers to Youth Exchanges in the European Community.* Luxembourg: Commission of the European Communities.

Leeman, Y. (1982). *Intercultureel Onderwijs.* Amsterdam: Universiteit van Amsterdam.

Lynch, J. (1983a). *The Multicultural Curriculum.* London: Batsford Academic.

Lynch, J. (1983b). "Multiethnic Education in Europe." *Phi Delta Kappan* (April), pp. 576–579.

Lynch, J. (1986a). "Multicultural Education in Western Europe." In J. A. Banks and J. Lynch (eds.), *Multicultural Education in Western Societies* (pp. 125–152). New York: Praeger.

Lynch, J. (1986b). *Multicultural Education: Principles and Practice.* London and Routledge, N.Y.: Methuen.

Lynch, J. (1987). *Prejudice Reduction and the Schools*. London and New York: Cassell.

Lynch, J. (1990). "Cultural Pluralism, Structural Pluralism and the United Kingdom." *Britain: A Plural Society* (seminar report). London: Commission for Racial Equality.

Lynch, J. (1991). *Multicultural Education in a Global Society*. London: Falmer Press.

Lynch, J. (1992). *Education for Citizenship in a Multicultural Society*. London: Cassell.

Lynch, J., Modgil, C., and Modgil, S. (eds.). (1992). *Human Rights, Education and Global Responsibilities*. London/Washington, D.C.: Falmer Press.

Mitter, W., Doebrich, P., Kodron, C., and Lynch, J. (1982). *Lehrerbildung fuer multikulturelle schulen*. Frankfurt am Main: Deutsches Institut fuer Internationale Paedagogische Forschung.

National Curriculum Council. (1990). *Education for Citizenship* (Curriculum Guidance 8). New York: National Curriculum Council.

National Curriculum Council. (1991). *Environmental Education* (Curriculum Guidance 7). New York: National Curriculum Council.

Nye, A. (1988). *Feminist Theory and the Philosophies of Man*. New York: Croom Helm.

O'Connell, J. (1992). "Peace Education in the Schools: The Urgency of Study and the Necessity of Balance." In J. Lynch, C. Modgil, and S. Modgil (eds.), *Education for Cultural Diversity: Convergence and Divergence* (pp. 257–272). London and Washington, D.C.: Falmer Press.

Parliamentary Assembly of the Council of Europe (Thirty-Third Ordinary Session). (1981). *Recommendation 928 (1981) on the Educational and Cultural Problems of Minority Languages and Dialects in Europe*. Strasbourg: Council of Europe.

Plewis, I. (1988). "Assessing and Understanding the Educational Progress of Children from Different Ethnic Groups." *Journal of the Royal Statistical Society* (Series A: Statistics in Society), *151*(2), 306–326.

Porcher, L. (1983a). *L'Enseignement aux enfants migrants*. Paris: Didier.

Porcher, L. (1983b). *Report of the Project Group to the CDCC*. Strasbourg: Council of Europe.

Porter, M. E. (1990). *The Competitive Advantage of Nations*. New York: Free Press.

Ramirez, F. O., and Boli, J. (1987). "The Political Construction of Mass Schooling: European Origins and Worldwide Institutionalization." *Sociology of Education, 60*(1), 2–17.

Rey, M. (1984). *Une pédagogie interculturelle*. Berne: Commission Suisse Pour L'Unesco.

Rey, M. (1986). *Training Teachers in Intercultural Education. The Work of the Council for Cultural Cooperation*. Strasbourg: Council for Cultural Cooperation.

Rowe, D., and Thorpe, T. (1991). "New Law Materials Go on Trial." *Citizenship* (the Journal of the Citizenship Foundation), *1*(2), 24–25.

Selby, D. (1987). *Human Rights.* Cambridge: Cambridge University Press.

Soysal, Y. N., and Strang, D. (1989). "Construction of the First Mass Education Systems in Nineteenth-Century Europe." *Sociology of Education, 62*(4), 277–288.

Standing Conference of European Ministers of Education. (1979). *Eleventh Session: Committee of Senior Officials, Migrants' Education.* Strasbourg: Conference of European Ministers of Education.

Starkey, H. (1988). "Human Rights: The Values for World Studies and Multicultural Education." *Westminster Studies in Education, 9,* 57–66.

United Nations Educational, Scientific and Cultural Organization. (1987). *Meeting of Governmental and Non-governmental Officials Responsible for Programs of Youth Exchanges* (Working Document for Meeting in Rome, June 22–27, 1987). Paris: UNESCO.

Van den Berg-Eldering, L. (1987). *The CDCC's Project Number 7: The Education and Cultural Development of Migrants* (Final Conference Report). Strasbourg: Council for Cultural Cooperation.

Young, M.F.D. (1976). *Knowledge and Control.* London: Collier-Macmillan.

Part Two

---

# *The Shaping of Attitudes About Race and Ethnicity*

*Chapter Four*

# Developmental Processes and Their Influence on Interethnic and Interracial Relations

Cynthia T. García Coll
Heidie A. Vázquez García

Interethnic and interracial conflicts have been a salient part of human history. These conflicts have been so pervasive that some observers of human behavior have ascribed the underlying psychological processes, such as the formation of stereotypes and prejudices about members of other ethnic and racial groups, as basic to human nature. For example, as early as 1930, psychologists considered prejudice to be the result of the operation and integration of universal psychological processes such as projection, frustration, and the displacement of hostility (Dollard and others, 1939; MacCrone, 1937). More recently, universal cognitive processes such as categorization have been postulated as playing a part in the development of racial stereotypes (see, for example, Hamilton and Trolier, 1986; Lilli and Rehm, 1988).

The purpose of this chapter is to address the role of basic developmental processes in the development of interethnic and interracial attitudes. It is our contention that an understanding of basic developmental processes in the areas of cognition, social, and affective development can elucidate the development of negative/positive attitudes and behaviors toward members of other ethnic/racial groups. In other words, we are postulating that there are normative developmental processes that, under specific environmental circumstances, provide the foundation for and contribute to the formation of negative attitudes, prejudice, and stereotypes, which in turn may consequently lead to interethnic and interracial conflicts. However, it is our position that, although these processes are necessary, they are not sufficient conditions for the formation of negative attributions. In other words, while these basic processes might help explain the pervasiveness of negative attitudes toward ethnic/racial groups, the presence of environmental input is equally necessary to their development.

In this chapter we examine how developmental processes can lead to the acquisition of beliefs, attitudes, and behaviors toward members of other ethnic/racial and minority groups. The evidence suggests that these beliefs and attitudes start very early in a child's life. Studies done in the sixties and seventies among white and black children in northern and southern cities of North America report the existence of biases against blacks from preschool throughout the early school years (Morland, 1958; Williams, Best, and Boswell, 1975). Similarly, studies using dolls and pictures depicting children's own or other racial or ethnic groups indicate that preschool and young school-age children of various racial backgrounds demonstrate a pro-white bias in ethnic and racial preference, attitudes, and identification (Spencer and Markstrom-Adams, 1990). The early appearance of ethnic/racial attitudes and the prevalence and enduring qualities of interethnic and interracial conflicts pose challenges to the nature-nurture controversy. The basic question is, How inherent to human nature are underlying psychological processes (such as the formation of stereotypes and prejudices) that can lead to interethnic and interracial conflicts?

The complexity of these issues has made their study very difficult. Accordingly, many researchers have examined the effects of only one set of variables (for example, categorization) on attitudes and behaviors at a time (Duckitt, 1992). While this approach is necessary and useful, we feel that in order to have a better understanding of how antisocial or prosocial attitudes, capabilities, and behaviors are developed in an increasingly multiethnic and multiracial society, it is crucial to examine how different developmental processes interact with each other and provide the bases for such development. Thus our examination of the literature not only focuses on individual domains but also presents an integrated perspective on the development of interethnic and interracial relations. Two of the questions we will be addressing are as follows: How can we account for the emergence of cognitive, social, and affective patterns that underlie interethnic and interracial conflicts or prosocial interactions? And can socialization processes bring about fundamental changes not only at the individual level of our society but also at the collective level?

## Theoretical Perspectives

Throughout the twentieth century, various theories have been proposed to explain prejudice in the United States. In a review of the literature and theoretical perspectives to date, Duckitt (1992) identifies seven stages that have been significant in the evolution of the psychological understanding of prejudice. These theoretical orientations are as follows. (1) Prior to 1920, prejudice was perceived as a natural response to "inferior" and "backwards" people. (2) In the 1920s and 1930s, prejudice was conceptualized as a social problem and explained in terms of the stigmatization of minorities. (3) In the 1930s and 1940s, psychodynamic theory was used to identify universal processes underlying prejudice. (4) In the 1950s, prejudice-prone personality was identified and prejudice itself was considered to be an expression of a pathological need. (5) In the 1960s, theorists discussed the sociocultural transmission of prejudice as a social norm. (6) In the 1970s, the intergroup dynamics of prejudice were identified, and prejudice was construed as an expression of group interests. And (7) in the 1980s, when the cognitive perspective prevailed, prejudice was viewed as an inevitable outcome of social categorization. Duckitt argues that while both the onset and the motivation for each of these distinct theoretical frameworks have been due to social circumstances and historical events, their individual contribution to the understanding of prejudice is very important.

Concurrent to the search for the causation of prejudice, researchers have been focusing on theoretical frameworks that elucidate the development of prosocial dispositions. As with prejudice, research regarding the development of prosocial dispositions has followed the psychodynamic, social learning, and cognitive developmental perspectives. Although these paradigms concentrate on different yet important mechanisms in the development of prosocial characteristics (that is, psychodynamic theory emphasizes internal motives, social learning theory emphasizes overt responses to environmental factors, and cognitive developmental theory emphasizes interpretation and organization of stimuli), there are two points on which all three agree. They all propose that children move from egocentric thought to other-centered thought as they grow and mature (Mussen and Eisenberg-Berg, 1977). And they all propose that as the child matures, the control over moral behaviors reverses, shifting from an externalized system of reward (whereby, for example, parents reward the child for an appropriate behavior) to an internalized system of reward (whereby the child is internally motivated to act prosocially and reward him- or herself for such actions) (Mussen and Eisenberg-Berg, 1977).

However, maturity in moral reasoning does not necessarily mean that an individual will engage in prosocial, constructive behavior. Rather, the individual's behavioral expressions are dependent upon personal expectancies about the environment and his or her own behavior and subjective values (that is, about any stimuli that have the power to induce positive or negative emotional states [Mischel and Mischel, 1976]). In other words, we need to examine not only how intrinsic variables such as self-regulatory behavior, self-imposed goals, and standards affect prosocial behavior, but also how external motivations and consequences (that is, peer relations, authority figures, and environmental factors) shape prosocial interactions.

In short, the prevalent theories for explaining the development of both positive and negative attitudes and behaviors toward others must acknowledge the role of both individual as well as environmental factors. In the following sections, we examine the role of three intrinsic processes that provide the foundations for the development of negative/positive attitudes toward members of other ethnic/racial groups: categorization, group identification, and empathy. These sections are followed by an elaboration of the role of the environment and, finally, by recommendations for preventing interethnic/interracial conflict.

## Categorization

One of the main areas of growth during early development is that of cognition. A particular cognitive capacity that might make possible the development of stereotypes and other negative attributions toward other ethnic/racial groups is categorization. Children's ability to categorize and classify objects and persons increases with age. Yet recent studies show that the ability to create categories of objects and people based on physical attributes develops very early on. Research indicates that children as young as nine months can form and retrieve basic-level categories (Roberts and Cuff, 1989). By the first year of life, children can begin to group objects in a single category, for instance, they can place a group of squares in one pile (Ricciuti, 1965; Starkley, 1981; Sugarman, 1983). Furthermore, by eighteen months of age, children begin to form multicategory groupings (all the balls in one pile, all the squares in another [Gopnik and Meltzoff, 1987; Nelson, 1973; Ricciuti, 1965]). Thus, even though the capacity for categorization increases over time, even infants and toddlers are able to use categories as a basic means for information processing.

Fairly recently, researchers have indicated that perceptual categories in children, primarily basic-level categories, seem to be organized around prototypes (Roberts and Horowitz, 1986; Strauss, 1979; Younger, 1985). Several models have been advanced to explain cognitive organization and the processing of categorical information. For example, the featural model of categorization emphasizes that a concept's most salient features will be stored and that categorical decisions will be based on similarities between features (see Smith, Shoben, and Rips, 1974). And the prototypical model of categorization suggests that typical exemplars of the category will be stored and that category decisions are based on comparisons between category members and the prototypical "reference point" (see Rosch, 1975). Yet regardless of the model, there is increasing consensus that information processing relies on categories that have been established based on previous experiences.

Even more important is the fact that prototypes are formed not only about objects but about persons and social interactions as well. These social prototypes are also believed to be formed at a very young age—hence the research emphasis on the importance of early life experiences on future behavior toward others. Researchers suggest that in the first year of life, children's biological maturation allows them to continually monitor all incoming experiences, making it possible to classify and categorize all sorts of stimuli and experiences (Kagan, 1984). Sroufe (1983) states that while later experiences are important in the development of children, early parent-child interactions can have significant effects on their behavior because the children develop a prototype of future relationships based on the early interactions with their parents. Thus, once these prototypes or "internal working models" have been established, events and experiences that occur later in life are processed according to these models.

Therefore, it is the contention of some researchers and theorists that the presence or absence of stimuli at an early age can affect the development of cognitive processes, thereby also affecting future behavior. What these and other models suggest, then, is that cognitive organizations (that is, through features or prototypes) regulate not only present but also future information processing. In addition, they suggest that both object categorization as well as social categorization rely on cognitive structures to encode, represent, and retrieve information. We propose that the lack of early exposure to positive and meaningful interactions with members of other ethnic/racial minority groups might exclude these experiences from the internal models that govern children's future interactions with these populations. In other words, ethnicity or race, as expressed by physical attributes as well as by more subtle social interactions (preferred modes of communication, affect regulation, and so on), becomes part of the reference point, prototype, or features upon which future social interactions will be based.

In support of these assertions and speculations, studies have shown that there are similarities between object categorization and the representation of stereotypes in social categorization (see Dovidio, Evans, and Tyler, 1986; Gaertner and McLaughlin, 1983). Accordingly, a number of researchers are considering racial stereotypes as cognitive structures that are either created over time or are based on previous experiences (see Hamilton, 1981). Fiske and Neuberg (1989) suggest that individuals initially categorize others based on perceptual cues that are socially meaningful, such as a physical feature or a verbalized label (for example, "mentally ill"), which in turn activate cognitions, affect, and behavior. The premise for this process is that it provides the observer with useful information at a relatively low cost in terms of both time and cognitive effort (see Allport, 1954). Attributional categorization or individuating processes are secondary to category-based processes, then, because they require not only more attention to attributes but also an interpretation of the attributes (Fiske and Neuberg, 1989).

Furthermore, in addition to identifying the cognitive processes through which racial biases can affect social categorization, researchers have suggested that affective components of racial attitudes can affect racial stereotypes and influence behavior independent of the cognitive element (McConahay & Hough, 1976). In other words, whereas cognitive components of racial attitudes (that is, racial beliefs) may shift quickly over time, affective components may not change at the same rate and may in fact linger and change more slowly. For example, Gaertner and McLaughlin (1983) as well as Dovidio, Evans, and Tyler (1986) show that although overtly negative stereotypes of blacks are decreasing, antiblack sentiment persists.

Similarly, Bigler and Liben (1993) have found that children can remember more of a story if the details are consistent with cultural and racial stereotypes than if they are not. In addition, they have found that children are more likely to remember stereotypic traits than social relationships. Therefore, while social pressures along with other factors may have changed racial attitudes in a cognitive sense, these attitudes are being maintained on an affective level and continue to influence interracial interactions. In other words, although cognitive representations of one group may be changing in the eyes of another group (consider, for example, the decrease in blatant and overt stereotypes of blacks by whites), there is a residual element present on the affective level that continues to perpetuate ethnic/racial stereotypes in a subtle form. These findings also suggest that cognitive capacities are a necessary, though not sufficient, explanation for the formation of stereotypes or other negative attributions about ethnic/racial groups.

### Group Identification

Whether based on physiological, psychological, social, or economic needs, the relationships that children develop with others from the time they are born are very important predictors of their developmental outcome later in life. Parent-child relations, specifically maternal-child relations such as attachment, are considered cornerstones for developmental outcome (Bowlby, 1969). However, other relationships, especially those with peers, are also very important to later social interactions. Relationships with peers begin to develop during the first year of life and initially involve interactions such as smiling, touching, sharing, and some forms of imitation and turn-taking between infants (see Vandell, Wilson, and Buchanan, 1980; Vincze, 1971). Researchers have shown that by age three, children are able to have elaborate social exchanges with their peers, once they have progressed from independent play to group play (Parten, 1932). Thus the ability to behave competently in social situations with their peers is an important early developmental task for children.

Although early peer-group affiliations and preferences might not be marked by the child's race, ethnicity, and socioeconomic status, these variables are important later on in determining the nature of peer interactions and relationships. For example, around age ten, Native American children begin to show a greater preference toward and identification with their own ethnic group (Beuf, 1977). A parallel pattern of own-group preference for African Americans has been described by Spencer (1982). And social psychologists such as Lewin (1948) have stated that minority-group members need to feel an affinity with their own group in order to develop a sense of well-being. Evidence in support of that assertion comes from studies showing that high school students with a clearer sense of their own ethnicity have higher self-esteem than their peers who lack such a sense (see Phinney and Chavira, 1992).

Thus the sense of belonging to one's own group and the sense of exclusion from others based on variables such as class, ethnicity, race, and religion is part of the normative development, particularly for children of color. Researchers have shown that across ethnic groups, those individuals who reported having a strong ethnic identification held more separatist attitudes, engaged in less cross-ethnic contact, and experienced more cross-ethnic conflict (see Rotheram-Borus, 1990; Phinney, 1990). While research is unclear as to whether the level of own-group preference is inextricably linked to outgroup dislike, most studies assume that outgroup dislike implies a preference for one's own group (Masson and Verkuyten, 1993).

Following this line of research is another finding indicating that children who become friends tend to be genetically similar to one another (Rushton, Russell, and Wells, 1984; Segal, 1988). This finding suggests that genetic relatedness affects social preferences and friendship choices. In other words, the more similar two individuals are genetically, the more likely they are to be reciprocating and consequently altruistic toward one another (Rushton, Russell, and Wells, 1984).

However, once children enter a group setting, their criterion for association with others shifts from genetic relatedness to their position on the dominance hierarchy (Savin-Williams, 1987). Research indicates that this behavior may have collective benefits such as reduction of aggression (Carpenter, 1942) and the coordination of affiliative behavior (Chance, 1967). The former has been observed in preschool groups (Abromvitch, 1980; Strayer and Strayer, 1976; LaFreniere and Charlesworth, 1983), and the latter, in groups of five-year-olds (Strayer and Trudel, 1984).

In addition, researchers have found that even at the preschool level there is an association between rank and resource control (Charlesworth, 1988; Charlesworth and LaFreniere, 1983). Charlesworth (1988) has found that dominant children receive a number of physical privileges such as larger portions of food, as well as social privileges such as higher self-esteem and confidence and more input in the decision-making process of the group. Therefore, children as young as preschool age classify themselves based on personal characteristics, specific talents, or social status. But the question that remains is, When does race and ethnicity become part of this classification system of self and others, and a basic feature of peer relations and in-group identification?

Children's increasing ability to differentiate between things that are similar and dissimilar, and to identify themselves with those things, people, or experiences that are similar to them rather than with those that are not, brings up a variety of issues that may be relevant to interethnic and interracial relations. First, this ability leads to polar relationships between people, cultures, and other social concepts. The "us" and "them" distinction is one that has been programmed by both historical and contemporary factors, and it shapes our society not only at an individual level but at the institutional and cultural levels as well. Research has shown that people tend to favor other people who are like them (Zaleski, 1992) and thus to exhibit prosocial behavior toward those who are similar (Jarymowicz, 1988).

When translated into racial, cultural, and socioeconomic terms, these biases, differentiations, and categorization mechanisms can be expressed as prejudice, discrimination, and segregation. And when these processes use skin color, racial features, socioeconomic class, religious affiliation, and ethnicity as references, they can form the foundation for interethnic and interracial conflict.

## The Development of Empathy

The ability to identify with others is an important task not only in terms of social development but also in terms of affective development and the progression from egocentric thought to empathetic thought and behavior. Various models of empathy have been articulated (see Hoffman, 1982; Feshbach, 1975, 1978; Keefe, 1976); but, in general, empathy has been defined as an affective-cognitive-communicative system (Keefe, 1976). While some theorists believe that empathetic responsiveness in children does not begin to develop until early childhood (see Piaget, 1932), others indicate that infants as young as thirty-four hours will cry intensely when they hear another infant cry (Hoffman, 1976). Crying in response to another infant's cry has been regarded as a form of primitive empathy that may lay the foundation for future empathetic responsiveness and, consequently, prosocial behavior (Staub, 1979).

In addition, research suggests that children as young as nine to ten months demonstrate sharing behavior, which indicates some sort of role-taking ability (Rheingold, Hay, and West, 1976). The implication is that children show some understanding for the perspective of another person and are aware that this perspective is different from their own. Hoffman (1977) states that as the child's cognitive abilities begin to mature, the expression of empathy changes as a function of the way cognition mediates the original response.

Thus, the shift from self-centered to other-centered thought and behavior is a crucial one in understanding the evolution of prosocial, empathetic behaviors. Both psychoanalytic and cognitive theory state that the first stage of human life is characterized by self-gratification and egocentric behavior as well as by thought. In other words, the only world that an infant knows is that of him- or herself, so the only important and valid viewpoint is his or her own. When children begin to become aware of other people who have a separate existence, they are then able to cognitively take the perspective of these others, thereby increasing their understanding of their own thoughts, emotions, and motivations. While the ability to take the perspective of others does not necessarily mean non-egocentrism (Shantz, 1983), nonegocentric reasoning is an important aspect of cognitive empathy.

There are two implications of this evolution from egocentric thought to being able to take the perspective of others. First, if we draw an analogy between this concept and cultures, we find a similar phenomenon—namely, ethnocentrism. The same assumption that guides egocentric attitudes is present in ethnocentric attitudes: the assumption that one's own cultural patterns and practices are "normal" and natural and that the practices of different cultures are "abnormal" and therefore inferior (Schopmeyer and Fisher, 1993). Much like egocentrism can lead to disconnection from others, the intolerance of other, different cultural perspectives can be one of the causes of distortions and tensions among various groups. As with an individual child, the task for any particular group is to move from ethnocentric thought to a more pluralistic worldview in which the perspectives of other racial and ethnic groups can be understood and accepted, and not be considered a threat to either the group or the individual.

Another implication of the progression from egocentric to empathic thought is that we need to understand how these increasingly prosocial attitudes can become generalized to the interactions and thoughts about members of other ethnic/racial/socioeconomic groups. It is clear that having the capacity to be empathic does not guarantee that this response will be applied under all environmental conditions or as part of all human interactions. Two questions logically follow: How do we facilitate the application of these emerging capacities to interactions with members of other ethnic and racial groups? And how can the concurrently developing capacities for categorization, ingroup identification, empathic thoughts, and generalizations be combined with the increasing capacity to take the perspective of others in a way that will facilitate interethnic and interracial relations?

## The Role of the Environment

There are many implications of our increasing understanding of developmental processes and their potential impact on interethnic and interracial relations. It is evident that, even at the preschool level, children are not only making judgments about people based on ethnic, racial, and social categories, but they are also identifying themselves as members of particular groups, competing for resources, and segregating themselves based on social and physical characteristics. How then can we establish a common ground where these categorizations and associations are inclusive of members of other ethnic and racial groups?

Current developmental theories emphasize the transactional aspects of human development, whereby developmental outcome is as much a function of the unfolding individual processes as are the transactions with the environment (Sameroff and Fiese, 1990). These unique transactions explain in part the wide range of individual differences observed in human thought, emotional expressions, and behavioral responses within similar developmental periods that are categorized by the emergence of particular behaviors and the potential to develop certain traits or characteristics (Rathus, 1988). In other words, the capacity to make categorizations, to identify with a group, and to be empathic toward others will express itself in relation to environmental input. Therefore, while Piaget (1932) and Kholberg (1976) have asserted that all humans go through universal stages of cognitive and moral development, we can account for the development of racism and prejudice in some individuals and not others based on the interplay between environmental forces and personal capacities. Even if cognitive developmental stages are universal and consistent across cultures, we can begin to explain the variability within cultures, races, and ethnic groups regarding racist and prejudiced attitudes by examining the role of the environment.

Theorists have criticized this aspect of universality in the stages of moral development by emphasizing that content (personal, cultural, and social experience) is an essential component in the moral development of human beings. Some researchers have argued that there is an independent effect of content on moral development (see Lickona, 1976) that warrants an evaluation in its own right (see Wright, 1971). Others insist that the content of life experiences and personal beliefs, as well as the differences between individuals, are instrumental in shaping the moral lives of human beings and that attitude changes in people are not due necessarily to structural changes (Carini, 1968; Lickona, 1976). Still other researchers have postulated the idea that experiences may determine the movement of structure—in other words, that content can cause structural regression or arrest (Simpson, 1974). Finally, some researchers argue that situational influences affect not only how structures are operationalized behaviorally but what structures are affected (see Wright, 1971). Thus, while structural influences are important in moral development, we cannot dismiss the influences of content and personality characteristics in moral reasoning. This last argument can probably be applied to the other relevant developmental processes previously identified.

For example, current theoretical frameworks and empirical evidence suggest that the patterns of socialization to which young children are exposed within their families, among their peers, and in contact with other important institutions (such as schools, the media, the church, and so on) have enormous implications for the development of interethnic and interracial relations. Theories of socioemotional development suggest that the foundation for these processes is established during the earliest interactions experienced with others. After all, infants are constantly learning fundamental rules and regulations of social interactions with significant others that impact the subsequent development of prosocial interaction skills (Simmel, 1980).

Research guided by attachment theory provides evidence of how these early patterns of attachment influence the future development of prosocial skills. For example, studies have shown that while maternal warmth alone is not associated with offsprings' empathy (Janssens and Gerris, 1992; Koestner, Frantz, and Weinberger, 1990), parental support and empathic parenting is related to the development of empathy in children (see Kestenbaum, Farber, and Sroufe, 1989; Barnett, 1987). Empirical studies suggest that children who receive empathic, nurturing, responsive care as infants develop these qualities themselves (Kestenbaum, Farber, and Sroufe, 1989; Sroufe, 1983). Preschoolers who were securely attached as infants are more likely than insecurely attached children to respond to other children's distress and are also more socially competent with their peers (Sroufe, 1983; Lieberman, 1977). Sibling interactions have also been implicated in the acquisition of prosocial behaviors and verbal communications about feeling states in the infant as well as in the older sibling (Dunn, Bretherton, and Munn, 1987; Dunn and Munn, 1986).

In short, early patterns of interaction within the family system (however this system is defined) provide the foundation for later social interactions. From basic daily interactions with family members, children learn the rules and expectations for reciprocity, turn-taking, sensitivity, and responsivity to the needs of others. These rules are then utilized and transferred to situations involving other significant others in their lives, such as teachers, peers, and (one hopes) members of other ethnic and racial groups. As with the development of prosocial, empathic behaviors, we can assume that family, peer, and institutional influences permeate the individual and group differences observed in the formation of prejudices or other negative attitudes toward certain groups.

Parental directiveness is also associated with the development of empathy in children (Janssens and Gerris, 1992). Researchers have found that the children of parents who have an authoritative-reciprocal style of parenting tend to exhibit high levels of social and cognitive competencies such as open communication, negotiation, and reciprocity compared to parents who follow authoritarian, indifferent-uninvolved, or indulgent-permissive patterns of childrearing (see Maccoby and Martin, 1983; Baumrind, 1971).

In addition, there is empirical evidence suggesting that teachers play an important role in the development of empathy. Studies have shown that children who receive empathic understanding from teachers are more likely to exhibit positive social adjustment than those who have not received this understanding (see Traux and Tatum, 1966); they also tend to engage in more harmonious peer relationships (Diskin, 1956; Walter, 1977). Some researchers have found a strong positive relationship between teacher empathy and student academic gain (see Scheuer, 1971; Mantaro, 1971; Aspy, 1972). Others have discovered that, similar to high-empathy parents, high-empathy teachers use less controlling behaviors, enforce fewer deadlines, are more accepting of students' feelings, and tend to focus on creativity rather than on evaluation (Aspy and Roebuck, 1975).

It is crucial, then, to explore the impact of positive parental and teacher attitudes and behaviors on children's prosocial behaviors; but it is also necessary to examine the concept of socialization of aggression and its implications for interethnic and interracial relations. MacDonald (1988) states that while a positive social reward system has been dominant throughout most of human evolution, increased competition for resources as well as a shift into the nuclear family social organization promoted a move toward distant and hostile interpersonal relationships. Indeed, cross-cultural and historical data suggest that distant and hostile parenting is correlated with socialization of aggression (see George and Main, 1979; Reid, Taplin, and Lorber, 1981). In other words, parents who model and reinforce their children for aggressive behavior essentially socialize their children to be aggressive. What happens is that socialization of aggression—defined as the prevention of the development of a positive reward system through exploitative relationships, lack of empathy and altruism (MacDonald, 1988)—becomes a more adaptive mechanism than those mechanisms that rely on positive affective interactions. The literature on this subject is consistent with the notion that humans can be programmed to have a generalized tendency for aggression that can then be used for obtaining resources, thereby increasing personal and collective levels of success (MacDonald, 1988).

In short, it is clear that socialization practices and developmental processes interact to influence individual differences in the expression of competencies in the area of prosocial and altruistic development. How then can environmental input be effective as a tool in the reduction of stereotyping, prejudice, and other negative attitudes that are conducive to interethnic and interracial conflict?

## Recommendations

Given that the problem of interethnic and interracial conflict is as pervasive as it is profound, the solutions to this phenomenon must necessarily be complex. We need to operate from the assumption that, even though human beings exhibit an inherent cognitive bias toward developing categorizations of people and maintaining conceptualizations of "us" and "them," these categorizations and groupings can be modified with experiential input—because humans are also inherently capable of positive affective, prosocial, and altruistic behavior toward others. Accordingly, we recommend that cognitive, affective, and social needs be addressed by a combination of strategies designed to ameliorate interethnic and interracial relations and to diminish if not prevent interethnic and interracial conflict.

As previously noted, one of the most important inherent mechanisms that affect interethnic and interracial relations is categorization. As a cognitive function, categorization allows human beings to process, encode, and retrieve information in a quick and efficient way. However, an examination of the ways in which categorization can result in the formation of prototypes and stereotypes about people, races, and cultures leads us to conclude that there are social consequences of categorization as well as cognitive ones.

One way in which we can counter the process of categorization and its potential for developing prototypes and stereotypes in children is by exposing children to, and emphasizing the individual differences within, general categories of objects and people. Consider the category of people who are Hispanic. A child who has had the experience of interpersonal and intercultural encounters may be able to recognize and be sensitive not only to cultural differences between whites and Hispanics but also to individual differences among Hispanics. Redmond and Bunyi (1993) state that in order for two people to have an effective intercultural interaction, at least one of the persons involved must recognize, analyze, and adapt to the differences between their cultural/racial backgrounds.

Another way to combat the social consequences of categorization, especially in the context of interethnic and interracial conflict, is to deemphasize ingroup-outgroup distinctions. If empirical evidence suggests that children as early as preschool age make associations with others based on shared characteristics, early interventions may be beneficial before these associations form exclusively along ethnic, racial, and socioeconomic lines. One strategy that might improve this situation is early integration—that is, exposure to and creation of structures that create positive contact between different races and ethnic groups. According to Blau's macrostructural theory (1977), social associations depend upon contact opportunities, which in turn are necessary for meaningful social relationships. Blau argues that such conditions as group size, physical propinquity, group heterogeneity, and socioeconomic status can either constrain or create opportunities for members of different groups to engage in social relationships (Blau, 1977). Thus, if we provide children with the *opportunities* for developing positive, rewarding relationships with members of other ethnic/racial groups, we may be able to transcend some of the structural barriers that affect interracial and interethnic contact. For example, in a study examining peer interactions and friendships in ethnically diverse school settings, Howes and Wu (1990) found that kindergartners as well as third-graders were forming friendships with cross-ethnic as well as same-ethnic peers. Since such associations have already begun to develop during the preschool years, this is an important developmental period in which to start structuring these interventions.

While exposure alone does not guarantee that positive interaction between persons of different cultural and ethnic backgrounds will take place, it does increase the possibility that racial or ethnic misperceptions will be lessened. For example, Pettigrew (1979) states that in 1942 only 42 percent of whites believed that blacks had the same intelligence as whites; yet by 1956 the figure had risen to 78 percent. Similarly, Davis (1973) reports that in 1942 only 42 percent of whites thought that blacks should have the same opportunities as whites to get a job, but by 1972 this figure had risen to 95 percent. In short, racial and ethnic attitudes *are* changing, but they are doing so very slowly and in isolated instances. If parents, teachers, and community and government agencies worked together to provide children with balanced, integrated environments, the chances of constructive interethnic and interracial exchange could be increased. However, it is our position that these exchanges need to be structured carefully to support cooperation rather than competition among groups. Integration by itself is simply not enough.

In conjunction with integration, another strategy that could be employed to lessen ingroup-outgroup distinctions is to decrease social distance. Defined as "the grades and degrees of understanding and intimacy which characterize pre-social and social relations generally" (Park, 1924, p. 339), social distance pertains not just to groups of persons but to entire races and classes as well (Park, 1924). In our society, as well as in other societies around the world, it seems that when physical distance is not sufficient to bring about distinction between groups, such distinction is achieved instead through social distance (for example, through the limitation of intimacy between groups and the exclusion of others from social interaction). The notion that every group has a place in society and is "all right in that place" is the same notion that maintains and justifies institutions such as segregation and prejudice. We suggest that if ethnic and racial groups could manage to be not only in physical propinquity but in social proximity as well (through interpersonal relationships), both fear of the other group and competition between the groups would lessen, thereby increasing interethnic and interracial consciousness and erasing boundaries.

By deemphasizing ingroup-outgroup distinctions and decreasing social distance, not only are we able to expand categorizations so that they are more inclusive, but we are also in a position to encourage openness about the differences between people and to discourage judgmental attitudes about other ethnic/racial groups. If through experience and guidance we are able to sensitize children to their own biases, perceptions, and assumptions about their own ethnic/racial group as well as increase their awareness and sensitivity toward other groups, we can begin to move from an ethnocentric perspective to a more universal outlook on interethnic and interracial relations. In other words, by facilitating the process of perspective role-taking between members of different ethnic/racial groups, we are increasing the possibility that prosocial attitudes and empathetic behaviors will occur and be generalized across ethnic/racial lines.

In addition to interventions on the individual level, we suggest that contextual interventions can be effective in improving interethnic and interracial relations. For example, while it is the belief of Western societies that each individual alone is responsible for his or her behavior (Mancuso and Sarbin, 1976), situational influences seem to have a greater impact on prosocial and moral behavior than is usually recognized (Rosenhan, Moore, and Underwood, 1976). Several studies indicate that children around early adolescence conform most to group judgments on perceptual tasks (see Constanzo and Shaw, 1966; Iscoe, Williams, and Harvey, 1963). Although these studies focus on perceptual tasks, the assumption is that conformity or deviation on nonmoral issues comes in part from moral cognitions (Saltzstein, 1976). Given the fact that early adolescence is the period when children begin to show very strong own-group preferences, it follows that peer influences during this time may be crucial in influencing and maintaining conceptions and beliefs about racial and ethnic groups. This period of development, therefore, is also crucial for positive interventions around interethnic and interracial conflict.

Models can also have either a positive or negative influence on attitudes and behaviors toward other ethnic and racial groups and, hence, on interethnic and interracial relations. According to observational learning theorists, human behavior changes as a function of others' behavior either through direct (live modeling) or indirect (symbolic modeling) exposure (see Liebert and Wicks Poulos, 1976). But in addition to exposure, an individual has to acquire and then accept the modeling cues in order for subsequent actions to ensue (Liebert and Wicks Poulos, 1976). Therefore, whether at school, at home, or in the neighborhood, models are an important socialization agent for children. Studies show that, in observing a model obtain a positive consequence for his or actions, children are more likely to follow a response pattern similar to that of the model (Bandura, Ross, and Ross, 1963). In contrast, if a modeled behavior is punished, children are less likely to display similar behavior (Bandura, Ross, and Ross, 1963).

However, it is important to note that not all models have the same effect on all individuals. Researchers have discovered that the attributes of the observer and the model (for example, the status and power of the observer in relation to the model), as well as the relationship of the observer to the model, are important factors that may affect the level of influence a model has on the observer (Bandura and Walters, 1963; Grusec and Mischel, 1966). These basic learning principles can and should be applied to improve interethnic and interracial relationships: teaching about the destructiveness of stereotyping or prejudice only in the context of school or home will not generalize to other situations if important role models (such as parents, teachers, and peers) are not displaying attitudes and behaviors congruent with this knowledge.

In sum, our increasing knowledge about developmental processes points up the existence of certain human capacities (categorization and group affiliation, in particular) that, given certain
environmental conditions, are conducive to the formation of
stereotypes, prejudice, and competition among ethnic and racial
groups. However, this knowledge also points up the important role
of the environment in the expression of such capacities as well as
the simultaneous existence of prosocial and altruistic behaviors.
Early and continuous exposure to positive role models, positive
reinforcement for cooperation rather than competition among ethnic and racial groups, and movement toward a more pluralistic
view of human development are necessary not only to ameliorate
interethnic and interracial relations but also to prevent interethnic and interracial conflict.

# References

Abromvitch, R. (1980). Attention structures in hierarchically organized groups.
    In D. R. Omark, E. E. Strayer, and D. G. Freedman (eds.), *Dominance
    relations*. Hillsdale, N.J.: Erlbaum.

Allport, G. W. (1954). *The nature of prejudice*. Reading, Mass.: Addison-Wesley.

Aspy, D. (1972). *Toward a technology for humanizing education*. Champaign, Ill.:
    Research Press.

Aspy, D. N., and Roebuck, F. N. (1975). A discussion of the relationship between
    selected student behavior and the teacher's use of interchangeable
    responses. *Humanistic Education*, pp. 3–10.

Bandura, A., Ross, D., and Ross, S. A. (1963). Imitation of film-mediated aggres-
    sive models. *Journal of Abnormal and Social Psychology, 66*, 3–11.

Bandura, A., and Walters, R. H. (1963). *Social learning and personality develop-
    ment*. New York: Holt, Rinehart & Winston.

Barnett, M. A. (1987). Empathy and related responses in children. In N. Ei-
    senberg and J. Strayer (eds.), *Empathy and its development* (pp. 46–162).
    Cambridge, England: Cambridge University Press.

Baumrind, D. (1971). Current patterns of parental authority. *Developmental
    Psychology, 4*, 1–103.

Beuf, A. H. (1977). *Red children in white America*. University Park: Pennsylvania
    State University Press.

Bigler, R. S., and Liben, L. S. (1993). A cognitive-developmental approach to
    racial stereotyping and reconstructive memory in Euro-American chil-
    dren. *Child Development, 64*(5), 1507–1518.

Blau, P. M. (1977). *Inequality and heterogeneity*. New York: Free Press.

Bowlby, J. (1969). *Attachment and loss*. Vol. 1, *Attachment*. New York: Basic Books.

Carini, P. (1968). Studying thinking in children. Unpublished monograph. The Prospect School, North Bennington, Vermont.

Carpenter, C. R. (1942). Social behavior of free-ranging rhesus monkeys: Periodicity of estrus, homo- and autoerotic and nonconformist behavior. *Journal of Comparative Psychology, 33,* 147–162.

Chance, M.R.A. (1967). Attention structure as the basis of primate rank orders. *Man, 2,* 503–518.

Charlesworth, W. (1988). Resources and resource acquisition during ontogeny. In K. MacDonald (ed.), *Sociobiological perspectives on human development*. New York: Springer-Verlag.

Charlesworth, W., and LaFreniere, P. (1983). Dominance, friendship, and re-source utilization in preschool children's groups. *Ethology and Sociobiology, 4,* 175–186.

Constanzo, P. R., and Shaw, M. E. (1966). Conformity as a function of age level. *Child Development, 37,* 967–975.

Davis, J. A. (1973). *1972 General social survey*. Chicago, Ill.: National Opinion Research Center.

Diskin, P. (1956). A study of predictive empathy and the ability of student teachers to maintain harmonious interpersonal relations in selected elementary classrooms. *Dissertation Abstracts, 16,* 1399.

Dollard, J., and others. (1939). *Frustration and aggression*. New Haven, Conn.: Yale University Press.

Dovidio, J. F., Evans, N., and Tyler, R. B. (1986). Racial stereotypes: The contents of their cognitive representations. *Journal of Experimental Psychology, 22,* 22–37.

Duckitt, J. (1992). Psychology and prejudice. *American Psychologist, 47*(10), 1182–1193.

Dunn, J., Bretherton, I., and Munn, P. (1987). Conversations about feeling states between mothers and their young children. *Developmental Psychology, 23,* 132–139.

Dunn, J., and Munn, P. (1986). Sibling quarrels and maternal intervention: Individual differences in understanding and aggression. *Journal of Child Psychology and Psychiatry, 27,* 583–595.

Feshbach, N. D. (1975). Empathy in children: Some theoretical and empirical considerations. *Counseling Psychologist, 5,* 25–30.

Feshbach, N. D. (1978). Studies of empathetic behavior in children. In B. Maher (ed.), *Progress in experimental personality research* (pp. 1–47). New York: Academic Press.

Fiske, S. T., and Neuberg, S. L. (1989). Category-based and individuating processes as a function of information and motivation: Evidence from our laboratory. In D. Bar-Tal, C. F. Graumann, A. W. Kruglanski, and

W. Stroebe (eds.), *Stereotyping and prejudice* (pp. 83–103). New York: Springer-Verlag.

Gaertner, S. L., and McLaughlin, J. P. (1983). Racial stereotypes: Associations and ascriptions of positive and negative characteristics. *Social Psychology Quarterly, 46,* 23–30.

George, C., and Main, M. (1979). Social interactions of young abused children: Approach, avoidance and aggression. *Child Development, 50,* 306–318.

Gopnik, A., and Meltzoff, A. N. (1987). The development of categorization in the second year and its relation to other cognitive and linguistic developments. *Child Development, 58,* 1523–1531.

Grusec, J., and Mischel, K. (1966). Model's characteristics as determinants of social learning. *Journal of Personality and Social Psychology, 4,* 211–215.

Hamilton, D. L. (1981). Stereotyping and intergroup behavior: Some thought on the cognitive approach. In D. L. Hamilton (ed.), *Cognitive processes in stereotyping and intergroup behavior* (pp. 333–353). Hillsdale, N.J.: Erlbaum.

Hamilton, D. L., and Trolier, T. K. (1986). Stereotypes and stereotyping: An overview of the cognitive approach. In J. F. Dovidio and S. L. Gaertner (eds.), *Prejudice, discrimination and racism* (pp. 127–164). San Diego: Academic Press.

Hoffman, M. L. (1976). Empathy, role-taking, guilt, and development of altruistic motives. In T. Lickona (ed.), *Moral development and behavior* (pp. 124–143). New York: Holt, Rinehart & Winston.

Hoffman, M. L. (1977). Sex differences in empathy and related behaviors. *Psychological Bulletin, 84,* 712–720.

Hoffman, M. L. (1982). Development of prosocial motivation: Empathy and guilt. In N. Eisenberg (ed.), *The development of prosocial behavior.* New York: Academic.

Howes, C., and Wu, F. (1990). Peer interaction and friendships in an ethnically diverse school setting. *Child Development, 61*(2), 537–541.

Iscoe, I., Williams, M., and Harvey, J. (1963). Modification of children's judgments by a simulated group technique: A normative developmental study. *Child Development, 34,* 963–978.

Janssens, J.M.A.M., and Gerris, J.R.M. (1992). Childrearing, empathy and prosocial behavior. In J.M.A.M. Janssens and J.R.M. Gerris (eds.), *Childrearing: Influence on prosocial and moral development* (pp. 31–55). Amsterdam: Swets.

Jarymowicz, M. (1988). *Studia nad spostrzeganiem relacji JA-INNI: Tozsamosc, indywiduacja-przynaleznosc* [Studies on perception of relations: Self-other, identity, individuation-belongingness]. Wroclaw, Poland: Ossolineum.

Kagan, J. (1984). *The nature of the child.* New York: Basic Books.

Keefe, T. (1976). Empathy: The critical skill. *Social Work, 21,* 10–14.

Kestenbaum, R., Farber, E. A., and Sroufe, L. A. (1989). Individual differences in empathy among preschoolers: Relation to attachment history. In N.

Eisenberg (ed.), *New direction for child development*. Vol. 44, *Empathy and related emotional responses* (pp. 51–64). San Francisco: Jossey-Bass.

Kholberg, L. (1976). Moral stages and moralization. In T. Lickona (ed.), *Moral development and behavior* (pp. 31–53). New York: Holt, Rinehart & Winston.

Koestner, R., Franz, C., and Weinberger, J. (1990). The family origins of empathetic concern: A 26-year longitudinal study. *Journal of Personality and Social Psychology, 58,* 709–717.

LaFreniere, P. J., and Charlesworth, W. R. (1983). Dominance, affiliation and attention in a preschool group: A nine-month longitudinal study. *Ethology and Sociobiology, 4,* 55–67.

Lewin, K. (1948). *Resolving social conflicts*. New York: Harper & Row.

Lickona, T. (1976). Critical issues in the study of moral development and behavior. In T. Lickona (ed.), *Moral development and behavior* (pp. 219–240). New York: Rinehart & Winston.

Lieberman, A. F. (1977). Preschoolers' competence with a peer: Relationship with attachment and peer experience. *Child Development, 48,* 1277–1287.

Liebert, R. M., and Wicks Poulos, R. (1976). Television as a moral teacher. In T. Lickona (ed.), *Moral development and behavior* (pp. 284–298). New York: Holt, Rinehart & Winston.

Lilli, W., and Rehm, J. (1988). Judgmental process as bases of intergroup conflict. In W. Stoebe, A. W. Kruglanski, D. Bar-Tal, and M. Hewstone (eds.), *The social psychology of intergroup conflict* (pp. 29–46). Berlin: Springer.

Maccoby, E., and Martin, J. (1983). Socialization in the context of the family: Parent-child interaction. In P. Mussen and M. Hetherington (eds.), *Handbook of child psychology*. Vol. 4, *Socialization and personality development*. New York: Wiley.

McConahay, J. B., and Hough, J. C. (1976). Symbolic racism. *Journal of Social Issues, 32,* 23–45.

MacCrone, I. D. (1937). *Race attitudes in South Africa: Historical, experimental and psychological studies*. London: Oxford University Press.

MacDonald, K. B. (1988). *Social and personality development*. New York: Plenum Press.

Mancuso, J. C., and Sarbin, T. R. (1976). A paradigmatic analysis of psychological issues at the interface of jurisprudence and moral conduct. In T. Lickona (ed.), *Moral development and behavior* (pp. 326–341). New York: Holt, Rinehart & Winston.

Mantaro, C. A. (1971). An investigation of the relationship between the interpersonal relationships perceived by a pupil to exist between himself and his reading teacher and (1) his reading achievement and (2) his self-concepts. Unpublished doctoral dissertation, Syracuse University.

Masson, C. N., and Verkuyten, M. (1993). Prejudice, ethnic identity, contact and ethnic group preference among Dutch young adolescents. *Journal of Applied Social Psychology, 23*, 156–168.

Mischel, W., and Mischel, H. N. (1976). A cognitive social-learning approach to morality and self-regulation. In T. Lickona (ed.), *Moral development and behavior* (pp. 84–107). New York: Holt, Rinehart & Winston.

Morland, J. K. (1958). The development of racial bias in young children. *Theory into Practice, 26*, 472–479.

Mussen, P., and Eisenberg-Berg, N. (1977). *Roots of caring, sharing, and helping.* San Francisco: W. H. Freeman.

Nelson, K. (1973). Some evidence for the cognitive primacy of categorization and its functional basis. *Merrill-Palmer Quarterly, 19*, 21–39.

Park, R. E. (1924). The concept of social distance. *Journal of Applied Sociology, 8*(6), 339–344.

Parten, M. B. (1932). Social participation among preschool children. *Journal of Abnormal Social Psychology, 27*, 243–269.

Pettigrew, T. F. (1979). Racial change and social policy. *Annals of the American Academy of Political and Social Science, 441*, 114–131.

Phinney, J. S. (1990). Ethnic identity in adolescents and adults: Review of research. *Psychological Bulletin, 108*, 499–514.

Phinney, J. S., and Chavira, V. (1992). Ethnic identity and self-esteem: An exploratory longitudinal study. *Journal of Adolescence, 15*(3), 271–281.

Piaget, J. (1932). *The moral judgment of the child.* London: Routledge & Kegan Paul.

Rathus, S. A. (1988). *Understanding human behavior.* New York: Holt, Rinehart & Winston.

Redmond, M. V., and Bunyi, J. M. (1993). The relationship of intercultural communication competence with stress and the handling of stress as reported by international students. *International Journal of Intercultural Relations, 17*, 235–254.

Reid, J. B., Taplin, P. S., and Lorber, R. (1981). A social interactional approach to the treatment of abusive families. In R. B. Stuart (ed.), *Violent behavior: Social learning approaches to prediction, management and treatment.* New York: Brunner/Mazel.

Rheingold, H. L., Hay, D. F., and West, M. J. (1976). Sharing in the second year of life. *Child Development, 47*, 1148–1158.

Ricciuti, H. N. (1965). Object grouping and selective ordering behavior in infants 12–24 months old. *Merrill-Palmer Quarterly, 11*, 129–148.

Roberts, K., and Cuff, M. D. (1989). Categorization studies of 9- to 15-month old infants: Evidence for superordinate categorization? *Infant Behavior and Development, 12*, 265–288.

Roberts, K., and Horowitz, F. D. (1986). Basic-level categorization in seven- and nine-month-old infants. *Journal of Child Language, 13*, 191–208.

Rosch, E. (1975). Cognitive reference points. *Cognitive Psychology, 7*, 532–547.

Rosenhan, D. L., Moore, B. S., and Underwood, B. (1976). The social psychology of moral behavior. In T. Lickona (ed.), *Moral development and behavior* (pp. 241–252). New York: Holt, Rinehart & Winston.

Rotheram-Borus, M. J. (1990). Adolescents' reference-group choices, self-esteem, and adjustment. *Journal of Personality and Social Psychology, 59*, 1075–1081.

Rushton, J. P., Russell, R.J.H., and Wells, P. A. (1984). Genetic similarity theory: Beyond kin selection. *Behavior Genetics, 14*, 179–193.

Saltzstein, H. D. (1976). Social influence and moral development: A perspective on the role of parents and peers. In T. Lickona (ed.), *Moral development and behavior* (pp. 253–265). New York: Holt, Rinehart & Winston.

Sameroff, A. J., and Fiese, B. H. (1990). Transactional regulation and early intervention. In S. J. Meisels and J. P. Shonkoff (eds.), *Handbook of early childhood intervention* (pp. 119–191). New York: Cambridge University Press.

Savin-Williams, R. (1987). *Adolescence: An ethological perspective.* New York: Springer-Verlag.

Scheuer, A. L. (1971). The relationship between personal attributes and effectiveness in teachers of the emotionally disturbed. *Exceptional Children, 37*, 723–731.

Schopmeyer, K. D., and Fisher, B. J. (1993). Insiders and outsiders: Exploring ethnocentrism and cultural relativity in sociology courses. *Teaching Sociology, 21*, 148–153.

Segal, N. (1988). Cooperation, competition and altruism in human twinships: A sociobiological approach. In K. B. MacDonald (ed.), *Sociobiological perspectives on human development.* New York: Springer-Verlag.

Shantz, C. (1983). The development of social cognition. In J. Falvell and E. Markman (eds.), *Handbook of child psychology* (pp. 495–555). New York: Wiley.

Simmel, E. C. (1980). *Early experiences and early behavior.* New York: Academic Press.

Simpson, E. L. (1974). Moral development research: A case of scientific cultural bias. *Human Development, 17*(2), 81–106.

Smith, E. E., Shoben, E. J., and Rips, L. J. (1974). Structure and process in semantic memory: A featural model from semantic decisions. *Psychological Review, 81*, 214–241.

Spencer, M. B. (1982). Personal and group identity of black children: An alternative synthesis. *Genetic Psychology Monographs, 103*, 59–84.

Spencer, M. B., and Markstrom-Adams, C. (1990). Identity processes among racial and ethnic minority children in America. *Child Development, 61*(2), 290–310.

Sroufe, L. A. (1983). Infant-caregiver attachment and patterns of adaptation in preschool: The roots of maladaptation and competence. In M. Perlmutter (ed.), *Minnesota symposia on child psychology.* Vol. 16,

*Development and policy concerning children with special needs*. Hillsdale, N.J.: Erlbaum.

Starkley, D. (1981). The origins of concept formation: Object sorting and preference in early infancy. *Child Development, 52*, 489–497.

Staub, E. (1979). *Positive social behavior and morality*. Vol. 2, Socialization and development. New York: Academic Press.

Strauss, M. (1979). Abstraction of prototypical information by adults and 10-month-olds. *Journal of Experimental Psychology: Human Learning and Memory, 5*, 618–632.

Strayer, F. F., and Strayer, J. (1976). An ethological analysis of social agonism and dominance relations among preschool children. *Child Development, 47*, 980–989.

Strayer, F. F., and Trudel, M. (1984). Developmental changes in the nature and function of social dominance among young children. *Ethology and Sociobiology, 5*, 279–295.

Sugarman, S. (1983). *Children's early thought*. Cambridge, England: Cambridge University Press.

Traux, C. B., and Tatum, C. D. (1966). An extension from the effective psychotherapeutic model to constructive personality change in preschool children. *Childhood Education, 42*, 456–462.

Vandell, D., Wilson, K., and Buchanan, N. (1980). Peer interaction in the first year of life: An examination of its structure, content, and sensitivity to toys. *Child Development, 51*, 481–488.

Vincze, M. (1971). The social contacts of infants and young children reared together. *Early Child Development and Care, 1*, 99–109.

Walter, G. H. (1977). The relationship of teacher-offered empathy, genuineness, and respect to pupil classroom behavior. Unpublished doctoral dissertation, University of Florida.

Williams, J. W., Best, D. L., and Boswell, D. A. (1975). The measurement of children's racial attitudes in the early school years. *Child Development, 46*, 494–500.

Wright, D. (1971). *The psychology of moral behavior*. Baltimore, Md.: Penguin Books.

Younger, B. (1985). The segregation of items into categories by ten-month-old infants. *Child Development, 56*, 1574–1583.

Zaleski, Z. (1992). Ethnic identity and prosocial attitudes. *Journal of Psychology, 126*(6), 651–659.

*Chapter Five*

# Ethnic Identity and Multicultural Competence: Dilemmas and Challenges for Minority Youth

Nancy A. Gonzales
Ana Mari Cauce

Any discussion of race relations, whether it concerns school-aged populations and educational policy, or national and international political concerns, inevitably invites speculation regarding the role of "ethnic identity." Ethnic identity has been broadly defined in scholarly discourse as "those aspects of an individual's thinking, feelings, perceptions, and behavior that are due to [his or her] ethnic group membership, as well as a sense of belonging and pride in [his or her] ethnic group" (Rotheram and Phinney, 1987). That ethnic identity plays a fundamental role in race relations in American schools is certain. And, indeed, if intergroup divisions are to occur, students must be aware of group memberships and distinctions. [*ethnic awareness*]

Some educators have argued, therefore, that the best strategy to eliminate interethnic tension and school violence is to minimize group differences in the school setting—that is, to essentially ignore race and ethnicity, so as to reduce their salience as dimensions of group identification. Yet this approach, though based on sound principles that should not be wholly disregarded, is unlikely to produce the desired "color-blind" goal. To understand why, we must consider more broadly the role of ethnic identity in the lives of developing adolescents. [*minimize difference + ignorance*]

What does it mean to a developing adolescent to be "identified" as black? African American? Korean American? Puerto Rican, Chicano, or Latino? How are these meanings shaped? And, once shaped, how do they determine the behavior of youths within their own group, and with members of other groups? Do these definitions anchor an individual in a gratifying relationship to self, or do they create internal states of doubt and low self-regard? How do social contexts and political forces shape the answers to these questions, potentially placing youths at risk for identity conflicts, or identity choices that limit their ability to participate fully in a multicultural American society?

The questions that surface in discussions about ethnic identity and cross-ethnic relations are always complex and inevitably political, often provoking emotionally charged responses. Unfortunately, empirical findings that can be brought to bear on these issues frequently fall short of effectively addressing the complexities and subtleties that are at the very heart of the most pressing of these questions. Accordingly, the present chapter will not attempt to provide definitive answers. Nor will it attempt to provide a comprehensive review of the research on ethnic identity (see Phinney [1990] for a recent review). This chapter will, however, explore the supposition that ethnicity is a salient component of the self-concept of adolescents from particular ethnic groups, and that concerns regarding ethnic identity have direct implications not only for interethnic relations but also, potentially, for the psychological health and well-being of these individuals.

In exploring these issues, we draw heavily from three related areas of research—ego identity theory, social identity theory, and acculturation theory—all of which have previously been used to illustrate the psychological and social significance of ethnic identity. Together, these research paradigms, respectively representing analytical frameworks at the level of individual, social group, and culture, will be used to illustrate potential challenges and choices that many adolescents face today as they attempt to forge an understanding of themselves as "ethnic" individuals. In addition, data from a study of African American students will be presented to further examine the links among ethnic identity, social relationships, and personal adjustment. (A full discussion of the differences and similarities between such terms as *ethnicity, culture,* and *race* is beyond the scope of this chapter. We use the term *ethnic people* herein to refer to those for whom ethnicity is a salient aspect in their lives. In this country, at this time, we assume that this encompasses most, if not all, people of color. In all likelihood it also encompasses first-generation immigrants. However, it may be applicable as well to other individuals or groups who are not either of the above.)

## Ego Identity Development

Identity achievement has long been regarded as one of the most important life-span developmental tasks, and as the single most important issue that defines the adolescent experience (Erikson, 1968; Marcia, 1976; Waterman, 1982). The consolidation of identity serves a critical organizing function for an individual: it provides a sense of meaning and personal continuity through time, a set of guidelines in making lifestyle and value choices, and the basis upon which personality integration and psychological well-being are established. Identity choices also circumscribe the possibilities of one's roles throughout life, thus providing a framework within which to prepare for one's potential place in society.

Research on ego identity supports the conceptualization of identity development as an ongoing process, beginning with self-concept development during early childhood and continuing well beyond adolescence (Harter, 1990; Waterman, 1985). The available evidence also suggests that identity development does not progress in a strictly linear fashion, culminating in an achieved adult status that is stable and enduring. Rather, commitments within different identity domains may be subject to reevaluation throughout the life span, typically in response to disequilibrating life events and changing contexts (Adams and Fitch, 1982). Thus, adolescents cannot stake an exclusive claim to the domain of identity development. It is during this period, however, that identity needs first emerge and assume a prominent role in shaping behavior, attitudes, and future possibilities. It is also during adolescence that individuals are initially capable of actively restructuring and shaping their own sense of self, at a time when they simultaneously have the cognitive abilities to fully appreciate personal, social, and political realities.

Adolescent identity development, as originally conceptualized by Erikson (1968), optimally involves active exploration and experimentation with a number of identity possibilities, whose contents provide powerful symbols around which the self-concept takes form (Archer, 1985; Harter, 1990; Marcia, 1976). Because the models and roles from which an individual chooses derive from his or her interactions in the social world, they are dependent on the opportunities and/or limitations present in that individual's sociocultural milieu. Sources of information and socialization central to this process include the primary influences of the family and peer group, as well as one's involvement with a number of nonfamilial agents and social institutions such as schools and the mass media (Cooper and Ayers-Lopez, 1985; Harter, 1990; Youniss, 1980).

### Ethnicity and Identity Development

Numerous writers have asserted that "ethnic identity" is an essential component of the identity process for many ethnic adolescents (Aries and Moorehead, 1989; Phinney, Lochner, and Murphy, 1987; Spencer, 1987). In a survey of high school and college students attending diverse educational institutions, Phinney and Alipuria (1990) report that as many as two-thirds of African American, Mexican American, and Asian American students rate ethnicity as "quite important" or "very important" to their identity—in contrast to only one-fourth of the white students surveyed. Other researchers have reported similar findings, indicating that most ethnic minority adolescents identify themselves as ethnic; at the same time, however, wide variations are reported between groups, a point to which we will later return (Rotheram-Borus, 1993).

For those adolescents who do choose to derive a sense of belonging and personal meaning from their ethnic group membership, the process by which this occurs is poorly understood. Much of the research has focused on either young children or late adolescents and adults for whom ethnic identity is symbolically and functionally distinct (see Chapter Six and Chapter Seven in this volume). Research with younger populations suggests that initial awareness of ethnic identity usually occurs between five and seven years of age, although ethnic attitudes, concepts, and preferences become evident much earlier (Aboud, 1987; Bernal and others, 1990). Children's understanding of their ethnicity is primarily absorbed directly from the family. When parents are themselves strongly ethnically identified, they are more likely to actively socialize their children to maintain ethnic values, customs, and preferences (Knight and others, 1993). Children's emerging views, however, also include the values and attitudes of the majority culture. Thus, even before they enter adolescence, children are well aware of specific labels, attitudes, and behavior patterns that are associated with their own group as well as with other ethnic groups, and many will have accepted negative views of their own group as self-defining features (Clark and Clark, 1939; Cross, 1978; Rotheram-Borus, 1993).

During adolescence, when individuals are able to actively reshape their concept of self, these internalized views may be reexamined and challenged. Similar models of ethnic identity formation that capture this process of redefinition have been described by researchers working within different ethnic populations (Cross, 1978; Helms, 1990; Phinney, 1989). These models suggest that identity exploration is typically preceded by a period of "crisis" and then one of "immersion" in ethnic exploration. During the latter period, individuals actively seek out experiences, information, and models to provide the basis for establishing an ethnic identity. The exploration stage of ethnic identity development is often accompanied by heightened feelings of alienation from the mainstream culture, and by separatist attitudes and behaviors, as individuals strive to assert their own distinctiveness and pride. Eventually, this process of "ethnic awakening" may lead to a more integrated understanding and acceptance of their own ethnicity, as well as greater appreciation and respect for other groups.

The problem with stage models of ethnic identity development, however, is that they have focused primarily on college students, and little is known about how ethnic identity is negotiated in non-college populations or during earlier stages of development. Indeed, only Phinney's research (1989, 1990) includes junior and senior high school students. Her findings suggest that active identity exploration is rarely in evidence among junior high school students, may be initiated by some adolescents during the high school years, but often does not begin until college. What, then, is the meaning of ethnic identity for youths who have not experienced an "ethnic awakening"?

## The Peer Context of Ethnic Identity: Belonging to an Ethnic Peer Group

Rotheram-Borus (1993) suggests that ethnic identity in younger adolescents is primarily tied to their choice of an "ethnically oriented reference group." Indeed, the powerful pull of this form of identification can be readily observed on campuses across the country as ethnicity persists as the most consistent category upon which the formation of adolescent "cliques" and "crowds" is based (Berndt, 1982), often despite focused efforts to increase cross-ethnic contact and decrease segregation in schools (Schofeld, 1981). Furthermore, developmental trends suggest that these preferences, which are already present to some extent during elementary school, become magnified during junior high school, and further increase during high school as identity development itself intensifies (Hallinan, 1982; Hallinan and Teiveira, 1987).

Once the predominant social structure of adolescent youth groups becomes established, the peer reference group provides a ready set of guidelines for behavior, attitudes, role models, and affiliation with other groups, along with powerful social pressures to conform to group expectations (Erikson, 1968; Brown, Clasen, and Eicher, 1986). To the extent that one's reference group has rigid boundaries and rules, separatist attitudes may be modeled and reinforced. Indeed, the resulting exclusivity may itself provide a strong sense of cohesion, loyalty, and ethnic pride. In our work with junior high school students in the Southwest, for example, we have found not only that adolescent peer groups are divided along black, Anglo, and Latino lines, but also that students of Mexican descent categorize themselves and one another with such distinct labels as "Chicano," "Mexicano," and "Mexican American." An extensive body of research suggests that these ethnic labels also symbolize a group's generation status, language preference, activities, style of dress, cultural values, political beliefs, and socioeconomic status, as well as ethnicity (Buriel, 1987). Furthermore, for those who identify as Mexican American, it is very important not to be viewed as "Mexicano" or "Chicano" because of the symbolic significance of these group-based identifications.

Whether a particular adolescent will choose to become exclusively aligned with an ethnically oriented reference group, and thereafter integrate this identification into his or her emerging self-concept, ultimately depends on a wide range of factors. The direct socializing influences of family members are paramount, but they are not exclusively responsible for the formation of ethnically based peer preferences. Ethnicity will also be rendered more or less salient for adolescents from different ethnic groups depending on the contextual and social pressures to which they are exposed in their communities and schools.

This latter fact is illustrated by Matute-Bianchi's fieldwork (1986), which highlights marked differences between Japanese-descent and Mexican-descent students in central California in terms of the extent to which they identify with their ethnic heritage. To explain the tendency for Mexican-descent students to be more strongly identified than the Japanese-descent students,

Matute-Bianchi suggests that ethnic identity is a "reactive process" that is strategically employed by certain ethnic groups in response to differential contextual pressures. She goes on to explain that for the Mexican-descent students in her study, a collective group identity, and the strong sense of cohesion that it provided, was needed to counteract negative stereotypes and expectations within a school community in which they held a subordinate status. By contrast, the Japanese-descent students did not require an ethnically explicit strategy (that is, collective group identity) to protect themselves in their interactions with others, because they generally enjoyed positively stereotyped reputations and did not occupy a subordinate status in the school.

Similar differences have been reported by other researchers who have drawn comparable conclusions about the importance of social context and, more specifically, about the degree to which economic and political power moderates the development and function of ethnic identity (Cross, 1991; Maharaj and Connolly, 1994; Spencer, 1987; Tajfel, 1978). Among minority children as well as adults, social disadvantage operates to increase ethnic identification and to compound prejudice toward outgroup members (Demo and Hughes, 1990). Thus, for some ethnic youths, particularly those who occupy lower-status positions relative to the larger community, it may be important to view ethnic identity both as an adaptive social-psychological response to external influences and as an essential component of the adolescent identity process (Spencer, 1987).

## Intergroup Relations and Ethnic Identity: Social Identity Theory

By framing ethnic identity as an essentially social phenomenon, social identity theory attempts to explain the social-psychological motivations underlying intergroup dynamics as a function of ethnic group membership and social context. Social identity is defined by Tajfel (1981, p. 255) as "that part of an individual's self-concept which derives from his or her knowledge of membership in a social group (or groups), together with the value and emotional significance attached to that membership." All people have multiple social identities (such as gender, social status, race, and ethnicity) that provide the basis for self-concept development and function to guide their behavior, particularly in instances of intergroup relations. In subsequent sections, we will rely on the principles of social identity theory, as well as those of ego identity theory, to explain the various struggles that ethnic minority youth may encounter as they attempt to forge a positive self-concept, and to clarify the strategies or adaptations that are likely to be used in the face of such struggles. Before proceeding, however, we offer the following brief outline of the processes that are central to social identity theory.

Social identity theory begins with the assumption that individuals are motivated to achieve a positive self-concept. Related to this psychologically based motivation are two fundamental social-psychological processes—social categorization and social comparison (Tajfel, 1982). The first of these processes suggests that individuals are naturally predisposed to categorize and order the social environment, and other individuals within that environment, into units composed of similar others (ingroups) and dissimilar others (outgroups). Social categorization then provides the basis for determining appropriate behaviors with those other individuals depending on their status as ingroups or outgroups—a distinction that potentially leads to very different behaviors with ingroup members (for example, greater warmth, trust, communication) than with outgroup members (Brewer, 1979; Tajfel, 1982). These different behavior patterns may result from the amount of shared knowledge between individuals and/or from the relative preference for the ingroup over the outgroup.

Once categorization has taken place and group membership is affirmed, individuals engage in social comparison as a means of determining self-evaluations and self-worth (Festinger, 1954). That is, they derive the value of their own group, and therefore of themselves, by comparing it to other groups. Since the value status of most groups, particularly ethnicity-based groups, is largely externally imposed, some individuals will find themselves identified with groups that are negatively valued relative to other groups within the larger social matrix. Consequently, group membership may produce uncomfortable tensions requiring some form of self-protective adaptation at the individual or group level.

According to Tajfel (1978), when one's social identity is perceived to be unsatisfactory, as in members of low status or low-power social groups, individuals will seek either to change their group affiliation or to change the evaluation of the group they perceive as their ingroup. Social mobility represents an example of the former strategy, an option that is not available to all individuals, particularly those who are tied to their group identity by visible markers (that is, physical features), life circumstances (such as poverty), or strong cultural or emotional ties to the group. The latter strategy involves attempts to reinterpret assumed derogatory features of one's group in a more positive, self-enhancing light. "Black is beautiful," for example, is a slogan depicting the positive reconstruction of the social identities of African Americans in the 1960s, when group members attempted to redefine the most obvious symbol of their group identification.

The increasingly segregated peer groups that evolve during the adolescent years may also provide a context within which ethnically homogeneous peer groups can establish values, norms, and standards of evaluation that facilitate identity development and support the maintenance of a positive self-concept. In a study of 330 adolescents from diverse ethnic groups, Rotheram-Borus (1990) found that adolescents choosing a strong ethnic identification reported significantly more separatist attitudes, were less likely to engage in cross-ethnic contacts out of school, and were more likely to perceive cross-ethnic conflict. Furthermore, those with strong ethnic identifications were also more likely to report feelings of pride in their ethnic group than were ethnic individuals who identified themselves as mainstream. Herein lies the crux of the difficulty that we face in trying to deal effectively with race and ethnicity within the educational system: How does one recognize ethnic differences and support ethnicity as an important dimension of self-definition without paradoxically encouraging group divisions and intergroup tensions that often result when ethnic categories are emphasized?

## Challenges to Ethnic Identity Development and Intergroup Relations

For the reasons already noted, many adolescents will face considerable challenges as they attempt to establish meaningful social ties and a positive identity. Phinney (1990) suggests that, in the process of articulating their identity, ethnic minority youth must resolve two primary issues or conflicts that stem from their status as members of a nondominant group in society and pose a serious threat to their self-concept: (1) the existence of two different sets of norms and values between dominant and nonmainstream cultures, and (2) the negative views and disparaging images of ethnic groups that pervade mainstream society. As Ogbu (1978) points out, the nature and magnitude of threat to any single individual will of course depend on a number of factors, such as whether the individual is a member of an autonomous, immigrant, or castelike minority. (The term *minority* is used herein to refer to a nonmainstream, low-power status, relative to the dominant society, that may not always represent the "statistical" minority.)

### Acculturation and Ethnic Identity: The Immigrant Experience

The pressures of adapting to two cultures simultaneously are most pronounced for immigrant youths, or for those whose parents were immigrants (Berry, 1980; Phelan, Davidson, and Cao, 1991; Semons, 1991). These youths may experience daily conflict and stress as they discover that their cultural values and behaviors at home are not necessarily recognized or valued among peers or at school, and as they encounter among their peers a wide range of values and cultural orientations that may conflict with and challenge the values and expectations of their families. Specific stresses may result from cultural discontinuities such as non–English speaking ability, unfamiliarity with school rules and expectations, and differences in learning styles to which immigrant children must adapt (Chavez, Moran, Reid, and Lopez, 1994; Berry and Kim, 1988; Derbyshire, 1980). When combined with the pressures to which all youths are exposed, particularly during adolescence, "acculturative" stress may lead to an increased risk for physical and mental health problems as well as to academic and social difficulties (Cervantes and Castro, 1985; Schinke and others, 1988; Shuval, 1982).

Acculturation, which is defined as a process of culture change that takes place as the result of contact between two cultures, represents a third framework within which to analyze ethnically based adaptations to sociocultural pressures (Berry, 1991; Padilla, 1980). This level of analysis seeks to understand the process by which coexisting cultural groups come to influence one another at both the group and individual levels. Broad cultural change is expected to occur as the result of inevitable conflict between groups, particularly when large differences exist in beliefs, customs, values, and language.

The adaptational options available to acculturating individuals are largely structured by the implicit model of culture change that has been adopted by the host culture as well as by the explicit policies of that culture regarding country, community, and school system. An assimilationist model, for example, views the task of immigrants as one of learning and adopting the cultural norms, values, and behavior patterns of the host society as quickly as possible in an effort to "fit in" as much as possible. From this perspective, adaptation is viewed in an either-or fashion; one can be oriented toward either the mainstream "host" culture or their own culture, but not toward both. Those individuals who resist assimilation and remain strongly identified with their culture of origin are viewed as poorly adjusted. And those who attempt to establish meaningful ties to both cultures are viewed as "marginal" individuals whose adjustment will also be compromised (Stonequist, 1953).

Ultimately, the assimilationist model has been unworkable in the United States, either as a political ideology or as an approach that accurately represents observable patterns of culture change (Glazer and Moynihan, 1970). While a consistent decline in the retention of cultural beliefs and ethnic group identification from the first to the third generation of immigrants has been demonstrated among many groups, other aspects of ethnic behavior and identity persist. As a visit to any major U.S. city will demonstrate, the American "melting pot" ideology has not prevailed. The dominant group has not readily accepted others into the mainstream ingroup, and most ethnic groups do not easily give up all aspects of their own culture in the process of becoming "Americanized."

The goals and assumptions of the assimilationist model have thus been challenged in more recent years by alternative models that are able to account for a wider variety of culture change patterns. Berry (1980), for example, conceptualizes acculturation as involving cultural shifts along two orthogonal dimensions, in which individuals may develop an identification to the mainstream culture independent of their ties to their ethnic culture. Within this model, four types of adaptations are possible: (1) assimilation, in which individuals take on dominant cultural characteristics and cultural identity and move into the dominant society, thereby relinquishing their own ethnic identification; (2) biculturalism, in which individuals have a positive relationship to the dominant culture and take on its characteristics and identity, while at the same time retaining their own culture and identity; (3) rejection, in which individuals reject the dominant culture and retain their own ethnic culture and identity; and (4) marginalization, in which individuals reject and dissociate from both their ethnic culture and the dominant culture.

Berry's model of acculturation has provided a valuable framework for understanding the varieties of adaptation possible for acculturating individuals, making several contributions to our understanding of ethnic identity and interethnic relations. First, the model makes a significant contribution in its implication that change occurs in both directions between coexisting cultural groups. Over time, the norms, values, and behaviors of both groups can and will be modified through contact. This is an important distinction; so often we talk about whether minorities are achieving a positive adjustment to the majority, yet we fail to ask whether majority-group individuals have learned to adjust to the minority perspective.

Berry's model has also been influential as an articulation of "biculturalism" as a viable solution to multiethnic demands. The bicultural individual was previously characterized as suffering from an inability to decide between the mainstream and Anglo culture; now, however, biculturalism has been recast as potentially the most satisfactory adaptation. The available research has generally demonstrated that bicultural youth have the best psychological outcomes and marginal youth the worst, with assimilation and integration falling at an intermediate level of adjustment (Berry and Kim, 1988). Research on biculturalism has thus emerged in recent years as theorists have attempted to elucidate those factors that promote successful interactions within two distinct cultural contexts, skills that are referred to collectively as "bicultural competence" (Cross, 1987; Ramirez, 1984; Rotheram-Borus, 1993; Szapocznik, Kurtines, and Fernandez, 1980).

Bicultural competence is perhaps most important during adolescence, when children (particularly recent arrivals to a new country) become exposed to a wider social world and begin to choose critical identity orientations. There is a sizable literature documenting the difficulties experienced by immigrant families when children acculturate at a faster rate, and exhibit greater participation in the mainstream culture, than do parents who remain tied to their culture of origin (Szapocznik and Kurtines, 1980). These differences are thought to result in heightened intergenerational conflict, which disrupts family functioning, inhibits parents' ability to effectively socialize their children, and may lead to the development of serious problems. Intergenerational conflict also poses a specific challenge to identity development for youths who may feel that they have to choose between belonging to their parents' culture or to that of their peers. The option of biculturality, however, suggests that youths may be able to integrate into the mainstream culture without experiencing a concomitant weakening of ethnic identification.

## "Minority Status" and Ethnic Identity Development

Even the notion of bicultural adaptation may underestimate the complexity of cultural context in this country. For instance, Boykin (1986) has talked of African Americans in terms of the "triple quandary," referring to the fact that African Americans are exposed not only to the African American experience and the mainstream Anglo experience but to the "minority" experience as well. The latter refers to the discrimination, social injustice, and oppression that are shared by many people of color, though to varying extents.

As suggested by social identity theory, when the dominant group in a society holds in low esteem the traits or characteristics of a particular ethnic group, the members of that group are potentially faced with a negative social identity. Constantly reminded of their negative image within the eyes of the larger society, minority youth are indeed faced with the very difficult task of trying to derive a positive self-concept. Powerless to counteract media images and social expectations, some of these young people will accept the negative judgments about their group and internalize them as self-evaluative features (Cross, 1987). The early literature on internalized racism suggested that this outcome was inevitable for certain groups (see, for example, Clark and Clark, 1939); however, this literature has received widespread criticism. When it does occur, internalized racism may lead some students to dissociate from their ethnic heritage, although for most this strategy is impossible to achieve, and the attempt to do so may itself undermine one's self-concept (Semons, 1991).

Other youth may adapt to the disparagement of their group by affirming their group identification and repudiating the standard of evaluation set by the dominant group—a standard that, for many minority youth, is ultimately of little relevance to their own lives. Ogbu (1978, 1987) suggests that lack of status, political power, and economic opportunity in minority communities result in the perception among minority youths that American society is not an open opportunity structure, and that it does not provide a viable set of norms or values upon which to formulate their own identities. This perception is in fact an accurate reflection of what they have witnessed within their own families and communities, such that these youth may have nothing to lose and much to gain by rejecting "mainstream" ideals.

Fordham and Ogbu (1986) take this argument one step further by suggesting that the "minority experience" leads to the development of an "oppositional identity," a pattern that has also been referred to as *cultural inversion*. They note that many African American youths appear to base their identity in opposition to the mainstream Anglo culture, and for these youths "acting white" has very negative connotations and consequences. Unfortunately, doing well in school is usually one of the things associated with "acting white"—a poignantly unfortunate turn of events given that education still represents one of the few viable means of overcoming socioeconomic disadvantage.

The minority experience in this country may also deliver disproportionate numbers of individuals to the marginal category defined by Berry's model of acculturation. In addition to rejecting mainstream values, individuals may attempt to dissociate from their own cultural background in what appears to be the most maladaptive strategy. A number of researchers suggest, for example, that members of Mexican American gangs are most frequently those boys who reject white American cultural standards while at the same time holding the most extreme feelings of ambivalence toward Mexican culture (Matute-Bianchi, 1986; Moore, 1985; Vigil, 1988). It is difficult, of course, to determine whether these youth are "marginal" in the true sense of the term. Many so-called marginal youths may be capable of forming significant attachments within alternative cultures such as the "street culture," which provides a ready and powerful source of group identification and acceptance.

## Correlates of Ethnic Identity and Bicultural Competence

Most scholars of ethnic identity agree with the view that a strong sense of connection and pride in one's ethnicity is related to healthy developmental outcomes, and that ethnic identity should therefore be reinforced whenever possible. For example, Tajfel (1978) argues that ethnic identity provides a sense of social connectedness that is the basis for psychological well-being. In addition, because ethnic identity is viewed as a necessary defense for disparaged minority groups against the inevitable psychological insults of a racist society, it is considered critical to the development of a positive self-concept (Cross, 1991). Some theorists also believe that a secure ethnic identity may help to reduce prejudice toward others (Aboud and Doyle, 1993), and emerging evidence suggests that biculturalism is related to a number of positive outcomes including cognitive flexibility, social adjustment, and enhanced coping abilities (Ramirez, 1984; Rotheram-Borus, 1993; Szapocznik, Kurtines, and Fernandez, 1980).

Despite the general consensus of opinions regarding the psychological benefits of ethnic identity, its contribution to psychological well-being is a topic that remains open to empirical debate. While some studies suggest that ethnic identity promotes a positive self-concept and is related to higher levels of self-esteem, others find a negative association, and still others find no relation at all (Phinney, 1990). Such discrepant results may be due to the possibility that each study examined different aspects of ethnic identity, employed different measures, and utilized different indicators of self-esteem. Indeed, as both ethnic identity and self-esteem are multidimensional constructs, it may be that some aspects of ethnic identity affect particular areas of self-esteem more than others. Studies on the relation of ethnic identity or biculturality to adolescent mental health outcomes are even fewer in number and equally inconclusive (Phinney, Lochner, and Murphy, 1987; Rotheram-Borus, 1993).

In a previously reported study involving adolescents from diverse backgrounds, we and our associates examined family, school, and neighborhood factors that contribute to a broad range of both self-esteem and psychological adjustment outcomes (Mason, Cauce, Gonzales, Hiraga, and Grove, 1994; Gonzales, Cauce, Friedman, and Mason, 1994). Like many researchers, however, we have not yet reported on the role of ethnic identity as it relates to these outcomes. As a way of further highlighting the issues raised in this chapter, we provide the following sets of analyses, which examine aspects of ethnic identity as they relate to self-esteem and psychological adjustment within a sample of African American junior high school students.

## Description of the Study

The participants in this study were 106 African American adolescents (73 females, 33 males) who were in either the eighth or ninth grade. Sample recruitment and the study's procedures have been previously reported (Cauce and Gonzales, 1993; Mason and others, 1994). We assessed ethnic identity using the Multidimensional Ethnic Identity Scale for African American Adolescents, or MESAA (Cauce, Hiraga, Gonzales, and Mason, 1990), which was based on an adaptation of the Suinn-Lew Asian Self-Identity Acculturation Scale, or SL-ASIA (Suinn, Rickard-Figueroa, Lew, and Vigil, 1987). The MESAA was designed to assess multidimensional aspects of ethnic identity and covered such areas as self-identification, friendship choice, involvement in ethnic cultural activities, ethnic socialization, and ethnic attitudes. Two subscales measuring interrelated, but separable, aspects of ethnic identity were identified based on a combination of theoretical inspection and factor analysis. In the Ethnic Pride subscale, for instance, higher scores indicate a more positive and affirming attitude toward African

Americans. Sample items include "How much pride do you feel in your Black/African American identity?" and "My Black/African American heritage is an important part of who I am." Higher scores on the Ethnic Social Involvement subscale indicate higher levels of participation in the African American community as indicated by the race/ethnicity of parents' friends, one's own friends while growing up, and one's present set of friends. Sample items in this subscale include "What was the ethnic origin of friends and peers you had as a child, up to the age of 6?" and "Most of your parents' close friends are _____." Within this group of African American adolescents, each subscale demonstrated adequate levels of internal reliability (Cronbach's alpha was .62 and .69, respectively). A two-item measure, which we appended to the MESAA, was also used as an index of "biculturalism." One item asked adolescents to rate on a 5-point scale how well they fit into a primarily white group; the other asked the same with respect to a primarily black/African American group. Adolescents were coded as bicultural if they indicated that they would fit at least moderately well (given a rating of 3 or above) into *both* groups.

Self-esteem was assessed by means of the Harter Self Perceived Competence Scale for Adolescents, or SPCS (Harter, 1982), a widely used measure based on the conceptualization of self-esteem as a multidimensional construct. Other widely used indices of adjustment included the Child Depression Inventory, or CDI (Kovacs, 1981); the State-Trait Anxiety Scale, or STAIC (Spielberger, Gorsuch, and Lushene, 1970); and the Internalizing and Externalizing subscales of the Child Behavior Checklist, or CBCL (Achenbach and Edelbrock, 1983). Grade point average (GPA) was assessed based on adolescent self-reports of grades in mathematics and English.

### Study Results and Discussion

In the first set of analyses, we examined the correlations of scores on the Ethnic Pride (PRIDE) and Ethnic Social Involvement

(SOCIAL) subscales, using indices of self-esteem and emotional and behavioral adjustment. Correlations were examined separately for girls and boys. The results are presented in Tables 5.1 and 5.2.

As these results suggest, ethnic pride was related to positive outcomes for both girls and boys. For both genders, it was positively related to romantic competence, an index of adolescents' feelings about their desirability as a date or romantic partner. This area of self-esteem is especially important during adolescence. In addition, for boys, ethnic pride appeared to enhance job competence (the belief that one can and will be a good "worker") and school performance as indicated by self-reported grade point average. Given the high rates of school dropout and unemployment in the African American community, particularly among young African American men, these findings are notable.

In contrast, ethnic social involvement yielded a mixed pattern of results. For boys, it was positively related to social, behavioral, and job competence. For girls, however, it was generally related to negative outcomes. More specifically, ethnic social involvement was negatively related to behavioral competence and grade point average, and positively related to anxiety and depression. There is no easy explanation for these disparate results. Future investigation is needed to help us understand why growing up and living in a primarily African American social environment seems to enhance boys' self-esteem during adolescence but appears to be related to negative consequences for girls.

In our second set of analyses we examined the role that "biculturality" plays in self-esteem and adjustment. First, it is worth noting, as reported in Table 5.3, that both ethnic pride and ethnic social involvement were positively correlated with self-reported ability to fit into both an all-black/African American *and* an all-white group. These results would suggest that positive views of one's culture and a strong ethnic heritage enhance, rather than detract from, one's abilities to relate to the majority culture.

The benefits of a strong ethnic heritage and pride may be most important when they are part of a bicultural identity. We did not

**Table 5.1. Correlations of Pride and Socialization
with Perceived Self-Competence.**

|  | SCH | SOC | BEH | FRN | ROM | JOB | SELF |
|---|---|---|---|---|---|---|---|
| Boys (P) | .14 | .04 | .16 | .22 | .25# | .35* | .09 |
| (S) | .01 | .29# | .25# | .16 | .02 | .34* | .07 |
| Girls (P) | .13 | .07 | −.06 | −.06 | .25* | .17 | .08 |
| (S) | −.07 | .04 | −.27* | −.05 | .32** | −.15 | −.14 |

*Note:* SCH = School, SOC = Social, BEH = Behavioral, FRN = Friend, ROM =
Romantic, JOB = Job, SELF = Self. (All these are perceived-competence subscales
from the Harter measure).
#$p < .10.$
*$p < .05.$
**$p < .01.$

**Table 5.2. Correlations of Pride and Socialization
with Emotional and Behavioral Adjustment.**

|  | ANX | CDI | INT | EXT | PROB | GPA |
|---|---|---|---|---|---|---|
| Boys (P) | .06 | .06 | .05 | −.08 | .04 | .35* |
| (S) | −.07 | −.06 | −.04 | −.12 | .12 | .18 |
| Girls (P) | .15 | −.04 | .08 | .14 | .02 | −.18 |
| (S) | .20* | .28* | −.04 | .05 | .19 | −.30** |

*Note:* ANX = Anxiety, CDI = Depression, INT = Internalizing, EXT = Externalizing,
PROB = Problem Behavior, GPA = Self-Reported Grade Point Average.
*$p < .05.$
**$p < .01.$

measure bicultural identity per se; but by combining responses to the
two questions about fitting into a white or a black/African American
group, we were able to classify participants as either bicultural or not
bicultural. We then conducted a series of t-tests to examine whether
individuals in these groups differed on our indices of self-esteem and
psychological adjustment. As reported in Table 5.4, these results
clearly indicate that bicultural individuals were at an advantage.
Bicultural girls evidenced greater perceived behavioral competence,
greater job competence, and lower levels of anxiety, depression, and
problem behavior. Although the results were not as striking for boys,
who evidenced lower levels of only anxiety when they were bicul-

Table 5.3. Correlations of Pride and Socialization
with Inter- and Intraethnic Group Comfort.

| | White[a] | Black[b] |
|---|---|---|
| Boys (P) | .35[c] | .26[f] |
| (S) | .25 | .28 |
| Girls (P) | .29[d] | .28[d] |
| (S) | .44[e] | .31[d] |

[a]White = How well do you fit into a group that is primarily white?
[b]Black = How well do you fit into a group that is primarily black or African American?
[c]p < .05.
[d]p < .01.
[e]p < .001.
[f]p < .10.

tural, this outcome was due in part to the relatively small sample size. In fact, an inspection of the means for both groups suggested that bicultural boys were also at an advantage.

In sum, these preliminary findings support the view that the relation of ethnic identity to adjustment and self-esteem may vary according to gender, as well as to which aspect of ethnic identity is examined. We also suspect that results would vary according to age, ethnic group, and social context. Among these early adolescents, ethnic pride and bicultural competence appeared to enhance at least some aspects of adjustment for both boys and girls. The advantages of bicultural competence were especially striking. But the effects of ethnic social involvement within an African American environment were less straightforward, suggesting the need for more research in this area.

We will continue to explore the relation of ethnic identity to adolescent development and well-being within diverse populations, and we urge other researchers to do the same. Yet to be answered are a number of important questions about the relation of ethnic identity to self-concept development and psychological well-being, about the specific skills and competencies that define a biculturally competent individual, and about the specific contexts that may fos-

Table 5.4. Correlations of Bicultural Orientation
with Self-Competence and Adjustment.

|  | Boys | | Girls | |
|  | Bicultural (N = 16) | Nonbicultural (N = 17) | Bicultural (N = 38) | Nonbicultural (N = 34) |
|---|---|---|---|---|
| EXT[a] | 55.58 | 57.25 | 51.75 | 52.94 |
| INT | 54.35 | 58.00 | 53.46 | 52.92 |
| SCH | 14.40 | 14.00 | 14.09 | 14.61 |
| BEH |  |  | 14.88 | 13.72[b] |
| ROM | 13.88 | 14.07 | 13.55 | 13.27 |
| JOB |  |  | 16.73 | 15.35[c] |
| ANX | 33.31 | 37.82[b] | 32.77 | 37.85[d] |
| CDI | 32.80 | 35.61 | 34.03 | 37.65[c] |
| PROB | 21.25 | 27.75 | 19.97 | 22.90[b] |

[a]EXT = Externalizing, INT = Internalizing, SCH = School, BEH = Behavioral, ROM = Romantic, JOB = Job, ANX = Anxiety, CDI = Depression, PROB = Problem Behavior.
[b]$p < .05$.
[c]$p < .01$.
[d]$p < .001$.

ter ethnic pride while at the same time encouraging positive interethnic relations. Continued investigation in this area should prove valuable to future efforts directed toward the development of culturally informed and effective policies and interventions that promote the welfare of adolescents growing up in multicultural environments.

## Conclusions and Policy Recommendations

As part of our current mission to inform policy recommendations regarding interethnic relations, the preceding discussion outlines areas that are difficult to translate into straightforward guidelines. We believe that efforts to develop programs intended to facilitate race relations among adolescents must be based on a solid understanding of those developmental and social-psychological processes that either advance or undermine such efforts, especially with respect to adolescents' fundamental needs for group acceptance and self-worth. Empirical findings and historical patterns of race relations clearly suggest that individuals will continue to categorize themselves, and that these categories will then provide the basis for both positive and negative group-based responses. As such, educators and policy planners must acknowledge that "race" and "color" remain unavoidable social issues, as well as important dimensions of identity formation, and should be openly addressed. Failure to do so may result in interventions that are at best ineffective and at worst deleterious to the self-concept development of ethnic youth.

*educators cannot ignore ethnic development*

Unfortunately, the strategies that one might employ to facilitate these needs often seem at cross-purposes. The literature on social identity extensively documents the profound effects of social categorization, suggesting that simply creating boundaries, or accentuating existing ones, can have strong effects on the perceptions, evaluations, and judgments of members of both ingroups and outgroups (Brewer, 1979; Tajfel, 1982). Based on this factor alone, educational settings might be designed to minimize ethnic group membership and differences, thus weakening the relevance of category boundaries based on ethnicity (Worchel, 1986). Indeed, if viewed solely from this vantage point, traditional prejudice-reduction programs that stress ethnic origin may have the unintended effect of increasing own-group orientations and, hence, fueling the very prejudice they are designed to eliminate. Downplaying ethnicity as a social identity is also to be recommended, in light of the tendency among individuals to internalize disparaging ethnic images that have been reinforced in ethnicity-related contexts (Steele, 1993).

On the other hand, efforts aimed at fostering intergroup relations by minimizing ethnic differences are typically not sufficient to counteract the strong pull inherent in shared ethnic group membership (Schofeld, 1986). This is likely to remain the case, even in the face of well-organized efforts to desegregate or to create "color-blind" environments, as long as ethnic boundaries and social inequalities are reinforced to such an extent within the larger society, and as long as youths derive such benefits from a sense of belonging to their chosen peer group.

Furthermore, a policy that ignores ethnicity also fails to appreciate and accommodate the very real differences between individuals in cultural values, behaviors, and history that make it difficult for many ethnic youth, particularly those who are recent immigrants, to successfully adapt to a mainstream environment. Educators are increasingly realizing that a child's ethnic identity must be appreciated in the school setting if the goal of equal opportunity through equal achievement is to be attained (Banks, 1993). The climate and structure of the school, the mode of classroom interaction, and teaching styles must take into account the ethnic membership of students and the ways in which this membership affects their academic and social needs.

Failure to appreciate ethnic difference would also preclude the potential benefits to be gained from awareness by all individuals, including "nonethnic" individuals, of the unique characteristics and strengths of their cultural background. Individuals, particularly adolescents, have a need to understand and explore their "uniqueness," and clear ethnic boundaries are often necessary for an articulated sense of ethnic identity to develop. Even more to the point, emerging perspectives on bicultural development suggest that a secure ethnic identity may reduce prejudice toward others, because confidence in one's own ethnicity allows one to respect others who are ethnically different (Aboud and Doyle, 1993; Ramirez, 1984). Our findings also suggest that a positive identification with one's ethnic group does not detract from relations with the dominant group, but may in fact facilitate them.

Thus, multiethnic environments should strive to foster ethnic pride while at the same time facilitating mutual respect and cooperative existence (Slavin, 1990). Successful school-based interventions might include instruction that is culturally contextualized and features multiple ethnic perspectives without overemphasizing category boundaries. In addition, interventions designed to directly minimize racial tensions can be developed and integrated into the curriculum. For example, efforts to decrease status differences and promote equality in the classroom may reduce the social-psychological motivations underlying the self-protective, defensive reactions expressed by members of both the outgroup and the ingroup. Students might also be provided with meaningful opportunities to participate in cross-cutting categories that facilitate a sense of belonging to multiple social groups.

Our findings, and those of others, suggest potential gains from programs that actively promote the "ideology of multiculturalism" (Banks, 1993). As long as becoming more comfortable in a white group means losing one's "blackness," many black youth will not choose more integrated settings (Fordham, 1991). Thus it becomes important to identify and develop approaches that cultivate comfortable, and fully integrated, multiethnic school environments. Some researchers have referred to "bicultural competence" as a means of describing youths' ability to function effectively in two distinct cultural environments. Indeed, the available evidence suggests that a substantial proportion of adolescents will choose to identify themselves as bicultural when given the option (Rotheram-Borus, 1993). Perhaps within the increasingly multiethnic settings where most children obtain an education, "multicultural competence" is the appropriate term and goal—not just for minority members but for all youths and educators who would benefit both from a greater appreciation of diverse values and norms and from the ability to comfortably cross cultural boundaries.

## Final Reflections: "The Triple Quandary"

At the risk of ending on a pessimistic note, it is important that we emphasize the great difficulty that educators face in attempting to integrate the nation's most disenfranchised youth, particularly in the absence of substantial macro-level changes. Identity development, at its best, is conceptualized as a process by which individuals make choices in asserting their own self-definition. For many minority youth, however, true "choices" are severely limited, and self-definitions are bound by powerful, externally imposed symbols. Thus, without substantial changes in the opportunity structure for minority youth, there is a sizable segment of the population for whom interventions at any other level will be grossly ineffective. What incentives do these youth have for becoming more integrated into the fabric of American society when integration is accompanied by disparagement and self-doubt? We must appreciate this fact, this "triple quandary" of the minority experience, along with the compelling motivations for these youth to derive self-esteem and identity outside the dominant culture.

# References

Aboud, F. (1987). The development of ethnic self-identification and attitudes. In J. Phinney and M. Rotheram (eds.), *Children's ethnic socialization: Pluralism and development* (pp. 32–55). Newbury Park, Calif.: Sage.

Aboud, F. E., and Doyle, A. B. (1993). The early development of ethnic identity and attitudes. In M. E. Bernal and G. P. Knight (eds.), *Ethnic identity: Formation and transmission among Hispanics and other minorities* (pp. 47–59). Albany, N.Y.: SUNY Press.

Achenbach, R. M., and Edelbrock, C. S. (1983). The child behavior profile: Boys aged 12–16 and girls aged 6–11 and 12–16. *Journal of Consulting and Clinical Psychology, 47,* 223–233.

Adams, G., and Fitch, S. (1982). Ego stage and identity status development: A cross-sequential analysis. *Journal of Personality and Social Psychology, 43,* 574–583.

Archer, S. L. (1985). Identity and the choice of social roles. *New Directions for Child Development; Identity in Adolescence: Process and Contents, 30,* 79–100.

Aries, E., and Moorehead, K. (1989). The importance of ethnicity in the development of identity of black adolescents. *Psychological Reports, 65,* 75–82.

Banks, J. (1993). Multicultural education: Historical development, dimensions, and practice. In L. Darling-Hammond (ed.), *Review of research in education,* Vol. 19, pp. 3–50.

Bernal, M. E., and others. (1990). The development of ethnic identity in Mexican American youth. *Hispanic Journal of Behavioral Sciences, 12,* 3–24.

Berndt, T. (1982). The features and effects of friendship in early adolescence. *Child Development, 53,* 1447–1460.

Berry, J. (1980). Acculturation as varieties of adaptation. In A. Padilla (ed.), *Acculturation: Theory, methods, and some new findings* (pp. 9–25). Boulder, Colo.: Westview Press.

Berry, J. (1991). Ethnic identity in plural societies. In M. E. Bernal and G. P. Knight (eds.), *Ethnic identity: Formation and transmission among Hispanics and other minorities* (pp. 271–296). Albany, N.Y.: SUNY Press.

Berry, J., and Kim, U. (1988). Acculturation and mental health. In P. R. Dasen, J. W. Berry, and N. Sartorius (eds.), *Health and cross cultural psychology*, Vol. 10. Newbury Park, Calif.: Sage.

Boykin, A. W. (1986). The triple quandary and the schooling of Afro-American children. In U. Neisser (ed.), *The school achievement of minority children* (pp. 57–92). Hillsdale, N.J.: Erlbaum.

Brewer, M. B. (1979). In-group bias in the minimal intergroup situation: A cognitive-motivational analysis. *Psychological Bulletin, 86,* 307–324.

Brown, B. B., Clasen, D. R., and Eicher, S. A. (1986). Perceptions of peer pressure, peer conformity dispositions, and self-reported behavior among adolescents. *Developmental Psychology, 22,* 521–530.

Buriel, R. (1987). Ethnic labeling and identity among Mexican Americans. In J. Phinney and M. J. Rotheram (eds.), *Children's ethnic socialization: Pluralism and development* (pp. 134–152). Newbury Park, Calif.: Sage.

Cauce, A. M., and Gonzales, N. A. (1993). Slouching towards culturally competent research: Adolescents and families of color in context. *Focus: Psychological Study of Ethnic Minority Issues, 7,* 8–9.

Cervantes, R. C., and Castro, F. G. (1985). Stress, coping, and Mexican American mental health: A systematic review. *Hispanic Journal of Behavioral Sciences, 7,* 1–73.

Chavez, D. V., Moran, B. R., Reid, S. L., and Lopez, M. (1994). Acculturative stress in children: A modification of the SAFE scale. *Hispanic Journal of Behavioral Sciences.*

Clark, K. B., and Clark, M. P. (1939). The development of consciousness of self and the emergence of racial identification in Negro preschool children. *Journal of Social Psychology, 10,* 591–599.

Clark, K. B.,and Clark, M. P. (1947). Racial identification and preference in Negro children. In T. M. Newcomb and E. L. Hartler (eds.), *Readings in social psychology* (pp. 169–178). New York: Holt.

Cooper, C. R., and Ayers-Lopez, S. (1985). Family and peer systems in early adolescence: New models of the role of relationships in development. *Journal of Early Adolescence, 5,* 9–21.

Cross, W. (1978). The Thomas and Cross models of psychological nigrescence: A literature review. *Journal of Black Psychology, 4,* 13–31.

Cross W. (1987). A two-factor theory of Black identity: Implications for the study of identity development in minority children. In L. Phinney and M. Rotheram (eds.), *Children's ethnic socialization: Pluralism and development* (pp. 117–133). Beverly Hills, Calif.: Sage.

Cross, W. (1991). *Shades of Black: Diversity in African American identity.* Philadelphia, Penn.: Temple University Press.

Demo, D. H., and Hughes, M. (1990). Socialization and racial identity among Black Americans. *Social Psychology Quarterly, 53*(4), 364–374.

Derbyshire, R. L. (1980). Adaptation of adolescent Mexican-Americans to the United States society. In E. B. Brady (ed.), *Behavior in new environments: Adaptation of migrant populations* (pp. 275–290). Beverly Hills, Calif.: Sage.

Erikson, E. (1968). *Identity: Youth and crisis.* New York: Norton.

Festinger, L. (1954). A theory of social comparison processes. *Human Relations, 7,* 117–140.

Fordham, S. (1991). Peer-proofing academic competition among Black adolescents: "Acting White" Black American style. In C. E. Sleeter (ed.), *Empowerment through multicultural education.* Albany, N.Y.: State University of New York Press.

Fordham, S., and Ogbu, J. U. (1986). Black students' school success: Coping with the "burden of acting White." *Urban Review, 18,* 176–206.

Glazer, N., and Moynihan, D. P. (1970). *Beyond the melting pot,* 2nd ed. Cambridge, Mass.: MIT Press.

Gonzales, N. A., Cauce, A. M., Friedman, R., and Mason, C. A. (1994). *Parent and peer support for academic achievement in high risk neighborhoods.* Manuscript submitted for publication.

Hall, C.C.I. (1992). Please choose one: Ethnic identity choices for biracial individuals. In M.P.P. Root (ed.), *Racially mixed people in America.* Newbury Park, Calif.: Sage.

Hallinan, M. (1982). Classroom racial composition and children's friendships. *Social Forces, 61*(1), 56–71.

Hallinan, M., and Teiveira, R. (1987). Student's interracial friendships: Individual characteristics, structural effects, and racial differences. *American Journal of Education, 95,* 563–583.

Harter, S. (1982). The perceived competence scale for children. *Child Development, 53,* 87–97.

Harter, S. (1990). Identity and self development. In S. Feldman and G. Elliot (eds.). *At the threshold: The developing adolescent* (pp. 352–387). Cambridge, Mass.: Harvard University Press.

Helms, J. (1990). *Black and white racial identity: Theory, research, and practice.* New York: Greenwood.

Knight, G. P., and others. (1993). Family socialization and Mexican American identity and behavior. In M. E. Bernal and G. P. Knight (eds.), *Ethnic identity: Formation and transmission among Hispanics and other minorities* (pp. 105–129). Albany, N.Y.: SUNY Press.

Kovacs, M. (1981). The Children's Depression Inventory (CDI). *Psychopharmacology Bulletin, 21,* 995–999.

Maharaj, S. I. and Connolly, J. A. (1994). Peer network composition of acculturated and ethnoculturally-affiliated adolescents in multicultural settings. *Journal of Adolescent Research, 9*(2), 218–240.

Marcia, J. (1976). Identity in adolescence. In J. Adelson (Ed.), *Handbook of adolescent psychology*. New York: Wiley.

Mason, C. A., Cauce, A. M., Gonzales, N. A., Hiraga, Y., and Grove, K. (1994). An ecological model of externalizing in African American adolescents: No family is an island. *Journal of Adolescent Research, 4*, 639–655.

Matute-Bianchi, M. E. (1986). Ethnic identities and patterns of school success and failure among Mexican-descent and Japanese-American students in a California high school: An ethnographic analysis. *American Journal of Education, 95*, 233–255.

Moore, J. (1985). Isolation and stigmatization in the development of an underclass: The case of Chicano gangs in East Los Angeles. *Social Problems, 33*, 1–12.

Ocampo, K. A., Bernal, M. E., and Knight, G. P. (1993). Gender, race, and ethnicity: The sequencing of social consistencies. In M. E. Bernal and G. P. Knight (eds.), *Ethnic identity: Formation and transmission among Hispanics and other minorities* (pp. 11–30). Albany, N.Y.: SUNY Press.

Ogbu, J. U. (1978). *Minority education and caste: The American system in cross-cultural perspective*. New York: Academic Press.

Ogbu, J. U. (1987). Variability in minority school performance: A problem in search of an explanation. *Anthropology and Education Quarterly, 18*, 312–334.

Padilla, A. (1980). *Acculturation: Theory, methods, and some new findings*. Boulder, Colo.: Westview Press.

Phelan, P., Davidson, A. L., and Cao, H. T. (1991). Students' multiple worlds: Negotiating the boundaries of family, peer, and school cultures. *Anthropology and Education Quarterly, 22*, 225–250.

Phinney, J. S. (1989). Stages of ethnic identity development in minority group adolescents. *Journal of Early Adolescence, 9*, 39–49.

Phinney, J. S. (1990). Ethnic identity development in adolescents and adults: Review of research. *Psychological Bulletin, 108*, 499–514.

Phinney, J. S. (1992). The multigroup ethnic identity measure: A new scale for use with diverse groups. *Journal of Adolescent Research, 7*, 156–176.

Phinney, J. S., and Alipuria, L. (1990). Ethnic identity in older adolescents from four ethnic groups. *Journal of Adolescence, 13*, 271–281.

Phinney, J. S., and Chavira, V. (1992). Ethnic identity and self-esteem: An exploratory longitudinal study. *Journal of Adolescence, 15*, 271–281.

Phinney, J. S., Lochner, B. T., and Murphy, R. (1987). Ethnic identity development and psychological adjustment in adolescence. In J. Phinney and M. J. Rotheram (eds.), *Children's ethnic socialization: Pluralism and development* (pp. 53–72). Newbury Park, Calif.: Sage.

Ramirez II, M. (1948). Assessing and understanding biculturalism-multiculturalism. In J. L. Martinez and R. H. Mendoza (eds.), *Chicano psychology*, 2nd ed. (pp. 77–94). New York: Academic Press.

Rotheram, M. J., and Phinney, J. S. (1987). Ethnic behavior patterns as an aspect of identity. In J. Phinney and M. J. Rotheram (eds.), *Children's ethnic socialization: Pluralism and development* (pp. 201–217). Newbury Park, Calif.: Sage.

Rotheram-Borus, M. J. (1993). Biculturalism among adolescents. In M. E. Bernal and G. P. Knight (eds.), *Ethnic identity: Formation and transmission among Hispanic and other minorities* (pp. 81–102). Albany, N.Y.: SUNY Press.

Schinke, S. P., and others. (1988). Hispanic youth, substance abuse, and stress: Implications for prevention research. *International Journal of the Addictions, 23,* 809–826.

Schofeld, J. W. (1981). Complementary and conflicting identities: Images and interaction in an interracial school. In S. Asher and J. Gottman (eds.), *The development of children's friendships.* Cambridge, England: Cambridge University Press.

Schofeld, J. W. (1986). Causes and consequences of the colorblind perspective. In J. F. Dovidio and S. L. Gaertner (eds.), *Prejudice, discrimination, and racism* (pp. 231–253). Orlando, Fla.: Academic Press.

Semons, M. (1991). Ethnicity in the urban high school: A naturalistic study of student experiences. *Urban Review, 23,* 137–157.

Shuval, J. T. (1982). Migration and stress. In L. Goldberger and S. Breznitz (eds.), *Handbook of stress: Theoretical and clinical aspects* (pp. 677–691). New York: Free Press.

Slavin, R. E. (1990). *Cooperative learning: Theory, research, and practice.* Englewood Cliffs, N.J.: Prentice-Hall.

Spencer, M. B. (1982). Personal and group identity of black children: An alternative synthesis. *Genetic Psychology Monographs, 106,* 59–84.

Spencer, M. B. (1987). Black children's ethnic identity formation: Risk and resilience of castelike minorities. In J. Phinney and M. J. Rotheram (eds.), *Children's ethnic socialization: Pluralism and development* (pp. 103–116). Newbury Park, Calif.: Sage.

Spielberger, C. D., Gorsuch, R. L., and Lushene, R. E. (1970). *STAI Manual for the State-Trait Anxiety Inventory.* Palo Alto, Calif.: Consulting Psychologists' Press.

Steele, C. (1993). Collective prejudice: How stereotypes shape achievement and performance in American schools. Paper presented at the 73rd Annual Convention of the Western and Rocky Mountain Psychological Associations, Tempe, Arizona.

Stonequist, E. (1953). The problem of a marginal man. *American Journal of Sociology, 41,* 1–12.

Suinn, R. M., Rickard-Figueroa, K., Lew, S., and Vigil, P. (1987). The Suinn-Lew Asian Self Identity Acculturation Scale: An initial report. Unpublished manuscript.

Szapocznik, J., and Kurtines, W. (1980). Acculturation, biculturalism and adjustment among Cuban Americans. In A. M. Padilla (ed.), *Psychological dimensions of the acculturation process: Theory, models, and some new findings* (pp. 139–160). Boulder, Colo.: Westview Press.

Szapocznik, J., Kurtines, W., and Fernandez, A. (1980). Bicultural involvement and adjustment in Hispanic-American youth. *International Journal of Intercultural Relations, 4,* 353–365.

Tajfel, H. (1978). *The social psychology of minorities.* New York: Minority Rights Group.

Tajfel, H. (1981). *Human groups and social categories.* Cambridge, England: Cambridge University Press.

Tajfel, H. (1982). *Social identity and intergroup relations.* Cambridge, England: Cambridge University Press.

Tajfel, H., and Turner, J. (1979). An integrative theory of intergroup conflict. In W. Austin and S. Worchel (eds.), *The social psychology of intergroup relations* (pp. 33–47). Monterey, Calif.: Brooks/Cole.

Vigil, J. D. (1988). Group processes and street identity: Adolescent Chicano gang members. *Ethos, 15,* 421–445.

Waterman, A. (1982). Identity development from adolescence to adulthood: An extension of theory and a review of research. *Developmental Psychology, 18,* 341–358.

Waterman, A. (1985). Identity in the context of adolescent psychology. *New Directions for Child Development, Identity in Adolescence, Process and Contents, 30,* 5–24.

Worchel, S. (1986). The role of cooperation in reducing intergroup conflict. In S. Worchel and W. G. Austin (eds.), *Psychology of intergroup relations,* 2nd ed. (pp. 88–304). Chicago: Nelson-Hall.

Youniss, J. (1980). *Parents and peers in social development.* Chicago: University of Chicago Press.

## Chapter Six

# Becoming American: A Review of Current Research on the Development of Racial and Ethnic Identity in Children

Eugene E. Garcia

Aída Hurtado

The increasing cultural diversity in the United States poses serious questions as to how different ethnic groups will coexist in our society. The key to avoiding interethnic conflict is to identify the mechanisms by which individuals are able to develop a strong sense of themselves within their own groups while simultaneously not derogating other groups. Becoming American now involves much more complexity than in the recent past, precisely because of the availability of multiple identifications. The school system, as one of the main institutions in charge of socializing future citizens, will play a central role in the mediation of interethnic conflict and collaboration.

In this chapter we propose to highlight the most current and important developments regarding the ways in which children acquire their sense of belonging to different ethnic and racial groups. But first, we begin by reviewing the main framework through which schools deal with economic, racial, and cultural diversity—"Americanization." Implicit in this term is the notion that there is a white, middle-class mainstream culture that accounts for the economic and cultural success of the United States. The predominance of this framework, in turn, has affected the societal context in the United States under which various socializing agents, such as parents and schools, make decisions as to how they should teach children about their ethnicity and race. We then follow with an overview of the most recent research on children's racial/ethnic identity development. The chapter concludes with a series of proposals for future research.

## Americanization

Historically, Americanization has been a prime institutional educational objective for culturally diverse children (Wagner, 1981; Gonzalez, 1990). Americanization schooling practices were adopted whenever the population of these students rose to significant numbers in a community. The special programs that resulted were applied to both children and adults in urban and rural schools and communities. The desired effect of "Americanizing" students was to socialize and acculturate diverse communities. In essence, if schools could teach these students English and "American" values, then educational failure could be averted. Ironically, social economists have argued that Americanization was historically coupled with systematic efforts to maintain disparate conditions between whites and "minority" populations. Indeed, more than anything else, past attempts at addressing the educational problems of blacks, Hispanics, Indians, and Asians have actually preserved the political and economic subordination of these communities (Spencer, Dobbs, and Phillips-Swanson, 1988).

Proceeding as it does from a sociological theory of assimilation, Americanization has traditionally been recognized as a solution to the problem of immigrants and ethnicity in the modern industrialized United States. Americanization was intended to merge small ethnic and linguistically diverse communities into a single dominant national culture. Decades ago, Thomas and Park (1921) argued that the "Old World" consciousness of immigrants would eventually be overcome by "modern" American values. Although space limitations preclude a detailed review of the literature regarding the historical circumstances of the many immigrant populations that have come to the United States, we do rely on recent analyses by Gonzalez (1990) and Spencer (1988). According to Gonzalez, there are important distinctions between the way assimilation has been experienced by European immigrants and the way other immigrant groups have experienced it. First, the Americanization of the non-European community has been attempted in a continuously highly segregated social context. Indeed, African American, Latino, and other nonwhite students are more segregated today than three decades ago. Second, the assimilation of these non-European groups has had both rural and urban aspects, whereas the European experience has been overwhelmingly urban. Third, the assimilation of non-European immigrants has been heavily influenced by the regional agricultural economy, which retarded the "natural" assimilation process. Finally, slaves and immigrants from Africa, as well as from Mexico, Puerto Rico, and other Latin and Asian countries, could not escape the effects of the economic and political relationship between the United States' advanced industrialization and their countries' semi-industrialized, semi-feudal economies, most of which are under the political and economic sway of the United States. This relationship has led to a very constrained immigration pool, with only farm and low-skilled labor immigrating continuously to this country. Since none of the economies of the contributory European nations had such a relationship with that of the United States, their national cultures tended to be judged more on an equal footing with nations struggling to realize their interests. This factor alone would have made for a significant modification in the objectives and manner in which Americanization was applied to non-European background communities.

Americanization is arguably still the goal of many programs aimed at culturally diverse students (Weis, 1988; Rodríguez, 1989). But for these students, Americanization unfortunately still means the elimination of linguistic and cultural differences that are deemed undesirable. Americanization programs seem to assume a single homogeneous ethnic culture in contact with a single homogeneous modern one, and the relationship between the two is not that of equals. The dominant community, enjoying greater wealth and privileges, claims its position by virtue of cultural superiority (Ogbu, 1987). In one way or another, nearly every child who deviates from the dominant culture, whether born in the United States or elsewhere, is likely to be treated as a foreigner, an alien, or an intruder. As far back as 1923, a Los Angeles school superintendent voiced this common complaint in an address to district principals: "We have the [Mexican] immigrants to live with, and if we Americanize them, we can live with them" (quoted in Matute-Bianchi, 1990). Unfortunately, even today the objective is to transform the diversity in our communities into a monolithic English-speaking and American-thinking and -acting community. This attitude was recently articulated by Ken Hill, a California superintendent who has received state and national distinction for his efforts in a district serving a large number of African American, Mexican American, and Asian American students: "We've got to attend to the idea of assimilation and to make sure that we teach English and our values as quickly as we can so these kids can get in the mainstream of American life" (quoted in Walsh, 1990, p. B1, B4). In making this statement, Hill echoes the Americanization solution articulated repeatedly over the past century. It is important to note that the dropout rate for non-white students in Hill's school district was recently reported to be more than 40 percent (Matute-Bianchi, 1990).

In short, the Americanization solution has not worked. Having depended on the mistaken notion of a single, mainstream group culture, it presumes that children who are not part of the "mainstream" are, as a group, culturally flawed. To "fix" them individually, we would have to change their values, language, identity, and behavior—thus theoretically preventing their educational underachievement. In essence, all such disparate groups would "melt" into one large and more beneficial "American" culture. Clearly, however, the challenge facing educators with regard to culturally diverse students is not to "Americanize" them. Instead, it is to welcome each of the unique cultural contributions they make to the educational goal of academic success for all students.

## Social Context for Ethnic/Racial Socialization

Following Erickson (1987), it is important that we understand the nature of the lines separating cultures and settings. Some boundaries are neutral, as when sociocultural components are perceived to be equal by the people on each side. When such borders exist, movement between cultures occurs with relative ease: social and psychological costs are minimal. Alternatively, when these borders, whether real or perceived, are *not* neutral and separate cultures are *not* perceived to be equal, movement and adaptation are frequently difficult because the knowledge and skills in one culture are more highly valued than those in another. However successful students may appear to be navigating between borders, these transitions can incur personal and psychic costs invisible to teachers and others. Moreover, the borders can become impenetrable barriers when the psychosocial consequences of adaptation become too great.

Although the concepts referred to here are not new, prior research has generally focused on families, peers, and schools as distinct entities. We now know that any one of these categories can powerfully affect the direction in which students will be pulled. For example, dynamic teachers, vigorous schools, and programs designed to override the negative effects associated with low socioeconomic status and language and cultural barriers can produce committed, interested, and academically engaged individuals (Abi-Nader, 1990; Edmonds, 1979; Heath, 1982; Johnson and Johnson, 1981; Joyce, Murphy, Showers, and Murphy, 1989; Rutter, Maughan, Mortimore, and Ouston, 1979; Sharan, 1980; Slavin, 1988, 1989; Vogt, Jordan, and Tharp, 1987; Walberg, 1986). Likewise, research has described the potency and force with which peer-group members pull young people toward the norms of such groups (Clasen and Brown, 1985; Clement and Harding, 1978; Coleman, 1963; Eckert, 1989; Larkin, 1979; Ueda, 1987; Varenne, 1982). We know too that family structural position, such as socioeconomic status and parents' educational levels are important predictors of students' engagement with educational settings (Jencks and others, 1972), as are cultural expectations and beliefs (Clark, 1983; Erickson, 1987; Fordham, 1988; Gibson, 1987; Hoffman, 1988; McDermott, 1987; Ogbu, 1983, 1987; Spindler, 1987; Spindler and Spindler, 1989; Suarez-Orozco, 1985, 1987; Trueba, Moll, Diaz, and Diaz, 1982; Trueba, 1988). In other words, we know a great deal about how aspects of families, schools, teachers, and peer groups independently affect educational outcomes. But we also need to know how these worlds *combine* in the day-to-day lives of students, thus affecting their engagement with school and classroom contexts.

As educators attempt to create optimal school environments for increasingly diverse populations, they need to understand how students negotiate borders successfully or, alternatively, how they are impeded by them in a way that prevents their connection with institutional contexts as well as with peers who are different than themselves. Figure 6.1 graphically portrays this intricate interaction.

Recent recognition of cultural differences, particularly by educational institutions, combined with theoretical and empirical interest expressly concerned with extrapolating the cause of such differences (Mead, 1937), has led to research on differences in socialization practices. In particular, such research has attempted to relate familial characteristics to the emergence of particular social attributes that distinguish populations (Tharp, 1989). It is this effort to understand ethnic identities that start in the family and home, along with their relationship to schooling, that will be discussed in the remainder of the chapter.

## Ethnic Images and Their Effects

### Ethnic Images in Society

In recent decades the United States has made considerable progress in the area of race relations. Lynching, de jure segregation, and

Figure 6.1. The Students' Multiple Worlds Model

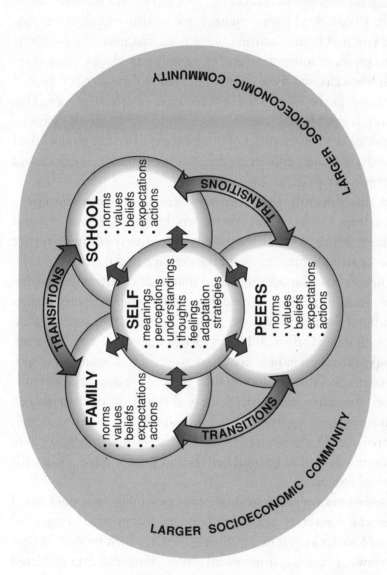

Source: Reprinted by permission of the publisher from "Students' Multiple Worlds: Navigating the Borders of Family, Peer, and School Cultures" by P. Phelan, A. L. Davidson, and H. C. Yu, Renegotiating Cultural Diversity in American Schools (p. 56) by P. Phelan and A. L. Davidson, © 1993 by Teachers College, Columbia University, New York: Teachers College Press. All rights reserved.

Jim Crow laws have been abolished. Whites have become more supportive of integration and racial equity (Smith and Sheatsley, 1984; Schuman, Steeh, and Bobo, 1985; Jaynes and Williams, 1989; Smith, 1990). And governments have instituted numerous programs (such as busing, affirmative action, and minority contracting) to promote integration and assist minority groups. Recent research has addressed these changes in racial tolerance as evidenced by changes in the images that people have of ethnic groups. This research has addressed two questions: (1) What are the various dimensions or characteristics of these images of ethnic groups? And (2) do these images influence other attitudes and behaviors toward the ethnic groups in question?

In this research, the term *ethnic* encompasses six groups— whites, Jews, blacks, Asian Americans, Hispanic Americans, and Southern whites)—that have been extensively studied and are defined partly by race, religion, nationality, and region. And the term *images* has a broader meaning than that of *stereotypes* or *prejudices*, so as to avoid heated debates that would detract from a meaningful discussion of how images about different ethnic/racial groups do indeed affect children's identity development. After all, stereotypes and prejudices are often assumed to contain a component of irrationality, including such fallacies as improper generalization, excessive categorization, and rejection or disregard of counterevidence (Allport, 1954; Schuman and Harding, 1964; Jackman, 1973). As referred to here, then, ethnic images include stereotypes as well as general beliefs that people have about ethnic/racial groups.

Despite enormous improvements in racial relations, the United States is far from color- and creed-blind, as documented in the *1990 General Social Survey* (cited in Smith, 1990), which focuses on people's views of various ethnic/racial groups. First, the data collected in this survey indicate that people are able to rate group members on the basis of their ethnicity. African Americans seem to be the easiest minority group to categorize and Asian Americans are the most difficult.

Second, with the exception of Jews, ethnic/racial groups of color are evaluated more negatively than whites. But even Jews, who are rated more favorably than whites on each characteristic, are rated as less patriotic. No other group scores above whites on any characteristic. Looking at overall ratings (including those for ingroup members), we find that Jews are rated positively in most categories (first in wealth, industry, nonviolence, intelligence, and self-support and third in patriotism). Asian Americans and white Southerners are ranked next (second or third) on almost every dimension. And, finally, blacks and Hispanic Americans are ranked last or next to last on almost every characteristic. In short, Jews are the only positively rated "minority" group.

Ethnic images are also related to the social distance that people prefer to maintain between themselves and other groups. As the image scale for each group moves from positive to negative, people are less favorable toward living in a neighborhood where half of the neighbors are from particular groups and less favorable toward having a close relative marry a group member. While all of the statistical correlations are significant, the relationship between images and social distance for Jews and white Southerners is modest, whereas that for blacks, Asian Americans, and Hispanic Americans is much more substantial.

In short, images of ethnic groups are significant predictors of support for racial integration and desired social distance. Despite the demonstrable progress in intergroup tolerance over the last several decades, ethnic images are still commonplace in contemporary society. On the whole, these images are neither benign nor trivial. Many whites in the United States see ethnic/racial groups in a decidedly negative light on a number of important characteristics. Only the images of Jews are generally positive—and even then, people seem to question their patriotism. All other groups—including the "old stock," white Southerners—are seen more negatively than whites in general. Hispanic Americans and blacks receive particularly low ratings. These negative ethnic images, in turn, help shape attitudes toward civil rights, racial integration policies, affirmative action, school desegregation, social distance, foreign countries, and presumably other group-related issues. Indeed, contemporary intergroup relations cannot be understood without taking into account the images that people have in their minds about the various ethnic groups that make up this country. This, then, is the human ecology (Bronfenbrenner, 1979; Garbarino, 1982) under which parents socialize their children to be part of their ethnic and racial groups.

## Effects on the Individual

How do these images shape an individual's self-identity? It is through self-identity that children's interpreted experiences are reconciled with their emotional states. Those experiences, in turn, are shaped by the social categories through which the child is interpreted by the socializing environment. A sense of ethnic identity is part of that synthesis, whereby ethnic identity is defined as the accurate and consistent use of an ethnic label to denote being part of the group (Phinney and Rotheram, 1987, p. 17). In a world populated by people of many different ethnic backgrounds who often interact, and conflict, with each other, children's developing sense of their ethnic group identity is an important social issue (Harrison and others, 1990). Accordingly, several studies on the development of ethnic identity have focused both on children's ability to identify their own ethnic group and on their attitudes toward their own and other groups (McAdoo and McAdoo, 1985; Bernal and Knight, 1993; Phinney and Rotheram, 1987).

Perhaps the best-known research on the development of ethnic identity was that carried out by Kenneth and Mamie Clark (1939, 1940), because its results were used as evidence that led the U.S. Supreme Court to declare racially segregated education illegal. African American and white children three years of age and older were presented with pairs of dolls representing the two ethnic groups. On successive trials the children were asked to choose "which boy [doll] you would like to play with" or "which girl you don't like." They reported that most of the youngest children distinguished between the gender categories of the dolls and that both the white and African American children displayed a preference for the white dolls. These results were interpreted by the justices of the Supreme Court as evidence that segregation resulted in the development of a negative sense of self among African American children. Studies conducted since the 1950s have not only confirmed the Clarks' original findings (McAdoo, 1985; Spencer, 1985) but have also extended them to include other minority ethnic groups, including Native Americans (Beuf, 1977) and Bantu children in South Africa (Gregor and McPherson, 1966). In all of these cases, the minority group children were more likely to prefer white dolls.

The same studies have cast doubt on the notion that minority group children acquire a generalized negative self-concept. Beuf (1977), for example, reports incident after incident in which Native American children who displayed a preference for the white dolls accurately portrayed the economic and social circumstances that make their lives difficult in contrast to the lives of whites. Five-year-old Dom, for example, was given several dolls representing whites and Native Americans (the latter were brown in color) to put into a toy classroom (Beuf, 1977, p. 80).

> *Dom:* (*holding up a white doll*) The children's all here and now the teacher's coming in.
> *Interviewer:* Is that the teacher?
> *Dom:* Yeah.
> *Interviewer:* (*holding up a brown doll*) Can she be the teacher?
> *Dom:* No way! Her's just an aide.

In Beuf's view, children's choices when presented pairs of dolls are less an expression of their self-concept than one of desire for the power and wealth of whites with whom they have come in contact.

Other recent research has shown that, when social- and self-conceptions are tested, young children's expressed ethnic preferences change according to the method of data collection. For example, Morgan (1991) demonstrates that children's race "preference" is affected by the method of measurement. Whereas black and white first-and second-graders will select more white pictures to depict a hypothetical family, they will seldom or never mention race in a discussion about a hypothetical family. And with respect to historical changes, Harriet McAdoo (1985) reports that the degree to which African American preschoolers show a preference for white dolls has decreased relative to the results obtained prior to the 1960s. She does not speculate on the reasons for this trend, but the end of racial segregation and several decades of political and cultural activism in the African American community are likely candidates. This conclusion is reinforced by Beuf's finding (1977) that young children of parents who were active in promoting Native American cultural awareness and civil rights displayed relatively high levels of choice of dolls representing Native Americans compared to children of parents who took little interest in Native American affairs.

Additional evidence of the power of the environment to shape children's ethnic preferences comes from an experimental study in which three- to five-year-old children were rewarded for choices of black versus white pictures of animals and people (Spencer and Horowitz, 1973). Initially all of the children showed a preference for white stimuli (both animals and people), but after training sessions in which the researchers rewarded them symbolically (by giving them marbles that could be traded for cookies) they displayed a marked preference for black stimuli that remained intact over a period of several weeks. Still other evidence for the power of the environment comes from Bowman and Howard's analyses (1985) of the socialization practices of a national sample of African American trigenerational families. Parents of *academically successful* children emphasized in their socialization practices ethnic pride, self-development, awareness of racial barriers, and egalitarianism. However, the majority of ethnic/racial families want their children to function well not only within their own group but with members of the majority group as well (Harrison, Serafica, and McAdoo, 1984;

Peters, 1988). Developing biculturalism in its practical form involves the *synthesis* of two cultures rather than the use of two cultural modalities in an additive manner (Gutierrez, Sameroff, and Karrer, 1988). Children performing this synthesis require greater cognitive and social flexibility. The added "work," if successful, allows these children to develop into adults who can be part of two cultures while simultaneously standing outside of both. As Harrison and her colleagues (1990) point out, "Achieving the new synthesis is a complex process fraught with many obstacles and conflict" (p. 356).

An important development in the conceptualization of ethnic identity is the notion that ethnicity is not the only group membership factor of importance in determining individuals' behavior (Hurtado, Rodríquez, Gurin, and Beals, 1993). Indeed, ethnicity is only one of many such factors with emotional and cognitive significance for individuals (Rodríguez-Scheel, 1980). Bernal and her colleagues (1990) have further developed this notion by distinguishing between children's ethnic and racial identification. Clearly, then, the study of ethnicity has shifted from examining only the development of ethnic identity in children to examining other group memberships simultaneously. Researchers have concluded that *gender awareness* happens very early, usually by the age of two; that *racial awareness* happens next, usually by the age of four; and that *ethnic awareness* happens much later, usually between the ages of five and ten.

Furthermore, children's cognitive development is involved in all of these identification processes. Very young children, under the age of five, do not have the cognitive capacity to understand the many different dimensions of ethnicity, including language, cultural preferences, and practices. Yet they do have the cognitive ability to understand the concrete identification necessary for gender, based mostly on secondary sex characteristics, or for race, which is largely based on skin color and other phenotypic attributes.

Gender, racial, and ethnic *constancy* is also related to the level of social cognitive development. That is, besides identifying with different social groups, children have to develop the notion that those memberships are not easily changed—a boy does not become a girl by wearing a dress, and a Mexican American child does not become white by speaking English. The development of gender, racial, and ethnic constancy for group memberships follows the same pattern as identification, with gender constancy happening first, racial constancy second, and ethnic constancy last (Knight, Bernal, Garza, and Cota, 1993).

Two basic processes have been identified to explain how children develop their ethnic/racial identities. The first of these has been termed *enculturation* by Bernal and Knight (1993). Enculturation, or ethnic socialization, "refers to the cultural teaching that parents, families, peers, and the rest of the ethnic community provide to children during the childhood years" (p. 3). The second process they identify as affecting the persistence of ethnic/racial identity is *acculturation*, "which refers to the adaptation of ethnic minority people to the dominant culture and its members. In the process of adaptation, there often is some sort of cultural change that occurs in people, and that change could affect their ethnic identity" (p. 3).

An integral part of both processes—enculturation and acculturation—is the use of the ethnic/racial group's language. Not all ethnic/racial groups use a non-English language, but many do. Others, such as African Americans, use a variety of English that is distinctive from the one spoken by the majority (Kochman, 1987). The use of the ethnic/racial language adds to the discontinuity a child may experience between the home and school environment (Harrison and others, 1990). Yet that language is an integral part of the child's ethnic/racial identity. The acquisition of standard English by an ethnic/racial group member has been consistently used by researchers as a measure of acculturation to mainstream U.S. society (Marín, 1993). At the same time, bilingualism is one of the most important indicators of biculturalism (Hakuta and Garcia, 1989). Children perform better and have a better sense of their own group as well as of other groups when there is less discontinuity, including that in languages used, between home and school (Delgado-Gaitan, 1987; Laosa and Sigel, 1982; Marcias, 1987).

Language is a powerful carrier of ethnic identity. As Heller (1987) indicates: "Shared ways of speaking become symbolic of shared background knowledge, of shared culture" (p. 187). Therefore, parents who want their children to maintain their group's culture and traditions often insist that they speak the ethnic group's language (Hurtado, Rodríguez, Gurin, and Beals, 1993). Furthermore, children's racial/ethnic preferences are influenced by language. For example, American Indian children show greater preference for their own race when tested in their native language (Annis and Corenblum, 1987). Children's use of their ethnic language is also related to their ethnic identity. For example, children growing up in a predominantly Spanish-speaking environment tend to identify with Mexican American culture, to know more about their culture, and to engage in other ethnic behaviors such as eating Mexican food, watching Spanish television, and having a piñata for their birthdays (Knight and others, 1993). The advantages of bilingualism over monolingualism are greater cognitive flexibility (McShane, 1986), metalinguistic awareness (Diaz, 1983), and flexibility in using several formats for learning (Boykin, 1979).

In summary, research indicates that children are aware of ethnic differences by four years of age. At the same time, or not long after, they also become aware of, and form judgments about, their own ethnicity. Their attitudes toward their own and other people's ethnicity seem to depend both on the attitudes of their adult caregivers and on the perceived power and wealth of their own ethnic group. An integral part of this process is the children's cognitive ability to make inferences about their group memberships in comparison to other ethnic/racial groups in the environment (Spencer and Markstrom-Adams, 1990).

## Conclusions and Future Research

Families from various ethnic backgrounds make decisions about how to socialize their children within the context of an Americanization policy that not only persists in most institutions in this country but also contributes to the images that U.S. residents hold of different ethnic groups. Within that context, children are very aware, as they develop their identities, that not all groups are held in equal esteem and that there are negative consequences to being members of particular groups. The ways in which children interpret these negative attributions are largely dependent on the context (Harrison and others, 1990). Children whose ethnicity is valued, and who have positive role models from their own group, are less likely to experience their ethnic group membership as problematic (McAdoo, 1985; Beuf, 1977). Children who do not have these positive experiences tend to choose outgroup members as more valued than their own. Several factors influence children's identity formation, including phenotype (for example, dark skin or Indian facial features), language differences, social stereotypes, and cultural differences as reflected in social behaviors (Spencer and Markstrom-Adams, 1990).

A number of important questions relating to the linkage between school and home environment help explain how children acquire their sense of belonging to different ethnic/racial groups. For example, how does multicultural education influence children's acquisition of positive views of their ethnicity? How are white children influenced by exposure to different ethnic/racial groups in their own development of self? Do white children become bicultural or multicultural in their identities and in their behaviors? And most important, what are the long-term effects on identity for those children whose home and school environments reinforce multiculturalism in all its different dimensions, including language, and knowledge about the history, culture, and customs of ethnic/racial groups?

At the risk of repeating what has now become obvious, we emphasize that the United States is on the verge of a sociocultural revolution whereby educational paradigms will have to address the issue of how to produce citizens of the world while at the same time allowing these citizens to retain their valued ethnic/racial uniqueness. Interethnic and interracial conflict does not have to be the outcome of increasing cultural and economic diversity.

# References

Abi-Nader, J. (1990). A house for my mother: Motivating Hispanic high school students. *Anthropology and Education Quarterly, 21*(1), 41–58.

Allport, G. (1954). *The nature of prejudice*. Reading, Mass.: Addison-Wesley.

Annis, R. C., and Corenblum, B. (1987). Effect of test language and experimenter race on Canadian Indian children's racial and self-identity. *Journal of Social Psychology, 126*, 1761–1773.

Bernal, M. E., Knight, G. P. (eds.). (1993). *Ethnic identity: Formation and transmission among Hispanics and other minorities*. Albany: State University of New York Press.

Bernal, M. E., and others. (1990). The development of ethnic identity in Mexican-American children. *Hispanic Journal of Behavioral Sciences, 12*(1), 3–24.

Beuf, A. H. (1977). *Red children in white America*. Philadelphia: University of Pennsylvania Press.

Boykin, A. W. (1979). Psychological behavioral verve: Some theoretical explorations and empirical manifestations. In A. W. Boykin, A. J. Franklin, and J. F. Yates (eds.), *Research directions of black psychologists* (pp. 351–367). New York: Russell Sage Foundation.

Bowman, P. J., and Howard, C. (1985). Race-related socialization, motivation, and academic achievement: A study of black youth in three-generation families. *Journal of the American Academy of Child Psychiatry, 24*, 134–141.

Bronfenbrenner, U. (1979). *The ecology of human development*. Cambridge, Mass.: Harvard University Press.

Clark, R. M. (1983). *Family life and school achievement: Why poor black children succeed or fail*. Chicago: University of Chicago Press.

Clark, K. B., and Clark, M. K. (1939). The development of consciousness of self and the emergence of racial identification in Negro preschool children. *Journal of Social Psychology, 10*, 591–599.

Clark, K. B., and Clark, M. K. (1940). Skin color as a factor in racial identification of Negro preschool children. *Journal of Social Psychology, 11*, 159–169.

Clasen, D. R., and Brown, B. B. (1985). The multidimensionality of peer pressure in adolescence. *Journal of Youth and Adolescence, 14*(6), 451–468.

Clement, D., and Harding, J. (1978). Social distinctions and emergent student groups in a desegregated school. *Anthropology and Education Quarterly, 9*(4), 272–283.

Coleman, J. S. (1963). *The adolescent society: The social life of the teenager and its impact on education*. New York: Free Press.

Delgado-Gaitan, C. (1987). Tradition and transitions in the learning process of Mexican children: An ethnographic view. In G. Spindler and K. Spindler (eds.), *Interpretative ethnography of education: At home and abroad* (pp. 333–359). Hillsdale, N.J.: Erlbaum.

Diaz, R. (1983). Thought and two languages: The impact of bilingualism on cognitive development. In E. Gordon (ed.), *Review of research in education*, Vol. 10. Washington, D.C.: American Educational Research Association.

Eckert, P. (1989). *Jocks and burnouts: Social categories and identity in the high school.* New York: Teachers College Press.

Edmonds, R. (1979). Some schools work and more can. *Social Policy* 9(5), 28–32.

Erickson, F. (1987). Transformation and school success: The politics and culture of educational achievement. *Anthropology and Education Quarterly*, 18(4), 335–355.

Fordham, S. (1988). Racelessness as a factor in Black students' school success: Pragmatic strategy or Pyrrhic victory? *Harvard Educational Review*, 58(1), 54–83.

Garbarino, J. (1982). *Children and families in the social environment.* New York: Aldine.

Gibson, M. A. (1987). The school performance of immigrant minorities: A comparative view. *Anthropology and Education Quarterly*, 18(4), 262–275.

Gonzalez, G. (1990). *Chicano education in the segregation era: 1915–1945.* Philadelphia: The Balch Institute.

Gregor, A. J., and McPherson, D. A. (1966). Racial attitudes among White and Negro children in a Deep-South standard metropolitan area. *Journal of Social Psychology*, 68(1), 95–106.

Gutierrez, J., Sameroff, A. J., and Karrer, B. M. (1988). Acculturation and SES effects on Mexican American parents' concepts of development. *Child Development*, 59, 250–255.

Hakuta, K., and Garcia, E. E. (1989). Bilingualism and education. *American Psychologist*, 44, 374–379.

Harrison, A. O., Serafica, S., and McAdoo, H. (1984). Ethnic families of color. In R. D. Parke (ed.), *The family: Review of child development research*, Vol. 7 (pp. 329–371). Chicago: University of Chicago Press.

Harrison, A. O., and others. (1990). Family ecologies of ethnic minority children. *Child Development*, 61, 347–362.

Heath, S. B. (1982). Questioning at school and at home: A comparative study. In G. D. Spindler (ed.), *Doing the ethnography of schooling: Educational anthropology in action* (pp. 102–131). New York: Holt, Rinehart & Winston.

Heller, M. (1987). The role of language in the formation of ethnic identity. In J. S. Phinney and M. J. Rotheram (eds.), *Children's ethnic socialization: Pluralism and development* (pp. 180–200). Newberry Park, Calif.: Sage.

Hoffman, D. M. (1988). Cross-cultural adaptation and learning: Iranians and Americans at school. In H. Trueba and C. Delgado-Gaitan (eds.), *School and society: Learning content through culture*. New York: Praeger.

Hurtado, A., Rodríguez, J., Gurin, P., and Beals, J. L. (1993). The impact of Mexican descendants' social identity on the ethnic socialization of children. In M. E. Bernal and G. P. Knight (eds.), *Ethnic identity: Formation and transmission among Hispanics and other minorities* (pp. 131–162). Albany: State University of New York Press.

Jackman, M. R. (1973). Education and prejudice or education and response-set. *American Sociological Review, 38,* 327–339.

Jaynes, G. D., and Williams, R. M., Jr. (eds.). (1989). *A common destiny: Blacks and American society*. Washington, D.C.: National Academy Press.

Jencks, C., and others. (1972). *Inequality: A reassessment of the effects of family and schooling in America*. New York: Basic Books.

Johnson, D., and Johnson, R. (1981). Effects of cooperative and individualistic learning experiences on interethnic interaction. *Journal of Educational Psychology, 73*(3), 444–449.

Joyce, B., Murphy, C., Showers, B., and Murphy, J. (1989). School renewal as cultural change. *Educational Leadership, 47*(3), 70–77.

Knight, G. P., Bernal, M. E., Garza, C. A., and Cota, M. K. (1993). A social cognitive model of the development of ethnic identity and ethnically based behaviors. In M. E. Bernal and G. P. Knight (eds.), *Ethnic identity: Formation and transmission among Hispanics and other minorities* (pp. 213–234). Albany: State University of New York Press.

Kochman, T. (1987). The ethnic component in Black language and culture. In J. S. Phinney and M. J. Rotheram (eds.), *Children's ethnic socialization: Pluralism and development* (pp. 180–200). Newberry Park, Calif.: Sage.

Laosa, L. M., and Sigel, I. E. (1982). *Families as learning environments for children*. New York: Plenum.

Larkin, R. W. (1979). *Suburban youth in cultural crisis*. New York: Oxford University Press.

McAdoo, H. P. (1985). Racial attitudes and self-concept of young Black children over time. In H. L. McAdoo and J. L. McAdoo (eds.), *Black children: Social, educational, and parental environments* (pp. 213–242). Beverly Hills, Calif.: Sage.

McAdoo, H. P., and McAdoo, J. L. (eds.) (1985). *Black children: Social, educational, and parental environments*. Beverly Hills, Calif.: Sage.

McDermott, R. P. (1987). The exploration of minority school failure, again. *Anthropology and Education Quarterly, 18*(4), 361–364.

McShane, D. (1968). Native North Americans: Indian and Inuit abilities. In J. H. Irvine and J. W. Berry (eds.), *Human abilities in cultural context* (pp. 385–426). Cambridge, England: Cambridge University Press.

Marcias, J. (1987). The hidden curriculum of Papago teachers: American Indian strategies for mitigating cultural discontinuity in early schooling. In

G. Spindler and L. Spindler (eds.), *Interpretive ethnography of education: At home and abroad* (pp. 363–380). Hillsdale, N.J.: Erlbaum.

Marín, G. (1993). Influence of acculturation on familialism and self-identification among Hispanics. In M. A. Bernal and G. P. Knight (eds.), *Ethnic identity: Formation and transmission among Hispanics and other minorities* (pp. 181–196). Albany: SUNY Press.

Matute-Bianchi, E. (1990). *A report to the Santa Clara county school district: Hispanics in the schools*. Santa Clara, Calif.: Santa Clara County School District.

Mead, M. (1937). *Cooperation and competition among primitive people*. New York: McGraw.

Morgan, H. (1991). Race preference studies: A critique of methodology. Doll studies revisited: Is the message in the method? *Western Journal of Black Studies, 15*(4), 248–253.

Ogbu, J. (1983). Minority status and schooling in plural societies. *Comparative Education Review, 27*(22), 168–190.

Ogbu, J. (1987). *Minority education and caste: The American system in cross-cultural perspective*. New York: Academic Press.

Peters, M. F. (1988). Parenting in black families with young children: A historical perspective. In H. P. McAdoo (ed.), *Black families*, 2d ed. (pp. 228–241). Beverly Hills, Calif.: Sage.

Phelan, P., Davidson, A. L., and Cao, H. T. (1991). Students' multiple worlds: Negotiating the boundaries of family, peer, and school cultures. *Anthropology and Education Quarterly, 22*(3), 224–250.

Phinney, J. S., and Rotheram, M. J. (eds.). (1987). *Children's ethnic socialization*. Newbury Park, Calif.: Sage.

Rodríguez, C. E. (1989). *Puerto Ricans born in the U.S.A.* Winchester, Mass.: Unwin Hyman.

Rodríguez-Scheel, J. (1980). An investigation of the components of social identity for a Detroit sample. Unpublished manuscript. Occidental College, Psychology Department, Los Angeles.

Rutter, M., Maughan, B., Mortimore, P., and Ouston, J. (1979). *Fifteen thousand hours: Secondary schools and their effects on children*. Cambridge, Mass.: Harvard University Press.

Schuman, H., and Harding, J. (1964). Prejudice and the norm of rationality. *Sociometry, 27*, 353–371.

Schuman, H., Steeh, C., and Bobo, L. (1985). *Racial attitudes in America: Trends and interpretations*. Cambridge, England: Cambridge University Press.

Sharan, S. (1980). Cooperative learning in small groups: Recent methods and effects on achievement, attitudes, and ethnic relations. *Review of Education Research, 50*(2), 241–271.

Slavin, R. E. (1988). Cooperative learning and student achievement. In R. E. Slavin (ed.), *School and classroom organization*. Hillsdale, N.J.: Erlbaum.

Slavin, R. E. (1989). What works for students at risk? A research synthesis. *Educational Leadership, 46*(3), 357–366.

Smith, T. W. (1990). *Ethnic images (GSS Topical Report No. 19)*. National Opinion Research Center, University of Chicago.

Smith, T. W., and Sheatsley, P. B. (1984). American attitudes towards race relations. *Public Opinion, 7,* 14–15, 50–53.

Spencer, M. B. (1985). Black children's race awareness, racial attitudes, and self-concept: A reinterpretation. *In Annual Progress in Child Psychiatry and Development* (616–630). New York: Brunner/Mazel Publishers.

Spencer, M. B., Dobbs, B., and Phillips-Swanson, D. (1988). African American adolescents: Adaptational process and socioeconomic diversity in behavioral outcomes. *Journal of Adolescence, 11,* 117–137.

Spencer, M. B., and Horowitz, F. D. (1973). Effects of systematic social and token reinforcement on the modification of racial and color concept attitudes in Black and White preschool children. *Developmental Psychology, 9*(2), 246–254.

Spencer, M. B., and Markstrom-Adams, C. (1990). Identity processes among racial and ethnic minority children in America. *Child Development, 61,* 290–310.

Spindler, G. D. (1987). *Education and cultural process: Anthropological approaches.* Prospect Heights, Ill.: Waveland Press.

Spindler, G. D., and Spindler, L. (1989). Instrumental competence, self-efficacy, linguistic minorities, and cultural therapy: A preliminary attempt at integration. *Anthropology and Education Quarterly, 20*(1), 36–50.

Suarez-Orozco, M. M. (1985). Opportunity, family dynamics and school achievement: The sociocultural context of motivation among recent immigrants from Central America. Paper read at the University of California Symposium on Linguistics, Minorities and Education, Tahoe City, California.

Suarez-Orozco, M. M. (1987). "Becoming somebody": Central American immigrants in U.S. inner-city schools. *Anthropology and Education Quarterly, 18*(4), 287–299.

Tharp, R. G. (1989). Psychocultural variables and $k$ constants: Effects on teaching and learning in schools. *American Psychologists, 44,* 349–359.

Thomas, S. V., and Park, B. (1921). *Culture of immigrants.* Cambridge, Mass.: Newcome Press.

Trueba, H. T. (1988). Peer socialization among minority students: A high school dropout prevention program. In H. Trueba and C. Delgado-Gaitan (eds.), *Schools and society: Learning content through culture.* New York: Praeger.

Trueba, H. T., Moll, L. C., Diaz, S., and Diaz, R. (1982). *Improving the functional writing of bilingual secondary students.* Washington, D.C.: National Institute of Education.

Ueda, R. (1987). *Avenues to adulthood: The origins of the high school and social mobil-*

*ity in an American suburb*. Cambridge, England: Cambridge University Press.

Varenne, H. (1982). Jocks and freaks: The symbolic structure of the expression of social interaction among American senior high school students. In G. Spindler (ed.), *Doing the ethnography of schooling: Educational anthropology in action*. New York: Holt, Rinehart & Winston.

Vogt, L. A., Jordan, C., and Tharp, R. G. (1987). Explaining school failure, producing school success: Two cases. *Anthropology and Education Quarterly*, 18(4), 276–286.

Wagner, S. T. (1981). The historical background of bilingualism and biculturalism in the United States. In M. Ridge (ed.), *The new bilingualism* (pp. 29–52). New Brunswick, N.J.: Transaction Books.

Walberg, H. (1986). What works in a nation still at risk. *Educational Leadership*, 44(1), pp. 7–11.

Walsh, D. (1990). California's newest students speaking in many tongues. *San Francisco Examiner*, pp. B1, B4.

Weis, L. (1988). *Class, race and gender in American education*. Albany: State University of New York Press.

## Chapter Seven

# Oppositional Identity and African American Youth: Issues and Prospects

## William E. Cross, Jr.

A major obstacle to unity within predominantly black student populations has been the growth of a black oppositional identity and culture (Solomon, 1992). What follows in this chapter is an attempt to differentiate black defensive oppositional identity from black alienated oppositional identity. The argument here is that defensive oppositional identity is a protective filter employed by blacks who are, or who seek to become, functional within the larger society. Its themes are protection and engagement, revealing a bicultural strategy that results in personal efficacy within both the black and white "worlds." Defensive oppositional identity has a long history in the black community and, until recently, was the normative type of protective strategy found in black America. The general term *oppositional identity*, as originally defined by Fordham and Ogbu (1986), captures a modern variation of the defensive form and, on close analysis, seems to be a corruption of the traditional stance.

## Slavery, Racism, and Defensiveness

One of the major functions of black identity in everyday life is protection against racism, although black identity and black culture are not solely defined by defensiveness. During slavery, a multidimensional mindset was devised that allowed blacks to oppose certain features of the American culture, while engaging, and even incorporating into black culture, other dynamics. This acculturation, which transformed Africans into African Americans, included mechanisms for protection against racism. In *Deep Like the Rivers*, Thomas Webber (1978) demonstrates that slaves evolved a worldview that let them discover and manipulate aspects of the "other world," while filtering out those aspects that denigrated and dehumanized. For example, black religious beliefs rejected the notion that the Bible sanctioned slavery and countered that "real" Christians would not own slaves, thus suggesting a mild sense of superiority rather than one of internalized inferiority. Equally important, blacks continued to accept the basic tenets of Christianity when they left slavery. While the black church has had a long history of assisting in the black community's struggle against racism, it also defines the nexus of black Americanism—not in a "patriotic" sense, but from a cultural vantage point. That is, it defends and protects, as it engages and selectively embraces.

Similar dynamics have been found in slaves' beliefs about education. Ex-slaves keenly valued formal education. As documented six decades ago by W.E.B. Du Bois (1935) in *Black Reconstruction*, and more recently by James Anderson (1988) in his compelling work *The Education of Blacks in the South, 1860–1935*, the ex-slaves spearheaded a social movement for public education in the South, between the end of the Civil War and the late 1870s. Meanwhile, Butchart (1980) has shown that this movement was driven by themes of protection (that is, by education that helps blacks avoid exploitation and oppose racism), ethnicity and pride (education that teaches African and African American history), and acculturation (education that leads to greater participation in the larger social order). This was not a movement involving just one age group, in which black adults imposed their will on resistive and oppositional children; rather, it relied on the entire community. As Anderson (1988) has documented, between 1900 and 1935 poor rural blacks, not just elites, double-taxed themselves to support the "public" education of their children. They paid taxes for which they received little return (this was the historical period during which white society funneled a disproportionate amount of public resources to support "white" education, while radically underfunding the education of black children); then they taxed themselves again, in the form of special collections and school building projects. (Blacks supplied the labor and materials, and in some cases, even the land!) Anderson further explains:

> Although we shall never know the precise amount in cash, land, and labor contributed by black southerners to public school authorities, a vast quantity of primary sources indicates that the double taxation of black southerners was a widespread and long-standing custom. We see a certain fineness and heroism in the sacrifices made by poor and ordinary men and women. . . . Their actions spoke volumes about their beliefs in learning and self-improvement. For black southerners, that particular way of living had been a common experience since slavery. . . . The process of double taxation also reflected the manner in which black southerners during the period 1900 to 1935 interpreted and dealt with their oppression. They submitted to the process because they felt that it was the only way they could secure an education for their children, a way to protect and develop their communities, a way to sustain passageways to better times [1988, pp. 184–185].

Note Anderson's stress on the themes of opposition (protection) and engagement (passageways). Although his analysis tails off around 1935, personal reflections by Kathryn Morgan (*Children of Strangers*), Clifton Taulbert (*Once Upon a Time When We Were Colored*), Chalmers Archer, Jr. (*Growing Up Black in Rural Mississippi*), and James Comer (*Maggie's Dream: The Life and Times of a Black Family*), to mention a few, give powerful testimony that after slavery and into the late 1950s, normative black culture stressed marriage, nuclear family life, and strong kinship bonds. These bonds linked blacks to community through leisure, sports, and religious and educational activities (in addition to a broad spectrum of nonreligious affiliations), as well as through an aesthetic capable of creating and sustaining gospels, rural blues, sophisticated jazz, and other modalities of artistic expression. Just as important, the children of this period did not stand in opposition to the experience of black culture. On the contrary, the fact that this culture was able to reproduce itself, from 1865 through the late 1950s, while keeping manageable the levels of social pathologies that inevitably accompany oppression, renders this one of the most remarkable social histories to be found in the evolution of any modern Western nation.

## The Alienation of the Black Underclass

Within the United States, the capacity for a people to carry on its culture is linked to employment, as well as to the positive "ripple effects" that accompany it. With employment, one can look forward to marriage, sustain one's family, make contributions to one's church and to self-help groups (which, in turn, can both service and reinforce the moral tone of the community), pay taxes (which gives one a larger say in the running of local schools and institutions), spend money in local businesses and gain a credit rating, make contributions to local and national protest groups (such as the NAACP, Black Caucus, and so on), provide spending money to one's children (who, because they are well fed and focused, can go to school with an academic rather than an oppositional agenda), and, finally, plan for one's retirement.

Blue-collar blacks gained access to solid union-scale jobs in the late 1940s. As Coontz (1992, p. 244) points out:

The economic and political gains of the postwar period allowed many poorly educated black Americans to find blue-collar jobs in which they could work up to a level of security and seniority that permitted them to establish families, buy homes, and contemplate sending their children to school for longer periods. This, contrary to myth, is the traditional route to mobility for all social and ethnic groups in American history, especially migrants to the cities: First they achieved income security; then they invested in education. For the first time in American history, some blacks were offered the same route to success, and they took advantage of it, during the short time it was available, in percentages at least as high as those for any other group.

In the 1960s and 1970s, the progeny of these blue-collar workers spearheaded, first, the civil rights movement and, then, the more urban-oriented black consciousness movement. Participants from both movements opposed racism, while demanding greater access to society rather than outright rejection of it. The black consciousness movement had the greater edge, given its militant opposition to racism and advocacy of a pluralistic, rather than assimilationist, model of change. With this pluralist orientation, it made demands on white institutions, not simply for access but for changes in everyday operations that facilitate an atmosphere friendly to nontraditional workers (that is, people of color and women). For African Americans with a high school education or better, these movements provided access to opportunities and employment, leading to the expansion of the black middle class between 1965 and the present. However, at the same time that society was opening up to people of color with advanced education, good-paying jobs for those with less education disappeared. As Coontz (1992, p. 245) notes, the employment rate for black men was 80 percent in 1930 but only 56 percent in 1983:

The average real income of young black men fell by almost 50 percent between 1973 and 1986. The biggest losers were unskilled or uneducated black men who could once by the dint of hard work and strenuous exertion make an adequate income to support a family. The bottom fell out of the market for poorly educated labor in the cities; by 1986, the average black high school dropout earned 61 percent less than he did in 1973.

Over time, these economic trends have pounded potential black factory workers into an unemployed underclass. At first glance, the term *black underclass*, which places poor blacks into a distinct category, seems unjustified, especially when one considers that the same economic forces are operating in the larger community as well. Although poorly educated whites are also suffering (Goozner, 1990), they tend to be less visible to the public eye, since they are "scattered" rather than concentrated in ghettoes. However, housing segregation has resulted in the hyperconcentration or ghettoization of blacks (Massey and Denton, 1993).

Protracted, widespread unemployment, in conjunction with intense residential segregation, tends to have devastatingly *negative* ripple effects, as Massey and Denton (1993, p. 146) explain:

> Concentrated poverty is inevitable when high rates of poverty and intense racial segregation are combined.
>
> The concentration of poverty, moreover, sets off a series of ancillary changes in the social and economic composition of neighborhoods. By concentrating poverty, segregation also concentrates other conditions that are associated with it. Deleterious conditions such as falling retail demand, increasing residential abandonment, rising crime, spreading disorder, increasing welfare dependency, growing family disruption, and rising educational failure are all concentrated simultaneously by raising the rate of poverty under a regime of high segregation.

The hyperconcentration of unemployed and undereducated black adults, along with their families and children, has characterized some urban areas since 1975. It is in the context of such neighborhoods that young people have evolved a psychology of alienation that reflects their redundancy as potential workers. In perceiving themselves as having no place in society, they see no value in belonging to it. This new form of oppositional identity is not a method for overcoming obstacles that impede one's entrance into or existence and functioning within the society. It is a strategy that achieves protection by rejecting involvement.

## Fordham and Ogbu's Oppositional Identity

The most powerful analysis of this new alienation-driven, black oppositional identity has been penned by Fordham and Ogbu (1986). Based on their case study of black high school students on the West Coast of the United States, Fordham and Ogbu (1986) claim that black children from low-income families have devised an identity that demarcates authentically black attitudes and behaviors from those that are white oriented. The list of concerns runs the gamut from speech patterns, styles of dress, body language, friendship patterns, and social networks to aspirations, school behavior, sexual attitudes, and gender relations. If whites are perceived to act one way, black identity is its reverse. If to study and achieve is white, then to be black is to resist being successful (that is, to fail); if whites are talkative and polite, but evasive, then blacks are direct, blunt, and confrontational; if whites are timid, then blacks are forceful and threatening; if whites are circumspect about sexuality, then blacks address it openly and freely.

As soon becomes apparent, this oppositional identity is at variance not only with white culture but with traditional black culture as well. In its sledge-hammer analysis of what is white and what is black, it bludgeons the more sophisticated, black-defined forms of resistance from the "past," if yesterday can be considered as such, and replaces them with simple-minded, either/or forms. The claim that it is white to study mathematics, at the same time that Afrocentric scholars are demonstrating the African origins of Western mathematics and science, reveals an identity grounded in a lack of knowledge about the true history and development of black culture.

At the surface level, key dimensions of the defensive and alienated identities overlap, for both address gender relationships; the conditions for discourse with other ethnic groups, such as with Jews; attitudes toward whites, as individuals and as a group; the duality of being a product of black as well as white culture, in terms of one's preferred speech patterns and ways to make it in school; and so on. However, the alienated oppositional identity shows itself to be a corruption of the traditional form in its flirtation with extreme misogynistic attitudes and behavior, hateful attitudes toward whites in general, crude anti-Semitism, profound anti-intellectualism, and appeal to racial purity. I refer here to an identity formulation produced by a sector of the black community that is disconnected and isolated from whites and, in its economic and social redundancy, finds itself no less estranged from those blacks who, through employment and education, continue to maintain multiple connections to both the black and white worlds, no matter how problematic. (In this connection, see Ellis Cose's new text [1993] on the "rage" of the black middle class.)

## The Clash Between Defensive and Alienated Oppositional Perspectives

It is not uncommon to hear of conferences and meetings in which black leaders, scholars, and activists specify as their agenda the destruction of structural barriers that are the root cause of the underclass (Holmes, 1994). However, whereas such participants have consciously chosen to remain in communication with those who are entangled in the underclass, most black people have no such option. Housing traditions in America have separated whites from blacks; but this same segregation has resulted in a situation whereby blacks from all walks of life share, if not the same or adjacent neighborhoods, at least the same schools (Massey and Denton, 1993; Kozol, 1991). Note, as well, that the so-called black underclass would be more multiracial if poor white people were equally hypersegregated by class and race. When "pockets" of poor and unemployed white people are studied (MacLeod, 1987), behaviors and attitudes thought to be "unique to blacks" take on a more social-class dynamic.

White middle-class children live in neighborhoods that buffer them from exposure to the oppositional identity, but the same is not true for blacks. Brooks-Gunn (1993, p. 9) has cited census data showing that in 1980, one in five black children and one in fifty white children lived in neighborhoods where 30 percent or more of the residents were poor. In contrast, three in five of white children and only one in ten black children resided in neighborhoods where fewer than 10 percent of the individuals were poor. These statistics suggest that white middle-class and wealthy parents can rest assured that their children will not interact with white, let alone black, children of the underclass. For members of the black middle class, however, sustained interactions between their children and those of the underclass are very probable and, as their children enter adolescence, increasingly problematic. In short, housing discrimination results in the hyperconcentration of poor blacks, but it also limits access for middle-class and traditional working-class families. The neighborhoods surrounding the two types of families are similar enough that their children are likely to attend the same schools. Consequently, predominantly black schools end up servicing two extreme student populations: one that, over time, has every reason to question the American dream, and the other for whom the dream remains a beacon of things to come. Housing segregation and the forced mixing of blacks from all walks of life are not new; however, in the past, the higher employment rate for blacks in general (recall that the employment rate among black males was 80 percent in 1930 but only 56 percent as of 1983) meant that the defensive or more optimistic oppositional identity tended to hold more sway than the alienated version, primarily because there were fewer blacks, even under segregation, who were economically redundant!

It appears that even today, both poor and middle-class black parents are able to socialize their infants and elementary-school-aged progeny in accordance with the more optimistic, biculturally oriented, defensive oppositional identity; but as their children grow older, the pull of the alienated version takes hold, reaching a crisis state during the middle school and high school years. In their oft-cited study, Fordham and Ogbu (1986) define the parameters of the oppositional identity, and most of their examples are of children who initially exhibited successful school behaviors and outcomes, and then, in middle school and high school, experienced conflict with their peers about being "eggheads" or "bookworms." Zweigenhaft and Domhoff's study (1991) of the effectiveness of the ABC Program, which was designed to place promising inner-city kids in prep schools, also cites examples of children who were successful at an early stage of their schooling, became drawn into the alienated oppositional identity at puberty, experienced an accompanying drop in school performance, and, then, through the ABC intervention, reclaimed their earlier commitment to positive school performance.

The push and pull of the two types of oppositional identities continues into the college years. At any point from adolescence throughout the life span (Parham, 1989), blacks may undergo a consciousness-raising experience that theorists and researchers have captured in models of *Nigrescence* (Thomas, 1971; Cross, 1971, 1991; Milliones, 1973; Jackson, 1976), a French word that, literally translated, means the process of developing a black consciousness. Such models reticulate the four or five stages that black people traverse in replacing an identity for which factors other than race are salient, with an identity for which black affairs, black creativity, and black culture define being and existence. Research on the transition stage, during which the old "white-oriented" identity is at war with the emerging "black" identity, provides examples of black college students who have come to terms with what is and is not appropriate black behavior (Napper, 1973; Williams, 1975; Cross, 1991; Brown, 1979; Denton, 1985). What is "appropriate" turns out to be anything that is the opposite of what whites think or believe, along with a glib acceptance of the notion that people from the "hood" have a better handle on what is reality than does anyone else. In proving their blackness to each other, and in showing their "connection" to the plight of black people off campus, many black student groups sponsor "lectures," by members of a particular black religious sect, in support of a worldview that is separatist, misogynist, anti-intellectual, homophobic, and openly anti-Semitic (Wilkins, 1994). However, unlike Fordham and Ogbu's oppositional identity, which seems to become more firmly rooted over time, advanced stages of Nigrescence show students moving toward a rapprochement with their biculturalism; some eventually affirm even a multicultural perspective (Cross, 1991). This is not to suggest that one would have a difficult time identifying alienated oppositional themes in the worldview of today's educated black adults, whose frustration over society's lack of response to the plight of poor blacks is fertile ground for reactionary machinations.

Bailey Jackson, the dean of the School of Education at the University of Massachusetts and a leading Nigrescence theorist, has noted that growth into the advanced stages of the identity carries with it a greater sense of psychological security and confidence, allowing blacks to reconnect with the nonracist aspects of the American experience. Furthermore, Jackson continues, "ownership of the acceptable aspects . . . does not preclude or override the ownership of black culture" (1976, p. 62).

It has been noted (by Cross, 1991; and Cross, Parham, and Helms, in press) that a fully developed black identity serves at least three functions in a person's daily life: (1) it defends the person from negative psychological stress that results from having to live in a society that is at times very racist; (2) it establishes a sense of purpose, meaning, and affiliation; and (3) it provides a psychological mechanism that facilitates social intercourse with people, cultures, and situations located outside the boundaries of blackness. A person's identity may acquire these functions over the course of socialization from childhood through early adulthood, provided that this person's parents or caretakers have strong black identities themselves. Otherwise, the functions may unfold as part of one's resocialization during Nigrescence. Let us take a closer look at each of these functional modes, for, taken together, they constitute a way of conceptualizing how the defensive and alienated versions of oppositional identity may be integrated.

## The Defensive Function of Black Identity

The defensive function of black identity provides a psychological buffer at times when the person encounters racist circumstances, especially those of a psychological nature. (Obviously, a psychological defense would be inadequate in the face of violence.) In its crudest manifestation, this mode engenders a siege mentality whereby the person sees all white people and all white institutions as inherently racist. In being hypersensitive about racism, the person gains "protection" simply by writing off all contact with whites.

With the mellowing influence of time, the defensive function becomes much more sophisticated and flexible. Instead of an iron shield of rejection, it becomes a translucent filter that is often "invisible" or undetectable, allowing nonthreatening information and experiences to be processed by the person, without distortion. Structurally, this protective function seems to involve (1) an awareness that racism is part of the American experience; (2) the anticipation that, regardless of one's station in American society, one could well be the target of racism; (3) well-developed ego defenses that one can employ when confronted with racism; (4) a system-blame and personal-efficacy orientation in which one is predisposed to find fault in one's circumstances, and not in oneself; and (5) a religious orientation that prevents the development of a sense of bitterness and the need to demonize whites.

The first two factors are at the heart of this function's protective capacity, for it is impossible to defend against something whose existence is denied or minimized; and, of course, if one sees oneself as a special Negro who is beyond the reach of racism, then one will hardly be in a position to anticipate being the target of a racist. For a person with a black identity and a well-developed defensive mode, racism is a given, and that person understands that he or she may well be the focus of racism. The third factor refers to the behavioral and attitudinal repertoire that one can employ in negotiating racist situations (withdrawal, assertion, counteraggression, passivity, avoidance, and so on). The stronger, more mature, and more varied one's ego defenses are, the greater one's capacity to handle a variety of racist configurations. For those blacks beset by poor and degrading living conditions, the fourth factor helps to maintain a sense of perspective and personal worth in the face of racism. In this way, they are able to distinguish between what is an extension of their self-concept (what they deserve and should be given credit for) and those elements that reflect the racist and oppressive system against which they must struggle to survive. Finally, the fifth factor, the spiritual and religious one, helps the black person avoid becoming embittered and filled with hatred toward whites. This is important because hatred originally directed toward whites often spills over into and poisons black-on-black relationships. In a sense, the focus of this fifth factor is on racism as a form of human evil, rather than on the demonization of white people, with its attendant hopelessness. (After all, one cannot negotiate with someone perceived as the devil.)

The defensive mode helps one to deal with the "hassle" of being black. It operates to minimize the pain, imposition, and stigma that come when one is treated with disrespect, rudeness, and insensitivity. Rather than being unduly hurt and caught off guard, the defensive mode allows the person to maintain control and avoid overreacting, thus being able to pay more attention to "who and what" are instigating the problem.

There are two extremes to this modality. On the one hand, the person may underplay the importance of racism, in which case the defensive function will be inadequately developed and the person's identity will provide little protection against racism. On the other, the person may be overly sensitive or even paranoiac, "seeing" racism where it does not exist.

## The Group-Affiliation Function of Black Identity

Most, if not every, human being needs to feel wanted, connected, accepted, and affiliated, although the group from which one may derive a sense of well-being need not be the group with which one is normally identified. For instance, many blacks derive their sense of affiliation from groups that have little to do with a nationalist or black identity. In other words, they gain personal fulfillment and happiness from being Christians, lawyers, doctors, gamblers, police officers, gays, or believers in obscure cults. Such people cannot be said to have a black identity because their sense of personal well-being is anchored in something other than their blackness.

Having a black identity means that the affiliation function of one's identity is grounded in one's blackness. In this case, being black has high salience to one's sense of well-being, one's purpose in life, one's sense of connection to other blacks. One's feeling of being wanted, accepted, appreciated, and affiliated are deeply rooted in black people, black culture, and the general black condition. And one's values, cultural preferences, artistic tastes, leisure activities, cooking styles, food choices, musical tastes, church affiliation, organizational membership, and social network are all influenced by one's perceived connection to black people. In brief, life's very meaning and the hope one has for living purposefully are linked to one's perception of oneself as an African American.

The affiliation function of black identity can lead to the celebration of black accomplishments, pressure to solve the problems of blacks, and a desire to promote black culture and history. In its more negative manifestations, however, it can lead to extreme social conformity, ethnic chauvinism, polarized attitudes, and reactionary social perspectives.

## The Bridging or Transcendent Function of Black Identity

The first two functions combine to form the type of ethnic identity that is fairly typical of people whose lives revolve around a particular culture, religion, or race. Indeed, such people often show very little concern for experiences outside their own. In the case of blacks, as long as one is operating (in terms of work, play, marriage, religion, and so on) in an all-black or predominately black human environment, there is no need to include in one's identity the functional skills and sensitivities that make one efficacious in interactions with nonblack peoples and cultures. However, it is one of the paradoxes of black life that, although blacks are subject to being "hypersegregated," many, if not most, black Americans, cannot escape having to negotiate repeated and often enduring contacts, transactions, and communications with ethnic whites, Asian Americans, Jews, Latinos, American Indians, and, of course, white Protestants. Another identity function that must be performed in the everyday life of many black people, then, involves bridging and making connections to other experiences, groups, organizations, and individuals who make up the larger nonblack world within which the black world is nestled. In addition, bridging helps blacks from different walks of life find ways to better communicate with each other.

Transracial and, especially, black-white bridging activities can lead to conflicts within the black community. Black nationalists may interpret such bridging (that is, other than the Pan-African variety) as a waste of limited time and resources, while those involved in transracial connections counter by stating that black life is inherently bicultural, if not multicultural, and that meaningful change cannot take place without bridging. Other blacks see the "to bridge or not to bridge" debate as silly, because their workplace and community environments are decidedly multiracial and multicultural; accordingly, they view the development of the bridging function of black identity as a necessity, not an option. Black women argue that the sexism of white as well as black men make it necessary to constantly bridge back and forth from a gender to a blackness orientation. Finally, bridging adds a crucial element of flexibility to black identity that allows one to better assimilate rapid culture and technological innovation (Cross, 1991; Cross, Parham and Helms, in press). Black Americans, like all Americans, must be able to keep abreast of transformations in American society, but a rigid, provincial identity structure cannot handle such changes.

Together, the defensive, affiliation, and bridging functions define a fully developed identity, although Parham (1989) has theorized that new identity questions are likely to confront a black person at various points in the life span, allowing for continuous growth of one's blackness. In working through these new challenges, the person may go through developmental progressions that are similar to the Nigrescence stages mentioned earlier, suggesting a "recycling" of sorts. The overall pattern, however, remains the same: the person seeks ways to better protect her- or himself in order to more effectively engage the larger society—the exact opposite of the actions of a person guided by an identity steeped in alienation.

## Conclusions

In this chapter, Fordham and Ogbu's important statement (1986) about oppositional identity has been refined to differentiate defensive from alienated opposition. The defensive pattern was shown to be the more traditional, normative identity; it defines the age-old struggle of black Americans to construct a psychological mechanism that, on the one hand, protects them from that which is racist about American life and, on the other, makes it possible for them to partake of, contribute to, change, and even assimilate that which is race-neutral. The defensive oppositional identity is a fundamentally bicultural dynamic because protection from racism is a prelude to engagement and attempts at inclusion. It takes a perspective of hope and expectation, initially fashioned by slaves and carried forth by generations of blacks, especially those who, through some form of employment, no matter how lowly, felt connected to the social order. And it is an identity pattern still very much in evidence today, even among the most successful of blacks, who, despite their educational and material advantages, must protect themselves against daily swipes at their personhood (Cose, 1993; Dividio, 1993).

Since the late 1950s, the restructuring of the American economy has closed off avenues of employment to Americans with limited education. As a consequence of historical racism, blacks find themselves disproportionately represented among this redundant layer of the work force. Although redundant workers have been pushed out of the workplace, they are described as *underclass*, a term that effectively masks the actual origin of their predicament, because it implies that their "dropping out" is a "personal choice." Historical and contemporary patterns of housing segregation have concentrated vast numbers of these surplus workers, their families, and their progeny in compacted ghettoes, and from this strained "human ecology" has arisen a new form of black oppositional identity grounded in alienation. The youth from these ghettoes have fought back with a psychology of rejection and opposition, within which there is hardly a hint of a desire to engage in "white" ways, other than for confrontational purposes. Those who possess this alienated oppositional identity also find themselves at odds with blacks operating within the more traditional perspective of protection and inclusion.

The more negative identity crosses racial boundaries, but housing discrimination creates barriers that "separate and protect" white middle-class and wealthy children from the influences of oppositionalism. However, these same discriminatory forces operate in the black community to increase the likelihood of sustained school-based interactions between black children of the underclass and black children from more advantaged circumstances. In the past, because nonalienated blacks outnumbered those who were alienated, this mix of poor and advantaged black children favored the spread of the more optimistic perspective. Today, the expansion of the underclass has all but kept pace with the rise of the middle class; consequently, the alienated oppositional perspective may have as much social presence in predominantly black schools as does the traditional view. In short, housing segregation makes it more diffi-

cult for black middle-class and stable working-class parents to reproduce themselves through their children, because in some instances
they "lose" their children to the underclass. Having failed to understand how the alienated oppositional identity has become influential across social classes, the media and spokespersons for the
conservative right explain the spread in terms of social pathologies
unique to all members of "the" black culture. Not surprisingly,
whites often fear racial integration, period, because they think that
all blacks are "infected" and capable of "spreading" the alienated
oppositional identity.

School-based programs aimed at breaking the influence of alienated oppositional identity have their work cut out for them, since
the backdrop of this perspective is a world of parents and significant adults who are redundant workers. Their dislocation and
hyperghettoization convey to their children the message that many
if not most of the significant adults from the neighborhoods have
no connection and value to the larger society. By the time these
children reach adolescence, when the situation becomes unambiguous, their alienation seems to be "locked in." Their bicultural
and bridging potential becomes buried in outright rejection. It is
possible, however, that this emerging perspective on the underclass
and their children is too categoric. Coontz (1992) and Duneier
(1992) point to evidence indicating that, just below the surface,
members of the so-called underclass continue to hold "traditional"
beliefs about making it in America.

School-based programs designed to promote greater unity
among black students must, at a minimum, acknowledge the proportion of students representing each identity. In theory, at least, a
student population with a 70 to 30 ratio of traditional to underclass
students should allow for a more aggressive biculturally oriented
model for change than one in which the reverse is true. Otherwise,
an ineffective needs analysis can quickly lead to failure, for a program designed to struggle with a defensive oppositional stance will
meet its match, should the students be operating with the more
alienated version.

# References

Anderson, J. D. (1988). *The Education of Blacks in the South, 1860–1935*. Chapel Hill: University of North Carolina Press.

Archer, C., Jr. (1992). *Growing Up Black in Rural Mississippi*. New York: Walker.

Brooks-Gunn, J. (1993). Growing up Poor: Context, Risk, and Continuity in the Brofenbrenner Tradition. Unpublished paper presented at the Conference Honoring Urie Bronfenbrenner (Sept. 8), Cornell University.

Brown, A. (1979). Black Consciousness Prototypes: A Profile of Developmental Stages of Black Consciousness. Doctoral dissertation, University of Pittsburgh.

Butchart, R. E. (1980). *Northern Schools, Southern Blacks, and Reconstruction*. Westport, Conn.: Greenwood Press.

Comer, J. P. (1988). *Maggie's Dream: The Life and Times of a Black Family*. New York: Plume.

Coontz, S. (1992). *The Way We Never Were*. New York: Basic Books and HarperCollins.

Cose, E. (1993). *The Rage of a Privileged Class*. New York: HarperCollins.

Cross, W. E., Jr. (1971). The Negro-to-Black Conversion Experience. *Black World, 20*, 13–27.

Cross, W. E., Jr. (1991). *Shades of Black*. Philadelphia: Temple University Press.

Cross, W. E., Jr., Parham, T. A., and Helms, J. E. (in press). *Nigrescence Revisited: Theory and Research*.

Denton, S. E. (1985). A Methodological Refinement and Validation Analysis of the Developmental Inventory of Black Consciousness. Doctoral dissertation, University of Pittsburgh.

Dividio, J. (1993). The Subtlety of Racism. *Training and Development, 47(4)*, 50–57.

Du Bois, W.E.B. (1935). *Black Reconstruction*. New York: S. A. Russell.

Duneier, M. (1992). *Slim's Table*. Chicago: University of Chicago Press.

Fordham, S., and Ogbu, J. (19486). Black Students' School Success: Coping with the Burden of Acting White. *The Urban Review, 18(3)*: 176–206.

Goozner, M. (1990). Pay Inequality Grew in '80s, Study Finds. *Chicago Tribune*, September 3, 1990, p. 1.

Holmes, S. A. (1994). Prominent Blacks Meet to Search for Answers to Mounting Crime. *New York Times*, January 8, 1994, p. 1.

Jackson, B. (1976). The Functions of Black Identity Theory in Achieving Relevance in Education. Doctoral dissertation, University of Massachusetts at Amherst.

Kozol, J. (1991). *Savage Inequalities: Children in America's Schools*. New York: Crown.

MacLeod, J. (1987). *Ain't No Makin' It*. Boulder, Colo.: Westview Press.

Massey, D. S., and Denton, N. A. (1993). *American Apartheid*. Cambridge, Mass.: Harvard University Press.

Milliones, J. (1973). Construction of the Developmental Inventory of Black Consciousness. Doctoral dissertation, University of Pittsburgh.

Morgan, K. L. (1980). *Children of Strangers*. Philadelphia: Temple University Press.

Napper, G. (1973). *Blacker Than Thou: The Struggle for Campus Unity*. Grand Rapids, Mich.: Eerdmans.

Parham, T. A. (1989). Cycles of Psychological Nigrescence. *Counseling Psychologist, 17*(2), 187–226.

Solomon, R. P. (1992). *Black Resistance in High School: Forging a Separatist Culture*. Albany: State University of New York Press.

Taulbert, C. L. (1989). *Once Upon a Time When We Were Colored*. Tulsa, Okla.: Council Oak Books.

Thomas, C. W. (1971). *Boys No More*. Beverly Hills, Calif.: Glencoe Press.

Webber, T. L. (1978). *Deep Like the Rivers*. New York: W. W. Norton.

Wilkins, R. (1994). A Loud Silence on Racism. *New York Times*, January 8, 1994, p. 23.

Williams, I. A. (1975). An Investigation of the Development of Stages of Black Consciousness. Doctoral dissertation, University of Cincinnati.

Zweigenhaft, R. L., and Domhoff, G. W. (1991). *Blacks in the White Establishment*. New Haven, Conn.: Yale University Press.

*Chapter Eight*

# Racialization and Panethnicity: From Asians in America to Asian Americans

Kenyon S. Chan

Shirley Hune

## Introduction

Where were you born? Where is your family from?

How did you learn to speak English so well?

Do you eat rice every day?

How can you tell the difference between Koreans and Chinese?

Why do your people do so well in school?

These and other seemingly innocuous questions are confronted by Asian Americans regularly. (We use the term *Asian Americans* to refer to Americans of Asian or Pacific Rim ancestry.) While they appear to be inoffensive and innocent, they imply an enduring belief that Asian Americans are "outsiders." Ronald Takaki (1989) entitled his work on the history of Asian Americans *Strangers from a Different Shore* in order to capture the idea that Asians in America are generally viewed as recent immigrants and sojourners despite their 150 years in this country.

The Asian American experience is more than just the recent phenomenon of large-scale migration to the United States. Beginning in the 1840s, Asian Americans have played an historic role in the formation of the American West. During the latter half of the nineteenth century and the early part of the twentieth, Chinese, Japanese, and Filipino workers, accompanied by smaller migrations of Koreans and Asian Indians, made contributions to the nation's economic development far out of proportion to their numbers.

The primary terms used to describe contemporary Asian American communities are *growth* and *diversity*. The Asian American population increased from 877,934 (less than 0.5 percent of the total U.S. population) in 1960 to 7,273,662 (2.9 percent) in 1990. The American landscape is being transformed by persons who trace their ancestry either to countries from the Asian continent such as China, Japan, Korea, India, Vietnam, Cambodia, Laos, and Thailand or to those of the Pacific Basin such as the Philippines, Samoa, and Micronesia. Hawaiians, native to the United States, are also included within this broad category of Americans.

The new demographics have changed older Asian American communities, American institutions, and everyday life. Asian American communities are different from one another in their historical origins, languages, religions, cultures, and institutions. The ancestors of Asian Americans may even have fought one another in Asia or the Pacific region. Each Asian community in America was established at different times, in different locales, and for different reasons. Nonetheless, Asian Americans are linked by a similar historical experience whereby racially defined ideologies, policies, and practices in the United States have treated them individually and collectively as the same as one another. Hence, although they vary both culturally and structurally, Asian Americans have been and continue to be viewed as almost identical by American society.

In the American racial order, Asian Americans are generally ignored by policy makers and institutional leaders. They have been convenient scapegoats in times of economic recession and social crisis. They continue to be excluded from curricula, media representations, and popular culture. They receive lower wages than their European American counterparts for the same work, even though their education and training are equal or greater. And they encounter a "glass ceiling" in employment created by racial stereotypes and prejudices. They also continue to face anti-immigrant sentiment and actions despite the fact that they have been born here or are even third- or fourth-generation Americans.

In the following pages, we analyze how America's race-based ideologies, policies, and practices have resulted in largely negative stereotypes of Asian Americans and have limited their full and equitable participation in American society. First, we discuss how this process of racialization has contributed to the rearticulation of older racial formations into a new panethnic coalition by Asian Americans. Then we provide a brief historical overview of Asians in America in order to demonstrate how their experiences in the United States have contributed to the formation of the Asian American construct. Next, we examine the effects of the contemporary growth and diversity of Asian American communities and the increase of anti-Asian violence on the creation and maintenance of Asian American panethnicity. After that, we analyze the popular misconception of Asian Americans as a successful "model minority" and discuss the impact of this racialized, socially constructed stereotype on the people who are subjected to it. Finally, we consider the possibilities and limitations of Asian American panethnicity and its practical application for understanding and furthering coalition building among other racial and ethnic groups in the United States.

## Racial Formation Theory and Asian Americans

Omi and Winant (1986) have employed the term *racialization* to describe an ideological and sociohistorical process whereby previously racially unclassified relationships, social practices, or groups are given racial meaning. Discussions about race and diversity in the United States have focused largely on the black/white paradigm (Hune, 1993; Martinez, 1993; Omi, 1993). Recent widely publicized tomes such as Andrew Hacker's *Two Nations: Black and White, Separate, Hostile, Unequal* (1992) and Studs Terkel's *Race: How Blacks and Whites Think and Feel About the American Obsession* (1992) exemplify America's tenacious view of race relations as beliefs and interactions involving blacks and whites. But the racialization of America has never been simply black and white. Early European settlers adopted race-based policies toward Native Americans long before Africans were introduced to this continent. The young American nation applied race-based discriminatory and exclusionary policies to Mexican residents and Chinese settlers in the western territories immediately upon contact. One of the outcomes of racism in America has been the creation of new racial formations—namely, the Asian American category as well as pan-Asian organizations and institutions that Espiritu (1992) has aptly described as elements of Asian American panethnicity.

Racial formation theory helps us understand how Asian groups of Chinese, Japanese, Filipinos, Koreans, and others with little in common with one another migrated to the United States and were similarly and collectively racialized. Omi and Winant (1986) define *racial formation* as a "process by which social, economic and political forces determine the content and importance of racial categories, and by which they are in turn shaped by racial meanings" (p. 61). Indeed, race-based ideologies, policies, and practices imposed by the state and other overarching structures have shaped and reshaped the substance and contours of Asian American communities. Communities of first-generation Asian immigrants were separated from one another by language, religion, and homeland politics, and all Asian communities were separated from mainstream American society by the racial order, its culture, and its laws.

Race consciousness is embedded in every aspect of American life. Racial meanings permeate our society from the micro-level of individual identities to the macro-level of economic, political, and cultural/ideological structures. These meanings—whether they reflect categories, interactions, organizations, or ways of thinking—

are not constant. For example, the concept of Asians in America has changed over time. Racial meanings are negotiated in a pattern of conflict and accommodation between the social movements of a nation's racial minorities and the state's policies and programs. In short, racial meanings are continuously being redefined and reconstructed over time through political struggle. On occasion, overwhelming social forces demand that the American racial order be transformed (Omi and Winant, 1986).

## The Historical Racialization of Asians in America

Early migration to the United States reached its height between the 1850s and the end of the 1920s. In the same period that thirty-five million European immigrants reached East Coast ports, nearly one million Asian immigrants entered the United States from across the Pacific. The nation's response to the Atlantic and Pacific migrations is a study in contrasts (Hune, 1977).

Asian immigration in this historical period consisted of the serial recruitment, country by country, of primarily young males, with the objective of developing the new territories of the Pacific West and Hawaii. First came the Chinese, about 370,000 of whom reached California and Hawaii between the late 1840s and the early 1880s. They were followed between the late 1880s and the 1920s by about 400,000 Japanese who were bound for Hawaii and major ports along the Pacific Coast. About 7,000 Koreans, 7,000 Asian Indians, and 180,000 Filipinos also arrived in these locations between the 1890s and the 1930s (Chan, 1991).

In Hawaii, the Chinese worked on sugar plantations. On the mainland, they mined gold, built railroads, planted and harvested fruits and vegetables, and formed the backbone of light manufacturing industries in urban areas. They opened laundries, restaurants, and small groceries. Chinese, Japanese, and Filipinos pioneered the West's fishing industries and worked in salmon canneries in the Pacific Northwest. They also worked as domestic workers and gardeners (Cheng and Bonacich, 1984).

Japanese, Koreans, and Filipinos played a significant role as plantation workers in Hawaii and as farm laborers in the Pacific Coast states. Some Japanese, Koreans, and Asian Indians made major contributions to agricultural production as tenant farmers. For a time, the Japanese in California produced much of the state's vegetables, fruits, cut flowers, and winery grapes through small farms they owned or leased until restricted from doing so by the discriminatory Alien Land Act of 1913. Whereas European immigrants were given homesteads, permitted to purchase farmland, and employed in heavy manufacturing industries with higher wages and union protection, Asian immigrants were limited in their economic opportunities by a regional economy centered on services and agriculture and by blatant discriminatory practices (Chan, 1991).

Racial ideologies defined Pacific immigrants as aliens ineligible for citizenship, unfair economic competitors, and socially unassimilable groups. For the first 100 years of "Asian America"—the 1840s to the 1940s—the images of each community were racialized and predominantly negative. The Chinese were called "Mongolians" and depicted in the popular press as heathens, gamblers, and opium addicts. The Japanese and Koreans were viewed as the "yellow peril." Filipinos were derogatorily referred to as "little brown monkeys," and Asian Indians, most of them Sikhs, were called "ragheads" (Chan, 1991; Takaki, 1989).

Race-based political, economic, and social policies coerced Asians into second-class membership in American society. Denied the right of naturalization because of their race, Asian immigrants were politically disenfranchised and received little support from authorities when their civil rights were violated. Asian economic opportunities were restricted by special taxes, licenses, and laws against employment, land ownership, and the leasing of farm land. Social segregation was enforced in a number of spheres. State and city legislation sought to drive Asians out of certain areas or to restrict them to specific parts of a town. Race defined which schools Asian Americans could attend in states, such as California and Mississippi, that incorporated "Orientals" into their segregated school systems. Race also prevented Asians from marrying whites (anti-miscegenation statutes persisted until 1967), although marriages with African Americans and Mexican Americans existed (Chan, 1991; Hing, 1993; Leonard, 1992; Loewen, 1988; Takaki, 1989).

Anti-Asian sentiment in this period sometimes erupted into acts of violence against individuals and even whole communities of Asian immigrants, resulting in losses of lives and thousands of dollars in property. In the meantime, members of anti-Asian organizations demanded that the government restrict Asian immigration to the United States.

U.S. immigration laws took on racial meanings. In adopting the Chinese Exclusion Act of 1882, the federal government ended open migration from Asia to the United States until 1965 and introduced a policy of immigration restriction based on race. The act suspended Chinese labor migration to the United States for ten years and was subsequently renewed and expanded to include the wives of laborers. It was not repealed until 1943, when the Chinese were given a token quota of 105 immigrants annually.

Federal actions to restrict other Asian groups followed. These injunctions included the "Gentlemen's Agreement" with Japan in 1907 to limit Japanese entry; the "Asiatic barred zone" in the 1917 Immigration Law, which excluded Asian Indians; the 1924 Immigration Act, which excluded all Asians, notably the Japanese; and the Tydings-McDuffie Act of 1934, which created an annual quota of fifty for Filipinos (Chan, 1991; Takaki, 1989). Clearly, immigration laws of this period were racialized and served to bar Asians from U.S. shores as well as to keep their numbers small.

Restrictive immigration policies shaped community formation not only in size but also gender ratio, family construction, geographical distribution, and residential pattern. For example, in consideration of Japan's military power, the United States permitted Japanese immigrants to bring and send for wives from their homelands. But all other Asian groups suffered from a significant gender-ratio imbalance. Hence prior to World War II, with the exception of Japanese Americans, the development of a second-generation Asian American community was severely restrained, in contrast to European immigrant communities (Hing, 1993).

It was not Asian cultural traditions but America's race-based attitudes and policies that first created Asian ethnic enclaves, sometimes viewed as ghettos. For self-protection from racism as well as for ethnic support, Chinatowns and Manilatowns were established—originally as "bachelor societies." Japanese, Koreans, and Asian Indians also formed clusters in specific farming areas where they were permitted to work the land (Hing, 1993). These communities founded in this hostile climate were spatially separated and socially estranged not only from white America but also from each another.

The politics of World War II and the Cold War was a turning point for American-born Asians. This small, emergent second generation, being American born and educated, anticipated that the racial order would be different for them, as citizens, than for their immigrant parents. But Asian American communities composed of long-time Americans continued to be defined by racial ideologies that had become fused with virulent political ideologies embodying America's new global role and ambitions. Decades of anti-Asian movements, combined with war hysteria during World War II reinforced by sensationalist journalism and movies, culminated in the relocation and internment of 120,000 Japanese Americans, 70 percent of whom were U.S. citizens. The civil and constitutional rights of Japanese Americans were violated simply because of their racial identification with America's enemy and competitor for control of the Pacific region.

On the other hand, politics briefly improved the situation of Americans of Chinese, Korean, Filipino, and Asian Indian descent when their motherlands became allies of the United States during World War II. To secure the support of its Asian allies, the United States ended its policies of Asian exclusion and introduced token quotas for Chinese immigrants in 1943 and for Filipinos and Asian Indians in 1946. The shortage of labor during the war also provided some Asian Americans with employment opportunities in technical, scientific, and skilled trades not previously open to them.

Cultural structures, especially the powerful influence of Hollywood movies, remade the "Oriental" image in this period. During the late 1930s, the benign but clever "Chinese" detective from Hawaii, Charlie Chan, began to replace the evil Dr. Fu Manchu. Neither role was played by an Asian actor. From the silent-screen actress Anna May Wong, who was limited to roles as harlots and villainesses in the 1920s, to the character of "Suzie Wong" in 1960, Asian women were largely depicted as exotic and erotic. The only other acceptable representation for Asian women was that of the subservient and sacrificing wife or housekeeper. To an extent, as Chow (1988) points out, the tensions of the racial order were softened by popular music as Americans learned to hum show tunes from *South Pacific* (1956) and *Flower Drum Song* (1961). These portrayals were all racial stereotypes. No one distinguished between Asians in Asia and Asian Americans.

Any favorable image of a particular Asian American community was quickly diminished by the politics of the Cold War. For example, race-based foreign policies led the U.S. government to link the Peoples' Republic of China with American Chinatowns. Policies to contain communism abroad were extended at home as the U.S. government spied on, interrogated, and sometimes deported Chinese Americans (Chan, 1991). Each Asian American community continued to have its image and well-being defined not by its activities in the United States but by a racial order that was both domestic and international. No other American immigrant community has had its domestic relations with the U.S. government so determined by the nation's foreign policies with homeland states.

In summary, the early history of Chinese, Japanese, Filipinos, Koreans, and Asian Indians in the United States was largely one of single ethnic communities from the 1840s through World War II. Though different from one another the dominant culture created racial ideologies, policies, and practices that treated these groups similarly as undesirable and inferior because of their race. Through a process of racialization, individuals from different Asian American ethnic groups recognized that they had a collective American experience and that they shared a similar political consciousness. In the late 1960s, as part of the social transformation of the racial order of the era, Asians in America came together in a panethnic coalition and rearticulated racial meanings to form the Asian American construct.

## The Emergence of the Asian American Construct

The U.S. racial order was critically challenged from both within and without during the 1950s and 1960s. At home, the civil rights movement began to dismantle legal racial discrimination. Joined by the anti–Vietnam War, Black Power, and student movements, civil rights activists demanded not only an end to race-based policies but also the increased participation of minority communities in all aspects of civic life. Mass protest, collective political mobilization, and coalition building were successful political strategies for social change (Omi and Winant, 1986). Abroad, political independence movements and wars of national liberation in the Third World forced Europe and the United States to make accommodations in the global racial order. Nationalism, self-determination, and coalition building among developing states served as oppositional tactics intended to redefine and restructure world politics (Singham and Hune, 1986).

Prior to the late 1960s, there was no such identity as Asian American. The development of this Asian American construct was partly an outgrowth of the civil rights movement and the social upheavals of the 1960s. Because of immigration restrictions, the Asian American population was then primarily a U.S.-born population of second- and third-generation Americans of Japanese, Chinese, and Filipino ancestry. Only 35 percent of the Asian population in the United States was foreign born, and English was the predominant language. In 1960 Japanese Americans, 464,332 strong, were the largest Asian ethnic group, followed by 237,292 Chinese Americans and 176,310 Filipino Americans. Including these groups, and much smaller numbers of Koreans and Asian Indians, Asian Americans made up barely 0.5 percent of the total U.S. population.

The Asian American construct originated with the student movements of the era. Young second- and third-generation Japanese, Chinese, and Filipino American college students joined with African Americans, Native Americans, and Mexican Americans to protest race-based social and political practices. Race-based access to education, public accommodations, governmental support, and political power were all on the agenda for change (Espiritu, 1992; Omatsu, 1989; Wei, 1993).

Racial identity and ethnic consciousness were fundamentally transformed, along with the racial order. The polarization of the civil rights protests required Asians in America to consider their identity, their self-definition, and their place in racialized America. They discovered that racial quotas and legal inequalities applied to them just as they did to other minorities. "Colored" was clearly defined as anyone nonwhite.

Asian American college students redefined racial meanings. They argued that the commonly used descriptor, "Oriental," was a dehumanizing construct more suited to describing rugs and objects than human beings. It implied the centrality of Europe and the colonization of Asia by the West. By extension, the "Oriental" in America had no identity outside of the Western context and was a product of and defined by internal colonialism.

More than a century of racialization had prompted the development of a new social concept unique to the United States. Individual Asian communities in America were too small to wield much political power separately as Chinese Americans, Japanese Americans, or Filipino Americans (Espiritu, 1992). Asians in America began to assert their American heritage and rights, and reconceptualized themselves by forming an ethnic and political identity that transcended traditional nationalistic, linguistic, and cultural boundaries. Second- and third-generation Japanese, Chinese, and Filipino Americans found similarities among themselves not previously experienced by their immigrant parents and grandparents. They also found much in common with the poor, the working class, and other racial minorities in the United States who were struggling for equality.

Thus, the term *Asian American* emerged as the unifying political construct encompassing all Americans of Asian and Pacific Island ancestry. Individuals worked across ethnic lines to form panethnic coalitions committed to empowering their communities and to securing economic, political, and social rights. These coalitions are found in many forms, including professional organizations, community service agencies, political interest groups, and student groups (Omatsu, 1989). Over the years, these coalitions have demanded structural changes in American society. For example, in the educational arena, Asian American panethnic groups have sought support for bilingual education, curricular reform, Asian American studies, and increased access and advancement for Asian Americans in every level of education. And in the arts, panethnic groups have opposed media misrepresentations and sought more opportunities for Asian Americans in theater, film, and television.

In the political and economic spheres, panethnic Asian American groups have demanded redistricting and bilingual ballots for a fairer political participation. They have formed coalitions to secure accurate, full, and quick enumeration of census data pertaining to as many specific Asian American communities as possible to ensure that Asian Americans share in the allocation of resources and funding. Panethnicity has also promoted economic rights through such efforts as improving the working conditions of garment and restaurant workers, supporting community-based development, and calling attention to the "glass ceiling" confronted by Asian Americans in corporate America.

The Asian American construct also serves as a powerful internal redefinition of racial and ethnic identity—a statement of pride in being both American *and* Asian. In the late 1960s, Asian Americans articulated a new racialized collectivity. Over the years, they have imposed it upon the new racial order to advance their political interests and personal identities. In so doing, they have given new meaning to being Americans of Asian descent. What has emerged is the Asian American as both a racial formation and a panethnic coalition to support and further political and social goals.

This evolving construct has always caused tensions among Asian Americans. Should the term be *Asian and Pacific Islander*, or *Asian Pacific American*, or simply *Asian American?* Should it be hyphenated or not? Many older members of the community see no difficulty with the term *Oriental*. Still the construct, Asian American, must be viewed as transitional. It represents the fluidity of racial identity and categories, as well as the process of racialization. As a political coalition initially formed by student and community activists, it must be flexible in confronting racialized social and political structures in the United States. For example, the pan-Asian concept has been subsequently institutionalized by community and professional organizations, as well as government agencies. Panethnicity is a "process of fusion as well as of fission" (Espiritu, 1992, p. 14).

## The New Diversity

The new Asian American diversity is placing demands on the Asian American construct. The end of exclusionary and discriminatory immigration policies in 1965, and the conclusion of the Vietnam War in 1975, reconstructed the ethnic, social, and political character of "Asian America" in less than one generation. The influx of hundreds of thousands of new immigrants and refugees from regions of Asia not yet represented in the United States sorely tested the infrastructure of existing Asian American communities. However, the new coalition of Asian and Pacific ethnic groups also drew strength from these demographic changes.

The impact of the shift in immigrant and refugee policies can be seen in the 1990 census. The Asian American population in the

United States increased by 140 percent from 1970 to 1980 and then by 108 percent from 1980 and 1990 (to a total of approximately 7,273,662), making it the fastest growing segment of the U.S. population (calculated from Barringer, Gardner, and Levin, 1993). The percentage of foreign-born Asian Americans grew from 35 percent in 1970 to 58 percent in 1980 to more than 65 percent in 1990 (Barringer, Gardner, and Levin, 1993; U.S. Bureau of the Census, 1993). Accordingly, an Asian language was more likely to be spoken than English in Asian American homes in 1990 than in 1970. This change in birthplace reversed the trend toward a stable third- and fourth-generation community; the community has become a dynamic one composed largely of continuous newcomers.

The Asian American community changed not only in size but in ethnic composition and diversity as well. In 1970 the three historical ethnic groups—Chinese, Japanese, and Filipinos—constituted 95.2 percent of the total Asian American population, of which Japanese Americans were the largest group (41.1 percent). By 1990 they made up only 56.7 percent of Asian Americans, 23.8 percent of whom were Chinese, 20.4 percent Filipino, and 12.3 percent Japanese. The new diversity is evident in the increased presence of Southeast Asians (8.5 percent Vietnamese, 5.8 percent Cambodian, 2.1 percent Lao, totaling 16.4 percent), Asian Indians (11.2 percent), and Koreans (11 percent).

Old Chinatowns have been revitalized by Chinese ethnic refugees from Vietnam. Entire new communities of Korean, Filipino, Vietnamese, Asian Indians, Thai, and Chinese from Taiwan, Hong Kong, and elsewhere are developing in urban cores and suburban areas on the West Coast and in the mid-Atlantic states. The ethnic character of almost every major city in the country has changed as a result of such cultural additions as Korean, Indian, Thai, and Vietnamese restaurants, Buddhist and Hindu temples, and multilingual television and radio stations, ethnic newspapers, and ethnic video rental stores.

This cultural shift and new racial order have not come easily in the United States. First, the new Asian diversity has forced established Asian American communities to reassess themselves. Relations between old and new Asian American communities and between U.S.-born Asian Americans and first-generation immigrants and refugees are being renegotiated. The new populations have placed additional, and sometimes different, demands on education, health, and social services. Political and economic priorities thus need to be redefined. The new Asian American communities have brought political strength to the panethnic coalition of Asian Americans. This coalition, in turn, seeks to mediate between its unified voice and the specific concerns of the ethnic and class *diversity* within it. Should individual groups not feel accommodated, the panethnic coalition is potentially weakened. Hence the Asian American community is a racial order within itself. It is shaped by its internal groupings, increasingly by relations with other minority communities, and, most important, by the dominant culture.

This rapid growth and diversity have resulted in increasing resentment by European Americans and other racial minorities. The rise in anti-immigrant and anti-Asian sentiment is quite evident from the halls of Congress to the general populace. The competition for scarce opportunities, whether in jobs or college placements, and the role of ethnic small businesses in low-income neighborhoods have strained and tested race relations, especially in politically charged situations and times of economic stagnation. The rise of anti-Asian violence, in particular, points up the need for Asian American panethnicity as a political coalition.

## Anti-Asian Violence

For many Asian Americans, the Vincent Chin case symbolized the workings of the contemporary American racial order. On the evening of June 19, 1982, a young Chinese American man named Vincent Chin was at a local bar in Detroit with his friends, celebrating his upcoming marriage. Chin was confronted by two white auto workers who mistook him for Japanese and accused him and his kind of being responsible for unemployment in the American auto industry. A barroom fight ensued. Unsatisfied with the results of the fight, the two auto workers went to their car, retrieved a baseball bat, searched for Chin, and brutally beat him to death.

Through a plea bargain arrangement, the two perpetrators received a small fine and probation. Asian Americans across the country were outraged by such a mild sentence for what many viewed as an unwarranted, vicious, and racially motivated murder. They formed the American Citizens for Justice, a panethnic coalition, to protest the handling of the Vincent Chin case. But their anger grew in the face of two subsequent trials in which the perpetrators were found not guilty of violating the civil rights of Vincent Chin.

Asian Americans had once again learned that despite cultural, language, religious, and class differences, anti-Asian sentiment did not distinguish among Asian Americans from China, the Philippines, Japan, India, Korea, Vietnam, or various Pacific Island regions. When the American justice system displayed its race-based bias in failing to consider the racial meaning of the crime, Asian Americans set aside ethnic and cultural differences to combat anti-Asian racist violence.

Unfortunately, the Vincent Chin case was not an isolated incident. Five years later, in 1987, Navroze Mody, an Indian American living in Jersey City, was attacked and bludgeoned to death by a gang of eleven youths. Several of them were well known as "Dotbusters," a name referring to youths who victimized the local Indian American community. Then, in 1989, Jim (Ming Hai) Loo was attacked and beaten to death by two brothers in Raleigh, North Carolina, who blamed him and other "gooks" and "chinks" for killing Americans in Vietnam. Early in the morning on August 9, 1990, a fifteen-year-old Vietnamese immigrant to Houston, Hung Truong, was beaten and killed by a "White Power" skinhead. These dramatic cases and others have confirmed for many Asian Americans the necessity and practicality of Asian American panethnicity.

Major cities such as Philadelphia, Los Angeles, Boston, and New York report that a disproportionate number of hate crimes are directed at Asian Americans. Race-based violence occurs in their places of worship, their small businesses, their homes, and their schools and colleges (U.S. Commission on Civil Rights, 1992). Although Vietnamese refugees have been particular targets, most hate crimes directed at Asian Americans do not distinguish one ethnic group from another.

Hate crimes are often sensational and random outbursts of racial prejudice and bigotry. But more subtle and pernicious forms of racism also exist on a symbolic level (Chan, 1994). The "model minority" construct is an example of an imposed race-based cultural definition of Asian Americans. As such, it requires particular analysis.

## The "Model Minority" Myth

Asian Americans are still defined by racial stereotypes. The "model minority" concept, a racial formation created by majority cultural and ideological structures, incorporates all Asian American communities without differentiating on the basis of national grouping, class, gender, generation in the United States, language skills, and other variables. This "yellow" equivalent of the Horatio Alger myth is an abrupt reversal from the pre-1965 vision of buck-toothed kamikaze "Japs," inscrutable Oriental villains, "gooks," Suzie Wong prostitutes, and quaint backward people out of Pearl Buck's *Good Earth*.

The first public presentation of this idea is generally credited to a 1966 article in the *New York Times Magazine* entitled "Success Story, Japanese-American Style" (Petersen, 1966). It reviewed the seemingly remarkable success of Japanese Americans in the aftermath of the indignities and illegalities they had suffered during the World War II internment. This article was soon followed by a feature in the *U.S. News and World Report* entitled "Success Story of One Minority in the U.S." (1966), which described the economic rise of Chinese Americans in spite of historic discrimination.

Both articles used extant statistics on rising educational and income levels among Asian Americans, and on presumably low rates of reported crime and mental illness, to conclude that

Asian cultural values enabled these minorities to overcome whatever obstacles they confronted in the United States (Osajima, 1988). Countless other cover stories and popular articles in the mainstream media have puzzled over this rather exceptional story of an American minority group. Even scholarly articles have focused on what would appear to be the unexpected achievement of Asian American children and youth in school (see, for example, Sue and Okazaki, 1990). Asian Americans, in essence, have been re-racialized and misrepresented into what appears to be a positive stereotype.

Osajima (1988) concludes, however, that the subtext of the "model minority" concept is symbolically negative and breaches any potential solidarity among minority groups. This subtext implies that minority status, in itself, is not a proxy for discrimination or racism in American society, nor does it necessarily result in discriminatory outcomes. It also suggests that if a racial minority such as Asian Americans can "make it," then what holds back African Americans and Latinos? If American institutional or cultural racism is not implicated, the argument goes, there may be something inherently wrong with the cultural character of African American and Latino communities. Accordingly, one is led to believe that equity and parity will come not through structural changes in the society at large but through fundamental cultural changes made by less successful communities. This reasoning has resulted in a direct assault on the integrity of the culture and family values of other minorities, as well as in fractured relationships between Asian Americans and other minority communities. In short, the "model minority" characterization of Asian Americans serves as a convenient political device to explain away the persistence of racial inequalities in a liberal democratic society that now legally prohibits racial discrimination.

This redefinition of inequitable outcomes has taken the place of overt or legal racialization, forming a subtler, softer type of racial meaning—what Sears (1988) calls "symbolic racism." As a consequence, discussions of economic and educational achievement continue to be racialized rather than focusing on the institutional barriers that inhibit the advancement of minorities. Furthermore, blind acceptance of the "model minority" concept ignores the tremendous heterogeneity of the Asian American community and denies the needs and problems of vast numbers of Asians in America who do not share in this so-called success.

Indeed, for Asian Americans whose everyday lives contradict the educational and economic attainments of the "model minority" construct, the "success story" is a myth. With each nationwide census since 1970, Asian American scholars have critically challenged the superficial interpretation of census data that seemingly support the "model minority" concept (see, for example, Chun, 1980; Suzuki, 1977). The Asian American revisionist interpretation has received panethnic support, a position we summarize and expand on using census data from 1990.

In that year, the U.S. Bureau of the Census reported that, at $42,250, the median family income for Americans of Asian descent was the highest of all groups. (The median family income for whites was $36,920.) These data, though consistent with the high rankings of Asian Americans found in the 1970 and 1980 censuses, have been promoted as evidence of an unbiased society by people interested in maintaining the "model minority" myth. However, the conclusion that Asian Americans are more economically successful compared to other Americans is false for at least three basic reasons.

First, median family income represents the combined income of all workers in the family unit. But it does not take into account the number of workers in that family unit—and, indeed, there are more workers per family in the average Asian American family unit than in the average non-Hispanic white family. In 1990, 20 percent of all Asian American families had three or more workers contributing to the overall family income, as contrasted to only 13.2 percent of all white families (Bennett, 1992).

Second, the average per capita income figures are even more revealing. As in 1970 and 1980, the per capita income for Asian Americans in 1990 was less than that for whites—$13,420 as compared to $15,260, amounting to a 12 percent difference (Bennett, 1992).

Third, median family income is greatly influenced by geographic location. The Asian American population remains concentrated in three regions of the country: the California/Pacific Coast, the mid-Atlantic states, and Hawaii. Almost 60 percent of all Asian Americans live in three high-income states: California (39.1 percent), New York (9.5 percent) and Hawaii (9.4 percent). Furthermore, Asian Americans tend to live in large urban areas where the cost of living and median income are higher than the averages for the entire country. In 1991, 94 percent of all Asian Americans lived in metropolitan areas as compared to only 77 percent of whites (Bennett, 1992). As Asian Americans are nonrandomly distributed across the country, their relative income is skewed upward and their effective income downward.

As noted, these three simple explanations for the apparent high level of median family income for Asian Americans have been offered by Asian American scholars after each nationwide census since 1970. Yet mainstream media pundits, politicians, and researchers continue to misrepresent and misinterpret the median family income data.

An analysis of the economic condition of Asian Americans also challenges the "model minority" construct. Bennett (1992) reports that, as of 1990, a larger proportion of Asian American families (11 percent) were below the poverty line than were white families (8 percent). And in a more detailed study, Ong and his colleagues (1993) examined the poverty rates of disaggregated Asian American groups in the Los Angeles region. This study used as a benchmark the poverty threshold for a family of four, defined in 1989 as $12,674. Seven percent of non-Hispanic whites fell under this threshold. Comparing 1990 census data for selected groups in Los Angeles, Ong and his colleagues also found that 16 percent of Koreans, 16 percent of Chinese, 24 percent of Pacific Islanders, 25 percent of Vietnamese, and 45 percent of other Southeast Asians (including Hmong, Cambodians, and Laotians) fell below the poverty threshold. These startling statistics not only contradict the myth of the "successful" Asian American community but also crystallize the need to understand its internal diversity.

Economic well-being is only one factor in defining parity. Successful completion of education is another. Many studies have documented the enviable educational achievements of Asian American children (see, for example, Caplan, Choy, and Whitmore, 1991; Steinberg, Dornbusch, and Brown, 1992). But their excellent performance is no mystery. As with most parents, a primary concern of Asian American parents is the educational welfare of their children. Anecdotal evidence suggests that Asian American parents will move, change jobs, or otherwise organize family life in order to maximize their children's educational opportunities. In addition, Asian American children spend more hours studying and doing homework, and opt to take more college preparatory classes than do their non-Asian counterparts (Caplan, Choy, and Whitmore, 1991; Escueta and O'Brien, 1991; Steinberg, Dornbusch, and Brown, 1992).

Mickelson, Okazaki, and Zheng (1993) have found that strong motivation and the willingness to work hard in school are neither innate qualities of Asian American youth nor signs of their cultural superiority; rather, they serve as functional tools. These researchers determined that African American and Asian American high school seniors shared the same high regard for education. At the same time, both groups understood that they would face inequities in employment opportunities, income, and career advancement that educational achievement could not overcome. The African American students, however, were discouraged by a history of oppression that would discriminate against them regardless of their best efforts in school. Cynicism and disillusionment about the possibility that schooling could improve their lives may account for the lower participation and achievement rate of many African American youth. Fordham and Ogbu (1986) have made a similar argument.

In contrast, Mickelson and her colleagues (1993) have

concluded that Asian American youth work harder in school and achieve better results because they continue to view education as the most functional means to future success, despite any discrimination or racism they may encounter. Sue and Okazaki (1990) concur in their analysis of the function of education in Asian American life.

Similarly, Chan (1994) has argued that differences in school performance by minority groups may be, in part, a function of different affective reactions to the trauma of racism. He suggests that children from different minority backgrounds react to racist acts and discrimination differently. Among Asian American children and their families, the reaction to racialized behavior may be intense concentration on school achievement at the risk of their mental health and personality—a reaction that can be seen as adaptive from one perspective and limiting from another (Sue and Okazaki, 1992; Uba, 1994).

Overall, the educational attainment rates for Asian Americans over the age of twenty-five appear to be promising. In 1990 the high school completion rate was 82 percent for Asian Americans compared with 80 percent for non-Hispanic whites. The rate of completion of four years of college was 35 percent for Asian Americans and 22 percent for non-Hispanic whites. And the rate of completion of at least one year of graduate studies was 16 percent for Asian Americans and 9 percent for non-Hispanic whites.

One might conclude that Asian Americans have indeed prospered in the American educational system. But it is only by disaggregating the data, as Asian American scholars argue, that the overall representation of the Asian American community can be revealed as a misrepresentation. For example, recent immigrants from Cambodia, Laos, and Vietnam have high school completion rates of approximately 35 percent, 36 percent, and 58 percent, respectively—well under the 82 percent group statistic for all Asian Americans (U.S. Bureau of the Census, 1993).

Media accounts of substantial overrepresentation of Asian Americans in elite universities also distort reality. For instance, the dramatic increase in college attendance among Asian Americans is due largely to immigration and the youthfulness of the total Asian American population. Indeed, Asian Americans, who represent about 4 percent of the college population, are only marginally (1.1 percent) more likely to attend college than one would predict based on their share of the population.

We might also ask, Do relatively higher rates of educational attainment translate to higher levels of economic success for Asian Americans? In 1990 the income of the average white high school graduate was approximately $26,530, while that of the average Asian American high school graduate was $21,060, or 79 percent of the white counterpart's income. Asian American male college graduates earned $37,550, or 10 percent less than white males, who earned $41,660. It is also important to note that both Asian American and white women college graduates earned about $29,000, or 30 percent less than their white male counterparts (Bennett, 1992). In other words, women in general experience more of a "cement floor" than a "glass ceiling." These data suggest that educational attainment does not lead to economic parity for either Asian Americans or women. Racialized social policies and behaviors, such as discriminatory labor practices, stereotyping, and the "cement floor" and "glass ceiling," would appear to dampen the optimism—and trust in education—often expressed by Asian Americans (Mickelson, Okazaki, and Zheng, 1993).

As we have seen, the "model minority" construct is accompanied by a host of racial stereotypes about Asian American behavior. Asian American students are thought to be overly studious, passive and conforming, diligent and hardworking—the quintessential representation of bookish nerds. Fearing unfair competition, non-Asian students have been known to transfer out of college math classes when they see Asian American students enrolled. Yet conscientious performance in math may mask poor English skills that push some Asian American students toward academic areas requiring less verbal fluency (Hsia, 1988). Instead of assisting these Asian American students, the "model minority" stereotype actually conceals their academic problems. As a result, such students find themselves stuck in a very narrow range of academic and employment options.

Contrary to the "model minority" myth, Asian Americans have not been able to break through the "glass ceiling." Asian Americans remain underrepresented in high level management and supervisory positions. For example, Asian Americans hold barely 1 percent of the executive and managerial positions in higher education (Escueta and O'Brien, 1991).

Asian American scholars have grown weary of contesting the inaccuracy of the "model minority" construct over two decades. Yet this construct persists, and through it Asian Americans have been re-racialized. Currently, they occupy a new and falsely positive but still "proper place" in the racial order.

In addition, the perpetuation of this stereotype not only exacerbates dissension between Asian Americans and other minority communities but also hinders coalition building that could advance all communities. At the same time, the "model minority" myth generates friction between individual Asian American communities that remain underserved and invisible because of the myth and communities that are relatively more successful. Meanwhile, the dominant society has managed to divest itself of responsibility for addressing the barriers that maintain racial and social inequality.

Writers on Asian American issues cannot afford to assume that other scholars, policy makers, educators, or general readers are immune to the selling of this enduring myth. Given the tenacity of this racial image of the overachieving successful Asian American, serious scholars and community leaders concerned about the racialization of Asian Americans must regularly reiterate why this perception of Asian Americans is fallacious.

## Conclusion

The Asian American community is a complex and fluid social phenomenon defined and shaped by both external and internal forces.

Throughout their history, Asians in America have experienced prejudice, discrimination, and institutional and cultural racism. In the late 1960s, Asian Americans sought proactively and reactively to renegotiate the unequal racial and social order. The result was the formation of the new racial construct "Asian American" not found anywhere else in the world. This construct has also led to a panethnic coalition of Asian and Pacific ethnic groups intent on contesting race-based ideologies, policies, and practices. At the same time, Asian American communities are developing a unique American identity through new cultural and social formations forged out of a common history and experience in the United States.

Reconstructing the definition of "American" may require racialized constructs, such as that of the Asian American, to be defined and rearticulated by the groups themselves. Evolving from Asians in America to Asian Americans, the group under discussion here has made major strides in bridging cultural, linguistic, political, and social differences and creating a panethnic coalition of Asians and Pacific Islanders.

As the size and diversity of the Asian American community continue to grow, its political strength also increases, placing new demands on the dominant society. Because the impact of the reconfiguration and expansion of this community has not been fully recognized by the political leadership of the United States, significant social policy problems may result in the future (see Leadership Education for Asian Pacifics, 1993).

As separate Asian American ethnic communities grow in number, however, panethnicity may be challenged. Each of these communities may be able to sustain its own viable social and political structures and pursue its own concerns. The tension between individual community and panethnic strategies still exists. Hence panethnicity as a strategy for social change may have limitations as well as great possibilities.

The growth and diversity of the Asian American community has enriched America, but not without social conflicts. Indeed, anti-Asian sentiment and violence have increased, along with friction between Asian Americans and whites. But the bigger picture reveals that confrontations in the United States have become multiracial and multiethnic in general. Tensions between African Americans and Jewish Americans, and among African Americans, Latinos, and Korean Americans, now occur on a national scale. Recall the multiracial riot in Los Angeles in April 1992, which involved whites, African Americans, Chicanos, and Koreans. These new types of conflict are an outgrowth of the racialization process whereby racial minorities internalize the ideologies and practices of the majority culture and view other groups through stereotypes defined by that culture. In situations where groups are in competition for scarce resources and the use of public space, such conflicts readily erupt into violence.

An understanding of racialization in bipolar black/white terms no longer reflects the reality of American society, now that the new social order is being contested among racial minorities as well as between racial minorities and the majority culture. However, the primary problem remains the reformulation of the dominant political, economic, and cultural/ideological structures in order to achieve equity. Past efforts at reordering American society through coalition building brought some measures of reform. Meanwhile, the further development of Asian American panethnicity can provide valuable insights into the formation of coalitions with other racial and ethnic communities. Contemporary race relations—and, for that matter, conflicts like the multiracial Los Angeles riot—will require multiracial and multiclass solutions. Much depends on the dominant political, economic, and social context in which all minorities, including Asian Americans live and interact.

# References

Barringer, H., Gardner, R. and Levin, M. (1993). *Asians and Pacific Islanders in the United States*. New York: Russell Sage Foundation.

Bennett, C. (1992). *The Asian and Pacific Islander Population in the United States: March 1991 and 1990*, Current Population Reports P20-459. Washington, D.C.: Government Printing Office.

Caplan, N., Choy, M., and Whitmore, J. (1991). *Children of the Boat People. A Study of Educational Success*. Ann Arbor: University of Michigan Press.

Chan, K. (1994). "Sociocultural Aspects of Anger: Impact on Minority Children." In M. Furlong and D. Smith (eds.), *Anger and Cynical Hostility in Children and Adolescents: Assessment, Prevention, and Treatment Strategies*. Brandon, Vt.: Clinical Psychology Publishing.

Chan, S. (1991). *Asian Americans: An Interpretive History*. Boston: Twayne.

Cheng, L., and Bonacich, E. (1984). *Labor Immigration Under Capitalism: Asian Workers in the United States Before World War II*. Berkeley: University of California Press.

Chow, C. (1988). "Sixty Years on the Silver Screen." *Rice* (September), pp. 11–22, 41.

Chun, K. (1980). "The Myth of Asian American Success and Its Educational Ramifications." *IRCD Bulletin, 15*(1, 2), 1–12.

Escueta, E., and O'Brien, E. (1991). "Asian Americans in Higher Education: Trends and Issues." In *Research Briefs*, Vol. 2, No. 4. Washington, D.C.: American Council on Education.

Espiritu, Y. (1992). *Asian American Panethnicity*. Philadelphia: Temple University Press.

Fordham, S., and Ogbu, J. (1986). "Black Students' School Success: Coping with the 'Burden of "Acting White." ' " *The Urban Review, 18*, 176–206.

Hacker, A. (1992). *Two Nations: Black and White, Separate, Hostile, Unequal*. New York: Charles Scribner's Sons.

Hing, B. (1993). *Making and Remaking Asian America Through Immigration Policy, 1850–1990*. Stanford, Calif.: Stanford University Press.

Hsia, J. (1988). *Asian Americans in Higher Education and at Work*. Hillsdale, N.J.: Erlbaum.

Hune, S. (1977). *Pacific Migration to the United States: Trends and Themes in Historical and Sociological Literature*. Washington, D.C.: Research Institute on Immigration and Ethnic Studies, Smithsonian Institution.

Hune, S. (1993). "An Overview of Asian Pacific American Futures: Shifting Paradigms." In Leadership Education for Asian Pacifics (LEAP), *The State of Asian Pacific America: Policy Issues to the Year 2020*. Los Angeles: LEAP Asian Pacific American Public Policy Institute and UCLA Asian American Studies Center.

Leadership Education for Asian Pacifics (LEAP). (1993). *The State of Asian Pacific America: Policy Issues to the Year 2020*. Los Angeles: LEAP Asian Pacific American Public Policy Institute and UCLA Asian American Studies Center.

Leonard, K. (1992). *Making Ethnic Choices: California's Punjabi Mexican Americans*. Philadelphia: Temple University Press.

Loewen, J. (1988). *The Mississippi Chinese: Between Black and White*, 2nd ed. Prospect Heights, Ill.: Waveland Press.

Martinez, E. (1993). "Beyond Black/White: The Racisms of Our Time." *Social Justice*, 10(1–2), 22–34.

Mickelson, R., Okazaki, S., and Zheng, D. (1993). "Different Tales Told at the Dinner Table: Asian, Black, and White Adolescents' Education Attitudes and High School Performance." Paper presented at the meeting of the American Educational Research Association, Atlanta (April).

Omatsu, G. (ed.). (1989). "Commemorative Issue." *Amerasia Journal*, 15(1).

Omi, M. (1993). "Out of the Melting Pot and Into the Fire: Race Relations Policy." In *The State of Asian Pacific America: Policy Issues to the Year 2020*. Los Angeles: LEAP Asian Pacific American Public Policy Institute and UCLA Asian American Studies Center.

Omi, M., and Winant, H. (1986). *Racial Formation in the United States*. New York: Routledge & Kegan Paul.

Ong, P., and others. (1993). *Beyond Asian American Poverty*. Los Angeles: Leadership Education for Asian Pacifics.

Osajima, K. (1988). "Asian Americans as the Model Minority: An Analysis of the Popular Press Image in the 1960's and 1980's." In G. Okihiro, S. Hune, A. Hansen, and J. Liu (eds.), *Reflections on Shattered Windows*. Pullman: Washington State University Press.

Petersen, W. (1966). "Success Story, Japanese-American Style." *New York Times Magazine* (January 9), pp. 20–21, 33, 36, 38, 40–41, 43.

Sears, D. (1988). "Symbolic Racism." In P. Katz and D. Taylor (eds.), *Eliminating Racism*. New York: Plenum Press.

Singham, A., and Hune, S. (1986). *Non-Alignment in an Age of Alignments*. Westport, Conn.: Lawrence Hill/London: Zed Books.

Steinberg, L., Dornbusch, S., and Brown, B. (1992). "Ethnic Differences in Adolescent Achievement: An Ecological Perspective." *American Psychologist*, 47, 723–729.

"Success Story of One Minority in the U.S." (1966). *U.S. News and World Report* (December 26), pp. 73–78.

Sue, S., and Okazaki, S. (1990). "Asian-American Educational Achievements: A Phenomenon in Search of an Explanation." *American Psychologist*, 45, 913–920.

Suzuki, B. (1977). "Education and Socialization of Asian Americans: A Revisionist Analysis of the 'Model Minority' Thesis." *Amerasia Journal*, 4(23), 23–51.

Takaki, R. (1989). *Strangers from a Different Shore*. Boston: Little, Brown.

Terkel, S. (1992). *Race: How Blacks and Whites Think and Feel About the American Obsession*. New York: New Press.

Uba, L. (1994). *Asian Americans: Personality Patterns, Identity, and Mental Health*. New York: Guilford Press.

U.S. Bureau of the Census. (1993). *The Foreign-Born Population in the United States (CP-3-1)*. Washington, D.C.: Government Printing Office.

U.S. Commission on Civil Rights. (1986). *Recent Activities Against Citizens and Residents of Asian Descent.* Washington, D.C.: U.S. Commission on Civil Rights.

U.S. Commission on Civil Rights. (1992). *Civil Rights Issues Facing Asian Americans in the 1990's.* Washington, D.C.: U.S. Commission on Civil Rights.

Wei, W. (1993). *The Asian American Movement.* Philadelphia: Temple University Press.

# Part Three

# Effective Strategies for Improving Race and Ethnic Relations

*Chapter Nine*

# Intercultural Contact and Race Relations Among American Youth

Jomills Henry Braddock II
Marvin P. Dawkins
George Wilson

## Introduction

The problem of the twentieth century is the problem
of the color-line.
—W.E.B. Du Bois, *The Souls of Black Folk*

As we come to the close of the twentieth century, W.E.B. Du Bois's assessment of U.S. race relations, written in 1903, remains prophetic. In recent decades, considerable progress has been made in combating racial inequality in American society. However, this society continues to be racially segregated and polarized. (For reviews of recent trends along various socioeconomic indicators, see Farley and Allen, 1987; Farley and Bianchi, 1985; and Jaynes and Williams, 1989.)

One manifestation of the deep racial divisions that persist in this country is found in perceptions of the racial problem. Perspectives on American race relations vary widely. They range from optimism that the main issues have been resolved, to the view that African American progress is largely an illusion, to assessments that the nation is retrogressing and moving toward increased racial disparities (Jaynes and Williams, 1989). A recent report published by the National Academy of Sciences, entitled *A Common Destiny*, makes this point best in noting that "the status of black Americans today can be characterized as a glass that is half full—if measured by progress since 1939—or as a glass that is half empty—if measured by the persisting disparities between black and white Americans since the early 1970's" (Jaynes and Williams, 1989).

Significantly, a growing body of evidence has established that adherence to these perspectives does not cut across lines of socio-economic status or levels of educational attainment but, rather, is largely a function of race (Kluegel and Smith, 1986; Sigelman and Welsh, 1991). The fact that whites hold optimistic views of racial progress and African Americans hold deeply pessimistic views is another indication that the races still inhabit different social worlds. The consequences of this racial division are far-reaching: it not only affects the tolerance and acceptance among racial groups both in informal social settings and in day-to-day affairs (Sigelman and Welsh, 1991), but it also makes problematic the implementation and efficacy of social programs designed to alleviate persisting inequalities (Bobo, 1991).

What is particularly disturbing is that this division seems to have taken hold among our nation's youth. A recent national survey by People for the American Way (1992) found that white youth and youth of color hold deeply divergent views on intergroup relations: young people of all races indicated in this survey that they see themselves as victims in the race relations arena, with nearly half of the white youth viewing affirmative action as unfair while more than half of the African American and Latino youth view discrimination in education and employment as the norm. The harmful results of this racial divide among our youth are becoming more apparent in the alarming increase of adolescent hate crimes, organized hate groups, and overt expressions of racial intolerance.

If race relations are to improve in subsequent generations, the youth of today must take the lead. Our nation's youth will not only assume the mantle of leadership in the future but will also have significant influence over the content of the values their children adopt. However, the magnitude of this task—of providing a foundation for positive race relations among today's youth—must be recognized. First, they are coming of age at a time when massive societal changes militate against the adoption of positive interracial attitudes. If recent American history is any guide, growing racial and ethnic heterogeneity, combined with acute economic competition and constricted employment opportunities, does not seem to be the ideal macro-context in which to initiate an era of interracial tolerance and cooperation (see Olzak and Nagel, 1986; Bonacich, 1972; Spear, 1967).

Second, the sources of socialization that imbue our youth with attitudes toward other groups are in a state of flux. Specifically, the role of traditional sources of socialization such as the family are declining (see Cherlin, 1992; Wilson, 1987). For example, in the last twenty years, the rate of female labor-force participation in America has more than doubled (Reskin and Roos, 1990). Furthermore, evidence to date indicates that the increased commitment to the workplace is neither class- nor race-specific. As a result, "dual earner" families are no longer the exceptional case but, rather, have become common at all levels of American society (Cherlin, 1992). Moreover, in the same period of time, the rate of marriages that have resulted in separation or divorce within four years of their inception has almost doubled (Cherlin, 1992). Again, the best evidence indicates that such changes have occurred independent of social class and race.

These changes have undoubtedly affected the ability of parents to maintain their former role as a socialization agent. Even when parents are present in the household, the time and energy they have available to give to their children are considerably less than in previous decades. Thus, it should not be surprising that more than 65 percent of parents recently interviewed indicated that they feel their influence on their children's lives is waning (Cherlin, 1992).

In the face of such changes, the exploration of other sources of socialization is of crucial importance; indeed, these other sources now serve a more fundamental role than ever. In this chapter, we explore the role that two of these sources—in-school and out-of-school contexts—can play as settings for promoting positive intercultural contact between youth. Our emphasis is on strategies for improving race and ethnic relations in both contexts.

Schools have long played a key role in providing a foundation for positive race relations. They go a long way toward determining the "life-chances" of future generations. Not only are they a primary agent of the socialization of our young (consider that most of the waking hours of five- to eighteen-year-olds are spent in schools), but they also sort individuals into colleges and jobs. Yet public schools have become highly, and increasingly, racially segregated institutions, despite social and legal action to promote racially balanced, if not racially integrated, educational opportunities. As a result, young people are socialized in settings that are either socially isolated or stratified in ways that often exacerbate intergroup conflict.

Children now spend increasing amounts of time outside of schools in afterschool child-care programs, on playgrounds, in shopping malls that provide entertainment and eating establishments, at sporting events and musical concerts, and in church-sponsored and other voluntary associations where they engage in activities during evenings and weekends. All of these contexts constitute opportunities for interracial contact. Hence it is fundamentally important that we understand how interracial contact in these contexts can promote harmonious racial attitudes. To date, little research has assessed the role of these nonstructured settings as arenas for intergroup contact among youth. Yet a determination of their effect appears timely and urgent.

Even less attention has been focused on intergroup contact among children and youth in nonstructured settings. These settings are especially important in assessing the outcomes of intercultural contact between children because they involve naturally occurring situations, which are encounters unlikely to present the conditions necessary for improved race relations and reducing prejudice. For example, cooperative-learning methods have been effectively introduced as planned interventions to improve intergroup relations in desegregated schools because it is possible, through such methods, to achieve the conditions necessary for positive outcomes of contact in the highly structured setting of the classroom. However, in non-structured settings outside of the classroom, planned interventions such as coooperative learning may be more difficult to implement.

In the process of exploring strategies for improving race and ethnic relations, we discuss major barriers—both normative and situational—to increased intergroup contact and improved interracial tolerance among young people. Our objective is to describe both "inclusion barriers," norms, policies, and practices that restrict young people's opportunities for participation in interracial contact situations, and "interaction barriers," which impede the development of positive intergroup relations in situations of interracial contact. Both types of barriers are examined in a variety of organizational settings and sociocultural contexts.

## Intergroup Contact and Intergroup Relations

The contact hypothesis has been a principal formulation for more than forty years in the study of intergroup relations. In addressing the primary question raised by this hypothesis (whether contact improves intergroup relations), the cumulative evidence from decades of research in different settings supports assumptions posited by Allport (1954) and others regarding the factors necessary for improvement of intergroup relations through contact. These factors include (1) equal-status contact between individuals from majority and minority groups in pursuit of common goals, (2) contact that is sanctioned by institutional supports (authority figures), and (3) the opportunity for minority and majority group members to interact as individuals. Whereas earlier studies of the contact hypothesis focused on adults in such settings as industry, the military, and housing (Brophy, 1946; Deutsch and Collins, 1951; Wilner, Walkley, and Cook, 1952), later attention turned to intergroup contact in schools (Aronson et al., 1978; Slavin, 1985). The latter studies underscored the importance of cooperation in inter-group contact. However, research on intergroup contact between children of different racial and ethnic backgrounds in desegregated schools has produced mixed results. While some reviews of the lit-erature indicate that the majority of studies on interracial contact in desegregated schools show no positive effects on intergroup rela-tions (Armor, 1972; St. John, 1975; Stephan, 1978), other reviews suggest that the positive benefits of interracial contact in desegre-gated schools are long term and tend to be reflected in such later outcomes as positive interracial experiences among adults in such settings as neighborhoods and the workplace (Braddock and Dawkins, 1984; Braddock, 1985).

## Contextual Effects and Intergroup Contact

Recent attention focusing on an organizational analysis of the inclu-sion of African American workers in previously all-white work set-tings raises new questions regarding the outcomes of interracial contact in various contexts (Pettigrew and Martin, 1987). Many nat-ural settings, including locations in proximity to schools that offer structured programs to improve race relations, have become much more important contexts for interracial contact between children.

A major obstacle to rapid and lasting progress in race relations among our nation's youth is the often vast gulf in social norms between the various social contexts in which the youth must func-tion. *Contextual dissonance* is a term we can use to describe an indi-vidual's social experience of strong conflicting and competing nor-mative pressures emanating from significant others. Today, young people from preschool age through adolescence are commonly con-fronted with racial dilemmas associated with dramatically differ-ing expectations from significant others in their communities, homes, and schools. And because many school-age youth attend schools outside their immediate neighborhoods, they often belong to differing school- and community-based friendship groups. These overlapping but potentially "dissonant" normative spheres of influence in young people's lives can operate as impediments to positive race relations.

The nature of intergroup contact between children in these settings must be better understood if we are to develop intervention strategies for improving race relations among children.

## Intercultural Contact Between Children in Schools

As earlier noted, education plays a critical role in the incorporation of diverse social groups into society's mainstream. Hence American schools have been viewed as both great socializers and great equalizers. Especially at the elementary and secondary levels, schools play an important role as socializing institutions in transmitting society's culture and values to its young as well as preparing them with appropriate knowledge and skills for leading productive and fulfilling adult lives (Bullivant, 1982). American schools, as equalizers (at least in principle), are designed to prepare all of the nation's youth to realize their full potential and to improve their individual and collective status. Thus, schools have traditionally been viewed by most as the route through which both individuals and groups can achieve social mobility.

Nevertheless, the American educational system has historically provided disproportionately greater benefits to whites than to students of color, and to the middle and upper classes than to the poor. In short, inner-city schools have characteristically failed to provide the kind and quality of educational experience required to help African American and Latino students overcome the effects and vestiges of racial and economic isolation, poverty, and discrimination.

Indeed, some observers have argued that the American educational system is designed to *maintain* race and class division in society, citing as evidence a number of pervasive school policies and practices that inherently reinforce the existing structure of racial and class privileges. Such policies and practices can operate at the very broadest levels, influencing federal, state, and local educational priorities and resource allocations across schools; but the present analysis focuses on policies and practices operating within individual schools that, intentionally or not, fail to foster the development of intergroup tolerance and understanding among students of diverse racial and cultural backgrounds.

Both theory and research suggest that good race relations in schools—and equal educational opportunities overall—depend upon equal-status contacts among students of diverse backgrounds. In the context of individual schools, equal-status contacts, and thus race relations, are affected by a number of school policies, practices, and organizational arrangements (Epps, 1974). School and classroom organization, curriculum and instruction, school climate and culture (including extracurricular and co-curricular programs)—all are key features of American schools and schooling that impact intergroup contact and race relations among students in important ways.

Each of these features involves particular practices, policies, or procedures that may operate as "exclusionary barriers," limiting the possibilities for intergroup contacts among diverse students, or as "interaction barriers," constraining student contacts in ways that limit opportunities for student interactions in heterogeneous settings to fulfill the cross-group conditions necessary to produce such contact-theory benefits as equal status and shared goals.

We will consider two examples—"tracking" and extracurricular activities (sports)—to illustrate this point. Each represents an important aspect of school organization and school climate or culture. Tracking, moreover, is often the defining feature of a school's instructional program, encompassing not only matters of instructional practice but often curriculum content and coverage as well. Because it shapes scheduling, tracking can also influence student opportunities for participation in extracurricular activities.

Insofar as it reflects classroom organization and student assignments, tracking is the ultimate determinant as to which students will enroll in the same programs and classes within a particular school. As such, it designates which students will have routine and frequent opportunities to interact with other students, like and unlike themselves. Likewise, it determines status relations among students both between classes (in grouped settings) and within classes (in ungrouped settings). And in defining curriculum content, tracking defines both group worth and student status associated with membership in a particular group. To the extent that extracurricular activities may be scheduled in ways that more optimally fit the needs of students enrolled in particular classes or programs, tracking can further limit student opportunities to participate in nonclassroom activities with other students beyond their own hierarchically defined groups. Between-class grouping is typically more limiting, unless it is used flexibly—that is, unless homogeneous placements are restricted to one or two subjects based on appropriately assessed criteria, and students are permitted to attend classes with different classmates for most subjects. It should be noted, however, that unless within-class grouping is consciously implemented with strategies (such as cooperative learning) designed to minimize distinctions, unequal-status relations and other factors in heterogeneous classes could lead to less desirable outcomes in intergroup relations. Research tends to support these propositions regarding the relation between tracking and various intergroup outcomes. In the following sections we discuss specifically those studies that deal with the consequences of tracking and extracurricula activities for integration and intergroup relations.

*Tracking.* Although American public education is based on a common school ideology that purports to promote equal access to all learners, pervasive tracking throughout our nation's schools often results in differentiated classroom opportunities for intergroup contact among students. Classrooms are somewhat more segregated than schools overall (Hochschild, 1984), and much of the classroom segregation that exists is, at least in part, a result of tracking and between-class ability grouping (Epstein, 1985). There is evidence that African Americans, Latinos, and American Indians are overrepresented in low-track, low-ability classes and programs and underrepresented in high-track college preparatory programs and classes for the gifted and talented (Braddock, 1989; Oakes, 1982,

1985, 1992). These groups are also overrepresented among the low tracks in junior high and middle schools (see, for example, Jones, Erickson, and Crowell, 1972), and in low-level reading groups in elementary school (Haller, 1985). Leaving aside race and ethnicity, students from low socioeconomic circumstances are also greatly overrepresented in the low tracks (Heyns, 1974; Alexander, Cook, and McDill, 1978).

Relatively little is known about the direct effect of ability grouping on attitudes among students of different ethnicities. One study compared interethnic attitudes in ability-grouped and heterogeneous sixth-grade classes in New Mexico schools containing Hispanic and Anglo students. Intergroup attitudes were consistently higher in the heterogeneous classes (Sarthory, 1968). However, the effects of between-class ability grouping are certainly much more profound than this. Because it separates students into classes that are predominantly composed of one or another ethnic group, ability grouping necessarily has a strong negative impact on the number of positive relationships that could possibly develop across ethnic group lines.

*Extracurricular Activities.* Extracurricular activities have been a feature of American education since the late nineteenth century or earlier. Beginning around 1910, athletics and the complex of activities that constitute the extracurricular program of many schools today became more formalized. Receiving increasing attention from educators, especially as reflected in the recommendations of the Commission on the Reform of Secondary Education in 1918 (Krug, 1964), these activities were elevated to a status nearly equal to that of the formal curriculum. They were viewed as essential to the reformed secondary school's ability to prepare students for their roles as adults in the corporate economy and in democratic society. The rationale of educational leaders calling for the enhancement of extracurricular programs at the turn of the century reveals several core themes: (1) cultivation in students of a commitment to the values of teamwork and cooperation, (2) accommodation (sacrifice) of individual goals and interests for the benefit of the group, (3) cultivation of a strong work ethic, (4) integration of physical and mental health, and (5) appreciation for class and ethnic diversity.

Participation in extracurricular activities has been examined in the context of desegregated schools for evidence of its potentially unifying effects. For example, Crain (1981) and Crain, Mahard, and Narot (1982) have found evidence to support the beneficial effects of extracurricular activities on race relations in desegregated schools. Indeed, the attitudes of African American and white students toward these schools tend to be positively influenced by higher rates of student involvement in extracurricular activities. In addition, Trent and McPartland (1981) examined reported rates of participation in extracurricular activities in segregated and desegregated schools to identify black-white differences in participation based on the racial composition of the school and the potential for cross-race contact in the extracurricular activities at the desegregated schools. Their results reveal complex regional, race, gender, and activity differences in self-reported participation. Generally, African American and white males and females exhibit comparable levels of participation in extracurricular activities in segregated schools, but different patterns in desegregated schools. In the latter, white males and females report slightly greater participation in honors clubs and student government, but less participation in sports, band, and similar activities compared to the participation patterns of African American students. For students in the same desegregated schools, the opportunity for cross-race contact was greatest in those activities where African American and white students were about equally represented. Such equal representation occurred across regions and involved both males and females, but only in vocational clubs. White students had the least access to African American students in honorary activities and the greatest in athletic activities, among which white students were overrepresented and underrepresented, respectively.

In short, extracurricular activities can offer unique and important opportunities for positive cross-race contacts among students if the various clubs and teams recruit from all groups and permit leadership roles to be held by students of diverse backgrounds.

## A Case Example

Both Bill Brown and David Gross grew up in middle-class Catholic families along the eastern seaboard and both loved football. But their lives did not intersect until Bill, who is black, and David, who is white, came to Xavier Catholic High School as freshmen.

David played defensive guard; Bill was a linebacker. In the spring, they also played baseball together—David on first base, Bill on third. They shared the exhilaration of becoming Metro Conference baseball champions two years in a row. And they fought side by side in a heart-wrenching loss to Xavier's archrival in the last game of their final baseball season.

"By the time we were in twelfth grade, we had a history of pulling for one another and coming through for one another and being there for one another that I don't think people who aren't part of a team get," David says.

Their companionship quickly reached well beyond sports. They became good friends who, like all good friends, influenced each other in unexpected ways.

It was at Bill's house that David discovered collard greens. Bill's Mom had him over for dinner and served collard greens and Cornish game hens. It was at David's house that Bill discovered Jim Morrison and The Doors. "We would sit there after a ballgame and talk and listen to music until the wee hours of the morning," Bill says.

When David won his two Emmys, he called Bill to tell him about it. When Bill got another coaching offer, he and David talked several times a day as Bill agonized about leaving Xavier.

When the riots erupted in Los Angeles in 1992, Bill called David, then living in Burbank, to make sure he was all right. When David came home for a visit shortly afterward, they got together and talked about it for hours.

"Lately, every time we see one another we spend our time talking about those things—race and our relationship and how it's grown," David says. "A lot of our talks gravitate toward race and prejudice and the hidden things that happen. I know for a fact that there are things that happened to Bill just because he's black."

"Speaking as a white male," David adds, "those are things I can never understand." And yet, he says, "You hurt when your friend hurts. You hurt when someone you love hurts."

This case example illustrates the potential of sports, and certain other extracurricular activities, to provide key social contexts for students of different backgrounds to interact (1) as equals, (2) in a cooperative way, and (3) with shared goals. These characteristics of team sports are precisely the conditions posited by contact theory as likely to lead to positive outcomes of intergroup contact. They are also attributes that served as the major stimulus in the development of cooperative-learning strategies—attributes that have proven quite effective in classroom contexts for promoting positive intergroup relations as well as enhanced student achievement.

## Intercultural Contact Between Children in Nonschool Settings

Since intergroup contacts in everyday life are less likely than school-based contacts to conform to the equal-status idea (Schaefer, 1993) or to other conditions necessary for achieving positive outcomes, intercultural contact in nonschool settings provides a greater challenge for developing means by which social interventions can contribute to positive outcomes of contact between children of different racial groups. In addition, recent demographic changes in the U.S. population indicate that for many regions there is a trend toward greater ethnic and racial diversity among school-age children, thus providing more occasions for intercultural contact in contexts other than schools. Schwartz and Exter (1989), after deriving population projections based on U.S. Census data, have reported that as many as 38 percent of Americans under the age of eighteen will be black, Hispanic, or Asian by 2010. And in several states, minorities will actually constitute the majority of children by the same year. These states are Hawaii (80 percent), New Mexico (77 percent), California (57 percent), Texas (57 percent), New York (53 percent), Florida (53 percent), Louisiana (50 percent), and the District of Columbia (93 percent). While most states (thirty-three out of fifty) will experience a decline in the total youth population (that is, all racial and ethnic groups combined), many of the largest states with the greatest diversity today will continue to experience increases in the minority share of their youth population (Schwartz and Exter, 1989). Some of these states, including New York, California, and Florida, have also witnessed youth involvement in negative outcomes of racial and ethnic contact. Racial violence and hostilities in Bensonhurst (New York), South Central Los Angeles (California), and Liberty City Miami (Florida) serve as recent cases in point. More attention has been focused on economic efforts to address the needs of communities in the aftermath of racial conflicts, such as the riots in Miami in 1989 and in Los Angeles in 1992, than on the needs of youth, especially in terms of devising ways to assist them in preparing for future intercultural contact. Although most occasions for intercultural contact in community contexts may not surround such explosive issues as these, the question of how to foster positive intercultural contact among youth in unstructured settings must be addressed so as to reduce the likelihood of negative responses to racial and ethnic tensions. Two brief examples of such settings will serve to illustrate the importance and potential possibilities for enhancing our understanding of intercultural contacts beyond schools.

*Afterschool Child-Care Programs.* A major portion of time is spent by children in afterschool child-care programs. Many children of elementary-school age may spend from one to five hours per day in an afterschool program during any given week. The importance of providing early multiethnic experiences in preparation for later intergroup contact among children has been suggested for children as young as preschool age (Harper and Dawkins, 1985). In child-care programs that accommodate children from different racial and ethnic backgrounds, the opportunities may exist for extending strategies that have been effective in improving intergroup relations in the school setting. However, despite the fact that providers of these programs must usually meet certain requirements related to space, cleanliness, food service, planned activities, and safety, child-care staffs tend to include few of the highly trained personnel who would be needed to implement the type of interventions that have been successful in the classroom. Nevertheless, this context may be important in helping to prepare children for intercultural contact in more unstructured nonschool settings. For example, techniques for improving friendship patterns across grade level, gender, race, and ability level may be more readily achieved in this context than in the classroom setting.

*Organized Youth Sports.* As children move toward adolescence, more unstructured settings can promote intergroup contact in nonschool environments. For example, community-based organized youth sports events at school facilities or neighborhood playgrounds provide a context for intercultural contact on the part of both spectators and participants who attend segregated schools or live in segregated communities. By contrast, competitive athletic events such as football, basketball, and track are rarely perceived as contexts for examining intergroup contact. Even though the contact in these contexts may be of short duration and under the control of adult authorities, the fierce competitive atmosphere characteristic of sports events from Little League to high school athletics may reflect strong expressions of ingroup loyalty and outgroup hostility. These expressions, in turn, may be transformed into racial and ethnic hostility when the opposing teams and their followers are members of different cultural groups from communities or schools that are polarized along racial or ethnic lines.

Of course, sporting events can also provide opportunities for developing interventions with the aim of promoting harmony between intercultural groups—especially in settings where the contact between groups is of short duration. For example, the universal appeal of popular professional athletes can be drawn upon in creating a climate for promoting such intergroup harmony in large sports-related gatherings where children of different racial backgrounds come into contact.

## Intervention Strategies and Policy Implications

Our examination of various school and nonschool contexts has emphasized the operation of both "exclusionary barriers" and "interaction barriers" as obstacles to positive intergroup contact among our nation's youth. We maintain that increasingly important agents of socialization—specifically, extracurricular school activities and community-based nonschool settings—can play a key role in fostering positive interethnic group relations. We also maintain that, given the potential for interethnic intolerance and conflict caused by the rapidly changing ethnic composition of the American population, an understanding of how these agents of socialization can promote positive intergroup relations is particularly important.

Youth sports are highlighted here as one potentially promising extracurricular school activity that may be used for promoting positive intergroup contact among American young people. The widespread appeal of sports is evident in both school and nonschool settings. Indeed, more than one-half of the males in middle grades and one-quarter of those in high school engage in sports as an extracurricular activity. Yet, despite the considerable potential for cross-race student contacts offered by sports programs, current school policies and practices often restrict such participation. As an example, consider the school policy of "no pass/no play," which limits extracurricular sports opportunities for large numbers of students. If anything, the potential for utilizing sports to promote opportunities for intergroup contact in nonschool settings should be expanded, not restricted.

The relatively informal nature of many nonschool community-based settings probably makes it difficult to design laboratory-like implementation strategies that foster positive intergroup relations. Nevertheless, such organizations as the Boys and Girls Clubs, YMCAs and YWCAs, and church- and business-sponsored groups offer a variety of structured programs that can be used to promote positive intergroup contacts. Particularly noteworthy is the multi-ethnic nature of these community-based organizations, long noted as settings in which individuals from different social class and ethnic backgrounds have opportunities to interact (Whyte, 1949; Liebow, 1967). As such, these settings allow for the development of intervention strategies with unprecedented potential to influence the interracial attitudes of youth.

This chapter has attempted to identity some neglected but important social contexts that may be important in structuring positive intergroup relations. We advocate a careful assessment of these settings as determinants of interracial attitudes. If they do not receive proper attention by academics and policy analysts, racial intolerance and the perpetuation of invidious stereotypes will continue to plague society.

# References

Alexander, K. L., Cook, M. A., and McDill, E. L. (1978). "Curriculum Tracking and Educational Stratification." *American Sociological Review, 43*, 47–66.

Allport, G. W. (1954). *The Nature of Prejudice*. Garden City, N.Y.: Doubleday.

Armor, D. J. (1972). "The Evidence on Busing." *Public Interest, 28*, 90–126.

Aronson, E., Stephan, C., Sikes, J., Blaney, N., and Snapp, M. (1978). *The Jigsaw Classroom*. Beverly Hills, CA: Sage.

Bobo, L. (1991). "Social Responsibility, Individualism, and Redistributive Policies." *Sociological Forum, 6*, 71–91.

Bonacich, E. (1972). "A Theory of Ethnic Antagonism: The Split-Labor Market." *American Sociological Review, 37*, 547–559.

Braddock, J. H. (1985). "School Desegregation and Black Assimilation." *Journal of Social Issues, 41*, 9–22.

Braddock, J. H. (1989). *Tracking of Black, Hispanic, Asian, Native American, and White Students: National Patterns and Trends*. Baltimore, Md.: Center for Research on Effective Schooling for Disadvantaged Students.

Braddock, J. H., and Dawkins, M. P. (1984). "Long-Term Effects of School Desegregation on Southern Blacks." *Sociological Spectrum, 4*, 365–381.

Brophy, N. (1946). "The Luxury of Anti-Negro Prejudice." *Public Opinion Quarterly, 9*, 456–466.

Brophy, J. E., and Good, T. L. (1986). "Teacher Behavior and Student Achievement." In M. C. Wittrock (ed.), *Handbook of Research on Teaching*, 3rd ed. (pp. 328–375). New York: Macmillan.

Bullivant, B. (1982). "Power and Control in the Multi-Ethnic School: Toward a Conceptual Model." *Ethnic and Racial Studies, 5*, 53–70.

Cherlin, A. (1992). *Marriage, Divorce, Remarriage*. Cambridge, Mass.: Harvard University Press.

Cottle, T. L. (1974). "What Tracking Did to Ollie Taylor." *Social Policy, 5*, 21–24.

Crane, R., Mahard, R., and Narot, R. (1982). *Making desegregation work*. Cambridge, Mass.: Ballinger.

Deutsch, M., and Collins, M. E. (1951). *Interracial Housing: A Psychological Evaluation of a Social Experiment*. Minneapolis: University of Minnesota Press.

Du Bois, W.E.B. (1903). *The Souls of Black Folk*. Chicago: A. C. McClurg.

Epps, E. (1974). "Impact of School Desegregation on Aspirations, Self-Concepts and Other Aspects of Personality." In M. Weinberg (ed.), *Minority Students: A Research Appraisal*. Washington, D.C.: National Institute of Education.

Epstein, J. (1985). "After the Bus Arrives: Resegregation in Desegregated Schools." *Journal of Social Issues, 41*(3), 23–43.

Esposito, D. (1973). "Homogeneous and Heterogeneous Ability Grouping: Principal Findings and Implications for Evaluating and Designing More Effective Educational Environments." *Review of Educational Research, 43*, 163–179.

Farley, R., and Allen, W. (1987). *The Color Line and the Quality of Life in America*. New York: Russell Sage Foundation.

Farley, R., and Bianchi, S. (1985). "Class Polarization: Is It Occurring Among Blacks?" *Research in Race and Ethnic Relations, 5*, 1–31.

Haller, E. J. (1985). "Pupil Race and Elementary School Ability Grouping: Are Teachers Biased Against Black Children?" *American Educational Research Journal, 22*, 465–483.

Haller, E. J. and Davis, S. A. (1980). "Does Socioeconomic Status Bias the Assignment of Elementary School Students to Reading Groups?" *American Educational Research Journal, 17*, 409–418.

Haller, E. J., and Davis, S. A. (1981). "Teacher Perceptions, Parental Social Status, and Grouping for Reading Instruction." *Sociology of Education, 54*, 162–174.

Harper, F. D., and Dawkins, M. P. (1985). "The Syphax Child Care Center." *Journal of Negro Education*, 54, 438–450.

Hawley, W. (1992). "Research, Public Opinion and Public Action: Thoughts on the Future of School Desegregation." Paper presented at the American Educational Research Association, San Francisco.

Heyns, B. (1974). "Social Selection and Stratification Within Schools." *American Journal of Sociology*, 79, 1434–1451.

Hochschild, J. (1984). *The New American Dilemma*. New Haven, Conn.: Yale University Press.

Jaynes, J., and Williams, R. (1989). *A Common Destiny*. Washington, D.C.: National Academy of Sciences.

Jones, J. D., Erickson, E. L., and Crowell, R. (1972). "Increasing the Gap Between Whites and Blacks: Tracking as a Contributory Source." *Education and Urban Society*, 4, 339–349.

Kluegel, J., and Smith, E. (1986). *Beliefs About Inequality*. New York: Aldine De Gruyter.

Liebow, E. (1967). *Tally's Corner*. Boston: Little, Brown.

Oakes, J. (1982). "The Reproduction of Inequity: The Content of Secondary School Tracking." *Urban Review*, 14, 107–120.

Oakes, J. (1985). *Keeping Track: How Schools Structure Inequality*. New Haven, Conn.: Yale University Press.

Oakes, J. (1992). "Grouping Students for Instruction." In M. Alkin (ed.), *Encyclopedia of Educational Research*. New York: Macmillan.

Olzak, S., and Nagel, J. (1986). "Competitive Ethnic Relations: An Overview." In S. Olzak and J. Nagel (eds.), *Competitive Ethnic Relations*. Orlando, Fla.: Academic Press.

Persell, C. H. (1977). *Education and Inequality: A Theoretical and Empirical Synthesis*. New York: Free Press.

Pettigrew, T. F., and Martin, J. (1987). "Shaping the Organizational Context for Black American Inclusion." *Journal of Social Issues*, 43(1), 41–78.

People for the American Way. (1992). *Democracy's Next Generation* (vol. 2). Washington, D.C.: Author.

Reskin, B., and Roos, P. (1990). *Job Queues, Gender Queues*. Philadelphia: Temple University Press.

Rosenbaum, J. E. (1976). *Making Inequality: The Hidden Curriculum of High School Tracking*. New York: Wiley.

Sarthory, J. A. (1968). "The Effects of Ability Grouping in Multi-Cultural School Situations." *Dissertation Abstracts*, 29, 451A (UME No. 68-11, 664).

Schwartz, J., and Exter, T. (1989). "All Our Children." *American Demographics* (May), pp. 34–37.

Schaefer, R. T. (1993). *Racial and Ethnic Groups* (5th ed.). New York: HarperCollins Publisher.

Sigelman, L., and Welsh, S. (1991). *The Dream Deferred: Black Americans' Views of Racial Inequality*. Cambridge, England: Cambridge University Press.

Slavin, R. E. (1985). "Cooperative Learning: Applying Contact Theory in Desegregated Schools." *Journal of Social Issues, 41*, 45–62.

Spear, A. (1967). *Black Chicago*. Chicago: University of Chicago Press.

St. John, N. (1975). *School Desegregation: Outcomes for Children*. New York: John Wiley.

Stephan, W. (1978). "School Desegregation: An Evaluation of Predictions Made in *Brown v. Board of Education*." *Psychological Bulletin, 85*, 217–238.

Trent, W., and McPartland, J. (1981). "Race Comparisons of Student Course Enrollment and Extracurricular Membership in Segregated and Desegregated High Schools." Paper presented at American Education Research Association meeting, Los Angeles.

Whyte, W. F. (1955). *Street Corner Society*. Chicago: University of Chicago Press.

Wilner, D. M., Walkley, R. P., and Cook, S. W. (1952). "Residential Proximity and Intergroup Relations in Public Housing Projects." *Journal of Social Issues, 8*, 45–69.

Wilson, W. J. (1987). *The Truly Disadvantaged*. Chicago: University of Chicago Press.

## Chapter Ten

# Promoting Positive Intergroup Relations in School Settings

## Janet Ward Schofield

Two facts undergird the vital importance of improving intergroup relations between children and youth from different racial and ethnic backgrounds. First, there is clear evidence from a wide variety of situations—ranging from conflict between youth gangs of different backgrounds to racial incidents on college campuses that, despite the marked improvement in many aspects of intergroup relations in the United States since the 1950s, serious problems still exist (Hurtado, 1992; Jaynes and Williams, 1989; Levin and McDevitt, 1993; Magner, 1989). Second, demographic trends make it clear that minority-group members are becoming an increasingly large proportion of the U.S. population (De Witt, 1991; O'Hara, 1993). Thus, the patterns of prejudice and discrimination that persist will exact a larger and larger social and economic toll, both in terms of the number of minority-group members affected and in terms of the

This paper was published in J. A. Banks and C. A. McGee Banks (eds.), *Handbook of multicultural education*. New York: Macmillan, 1995. A section of this paper originally appeared in J. W. Schofield, Promoting positive peer relations in desegregated schools, *Educational Policy, 7*(3), 297–317, copyright 1993 by Corwin Press. It is reprinted with permission from Corwin Press, Inc.

loss of their potential contribution to the broader society. Furthermore, the potential for increased political power inherent in these growing numbers makes it likely that minority-group members will be able to pursue their interests more effectively than has been the case in the past. While this outcome may well have many benefits, it could also exacerbate tensions as majority-group members are confronted with new realities. Thus, the question of how to build and maintain positive relations among the increasingly diverse racial and ethnic groups in the United States is one of major importance and will remain so in the foreseeable future.

Because of the pervasive residential segregation in our society (Farley and Allen, 1987; Jaynes and Williams, 1989), it is in school that children frequently have their first relatively close and extended opportunity for contact with those from different racial or ethnic backgrounds. Hence, whether hostility and stereotyping grow or diminish may be critically influenced by the particular experiences children have there. Accordingly, this chapter focuses on an exploration of policies and practices that are conducive to improving intergroup relations in school settings.

A good deal of what we know about intergroup relations in these settings stems from research in the late 1970s and early 1980s (Gerard and Miller, 1975; Hawley and others, 1983; Hewstone and Brown, 1986; Patchen, 1982; Prager, Longshore, and Seeman, 1986; Rist, 1979; Schofield, 1982/1989). Although there is much to be learned from this body of work, three important limitations must be acknowledged. First, this research is largely correlational in nature, thus leaving open the question of the causal direction of any empirical links found between school policies and student outcomes (Schofield, 1991). Second, as this work is a decade or two old, it tends to focus exclusively on the improvement of relations between whites and African Americans rather than on the more multifaceted situations that are common today. And, third, this work fails to reflect whatever generational changes in intergroup attitudes and behavior have occurred in the past ten to twenty years (for a discussion of these changes, see Jaynes and Williams, 1989). Nonetheless, since this latter time period has witnessed relatively little research focusing directly on the policies and practices that are likely to improve intergroup relations among children (with the notable exception of research relating to cooperative team learning, which is discussed in Chapter 11 of this volume), I rely heavily on this early body of work in the following discussion.

## Matching the Approach to Improving Intergroup Relations with the Current State of Such Relations

Before discussing what is known about improving intergroup relations in school contexts, I must make some conceptual distinctions since the strategies that are likely to be effective in meeting this goal vary on the basis of numerous factors. The first of these factors is the current state of relations between the groups in question. Clearly, those strategies that might work well in situations involving a degree of tension and hostility but no overt conflict are quite different from those that would be needed if two or more groups are engaged in or on the verge of intense conflict. Second, it is important to distinguish between approaches that emphasize ongoing structural features of the school situation and those that emphasize specially developed programs or other kinds of potentially valuable but circumscribed "human relations" interventions such as special-assembly programs. Third, the goal of reducing negative intergroup attitudes and behaviors and the goal of increasing positive intergroup attitudes and behaviors are far from identical. Indeed, studies by both Patchen (1982) and Schofield (1982/1989) suggest that quite different factors may be related to change in the amount of positive and negative intergroup behavior that occurs. As a simple example, consider that one can stop a fight by physically separating the combatants, thus at least temporarily eliminating the negative behavior. But of course such an action in and of itself does not foster positive attitudes or behaviors between members of the two groups involved.

In short, my goal in this chapter is to review strategies aimed at fostering positive relations and inhibiting negative relations between members of different racial and ethnic groups in situations where intergroup isolation and/or tensions exist although they have not precipitated major conflict. This state of affairs characterizes many of our racially and ethnically mixed schools. I have decided to consider primarily ongoing structural factors and policies rather than the design of specific "human relations" modules for insertion into the curriculum because I believe that attention to pervasive everyday policies and practices is likely to have a greater impact on intergroup relations than a focus on more limited special-purpose interventions. However, this is not to say that the latter effort would be fruitless. Quite to the contrary, recent work in social psychology and other fields provides a rich basis for assessing how such efforts might best be structured (Brewer and Kramer, 1985; Deutsch, 1993; Devine, Monteith, Zuwerink, and Elliot, 1991; Dovidio and Gaertner, 1991; Eurich-Fulcer and Schofield, 1995; Linville, Salovey, and Fischer, 1986; Park, Judd, and Ryan, 1991; Pruitt and Carnevale, 1993).

## Resegregation: A Common Barrier to Improved Intergroup Relations

The first question to ask about intergroup relations in any racially or ethnically mixed setting concerns the extent to which there is any kind of meaningful intergroup contact. This matter is especially challenging in situations involving youth whose native tongues are different. It is perfectly possible for a school or other setting with a rather diverse ethnic and racial makeup to be one in which individuals from the various groups have little or no contact with each other. Such resegregation can be extreme. For example, in one racially mixed school, a student remarked to a researcher, "All the segregation in this city was put in this school," reflecting the fact that although students from different backgrounds attended that school, they had little contact with each other (Collins and Noblit, 1978, p. 195). So it is important to be very aware of the possibility of "resegregation" and to plan actively to avoid or minimize it.

How does this resegregation occur? It is clear from research conducted in schools that a number of common educational practices lead, often inadvertently, to resegregation within desegregated schools. The most obvious and widespread of these are practices designed to reduce academic heterogeneity within classrooms. A host of social and economic factors contribute to the fact that minority-group students in desegregated schools tend to perform less well academically than their white peers. Thus, schools that categorize students on the basis of standardized tests, grades, or related criteria tend to have resegregated classrooms (Epstein, 1985).

Although much resegregation in schools stems from policies such as streaming or ability grouping, it is undeniable that children often voluntarily resegregate themselves in a variety of situations, from eating lunch in the school cafeteria to choosing playmates in their neighborhood. The extent of such voluntary resegregation is sometimes remarkable. For example, one set of studies of seating patterns in the cafeteria of a school whose student body was almost precisely half African American and half white, found that on a typical day only about 5 percent of the students sat next to someone of the other race (Schofield, 1979; Schofield and Sagar, 1977). This was so in spite of the fact that there was little overt racial friction. Other studies have reported similarly marked cleavage by race (Cusick and Ayling, 1973; Gerard, Jackson, and Conolley, 1975; Rogers, Hennigan, Bowman, and Miller, 1984).

On the one hand, there is nothing inherently deleterious to intergroup relations about a situation in which children who share particular interests, values, or backgrounds associate with each other to achieve valued ends. On the other hand, to the extent that grouping by race or ethnic group stems from fear, hostility, and discomfort, it is incompatible with the goal of breaking down barriers between groups and improving intergroup relations. As Stephan and Stephan's (1985) work suggests, anxiety about dealing with outgroup members is prevalent and can direct behavior in unconstructive ways. Other studies as well (Schofield, 1982/1989; Scherer and Slawski, 1979) point to numerous ways in which such anxiety can cause problems, including resegregation, in desegregated schools.

The very real importance of avoiding a pattern of resegregation, whether it stems from formal institutional policies or informal behavior patterns, is made clear by the theoretical and empirical work of many social psychologists (Pettigrew, 1969; Schofield, 1983,

1982/1989). As just one example, consider the body of work which suggests that when individuals are divided into groups they tend to favor the ingroup and discriminate against the outgroup, even when these groups have no previous history of antipathy (Doise, 1978; Tajfel, 1978; Tajfel and Turner, 1979). Thus, if racially or ethnically homogeneous groups are created through school policies that reseg-regate students, already-existing tendencies toward stereotyping and discrimination are likely to be magnified.

Thus great care should be taken not only to avoid institutional policies that lead to resegregation but also to adopt policies that may undercut children's tendency to cluster in racially homogeneous groups out of fear or uncertainty. Of course, the particular policies employed to discourage such resegregation would have to depend on the particular situation at hand. However, there are policies and practices that undercut resegregation, that can be very easily imple-mented. For example, teachers can assign seats in a way that creates substantial potential for interracial contact rather than letting stu-dents resegregate themselves. Specifically, teachers can assign seats on the basis of the alphabetical order of students' names rather than letting students select their own seats and then reinforcing the stu-dent's self-segregation with a seating chart (Schofield, 1982/1989). Furthermore, research shows that something as simple as occasion-ally changing assigned seats increases the number of friends students are likely to make during the school year (Byrne, 1961).

Another policy that can help to avoid resegregation is conscious planning to encourage both minority- and majority-group students to participate in extracurricular activities. Sometimes afterschool activities become the province of one or the other of these groups, such that one group participates in all or most activities and mem-bers of the other groups hardly participate at all. Another perhaps more common pattern is for particular activities to become associ-ated with students from a particular background such that, although all groups of students participate in some activities, there are few activities in which students from different backgrounds participate jointly (Collins, 1979; Gottlieb and TenHouten, 1965; Scherer and Slawski, 1979; Sullivan, 1979).

Again, appropriate strategies for preventing such outcomes clearly depend on the specific situation. But policies that really help can often be adopted. For example, if one group of students does not participate because its members live far away and transportation poses a problem, arrangements for transportation can be considered. Similarly, if the adult sponsors of school- or neighborhood-based clubs take clear steps to encourage both minority- and majority-group students to participate before the issue of whether this activity "belongs" to one group or the other emerges, these sponsors will be much more likely to succeed in encouraging a diverse membership than if they wait until the resegregation is complete and well known among the students.

A certain amount of resegregation may be an inevitable consequence of policies designed to advance important goals. For example, it is often hard to provide a desegregated education for children for whom English is not a first language without encountering a certain amount of resegregation, although constructive ways to deal with this complex situation have been suggested (California State Department of Education, 1983; Carter, 1979; Carter and Chatfield, 1986; Cazabon, Lambert, and Hall, 1993; Fernandez and Guskin, 1978; Garcia, 1976; Gonzalez, 1979; Haro, 1977; Heleen, 1987; Milan, 1978; National Institute of Education, 1977; Roos, 1978). Similarly, despite some recent movement away from the traditional ready acceptance of tracking policies on the part of policy makers and educators (Carnegie Council on Adolescent Development, 1989; National Governors' Association, 1990), many difficult pedagogical and political issues remain to be resolved about how best to serve students in classrooms in which skill levels vary widely (Oakes, 1992). In addition, certain extracurricular activities, such as gospel choirs or golf teams, are likely to be both highly valued by some parts of the community and more attractive to certain students than to others. Nevertheless, any examination of the functioning of a social environment encompassing children of very diverse racial or ethnic backgrounds needs to address the issue of resegregation, whether it has resulted from formal policies or from the choices of the children themselves. Indeed, it must devote serious attention to the question of how resegregation, if found, can be eliminated or at least reduced.

## Conditions Conducive to Improving Intergroup Relations

It is important to recognize that the mere absence of resegregation is not enough to create a set of experiences that fosters constructive rather than neutral or destructive relations between children from different backgrounds. The quality of those relations is the crucial factor, as Pettigrew (1969) points out in making his classic distinction between mere *desegregation*, which refers to the existence of a racially mixed environment, and true *integration*, which refers to the creation of a setting conducive to the development of positive relations between members of different groups.

If there is one thing that social psychological theory and research have taught us about racially and ethnically diverse environments during the last forty years, it is that simply putting children from different backgrounds together is not enough to ensure positive social outcomes (Allport, 1954; Cohen, 1972; Eddy, 1975; Orfield, 1975; Rist, 1979; Schofield, 1983). There are a great many actions that schools and other institutions serving diverse clienteles can take to promote positive intergroup relations and minimize intergroup conflict (Chesler, Bryant, and Crowfoot, 1981; Cohen, 1980; Crowfoot and Chesler, 1981; Epstein, 1985; Forehand and Ragosta, 1976; Forehand, Ragosta, and Rock, 1976; Hallinan, 1982; Hallinan and Smith, 1985; Hallinan and Teixeira, 1987; Hawley and others, 1983; McConahay, 1981; Mercer, Iadicola, and Moore, 1980; Miller, 1980; Patchen, 1982; Sagar and Schofield, 1984; Slavin and Madden, 1979; Wellisch, Carriere, MacQueen, and Duck, 1977; Wellisch, Marcus, MacQueen, and Duck, 1976). Precisely which specific practices are suitable depends on such factors as the children's ages, the institution's racial and ethnic mix, the degree to which minority and majority status are related to socioeconomic background, and so on. But since space limitations preclude a separate analysis of each of these myriad possibilities, I restrict my discussion to what theory and research suggest about the general underlying conditions that are conducive to building and maintaining positive intergroup relations.

The most influential social psychological perspective on the conditions conducive to these positive outcomes is called the "contact hypothesis." Since 1954, when Allport first proposed it, this approach has stimulated a great deal of research that, generally speaking, supports its basic elements. (A volume that reviews, extends upon, and revises this theory is Hewstone and Brown, 1986.) Basically, Allport argues that three aspects of the contact situation are particularly important in determining whether positive intergroup relations develop—namely, the existence of equal status within the situation for members of all groups; an emphasis on cooperative rather than competitive activities; and explicit support, expressed by relevant authority figures, for positive relations. In the sections that follow, I discuss each of these factors and illustrate briefly the types of policies and procedures that flow from them.

## Equal Status

First, Allport (1954) notes that the contact situation must be structured in such a way that equal status is given to both groups. If this is not done, he argues, then existing stereotypes and beliefs about the superiority or inferiority of the groups involved and the hostility engendered by these stereotypes will likely persist. Although other theorists have argued that equal status is not absolutely essential for improving intergroup relations, they generally see it as quite helpful (Amir, 1969; Riordan, 1978). In a school, as in most organizations, the various positions that need to be filled are ordered on the basis of a status hierarchy. Those on top, such as the superintendent at the system level or the principal at the school level, have more power and prestige than those who serve under them. Allport's argument suggests that, when the various positions in the organization

are filled, it is important that individuals from all groups are distributed throughout the status hierarchy rather than being concentrated
at a particular level. For example, one could hardly claim that major-
ity- and minority-group members have equal status in a school if
almost all the administrators and faculty are majority-group members and the teachers' aides are minority-group members.

Even if a school does its best to see that the formal status of
minority- and majority-group members is equal, the members
of the two groups are likely to have very different status outside of
that setting. This disparity can create real difficulties for achieving equal status within the setting. For example, given the sizable
and stubborn link between social class and academic achievement,
it is probable that unequal status outside of the school will translate into unequal distribution of students into academic tracks.
Even if the school administration recognizes this problem and
decides to avoid formalizing such group differences by eschewing
tracking, students' performance levels may still differ in ways
that affect their informal status both within the school and in their
peer groups.

It's not easy to find effective ways to prevent the unequal status
of majority- and minority-group members in the larger society from
creating unequal status within the school. However, concerted
efforts to achieve equal status within the contact situation do
appear to make a difference. For example, much has been written
about the way in which textbooks and other curriculum components have either ignored or demeaned the experiences and contributions of minority-group members (National Alliance of Black
School Educators, Inc., 1984; McAdoo and McAdoo, 1985; Oakes,
1985). Use of such materials is hardly conducive to an equal-status
environment. Although there are many barriers to remedying this
situation (Boateng, 1990), constructive change *is* possible. For example, Stephan and Stephan's review (1984) of the research conducted on multiethnic curriculum components concludes that a
substantial, if methodologically flawed, set of studies generally suggests that multiethnic curricula have a positive impact on inter-

group relations, at least when the program elements are of reasonable complexity and duration.

A very controversial issue relating to both equal status and resegregation is the issue of grouping students based on their academic performance. As mentioned previously, when desegregated schools group students on the basis of test scores, they often end up with heavily white high-status accelerated groups and heavily minority lower-status regular groups. In other words, the students are not only resegregated: they are resegregated in a way that can reinforce traditional stereotypes and engender hostility. Tracking is often instituted or emphasized in schools with heterogeneous student bodies as a mechanism for coping with that diversity. However, studies comparing tracked versus untracked schools have not yielded any consistent support for the idea that tracking generally benefits students academically (Oakes, 1992). Furthermore, there is reason to believe that it may sometimes undermine the achievement and motivation of students in the lower tracks and have a negative effect on intergroup relations (Collins and Noblit, 1978; Epstein, 1985; National Opinion Research Center, 1973; Oakes, 1992; Schofield and Sagar, 1977; Schofield, 1979). Epstein's study (1985) of grouping practices in desegregated elementary schools concludes that there is a clear positive link between equal-status programs (for example, programs that emphasize the equality and importance of both black and white students and avoid inflexible academically based grouping) and higher achievement for African American students. Furthermore, equal-status programs were found to positively influence both white and black students' attitudes toward desegregated schooling.

Although tracking is one of the most visible ways in which status differentials from outside the school get reinforced and formalized inside the school, there are myriad other ways in which this happens. Sensitivity to this issue can suggest seemingly minor, yet worthwhile, changes in practice that minimize the likelihood of this outcome. For example, schools can supplement the traditional practice of honoring students whose absolute level of achievement is outstanding with the practice of honoring students who have shown unusually large amounts of improvement in their academic performance. In this way, academic values are not only reinforced but also become more inclusive.

Such practices are trivial in some respects. Yet students often are very sensitive to these matters. For example, Schofield (1982/ 1989) reports an incident in which a racially mixed classroom of sixth-graders was shown a televised quiz show in which a team of students from their school competed against a team from another school. A usually well-behaved African American child refused to watch. Later, he explained that he did not want to see the program because the team from his school, which had a student body that was just over half black, consisted entirely of white children. He said bitterly, "They shouldn't call this school Wexler [a pseudonym]; they should call it White School."

## Cooperative Interdependence

Allport (1954) also argues that it is important that the activities occurring in the contact situation are cooperative rather than competitive. Cooperation is important for two reasons. First, given that discrimination is both a historical fact and a present reality in many spheres of life, the results of competition will frequently support traditional stereotypes. In addition, considerable research suggests that competition between groups can lead to stereotyping, to unwarranted devaluation of the other groups' accomplishments, and to marked hostility even when the groups initially have no history that might predispose them toward negative reactions to each other (Sherif and others, 1961; Worchel, 1979). It is reasonable to expect that this tendency for intergroup competition to lead to hostility and negative beliefs would be reinforced when the groups involved have a history that makes initial hostility or at least suspicion likely.

Both theory and research suggest that the type of cooperation most likely to lead to the reduction of intergroup tensions or hostility is cooperation toward achieving a shared goal that cannot be accomplished without the contribution of members of all groups (Bossert, 1988/1989; Sherif and others, 1961; Johnson and Johnson, 1992). This conclusion brings to mind a rich variety of activities that might be appropriate in settings such as the Girl Scouts, Boy Scouts, and other youth-oriented social, athletic, or service clubs. In the school setting, examples of activities likely to foster this type of cooperation would be the production of a school play, team sports, and the like. The important feature of such activities is that each individual is able to make a contribution to a whole that he or she could not possibly achieve alone. Even though different people may contribute different skills, each individual is necessary to and interested in the final product.

Historically, U.S. schools have stressed competition. However, this orientation is neither inevitable nor unchangeable. First, with the advent both of self-paced instructional approaches and of research on mastery learning, there has been an increasing acceptance of the idea that children may benefit from working at their own pace. Second, in recent years more and more theorists have emphasized the importance of teaching children how to work cooperatively with others to achieve a joint end product (Aronson and Osherow, 1980; Bossert, 1988/1989; Cohen, 1984; Hertz-Lazarowitz and Miller, 1992; Johnson and Johnson, 1987; Johnson, Johnson, and Maruyama, 1984; Kagan, 1991; Sharan and Sharan, 1992; see also Chapter 11 in this volume). Certainly this trend is a sensible one, given the increasing bureaucratization and complexity of our society—a society in which individuals, as adults, are more and more likely to work with others as part of an organization rather than as individual craftspeople, farmers, or entrepreneurs.

The use of class committees and teams to create joint projects comes very close to being the type of cooperation toward shared goals that appears to be so important for improving intergroup relations. A large number of experiments using a variety of cooperative structures suggest that such teamwork does indeed have a positive impact. For example, DeVries and Edwards (1974) found that students who participated in racially mixed work groups that were rewarded for their performance as groups were more likely to help and to be helped by members of the other race than were students who received rewards for their individual efforts. They were also somewhat more likely to name a person of the other race as a friend after one month of teamwork, even though the teams met for less than an hour a day. A whole host of other researchers have found similar results in more recent experiments on the impact of cooperative work in the classroom (Aronson and others, 1978; Aronson and Gonzales, 1988; Bossert, 1988/1989; Cook, 1985; Johnson and Johnson, 1982; Johnson, Johnson, and Maruyama, 1984; Sharan, 1980; Slavin, 1983a, 1983b, 1985). One very important feature of such cooperative groups is that they appear to foster not only improved intergroup relations but positive academic consequences as well (Johnson and others, 1981).

Although cooperative activities in the classroom and in other settings such as youth clubs hold great potential for improving intergroup relations, such cooperation must be very carefully structured (Hertz-Lazarowitz, Kirkus, and Miller, 1992; Miller and Harrington, 1992; Slavin, 1992). Indeed, it is crucial that the young people involved contribute to the group efforts in ways that do not reinforce traditional modes of interaction between majority- and minority-group members. For example, Cohen (1972) has found that when white and African American children who are equally capable interact with each other in certain kinds of situations, the white students tend to be more active and influential even though there is no rational basis for their dominance. Only through a carefully planned program of activities, such as one in which the African American children teach their white peers new skills, does this tendency diminish or disappear (Cohen, Lockheed, and Lohman, 1976). Hence educators must constantly be aware of the need to find ways of ensuring that all children contribute to the group's final product, rather than assuming that the existence of a cooperative group in and of itself will motivate all children to contribute and to allow others to contribute to the group's work.

The precise dynamics through which cooperation leads to a positive effect on intergroup relations are far from fully understood (Bossert, 1988/1989), although considerable attention has been devoted to the issue (see Hertz-Lazarowitz and Miller, 1992). Some factors are nevertheless worth individual consideration; to these we now turn.

**Cross-Cutting Social Identities.** One suggestion that is frequently made in the literature on intergroup relations is that one can undermine the tendency of individuals to show bias toward outgroup members by creating "cross-cutting social categories" (Brewer and Miller, 1984; Deschamps and Doise, 1978; Levine and Campbell, 1972; Schofield and McGivern, 1979; Vanbeselaere, 1987). The idea here is that one can mitigate the importance of any given basis of social categorization, such as race or ethnicity, by creating or making salient other social categories that those who differ with regard to the first category have in common. For example, in a situation where both African American and white students are members of two cooperative learning teams, racial background and team membership are said to be cross-cut. That is, students from different racial backgrounds now share something with some members of the racial outgroup and simultaneously differ on some dimension from some members of the racial ingroup. Insofar as the social category that cross-cuts racial or ethnic background is valued and salient, it may well undermine the tendency to discriminate that is based on the latter.

This phenomenon not only helps to account for some of the positive effects of cooperative-learning groups; it also points to other avenues for improving intergroup relations. For example, it suggests that finding ways to create and emphasize meaningful and valued shared social-category memberships for youths of different racial and ethnic backgrounds (as members of a particular school or community) should be constructive. In fact, laboratory work by Gaertner and his colleagues (Gaertner and Dovidio, 1986; Gaertner, Mann, Murrell, and Dovidio, 1989) suggests that bias between two initially separate groups can be mitigated when they later function in a new situation that gives them a unified identity. Thus, it seems reasonable to expect that the creation of signs and symbols of *shared* identity (ranging from school T-shirts and traditions to special songs) should be helpful in improving intergroup relations.

*Personalization of Outgroup Members.* Cooperative activities by their very nature require individuals to work together, thus providing an opportunity for them to come to know each other in ways that might not otherwise occur. This potential for cooperative work to lead to relatively close personal relationships with members of outgroups is frequently cited as one of its advantages (Miller and Harrington, 1992). The development of such personal relations, and the accompanying tendency to increasingly see the outgroup members as individuals with their own particular set of personality traits, skills, and experiences, is potentially important for several reasons. First, it can lead to the discovery of unexpected similarity between the self and outgroup members—and, indeed, there is evidence that perceptions of similarity play a strong role in attraction to others (Byrne, 1971; Byrne and Nelson, 1965). Second, to the extent the outgroup members behave in ways that are contrary to stereotypes of that group's behavior, such stereotypes may be weakened. This process, however, is far from simple. Behaviors tend to be perceived in ways that are consistent with stereotypes (Sagar and Schofield, 1980), apparently because stereotypes lead to the biased processing of social information (Bodenhausen, 1988; Hamilton and Trolier, 1986; Greenberg and Pyszczynski, 1985). Individuals may perceive those who act in ways unexpected for their group as "exceptions" whose existence does not challenge the validity of the basic stereotypes in question (Brewer, 1988; Hewstone, Hopkins, and Routh, 1992; Johnston and Hewstone, 1992; Taylor, 1981). Third, and perhaps most important, ongoing experience with several members of the outgroup may help to undermine the strong tendency to see outgroup members as relatively similar to each other, compared to ingroup members who are typically perceived to be much more varied (Judd and Park, 1988; Linville, Fischer, and Salovey, 1989). Recent work by Ryan, Judd, and Park (1993) demonstrates that a tendency to perceive outgroup members as quite homogeneous affects one's judgments of the characteristics of specific individuals belonging to that group in ways that are consistent with one's initial expectations. Thus, experiences that lead one to think of outgroup members as individuals who vary in many respects should be helpful in weakening stereotypes and lessening their impact on interactions with members of the outgroup.

Given the importance of increasing individuals' perceptions of similarity between ingroup and outgroup members, of exposing ingroup members to outgroup behavior that cannot be construed in a stereotypic fashion, and of expanding awareness of the individual variability of outgroup members, a number of potentially useful strategies can be recommended in addition to cooperative groups. Many of these strategies are embodied in "human relations" training programs or in attempts to produce multicultural curricula. Although there is little definitive evidence about the effectiveness of such approaches, fragmentary evidence suggests that they sometimes have weak positive effects on intergroup relations (Hawley and others, 1983; Longshore and Wellisch, 1982; Stephan and Stephan, 1984). The limited nature of many of these efforts, including the fact that they are often quick "one shot" attempts to create change, may help to account for their lack of strong impact. However, it is also likely that more specific attention to lessons drawn from the social psychological literature about the complexities of the process of attitude and behavior change would be fruitful.

*Creating Affectively Positive Environments.* One consequence of cooperation to achieve valued goals that would not otherwise be obtainable is the creation of a positive atmosphere when that goal has been accomplished. The importance of this factor is highlighted by the experimental work of Worchel, Andreoli, and Folger (1977), which demonstrates that for groups with a history of competition and conflict, successful cooperation increases intergroup attraction whereas cooperation that has led to failure decreases liking for outgroup members. Positive emotions caused by a wide variety of events have been demonstrated to lead to increased liking for others (Veitch and Griffitt, 1976; Griffitt, 1970; Gouaux, 1971) as well as to increased interaction with and disclosure about the self to previously unknown others (Cunningham, 1988; Clark and Watson, 1988). In a parallel fashion, negative emotions have been shown to lead to liking others less, to perceiving them as more different, and evaluating them negatively (May and Hamilton, 1980; Shapiro, 1988; Swallow and Kuiper, 1987). Patchen's finding (1982) that African American students who were generally satisfied with their life circumstances reported more positive change in intergroup attitudes in racially mixed high schools than others suggests that such processes may indeed operate in desegregated settings. Thus, by discovering ways to increase the enjoyment of situations in which different groups encounter each other, educators may well contribute to improved intergroup relations.

## Support of Authorities for Positive Relations

Finally, Allport (1954) suggests that the support of authority, law, and custom for positive equal-status relationships between members of all groups is vital to producing constructive change in intergroup attitudes and behavior as a result of intergroup contact. Certainly, a court ruling that requires desegregation (or a decision on the part of a school system to desegregate) is a very important sign of government authorities' support for this policy. However, in and of themselves, such events are not nearly enough. For schoolchildren, probably the most relevant authorities are their school's principal, their teachers, and their parents. Religious leaders can also be important authorities for some children. In addition, as children move from their early years into adolescence, their peers become increasingly important arbiters of opinion and exert a more and more potent influence on their behavior. Thus, although Allport clearly did not mean to include peers in his definition of "authorities," it seems sensible to point out that a potentially powerful approach lies in finding ways to mobilize the peer group to support positive intergroup relations. Blanchard, Lilly, and Vaughn's (1991) work, which shows that peers influence each others' expressions of racist opinions, demonstrates this point. Similarly, Patchen's finding (1982) that individuals' avoidance of outgroup members is clearly related to negative racial attitudes among their same-race peers suggests that concerns about peer disapproval of intergroup contact can contribute to resegregation.

In school settings, the importance of the principal as an authority who can facilitate improved intergroup relations can hardly be overemphasized (Orfield, 1975). Through their actions toward teachers, students, and parents, principals can influence the course that desegregation takes. Principals play at least four important roles in influencing the outcomes of desegregation. First, they can serve an enabling function; that is, they make choices that facilitate or impede practices that promote positive intergroup relations. For example, the principal can play an important role by encouraging teachers to adopt cooperative-learning techniques or by creating multiethnic committees designed to identify and solve problems before they turn into polarizing crises. Second, principals can serve a modeling function. It is clear that many people tend to emulate authority—and, indeed, the principal sets a model of behavior for teachers and students. There is no guarantee that others will follow this model, but its existence is certainly helpful. Third, principals can serve a sensitizing function. The principal is in a good position to argue for the importance of paying attention to the quality of intergroup relations and of placing this matter high on the school's list of priorities. Finally, of course, principals can serve a sanctioning function by actively rewarding positive practices and behaviors and discouraging negative ones. The prevention of negative intergroup behaviors is an issue of utmost importance, since negative incidents can spark similar behaviors in an escalating spiral. Research demonstrates that one of the strongest predictors of unfriendly intergroup contact for both white and African American students is the student's general aggressiveness (Patchen, 1982), thus highlighting the importance of the principal's role in creating a well-ordered environment in which aggressive behavior of any sort is minimized.

Teachers are also vital authority figures in the school. They, too, can facilitate or impede the development of positive relations at the classroom level through the processes of enabling, modeling, sensitizing, and sanctioning. For example, with regard to enabling, teachers often have it within their power to create conditions likely to improve intergroup relations between students. Epstein's research (1985) demonstrates that teachers with positive attitudes toward desegregation tend to use equal-status instructional programs more than others, and that students in such classrooms have more positive attitudes toward desegregation than peers in classrooms not using such approaches. Similarly, teachers with negative attitudes are more likely to use within-class ability grouping. Teachers, like principals, can also model respect for and equitable treatment of both ingroup and outgroup members. The importance of teachers' attitudes and behaviors is made clear in Patchen's work (1982), which found a clear relation between negative intergroup attitudes on the part of teachers and white students' tendency to avoid their African American classmates.

With regard to sanctioning, teachers and others in authority can foster positive intergroup relations by clearly articulating their expectation that children will respect each others' rights and by backing up this expectation with disciplinary measures. It is especially important that they make their expectation clear from the very beginning, so that children know they cannot violate others' rights with impunity. If this expectation of harmony and respect is not made clear initially, children are more likely to test the limits of the system and to feel that they are being treated unfairly when held accountable for their behavior.

One important way in which authorities such as principals and teachers can foster the development of positive relations through sensitizing is to be aware that individuals in a desegregated school may misunderstand each others' motives or intentions, either because of cultural differences or because of fears and uncertainties about outgroup members (Sagar and Schofield, 1980; Schofield, 1982/1989). Such awareness can indeed help in dealing with problems that arise.

Parents, too, are vital authority figures for most children, especially young ones. This is made clear by Patchen's finding (1982) that negative parental attitudes are likely to be associated with intergroup avoidance and unfriendly intergroup encounters, whereas positive parental attitudes are associated with friendly intergroup contact. Thus, it is important that educators find ways to encourage parents to involve their children in racially or ethnically diverse settings and to play a constructive role in encouraging positive intergroup contact. In the context of desegregated schools, they can employ practices such as involving parents early in the planning process, creating school and community-wide multiethnic committees that involve parents along with teachers and students, and providing information and opportunities for contact with the school (Hawley et al., 1983). Indeed, a study by Doherty and his colleagues (1981) suggests that parental involvement in school activities can create more positive attitudes toward majority-group members on the part of minority-group students. With respect to both school and nonschool activities, it seems reasonable to expect that issues relating to their children's safety will be very salient to parents, especially in communities where racial tensions are high. Thus, both practices that promote safety *and* information about these practices are useful in encouraging broad participation.

It is common for principals, teachers, and other authority figures involved with racially or ethnically diverse settings to feel that the best and fairest thing they can do is to adopt a viewpoint called the "color-blind" perspective (Rist, 1974). To be color-blind is to see racial and ethnic group membership as irrelevant to the way individuals are treated. From this perspective, taking cognizance of such group membership in decision making is seen as illegitimate and likely to lead to discrimination against minority-group members or reverse-discrimination. Two factors make serious consideration of the color-blind perspective worthwhile. On the one hand, it is widely endorsed as a desirable approach in institutions as diverse as the school system and the judicial system. On the other, although it is appealing in many respects—and consistent with the long-standing American emphasis on the importance of the individual—it easily leads to a misrepresentation of reality in ways that actually encourage discrimination against minority-group members. Accordingly, I now turn to a consideration of certain consequences of this perspective.

As noted, the color-blind perspective has some positive effects. It can reduce, at least in the short term, the potential for overt racial or ethnic conflict by generally deemphasizing the salience of race and encouraging the even-handed application of rules to all students (Miller and Harrington, 1992). It can also reduce the potential for discomfort or embarrassment in racially or ethnically mixed schools by vigorously asserting that race does not matter.

However, this perspective also has a number of potentially negative effects. The most important of these stems from the fact that the decision to try to ignore group membership, to act as if no one notices or should notice race or ethnicity, may lead to the unthinking acceptance of policies that are disadvantageous to minority groups (Schofield, 1986). For example, disproportionate suspension rates for minority students may fail to be seen as a sign of the need to examine discipline policies if school faculty and staff think of students only as individuals rather than facing the difficult issue of whether the school may be treating certain categories of students differently than others. Similarly, the color-blind perspective can readily lead to the adoption or tolerance of policies that lead to resegregation. Furthermore, this perspective makes it easy for a school to utilize textbooks and curricular materials that inadequately reflect the perspectives and contributions of minority- as well as majority-group members.

In raising questions about the color-blind perspective I am not arguing that it is desirable to constantly remind students of their group membership and continually emphasize group differences. On the contrary, both theory and experimental work suggest that practices which enhance the salience of such category memberships are bound to harm rather than to help intergroup relations (Brewer and Miller, 1984; Miller and Harrington, 1992). As just one example, consider the study by Miller, Brewer, and Edwards (1985), which found that when participants in cooperative groups believed that social-category membership was the basis for assignment, they were less likely to respond with favorable evaluations of the outgroup members than when they believed assignment to the groups was made on the basis of each individual's attitudes. Thus, the best course of action may be to encourage students to deal with each other as individuals while recognizing, in setting policies and making decisions, that attention to how various groups are faring is not only appropriate but likely to be constructive as well. The apparent contradiction here is mitigated by the fact that one thing likely to make group identities salient to students is the perception that their group is not being treated fairly in comparison to others. To the extent that group outcomes are equitable because attention has been paid to this issue in setting policies and making decisions, one very important source of polarization between members of different groups is lessened.

## Summary

In this chapter, I have discussed factors that theory and research in social psychology suggest are important in structuring racially and ethnically mixed environments so as to foster positive relations and minimize negative relations between different groups. First, it is important to avoid resegregation, which can occur either as a result of common school policies or as a result of students' negative attitudes toward members of other groups. However, avoiding resegregation is not enough. Policies and practices also need to be closely examined to ensure, to the extent possible, that they promote equal status and cooperative interdependence between minority- and majority-group members. Second, efforts to create cross-cutting group memberships and to heighten a sense of connection to superordinate group identities are likely to be beneficial, as are practices that encourage individuals to participate with outgroup members in enjoyable experiences conducive to getting to know each other as individuals. Finally, principals, teachers, and others in positions of authority can support the development of positive intergroup relations through such functions as enabling, modeling, sensitizing, and sanctioning. By recognizing that the improvement of intergroup relations is likely to require some attention to how groups as well as individuals are faring in a given setting, those in authority should be able to perform these functions effectively. However, in general, practices that heighten the salience of group membership should be avoided, unless they are the only means of making sure that other vital goals will be obtained.

# References

Allport, G. W. (1954). *The nature of prejudice*. Cambridge, Mass.: Addison-Wesley.

Amir, Y. (1969). Contact hypothesis in ethnic relations. *Psychological Bulletin*, 71(5), 319–342.

Aronson, E., and Gonzales, A. (1988). Desegregation, jigsaw, and the Mexican-American experience. In P. A. Katz and D. A. Taylor (eds.), *Eliminating racism: Profiles in controversy* (pp. 301–314). New York: Plenum Press.

Aronson, E., and Osherow, N. (1980). Cooperation, prosocial behavior, and academic performance: Experiments in the desegregated classroom. In L. Bickman (ed.), *Applied social psychology annual*, Vol. 1 (pp. 163–196). Beverly Hills, Calif.: Sage.

Aronson, E., and others. (1978). *The jigsaw classroom*. Beverly Hills, Calif.: Sage.

Blanchard, F. A., Lilly, T., and Vaughn, L. A. (1991). Reducing the expression of racial prejudice. *Psychological Science*, 2, 101–105.

Boateng, F. (1990). Combatting deculturalization of the African American child in the public school system: A multi-cultural approach. In K. Lomotey (ed.), *Going to school: The African American experience* (pp. 73–84). Albany: State University of New York Press.

Bodenhausen, G. V. (1988). Stereotypic biases in social decision making and memory: Testing process models of stereotype use. *Journal of Personality and Social Psychology, 55,* 726–737.

Bossert, S. T. (1988/1989). Cooperative activities in the classroom. In E. Z. Rothkopf (ed.), *Review of research in education,* Vol. 15 (pp. 225–250). Washington, D.C.: American Educational Research Association.

Brewer, M. B. (1988). A dual process model of impression formation. In T. Srull and R. Wyer (eds.), *Advances in social cognition,* Vol. 1 (pp. 1–36). Hillsdale, N.J.: Erlbaum.

Brewer, M. B., and Kramer, R. M. (1985). The psychology of intergroup attitudes and behavior. In M. R. Rosenzweig and L. W. Porter (eds.), *Annual review of psychology,* Vol. 36 (pp. 219–243). Palo Alto, Calif.: Annual Reviews, Inc.

Brewer, M. B., and Miller, N. (1984). Beyond the contact hypothesis: Theoretical perspectives on desegregation. In N. Miller and M. B. Brewer (eds.), *Groups in contact: The psychology of desegregation* (pp. 281–302). Orlando, Fla.: Academic Press.

Byrne, D. (1961). The influences of propinquity and opportunities for interaction on classroom relationships. *Human Relations, 14,* 63–69.

Byrne, D. (1971). *The attraction paradigm.* New York: Academic Press.

Byrne, D., and Nelson, D. (1965). Attraction as a linear function of proportion of positive reinforcements. *Journal of Personality and Social Psychology, 1,* 659–663.

California State Department of Education. (1983). *Desegregation and bilingual education—Partners in quality education.* Sacramento: California State Department of Education.

Carnegie Council on Adolescent Development. (1989). *Turning points: Preparing American youth for the 21st century.* Washington, D.C.: Carnegie Corporation of New York.

Carter, T. P. (1979). *Interface between bilingual education and desegregation: A study of Arizona and California.* Washington, D.C.: National Institute of Education (ERIC Document Reproduction Service No. ED 184 743).

Carter, T., and Chatfield, M. L. (1986). Effective bilingual schools: Implications for policy and practice. *American Journal of Education, 95,* 200–232.

Cazabon, M., Lambert, W. E., and Hall, G. (1993). *Two-way bilingual education: A progress report on the Amigos Program.* Santa Cruz, Calif.: National Center for Research on Cultural Diversity.

Chesler, M., Bryant, B., and Crowfoot, J. (1981). *Making desegregation work: A professional guide to effecting change.* Beverly Hills, Calif.: Sage.

Clark, L. A., and Watson, D. (1988). Mood and the mundane: Relations between daily life events and self-reported mood. *Journal of Personality and Social Psychology, 54,* 296–308.

Cohen, E. (1972). Interracial interaction disability. *Human Relations, 25,* 9–24.

Cohen, E. (1980). Design and redesign of the desegregated school: Problems of status, power, and conflict. In W. G. Stephan and J. R. Feagin (Eds.), *School desegregation: Past, present, and future* (pp. 251–278). New York: Plenum Press.

Cohen, E. (1984). The desegregated school: Problems in status power and interethnic climate. In N. Miller and M. B. Brewer (eds.), *Groups in contact: The psychology of desegregation* (pp. 77–96). Orlando, Fla.: Academic Press.

Cohen, E., Lockheed, M., and Lohman, M. (1976). The center for interracial cooperation: A field experiment. *Sociology of Education, 49,* 47–58.

Collins, T. W. (1979). From courtrooms to classrooms: Managing school desegregation in a Deep South high school. In R. C. Rist (ed.), *Desegregated schools: Appraisals of an American experiment* (pp. 89–114). New York: Academic Press.

Collins, T. W., and Noblit, G. W. (1978). *Stratification and resegregation: The case of Crossover High School, Memphis, Tennessee* (Final Report). Washington, D.C.: National Institute of Education.

Cook, S. W. (1985). Experimenting on social issues: The case of school desegregation. *American Psychologist, 40,* 452–460.

Crowfoot, J. E., and Chesler, M. A. (1981). Implementing "attractive ideas": Problems and prospects. In W. D. Hawley (ed.), *Effective school desegregation* (pp. 265–295). Beverly Hills, Calif.: Sage.

Cunningham, M. R. (1988). Does happiness mean friendliness? Induced mood and heterosexual self-disclosure. *Personality and Social Psychology Bulletin, 14,* 283–297.

Cusick, P., and Ayling, R. (1973, February). Racial interaction in an urban secondary school. Paper presented at the meeting of the American Educational Research Association, New Orleans.

Deschamps, J. C., and Doise, W. (1978). Crossed category membership in intergroup relations. In H. Tajfel (ed.), *Differentiation between social groups* (pp. 141–158). New York: Academic Press.

Deutsch, M. (1993). Educating for a peaceful world. *American Psychologist, 48*(5), 510–517.

Devine, P. G., Monteith, M. J., Zuwerink, J. R., and Elliot, A. J. (1991). Prejudice with and without compunction. *Journal of Personality and Social Psychology, 60*(6), 817–830.

DeVries, D. L., and Edwards, K. (1974). Student teams and learning games: Their effects on cross-race and cross-sex interaction. *Journal of Educational Psychology, 66,* 741–749.

De Witt, K. (1991). Large increase is predicted in minorities in U.S. schools. *New York Times* (Sept. 13), p. 14.

Doherty, W. J., Cadwell, J., Russo, N. A., Mandel, V., and Longshore, D. (1981). *Human relations study: Investigations of effective human relations strategies,* Vol. 2. Santa Monica, Calif.: System Development Corporation.

Doise, W. (1978). *Groups and individuals: Explanations in social psychology.* Cambridge, England: Cambridge University Press.

Dovidio, J. F., and Gaertner, S. L. (1991). Changes in the expression of racial prejudice. In H. Knopke, J. Norrell, and R. Rogers (eds.), *Opening doors: An appraisal of race relations in contemporary America* (pp. 119–148). Tuscaloosa: University of Alabama Press.

Eddy, E. (1975). Educational innovation and desegregation: A case study of symbolic realignment. *Human Organization, 34*(2), 163–172.

Epstein, J. L. (1985). After the bus arrives: Resegregation in desegregated schools. *Journal of Social Issues, 41*(3), 23–43.

Eurich-Fulcer, R., and Schofield, J. W. (1995). Correlated versus uncorrelated social categorizations: The effect on intergroup bias. *Personality and Social Psychology Bulletin, 21,* 147–157.

Farley, R., and Allen, W. (1987). *The color line and the quality of American life.* New York: Russell Sage Foundation.

Fernandez, R. R., and Guskin, J. T. (1978). Bilingual education and desegregation: A new dimension in legal and educational decision-making. In H. LaFontaine, B. Persky, and L. H. Glubshick (eds.), *Bilingual education* (pp. 58–66). Garden City Park, N.Y.: Avery Publishing.

Forehand, G. A., and Ragosta, M. (1976). *A handbook for integrated schooling.* Washington, D.C.: U.S. Department of Health, Education, and Welfare.

Forehand, G. A., Ragosta, M., and Rock, D. (1976). *Conditions and processes of effective school desegregation* (Final Report). Princeton, N.J.: Educational Testing Service.

Gaertner, S. L., and Dovidio, J. F. (1986). The aversive form of racism. In J. F. Dovidio and S. L. Gaertner (eds.), *Prejudice, discrimination, and racism* (pp. 61–89). New York: Academic Press.

Gaertner, S. L., Mann, J., Murrell, A., and Dovidio, J. F. (1989). Reducing intergroup bias: The benefits of recategorization. *Journal of Personality and Social Psychology, 57,* 239–249.

Garcia, G. F. (1976). The Latino and desegregation. *Integrated Education, 14,* 21–22.

Gerard, H., Jackson, D., and Conolley, E. (1975). Social context in the desegregated classroom. In H. Gerard and N. Miller (eds.), *School desegregation: A long-range study* (pp. 211–241). New York: Plenum Press.

Gerard, H. B., and Miller, N. (1975). *School desegregation.* New York: Plenum.

Gonzalez, J. M. (1979). *Bilingual education in the integrated school.* Arlington, Va.: National Clearinghouse for Bilingual Education.

Gottlieb, D., and TenHouten, W. D. (1965). Racial composition and the social systems of three high schools. *Journal of Marriage and the Family, 27,* 204–212.

Gouaux, C. (1971). Induced affective states and interpersonal attraction. *Journal of Personality and Social Psychology, 20,* 37–43.

Greenberg, J., and Pyszczynski, T. (1985). The self-serving attributional bias: Beyond self-presentation. *Journal of Experimental Social Psychology, 21,* 61–72.

Griffitt, W. (1970). Environmental effects on interpersonal affective behavior: Ambient effective temperature and attraction. *Journal of Personality and Social Psychology, 15,* 240–244.

Hallinan, M. T. (1982). Classroom racial composition and children's friendships. *Social Forces, 61*(1), 56–72.

Hallinan, M. T., and Smith, S. S. (1985). The effects of classroom racial composition on students' interracial friendliness. *Social Psychology Quarterly,* 48(1), 3–16.

Hallinan, M. T., and Teixeira, R. A. (1987). Students' interracial friendships: Individual characteristics, structural effects and racial differences. *American Journal of Education, 95,* 563–583.

Hamilton, D. L., and Trolier, T. K. (1986). Stereotypes and stereotyping: An overview of the cognitive approach. In J. F. Dovidio and S. L. Gaertner (eds.), *Prejudice, discrimination, and racism* (pp. 127–163). Orlando, Fla.: Academic Press.

Haro, C. M. (1977). Mexican/Chicano concerns and school desegregation in Los Angeles. Unpublished manuscript, University of California, Chicano Studies Center, Los Angeles.

Hawley, W., Crain, R. L., Rossell, C. H., Schofield, J. W., Fernandez, R., and Trent, W. P. (1983). *Strategies for effective desegregation: Lessons from research.* Lexington, Mass.: Lexington Books/D.C. Heath.

Heleen, O. (ed.). (1987). Two-way bilingual education: A strategy for equity. (Special issue.) *Equity and Choice, 3*(3).

Hertz-Lazarowitz, R., Kirkus, V. B., and Miller, N. (1992). Implications of current research on cooperative interaction for classroom application. In R. Hertz-Lazarowitz and N. Miller (eds.), *Interaction in cooperative groups* (pp. 253–280). Cambridge, England: Cambridge University Press.

Hertz-Lazarowitz, R., and Miller, N. (eds.). (1992). *Interaction in cooperative groups.* Cambridge, England: Cambridge University Press.

Hewstone, M., and Brown, R. (eds.). (1986). *Contact and conflict in encounters.* Oxford, England: Basil Blackwell Ltd.

Hewstone, M., Hopkins, N., and Routh, D. A. (1992). Cognitive models of stereotype change: Generalization and subtyping in young people's views of the police. *European Journal of Social Psychology, 22,* 219–234.

Hurtado, S. (1992). The campus racial climate: Contexts of conflict. *Journal of Higher Education, 63*(5), 539–569.

Jaynes, G. D., and Williams, R. M., Jr. (1989). *A common destiny: Blacks and American society.* Washington, D.C.: National Academy Press.

Johnson, D. W., and Johnson, R. T. (1982). The study of cooperative, competitive, and individualistic situations: State of the area and two recent con-tributions. *Contemporary Education, 1*(1), 7–13.

Johnson, D. W., and Johnson, R. T. (1987). *Learning together and alone*, 2nd ed. Englewood Cliffs, N.J.: Prentice-Hall.

Johnson, D. W., and Johnson, R. T. (1992). Positive interdependence: Key to effective cooperation. In R. Hertz-Lazarowitz and N. Miller (eds.), *Interaction in cooperative groups* (pp. 174–199). Cambridge, England: Cambridge University Press.

Johnson, D. W., Johnson, R. T., and Maruyama, G. (1984). Goal interdependence and interpersonal attraction in heterogeneous classrooms: A meta-analy-sis. In N. Miller and M. B. Brewer (eds.), *Groups in contact: The psychol-ogy of desegregation* (pp. 187–212). Orlando, Fla.: Academic Press.

Johnson, D. W., and others. (1981). Effects of cooperative, competitive, and indi-vidualistic goal structures on achievement: A meta-analysis. *Psycholog-ical Bulletin, 89*, 47–62.

Johnston, L., and Hewstone, M. (1992). Cognitive models of stereotype change: Subtyping and the perceived typicality of disconfirming group mem-bers. *Journal of Experimental Social Psychology, 28*(4), 360–386.

Judd, C. M., and Park, B. (1988). Outgroup homogeneity: Judgments of vari-ability at the individual and group levels. *Journal of Personality and Social Psychology, 54*, 778–788.

Kagan, S. (1991). *Cooperative learning resources for teachers*, 4th ed. San Juan Capistrano, Calif.: Resources for Teachers.

Levin, J., and McDevitt, J. (1993). *Hate crimes: The rising tide of bigotry and blood-shed*. New York: Plenum Press.

Levine, R. A., and Campbell, D. T. (1972). *Ethnocentrism: Theories in conflict, ethnic attitudes, and group behavior*. New York: John Wiley & Sons.

Linville, P. W., Fischer, G. W., and Salovey, P. (1989). Perceived distributions of characteristics of ingroup and outgroup members: Empirical evidence and a computer simulation. *Journal of Personality and Social Psychology, 57*, 165–188.

Linville, P. W., Salovey, P., and Fischer, G. W. (1986). Stereotyping and perceived distributions of social characteristics: An application to ingroup-outgroup perception. In J. Dovidio and S. L. Gaertner (eds.), *Prejudice, discrimination, and racism* (pp. 165–208). New York: Academic Press.

Longshore, D., and Wellisch, J. B. (1982). Human relations programs in deseg-regated elementary schools. *Evaluation Review, 6*, 789–799.

McAdoo, H. P., and McAdoo, J. W. (eds.). (1985). *Black children: Social, educa-tional and parental environments*. Beverly Hills, Calif.: Sage.

McConahay, J. (1981). Reducing racial prejudice in desegregated schools. In W. D. Hawley (ed.), *Effective school desegregation* (pp. 35–53). Beverly Hills, Calif.: Sage.

Magner, D. K. (1989). Blacks and whites on the campuses: Behind ugly racist incidents, student isolation and insensitivity. *Chronicle of Higher Edu-cation* (April 26), pp. 1, 28–31.

May, J. L., and Hamilton, P. A. (1980). Effects of musically evoked affect on women's interpersonal attraction and perceptual judgments of physical attractiveness of men. *Motivation and Emotion*, *4*, 217–228.

Mercer, J. R., Iadicola, P., and Moore, H. (1980). Building effective multiethnic schools: Evolving models and paradigms. In W. G. Stephan and J. R. Feagin (eds.), *School desegregation: Past, present, and future* (pp. 281–307). New York: Plenum Press.

Milan, W. G. (1978). *Toward a comprehensive language policy for a desegregated school system: Reassessing the future of bilingual education*. New York: Arawak Consulting Company.

Miller, N. (1980). Making school desegregation work. In W. G. Stephan and J. R. Feagin (eds.), *School desegregation: Past, present, and future* (pp. 309–348). New York: Plenum Press.

Miller, N., Brewer, M. B., and Edwards, K. (1985). Cooperative interaction in desegregated settings: A laboratory analogue. *Journal of Social Issues*, *41*(3), 63–79.

Miller, N., and Harrington, H. J. (1992). Social categorization and intergroup acceptance: Principles for the design and development of cooperative learning teams. In R. Hertz-Lazarowitz and N. Miller (eds.), *Interaction in cooperative groups* (pp. 203–227). Cambridge, England: Cambridge University Press.

National Alliance of Black School Educators, Inc. (1984). *Saving the African American child*. Washington, D.C.: National Alliance of Black School Educators, Inc.

National Governors' Association. (1990). *Educating America: State strategies for achieving the national educational goals*. Washington, D.C.: National Governors' Association.

National Institute of Education. (1977). *Desegregation and education concerns of the Hispanic community*. Washington, D.C.: U.S. Government Printing Office.

National Opinion Research Center. (1973). *Southern schools: An evaluation of the effects of the Emergency School Assistance Program and of school desegregation*, Vols. 1 and 2. Chicago: Author.

Oakes, J. (1985). *Keeping track: How schools structure inequality*. New Haven, Conn.: Yale University Press.

Oakes, J. (1992). Can tracking research inform practice? Technical, normative, and political considerations. *Educational Researcher*, *21*(4), 12–21.

O'Hara, W. T. (1993). America's minorities—The demographics of diversity. *Population Bulletin*, *47*(4), 1–48.

Orfield, G. (1975). How to make desegregation work: The adaptation of schools to their newly-integrated student bodies. *Law and Contemporary Problems*, *39*, 314–340.

Park, B., Judd, C. M., and Ryan, C. S. (1991). Social categorization and the representation of variability information. In W. Stroebe and M. Hewstone (eds.), *European review of social psychology*, Vol. 2 (pp. 211–245). Chichester, England: John Wiley.

Patchen, M. (1982). *Black-white contact in schools: Its social and academic effects.* West Lafayette, Ind.: Purdue University Press.

Pettigrew, T. (1969). The Negro and education: Problems and proposals. In I. Katz and P. Gurin (eds.), *Race and the social sciences* (pp. 49–112). New York: Basic Books.

Prager, J., Longshore, D., and Seeman, M. (eds.). (1986). *School desegregation research: New directions in situational analysis.* New York: Plenum Press.

Pruitt, D. G., and Carnevale, P. J. (1993). *Negotiation in social conflict.* Pacific Grove, Calif.: Brooks/Cole Publishing Company.

Riordan, C. (1978). Equal-status interracial contact: A review and revision of the concept. *International Journal of Intercultural Relations, 2*(2), 161–185.

Rist, R. C. (1974). Race, policy, and schooling. *Society, 12*(1), 59–63.

Rist, R. C. (ed.). (1979). *Desegregated schools: Appraisals of an American experiment.* New York: Academic Press.

Rogers, M., Hennigan, K., Bowman, C., and Miller, N. (1984). Intergroup acceptance in classrooms and playground settings. In N. Miller and M. B. Brewer (eds.), *Groups in contact: The psychology of desegregation* (pp. 213–227). New York: Academic Press.

Roos, P. D. (1978). Bilingual education: The Hispanic response to unequal educational opportunity. *Law and Contemporary Problems, 42,* 111–140.

Ryan, C. S., Judd, C. M., and Park, B. (1993). Effects of racial stereotypes on judgments of individuals: The moderating role of perceived group variability. Unpublished manuscript, University of Pittsburgh, Pittsburgh.

Sagar, H. A., and Schofield, J. W. (1980). Racial and behavioral cues in black and white children's perceptions of ambiguously aggressive acts. *Journal of Personality and Social Psychology, 39,* 590–598.

Sagar, H. A., and Schofield, J. W. (1984). Integrating the desegregated school: Problems and possibilities. In M. Maehr and D. Bartz (eds.), *Advances in motivation and achievement: A research manual* (pp. 203–242). Greenwich, Conn.: JAI Press.

Scherer, J., and Slawski, E. (1979). Color, class, and social control in an urban school. In R. C. Rist (ed.), *Desegregated schools: Appraisals of an American experiment* (pp. 117–153). New York: Academic Press.

Schofield, J. W. (1979). The impact of positively structured contact on intergroup behavior: Does it last under adverse conditions? *Social Psychology Quarterly, 42,* 280–284.

Schofield, J. W. (1982/1989). *Black and white in school: Trust, tension, or tolerance?* New York: Teachers College Press.

Schofield, J. W. (1983). Black-white conflict in the schools: Its social and academic effects. *American Journal of Education, 92,* 104–107.

Schofield, J. W. (1986). Causes and consequences of the colorblind perspective.

In S. Gaertner and J. Dovidio (eds.), *Prejudice, discrimination and racism: Theory and practice* (pp. 231–253). New York: Academic Press.

Schofield, J. W. (1991). School desegregation and intergroup relations: A review of the research. In G. Grant (ed.), *Review of research in education*, Vol. 17 (pp. 335–409). Washington, D.C.: American Educational Research Association.

Schofield, J. W., and McGivern, E. P. (1979). Creating interracial bonds in a desegregated school. In R. G. Blumberg and W. J. Roye (eds.), *Interracial bonds* (pp. 106–119). Bayside, N.Y.: General Hall.

Schofield, J. W., and Sagar, H. A. (1977). Peer interaction patterns in an integrated middle school. *Sociometry, 40*, 130–138.

Schofield, J. W., and Sagar, H. A. (1979). The social context of learning in an interracial school. In R. C. Rist (ed.), *Desegregated schools: Appraisals of an American experiment* (pp. 155–199). New York: Academic Press.

Shapiro, J. P. (1988). Relationships between dimensions of depressive experience and evaluative beliefs about people in general. *Personality and Social Psychology Bulletin, 14*, 388–400.

Sharan, S. (1980). Cooperative learning in teams: Recent methods and effects on achievement, attitudes, and ethnic relations. *Review of Educational Research, 50*, 241–272.

Sharan, Y., and Sharan, S. (1992). *Expanding cooperative learning through group investigation.* New York: Teachers College Press.

Sherif, M., and others. (1961). *Intergroup cooperation and competition: The Robbers' Cave experiment.* Norman, Okla.: University Book Exchange.

Slavin, R. E. (1983a). *Cooperative learning.* New York: Longman.

Slavin, R. E. (1983b). When does cooperative learning increase student achievement? *Psychological Bulletin, 94*, 429–445.

Slavin, R. E. (1985). Cooperative learning: Applying contact theory in desegregated schools. *Journal of Social Issues, 41*(3), 45–62.

Slavin, R. E. (1992). When and why does cooperative learning increase achievement? Theoretical and empirical perspectives. In R. Hertz-Lazarowitz and N. Miller (eds.), *Interaction in cooperative groups* (pp. 145–173). Cambridge, England: Cambridge University Press.

Slavin, R. E. (1994). Enhancing intergroup relations in schools: Cooperative learning and other strategies. In W. B. Hawley and A. Jackson (Eds.), *Toward a common destiny: Improving race and ethnic relations in America* (pp. 291–314). San Francisco: Jossey-Bass.

Slavin, R. E., and Madden, N. A. (1979). School practices that improve race relations. *American Educational Research Journal, 16*, 169–180.

Stephan, W. G., and Stephan, C. W. (1984). The role of ignorance in intergroup relations. In N. Miller and M. B. Brewer (eds.), *Groups in contact: The psychology of desegregation* (pp. 229–255). Orlando, Fla.: Academic Press.

Stephan, W. G., and Stephan, C. W. (1985). Intergroup anxiety. *Journal of Social Issues, 41*(3), 157–175.

Sullivan, M. L. (1979). Contacts among cultures: School desegregation in a poly-ethnic New York city high school. In R. C. Rist (ed.), *Desegregated schools: Appraisals of an American experiment* (pp. 201–240). New York: Academic Press.

Swallow, S. R., and Kuiper, N. A. (1987). The effects of depression and cogni-tive vulnerability to depression on judgments of similarity between self and other. *Motivation and Emotion, 11*, 157–167.

Tajfel, H. (ed.). (1978). *Differentiation between social groups*. London, England: Academic Press.

Tajfel, H., and Turner, J. C. (1979). An integrative theory of intergroup conflict. In W. Austin and S.Worchel (eds.), *The social psychology of intergroup relations* (pp. 33–47). Monterey, Calif.: Brooks/Cole.

Taylor, S. E. (1981). A categorization approach to stereotyping. In D. L. Ham-ilton (ed.), *Cognitive processes in stereotyping and intergroup behavior* (pp. 83–114). Hillsdale, N.J.: Erlbaum.

Vanbeselaere, N. (1987). The effects of dichotomous and crossed social catego-rization upon intergroup discrimination. *European Journal of Social Psy-chology, 18*, 143–156.

Veitch, R., and Griffitt, W. (1976). Good news, bad news: Affective and inter-personal effects. *Journal of Applied Social Psychology, 6*, 69–75.

Wellisch, J. B., Carriere, R. A., MacQueen, A. H., and Duck, G. A. (1977). *An in-depth study of Emergency School Aid Act (ESAA) schools: 1975–1976*. Santa Monica, Calif.: System Development Corporation.

Wellisch, J. B., Marcus, A. C., MacQueen, A. H., and Duck, G. A. (1976). *An in-depth study of Emergency School Aid Act (ESAA) schools: 1974–1975*. Santa Monica, Calif.: System Development Corporation.

Worchel, S. (1979). Cooperation and the reduction of intergroup conflict: Some determining factors. In W. G. Austin and S. Worchel (eds.), *The social psychology of intergroup relations* (pp. 262–273). Monterey, Calif.: Brooks/Cole.

Worchel, S., Andreoli, V. A., and Folger, R. (1977). Intergroup cooperation and intergroup attraction: The effect of previous interaction and outcome on combined effort. *Journal of Experimental Social Psychology, 13*, 131–140.

*Chapter Eleven*

# Enhancing Intergroup Relations in Schools: Cooperative Learning and Other Strategies

## Robert E. Slavin

The year 1994 marked the fortieth anniversary of *Brown* v. *Board of Education* (1954) and the 30th anniversary of the 1964 Civil Rights Act, the two most important events in the dismantling of legal barriers to racial integration in the United States. This year also saw the fortieth anniversary of an important event in the study of dismantling *interpersonal* barriers to racial integration: the publication of Gordon Allport's *The Nature of Prejudice* (1954). Just as the *Brown* decision set the stage for later judicial action against school segregation and the Civil Rights Act did the same for later legislative action against segregation and discrimination in society as a whole, *The Nature of Prejudice* has served for forty years as the basis for the study of intergroup relations.

At the time that Allport was writing, social scientists were debating the potential impact of desegregation, particularly *school* desegregation, on intergroup relations. Allport's work was central to the social science statement (Allport and thirty-four co-signers, 1953)

Adapted with permission from Robert E. Slavin, 1985, Cooperative learning: Applying contact theory in desegregated schools, *Journal of Social Issues*, 41(3), 45–60. Copyright 1985, The Society for the Psychological Study of Social Issues.

that played an important role in the deliberations of the court in the *Brown* case (see Cook, 1984).

In *The Nature of Prejudice*, Allport evaluated the experience of desegregation in industrial, military, and other nonschool settings to anticipate the effects of school desegregation on intergroup relations and other outcomes. In the early 1950s, integrated schools were illegal in the seventeen states (plus the District of Columbia) in which most African Americans lived, and they were rare elsewhere, so direct study of integrated schools was difficult. However, Allport did have available enough experience and research on various integrated settings to derive a set of principles to explain when interracial contact would lead to improved relationships and when it would not. He cited research indicating that superficial contact could be detrimental to race relations, as could competitive contact and contact between individuals of markedly different status. However, he also cited evidence suggesting that when individuals of different racial or ethnic groups worked to achieve common goals, when they had opportunities to get to know one another as individuals, and when they worked with one another on an equal footing, they became friends and did not continue to hold prejudices against one another. Allport's contact theory of intergroup relations is based on these findings. Contact theory, though updated by Amir (1969), Hewstone and Brown (1986), Pettigrew (1986), and others, has dominated social science inquiry on race relations for four decades. Allport's own summary of the essentials of contact theory is as follows: "Prejudice . . . may be reduced by equal status contact between majority and minority groups in the pursuit of common goals. The effect is greatly enhanced if this contact is sanctioned by institutional supports . . . and if it is of a sort that leads to the perception of common interests and common humanity between members of the two groups" (1954, p. 281).

Ever since *Brown v. Board of Education*, it has been assumed that desegregation would improve relations between students of different ethnic backgrounds. Yet all too often, desegregated schools are not really integrated schools: in most schools, African American, white, and Latino students remain much more likely to have friends of their own ethnic background than to make many cross-ethnic choices (Gerard and Miller, 1975; Schofield, 1991; Stephan, 1978). Although school desegregation does have a positive effect on racial toleration (Scott and McPartland, 1982), ethnicity is still a major barrier to friendship and respect in many desegregated schools.

Desegregation must be seen as an opportunity for improvement of intergroup relations, not as a solution in itself. Stuart Cook participated in the deliberations that led to the famous Social Science Statement ("Effects of Segregation," 1953) which in turn played a part in the *Brown* v. *Board of Education* decision. As he points out (Cook, 1979), in the early 1950s social scientists knew that school desegregation had to be accompanied by changes in school practices in order to have a positive effect on relations between African American and white students.

In traditionally organized schools, desegregation rarely fulfills the conditions outlined by Allport. Interaction between students of different ethnicities is typically superficial and often competitive. African American, Anglo, Latino, and other groups compete for grades, for teacher approval, and for places on the student council or the cheerleading squad. In the classroom, the one setting in which students of different races or ethnicities are likely to be at least sitting side by side, traditional instructional methods permit little contact between students that is not superficial. Otherwise, African American, Anglo, and Latino students usually ride different buses to different neighborhoods, participate in different kinds of activities, and go to different social functions. Thus, opportunities for positive intergroup interaction are limited. One major exception is sports; sports teams create conditions of cooperation and nonsuperficial contact among team members.

Correlational research by Slavin and Madden (1979) has shown that students who participate in sports teams in desegregated high schools are much more likely to have friends outside of their own race group and to have positive racial attitudes than students who do not participate in such sports teams. Hallinan and Teixeira (1987) and Patchen (1982) found a similar effect with respect to extracurricular activities in general. Sports teams fulfill the requirements of contact theory in that interaction among teammates tends to be nonsuperficial, cooperative, and equal status. However, there are only so many positions on teams, and schools below the high school level may not have sports teams at all.

Is there a way to change classroom organization to allow meaningful, cooperative contact to take place between students of different ethnicities? This chapter, adapted from an earlier review (Slavin, 1985), describes the results of several research programs designed to answer this question by applying a variety of classroom interventions, most of which are based on Allport's contact theory.

## Cooperative Learning

Cooperative-learning methods (Slavin, 1990b) explicitly use the strength of the desegregated school—the presence of students of different races or ethnicities—to enhance intergroup relations and other outcomes. Each of the groups in which students work is made up of four to five students of different races, sexes, and levels of achievement, and each reflects the composition of the class as a whole on these attributes. In most cooperative-learning methods, the groups receive rewards, recognition, and/or evaluation based on the degree to which they can increase the academic performance of each member. This approach stands in sharp contrast to the student competition for grades and teacher approval characteristic of the traditional classroom. Cooperation between students is emphasized both by the classroom rewards and tasks and by the teacher, who tries to communicate an "all for one, one for all" attitude. The various methods are structured to give each student a chance to make a substantial contribution to the team, so that teammates will be equal—at least in the sense of role equality specified by Allport (1954). The cooperative-learning methods are designed to be true changes in classroom organization, not time-limited "treatments." They provide daily opportunities for intense interpersonal contact among students of different races. When the teacher assigns students of different races or ethnicities to work together, he or she communicates unequivocal support for the idea that interracial or interethnic interaction is officially sanctioned. Even though race and race relations per se need not be mentioned (and rarely are) in the course of cooperative-learning experiences, it is difficult for a student to believe that the teacher supports racial separation when that teacher has assigned the class to multiethnic teams.

Thus, at least in theory, cooperative-learning methods satisfy the conditions outlined by Allport (1954) for positive effects of desegregation on race relations: cooperation across racial lines, equal-status roles for students of different races, contact across racial lines that permits students to learn about one another as individuals, and the communication of unequivocal teacher support for interracial contact.

The conditions of contact theory are not difficult to achieve in the laboratory, and a long tradition of laboratory studies has investigated and generally supported the main tenets of contact theory (see, for example, Cook, 1978; Miller, Brewer, and Edwards, 1985; Miller and Harrington, 1992). However, as Harrison (1976) points out, "200 million Americans cannot be run through the laboratory one by one [to reduce prejudice]" (p. 563). If a program designed to implement contact theory in classrooms is to be anything more than an academic exercise, it must not only improve intergroup relations but accomplish other educational goals as well. For example, research on cooperative-learning methods would be of little relevance to schools if these methods did not also improve (or at least not hinder) student achievement, or if they were too expensive, too difficult, too narrowly focused, or too disruptive of school routines to be practical as primary alternatives to traditional instruction. Accordingly, features of cooperative-learning methods other than the degree to which they are designed to improve race relations are of great importance.

Seven primary cooperative-learning methods embody the principles of contact theory. These have been compared to traditional methods over periods of at least four weeks in desegregated schools, and they have the practical characteristics outlined above: they are cheap, relatively easy to implement, widely applicable in terms of subject matter and grade levels, and easily integrated into an existing school without additional resources; in addition, most have been shown to improve achievement more effectively than traditional instruction (see Slavin, 1990a). Three of these methods were developed and evaluated at the Center for Social Organization of Schools at Johns Hopkins University—namely, Student Teams–Achievement Divisions, Teams-Games-Tournament (Slavin, 1986), and Team-Assisted Individualization (Slavin, Leavey, and Madden, 1984). A fourth technique, Jigsaw teaching (Aronson and others, 1978), has been evaluated in several desegregated schools and is widely used both in its original form and as modified by Slavin (1986) and Kagan (1991). The fifth method, developed and assessed at the University of Minnesota by Johnson and Johnson (1987), has been studied in desegregated schools; and the sixth, Group Investigation (Sharan and Sharan, 1992), has been studied in Israeli schools that include European and Middle Eastern Jews among their students. In addition, Weigel, Wiser, and Cook (1975) evaluated a cooperative-learning method in tri-ethnic (African American, Latino, Anglo) classes. These techniques are described below. (For more detailed descriptions, see Slavin, 1986, 1990.)

1. *Student Teams–Achievement Divisions (STAD)*. In STAD the teacher presents a lesson, and then students study worksheets in four-member teams that are heterogeneous on student ability, sex, and ethnicity. Following this, students take individual quizzes, and team scores are computed based on the degree to which each student improved over his or her own past record. The team scores are recognized in class newsletters.

2. *Teams-Games-Tournament (TGT)*. TGT is essentially the same as STAD in rationale and method. However, it replaces the quizzes and improvement score system used in STAD with a system of academic game tournaments, in which students from each team compete with students from other teams of the same level of past performance to try to contribute to their team scores.

3. *Team-Assisted Individualization (TAI)*. TAI combines the use of cooperative teams (like those used in STAD and TGT) with indi-

vidualized instruction in elementary mathematics. Students work in four- to five-member heterogeneous teams on self-instructional materials at their own levels and rates. The students themselves take responsibility for all checking, management, and routing, and help one another with problems, freeing the teacher to spend most of his or her time instructing small groups of students (drawn from the various teams) who are working on similar concepts. Teams are rewarded with certificates if they attain preset standards in terms of the number of units mastered by all team members each week.

4. *Jigsaw and Jigsaw II.* In the original Jigsaw method (Aronson and others, 1978) students were assigned to heterogeneous six-member teams, and each team member was given a unique set of information on an overall unit. For example, in a unit on Spain, one student might be appointed as an "expert" on Spain's history, another on its culture, another on its economy, and so on. The students read their information and then discuss it in "expert groups" made up of students from different teams who have the same information. The "experts" then return to their teams to teach the information to their teammates. Finally, all students are quizzed, and students receive individual grades.

Jigsaw II modified Jigsaw to correspond more closely to the Student Team Learning format (Slavin, 1986). Students work in four- to five-member teams (as in STAD, TGT, and TAI). All students read a chapter or story, but each team member is given an individual topic on which to become an expert. Students discuss their topics in "expert groups" and teach them to their teammates as in original Jigsaw. However, quiz scores in Jigsaw II are summed to form team scores, and teams are recognized in a class newsletter as in STAD. Kagan (1991) has described many additional variations of Jigsaw.

5. *Johnson Methods.* In the cooperative-learning methods developed by David Johnson and Roger Johnson (1987) students work in small, heterogeneous groups to complete a common worksheet, and are praised and rewarded as a group. These methods are the least complex of the cooperative-learning methods; they also come

closest to a pure cooperative model, as the other methods contain individualistic and/or competitive elements.

6. *Group Investigation*. Group Investigation (Sharan and Sharan, 1992), developed by Shlomo and Yael Sharan and their colleagues in Israel, is a general classroom-organization plan in which students work in small groups using cooperative inquiry, group discussion, and cooperative planning and projects. In this method, students form their own two- to six-member groups. The groups choose subtopics from a unit being studied by the entire class, further break their subtopics into individual tasks, and carry out the activities necessary to prepare a group report. The group then makes a representation or display to communicate its findings to the entire class. It is evaluated based on the quality of this report.

7. *The Method of Weigel, Wiser, and Cook*. In one study in junior and senior high schools containing African American, Mexican American, and Anglo students, Weigel and his colleagues (1975) used a combination of cooperative-learning methods, including information gathering, discussion, and interpretation of materials in heterogeneous groups. Prizes were given to groups on the basis of the quality of the group product.

## Research on Cooperative Learning and Intergroup Relations

The remainder of this chapter reviews field experiments in which the effects of cooperative-learning methods on intergroup relations are evaluated. This review emphasizes studies in which the methods were used in elementary or secondary schools for at least four weeks (the median duration was ten weeks), and in which appropriate research methods and analyses were employed to rule out obvious bias. Study Ns ranged from 51 to 424 (median = 164); grade levels, from four to twelve; and percentage of minority students, from 10 percent to 61 percent. Most of the studies used sociometric indices (such as questions like "Who are your friends in this class?" and "Who have you helped in this class?"), peer ratings, or behavioral observation to measure intergroup relations as pairwise positive relations between individuals of different ethnic backgrounds. And a few studies defined intergroup relations in terms of attitudes toward various ethnic groups. Because only students in the coooperative-learning classes were likely to have helped their classmates, such measures were biased toward the cooperative-learning treatments; thus, the results of these measures are not discussed here. Also, observations of cross-racial interaction during the treatment classes, another measure of implementation rather than outcome, are not considered as intergroup-relations measures.

## Main Effects on Intergroup Relations

The experimental evidence on cooperative learning has generally supported the main tenets of contact theory (Allport, 1954). With only a few exceptions, this research has demonstrated that when the conditions outlined by Allport are met in the classroom, students are more likely to have friends outside their own racial groups than they would in traditional classrooms, as measured by responses to such sociometric questions as "Who are your best friends in this class?"

**STAD.** The evidence linking STAD to an increased number of cross-racial friendships is strong. In two studies, Slavin (1977, 1979) found that students who had experienced STAD over periods of ten to twelve weeks gained more cross-racial friendships than did control students. Slavin and Oickle (1981) found significant gains in white friendships toward blacks as a consequence of STAD but found no differences in black friendships toward whites. Kagan and others (1985) found that STAD (and TGT) reversed a trend toward ethnic polarization of friendship choices among Anglo, Latino, and black students. And Sharan and others (1984) found positive effects of STAD on the ethnic attitudes of both Middle Eastern and European Jews in Israeli schools.

Slavin's study (1979) included a follow-up into the next academic year, in which students who had been in the experimental and control classes were asked to list their friends. Students in the control group listed an average of fewer than one friend of another race, or 9.8 percent of all of their friendship choices, whereas those in the experimental group named an average of 2.4 friends outside their own race, or 37.9 percent of their friendship choices. The STAD research covered grades two through eight and took place in schools ranging from 13 percent to 61 percent minority.

**TGT.** DeVries, Edwards, and Slavin (1978) summarized data analyses from four studies of TGT in desegregated schools. In three of these, students in classes that used TGT gained significantly more friends outside their own racial groups than did control students. In one, no differences were found. The samples involved in these studies varied in grade level from seven to twelve and in percentage of minority students from 10 percent to 51 percent. In addition, Kagan and others (1985) found positive effects of TGT on friendship choices among African American, Mexican American, and Anglo students.

**TAI.** Two studies have assessed the effects of TAI on intergroup relations. Oishi, Slavin, and Madden (1983) found positive effects of TAI on cross-racial nominations on two sociometric scales: "Who are your friends in this class?" and "Whom would you rather *not* sit at a table with?" Moreover, although they found no effects on cross-racial ratings of classmates as "nice" or "smart," TAI students made significantly fewer cross-racial ratings of "not nice" and "not smart" than did control students. In a similar study, Oishi (1983) found significantly positive effects of TAI on cross-racial ratings of "smart" and on reductions in ratings of "not nice." The effect on "smart" ratings was due primarily to increases in whites' ratings of African American classmates.

**Jigsaw.** The effects of the original Jigsaw method on intergroup relations are less clear than those for STAD, TGT, or TAI. Blaney and others (1977) did find that students in desegregated classes using Jigsaw preferred their Jigsaw groupmates to their classmates in general. However, since students' groupmates and their other classmates were about the same in ethnic composition, this cannot be seen as a measure of intergroup relations. In addition, no differences between the experimental and control groups in interethnic friendship choices were reported.

Gonzales (1979), using a method similar to Jigsaw, found that Anglo and Asian American students had better attitudes toward Mexican American classmates in the Jigsaw groups than in control groups, but he found no differences in attitudes toward Anglo or Asian American students. In a subsequent study, Gonzales (1981) found no differences in attitudes toward Mexican American, African American, or Anglo students in Jigsaw and control bilingual classes.

The most positive effects of a Jigsaw-related intervention were found in a study of Jigsaw II by Ziegler (1981) in classes composed of recent European and West Indian immigrants and Anglo Canadians in Toronto. She found substantially more cross-ethnic friendships in the Jigsaw II classes than in control classes both on an immediate posttest and in a ten-week follow-up. These effects were indicated for both *casual friendships* ("Who in this class have you called on the telephone in the last two weeks?") and *close friendships* ("Who in this class have you spent time with after school in the last two weeks?")

*Johnson Methods.* Two of the Johnsons' studies have examined intergroup relations outcomes. Cooper, Johnson, Johnson, and Wilderson (1980) found greater friendship across race lines in a cooperative treatment than in an individualized method in which students were not permitted to interact. However, they found no differences in cross-racial friendships between the cooperative condition and a competitive condition in which students competed with equals (similar to the TGT tournaments). Meanwhile, Johnson and Johnson (1981) found more cross-racial interaction in cooperative than in individualized classes during free time.

*Group Investigation.* In a study in Israeli junior high schools, Sharan et al. (1984) compared Group Investigation, STAD, and traditional instruction in terms of effects on relationships between Jews of Middle Eastern and European backgrounds. They found that students who experienced Group Investigation and STAD had much more positive ethnic attitudes than students in traditional classes. There were no differences between Group Investigation and STAD on this variable.

*The Method of Weigel, Wiser, and Cook.* One of the largest and longest studies of cooperative learning was conducted by Weigel, Wiser, and Cook (1975) in tri-ethnic (Mexican American, Anglo, black) classrooms. These researchers evaluated a method in which students in multiethnic teams engaged in a variety of cooperative activities in several subjects, winning prizes based on their team performance. They reported that their cooperative methods had positive effects on white students' attitudes toward Mexican Americans, but not on white-black, black-white, black-Latino, Latino-black, or Latino-white attitudes. They also found that cooperative learning reduced teachers' reports of interethnic conflict.

The effects of cooperative-learning methods are not entirely consistent, but sixteen of the nineteen studies reviewed here demonstrate that when the conditions of contact theory are fulfilled, some aspect of relationships between students of different ethnicities improves. Most of these studies operationalized intergroup relations as friendships between students of different ethnicities, but some found positive effects on general intergroup attitudes as well (see, for example, Sharan and others, 1984; Gonzales, 1979). A few studies indicate that cooperative learning resulted in improvements in majority-minority friendships but not minority-majority friendships (see, for example, Slavin and Oickle, 1981; Gonzales, 1979; Weigel, Wiser, and Cook, 1975), but in most studies improvements in intergroup relations were equally strong toward majority- and minority-group students.

## Effects on Academic Achievement

It is important to note that, in addition to positive effects on intergroup relations, cooperative-learning methods have had positive effects on student achievement in a wide variety of subjects and among students of different ethnicities and backgrounds. In particular, positive effects have been seen for methods that emphasize group goals and individual accountability, in which cooperating groups are recognized based on the individual learning performances of all group members (see Slavin, 1990a). In studies in desegregated schools, effects have often been particularly large for minority students. For example, in two studies of STAD (Slavin, 1977; Slavin and Oickle, 1981), African American students gained significantly more than white students in achievement (in comparison to control groups). And a study of Jigsaw by Lucker, Rosenfield, Sikes, and Aronson (1976) found positive achievement effects for African American and Latino students but not for white students. However, in other studies of STAD (for example, Slavin and Karweit, 1984), of TGT (for example, Edwards, DeVries, and Snyder, 1972), and of TAI (Slavin, Leavey and Madden, 1984), African American and white students gained from cooperative learning to the same degree. Similarly, Sharan and Shachar (1988) found that Israeli Jewish students of European and Middle Eastern backgrounds gained equally from Group Investigation.

## How Close Are the New Cross-Ethnic Friendships?

It is not surprising that friendships across racial or ethnic boundaries are rare, compared to friendships within these groups. Black, Hispanic, and Anglo students typically live in different neighborhoods, ride different buses, and prefer different activities. Secondary-school students of different ethnicities often come from different elementary schools. Socioeconomic and achievement differences further separate students. Indeed, these factors work against friendship formation even when race is not a factor (see Lott and Lott,

1965). Racial differences accentuate students' tendencies to form homogeneous peer groups, sometimes resulting in overt prejudice and interracial hostility.

Given the many forces operating against the formation of cross-racial friendships, it would seem that if cooperative learning influences these friendships, relatively weak relationships would be created rather than strong ones (see, for example, Schofield, 1991). In other words, it seems unlikely that a few weeks of cooperative learning would build strong interracial relationships between students in the classroom at the possible expense of prior same-race relationships.

A secondary analysis of the Slavin (1979) STAD study by Hansell and Slavin (1981) investigated this hypothesis. Their sample included 424 seventh- and eighth-grade students in twelve inner-city language arts classrooms. Classes were randomly assigned to cooperative-learning (STAD) or control treatments for a ten-week program. On both pre- and posttests, students were asked, "Who are your best friends in this class? Name as many as you wish," in a free-choice format. Choices were defined as "close" if they were among the first six made by students and as "distant" if they ranked seventh or later. The reciprocity and order of choices made and received were analyzed by multiple regression.

The results showed that the positive effects of STAD on cross-racial choices were primarily due to increases in strong friendship choices. Reciprocated and close choices, both made and received, increased more in STAD than in control classes. Thus, contrary to what might have been expected, this study showed positive effects of cooperative learning on close, reciprocated friendship choices, the kind of friendships that should be the most difficult to change.

### Effects on Social Networks

One limitation of existing research on cooperative learning, and on contact theory in general, is the concentration on dyadic relationships across racial lines or (to a lesser extent) attitudes toward entire racial groups. However, the impact of cooperative learning almost certainly involves networks of friendships rather than simple dyadic friendships. Secondary analyses of the data from Slavin's STAD study (1979) have revealed that many of the new cross-racial friendships made over the course of the STAD intervention were formed between students who had never been in the same cooperative group. A moment's reflection would support the inevitability of this result: in a four-member team consisting of two blacks and two whites, each student could only make two new friends from a different race if all of the new friends came from within his or her team. At least one of those teammates from a different race would also likely be of a different sex; norms against black-white dating aside, cross-sex friendships are even less frequent than cross-race friendships (Cooper, Johnson, Johnson, and Wilderson, 1980; DeVries and Edwards, 1974). It is also possible that two or more teammates of different races were already friends, thus further restricting the possible number of new cross-race, within-team choices; and any deviation from a fifty-fifty racial split reduces that possibility still further.

There are at least two ways in which cooperative learning might increase the number of cross-race friendships outside particular cooperative groups. First, a cooperative-learning experience often offers students their first (or best) cross-race friendships. Racial groups in classrooms are characterized by many friendship ties within each race group but by few outside of it. However, once a cross-race friendship is formed, the new friend's friends (of his or her own race) also become likely friendship candidates. For example, if a white student makes his or her first black friend, this relationship bridges between formerly isolated African American and white peer groups. It opens a new pool of potential African American friends, possibly reaching even beyond the confines of the classroom.

Second, even a small number of cross-race friendships may create less-defined peer-group boundaries, formerly based on racial (and sexual) criteria—thereby allowing new, smaller cliques to form based more on mutual liking than on race and sex. This pattern was found in an analysis of sociometric data conducted by Hansell, Tackaberry, and Slavin (1981); that is, clique size tended to diminish as a result of a cooperative intervention similar to STAD.

## Why Isn't Cooperative Learning Universally Used?

The research on cooperative learning is clear. It shows consistent and often substantial benefits for student achievement and many other important outcomes. In desegregated schools the rationale for cooperative learning is especially great, as the well-documented positive effects of cooperative learning on intergroup relations are particularly relevant. Cooperative learning is widely used in U.S. schools at all levels, but it is far from universal. Why might this be so?

One serious limitation is the unwillingness of schools and districts to spend more than token amounts of time and money on staff development. As a result, most training in cooperative learning is brief, is of poor quality, and is not accompanied by classroom follow-up. Important changes in teachers' practices rarely come about from such training. Indeed, real changes would require trainers who understand the models and the principles behind them, a series of training sessions, and peer coaching or other assistance with implementation in the classroom (Showers, Joyce, and Bennett, 1987). Many teachers try cooperative learning for a day or two without teacher's manuals and lacking a clear idea of what cooperative learning should look like. They then conclude that cooperative learning does not work.

Despite such evidence and the widespread acceptance of cooperative learning among opinion leaders in education, cooperative strategies may never become routinely implemented in a high proportion of classrooms until schools adopt a different approach to professional development. Then, once schools come to see improvements in their teachers' skills as a result of top-quality training in research-based methods, cooperative learning will finally become established in the teaching repertoires of most education professionals.

## Programs and Practices Other Than Cooperative Learning

Nearly all of the experimental research on programs designed to improve intergroup relations has focused on evaluation of cooperative-learning methods. However, some research on other promising strategies also exists, and there are several strategies that are often used to improve intergroup relations but have not been formally researched.

### Untracking

There is some evidence that ability grouping has a detrimental effect on intergroup relations. In one study in New Mexico schools containing Mexican American and Anglo students (Sarthory, 1968), the findings indicated that sixth-graders in heterogeneous classes had consistently better interethnic attitudes than did students in ability-grouped classes. In a secondary analysis of National Longitudinal Study data, Braddock and Slavin (1993) also found that, in comparison to students in untracked classes, those in ability-grouped classes perceived race relations in their school as being worse and reported more "racist remarks." Indeed, between-class ability grouping often creates classes predominantly composed of students of one or another ethnic group, thus reducing opportunities for positive contact (Jones, Erickson, and Crowell, 1972; Wenning, 1992). Between-class ability grouping has negative effects on many other outcomes as well, especially for students in the low-ability groups. In comparison with similar students in heterogenously grouped classes, students in low-ability groups usually exhibit lower achievement, lower self-esteem, more external locus of control, higher dropout rates, and higher delinquency rates (Braddock and Slavin, 1993; Oakes, 1992; Slavin, 1987, 1990a; Rosenbaum, 1980).

## Peer Tutoring

Cross-age peer tutoring, as when high school students tutor elementary- or middle-school students, has long been found to increase the achievement of the tutor as well as of the tutee (Allen, 1976; Devin-Sheehan, Feldman, and Allen, 1976). Research has also found very positive relationships between tutors and tutees. One might logically expect that when tutors and tutees are of different ethnic backgrounds, their interaction would lead to positive intergroup relations. One study, by Witte (1972), did find that tutoring in interracial dyads improved interracial acceptance and interaction, but much more research on this topic is needed.

## Other Practices

Many other practices are often used in attempts to improve intergroup relations among students, but their effects have not been extensively studied. A national study of integrated high schools found that the best predictors of positive intergroup relations among a set of school practices were responses to the questions "How often has your teacher assigned you to work on schoolwork with a student of another race?" and "How often have you played with a student of another race on a team at school?" Less consistent positive effects were found for class discussions about race. On the other hand, a study by Slavin and Madden (1979) revealed that attempts to change student attitudes, such as use of multiethnic texts, provision of minority-group history or culture courses, and establishment of biracial student committees, had no effects on intergroup relations. However, as this study was correlational rather than experimental, it should not be considered definitive. Descriptive studies of desegregated schools have found that such strategies as the use of multiethnic texts and multiracial advisory committees do contribute to racial harmony (Hawley and others, 1983; Schofield, 1991). Still other studies indicate that mediation of conflicts between students of different ethnicities can prevent or resolve serious friction between groups (Deutsch, 1992), and that multicultural education can have positive effects on students' intergroup attitudes (Banks, 1988, 1993).

## Conclusions

There are many promising approaches to improving relationships among students of different ethnicities. By far the most extensively studied are cooperative-learning strategies, but there is reason to believe that such practices as reducing the use of ability grouping and increasing that of peer tutoring, multicultural education, conflict resolution, and other strategies may contribute to positive intergroup relations as well.

The results of the studies relating cooperative learning to intergroup relations clearly indicate that when students work in ethnically mixed cooperative-learning groups, they gain cross-ethnic friendships. This research indicates that the effects of cooperative learning on intergroup relations are strong and long lasting, and are more likely to be associated with close, reciprocated friendship choices than distant or unreciprocated choices. There are no clear patterns indicating more consistent results for some cooperative-learning methods than for others. Indeed, all such methods have had some positive effects on intergroup relations.

Additional research is needed to discover the effects of cooperative learning on actual intergroup behavior, particularly behavior outside school. A few studies (for example, Oishi, 1983; Ziegler, 1981) have found positive effects of cooperative learning on self-reported cross-racial friendships outside class, but behavioral observation in nonclassroom settings is still warranted. Additional long-term follow-up data are also needed to establish the duration of the effects of cooperative learning

The practical implications of this chapter are unambiguous:

intergroup relations can be markedly improved by a variety of means. In particular, there is a strong positive effect of cooperative learning on intergroup relations. Four decades after Allport laid out the basic principles of contact theory, we finally have practical, proven methods for implementing this theory in the desegregated classroom. These methods are effective for increasing student achievement as well as for improving intergroup relations. However, much more work is needed to discover the critical components of cooperative learning and other strategies, and to inform a model of how these methods affect intergroup relations.

# References

Allen, V. L. (ed.) (1976). *Children as teachers: Theory and research on tutoring.* New York: Academic Press.

Allport, F. H., and thirty-four cosigners (1953). The effects of segregation and the consequences of desegregation: A social science statement. *Minnesota Law Review, 37*, 429–440.

Allport, G. (1954). *The nature of prejudice.* Cambridge, Mass.: Addison-Wesley.

Amir, Y. (1969). Contact hypothesis in ethnic relations. *Psychological Bulletin, 71*, 319–342.

Aronson, E., and others. (1978). *The Jigsaw classroom.* Beverly Hills, Calif.: Sage.

Banks, J. A. (1988). *Multiethnic education: Theory and practice.* Boston: Allyn & Bacon.

Banks, J. (1993). Multicultural education for young children: Racial and ethnic attitudes and their modification. In B. Spodek (ed.), *Handbook of research on the education of young children* (pp. 236–250). New York: Macmillan.

Blaney, N. T., and others. (1977). Interdependence in the classroom: A field study. *Journal of Educational Psychology, 69*(2), 121–128.

Braddock, J. H., and Slavin, R. E. (1993). *Life in the slow lane: A longitudinal study of effects of ability grouping on student achievement, attitudes, and perceptions.* Baltimore, Md.: Johns Hopkins University, Center for Research on Effective Schooling for Disadvantaged Students.

*Brown v. Board of Education* 347 U.S. 483 (1954).

Cook, S. W. (1978). Interpersonal and attitudinal outcomes of cooperating interracial groups. *Journal of Research and Development in Education, 12*, 97–113.

Cook, S. W. (1979). Social science and school desegregation: Did we mislead the Supreme Court? *Personality and Social Psychology Bulletin, 5*, 420–437.

Cook, S. W. (1984). The 1954 social science statement and school desegregation: A reply to Gerard. *American Psychologist, 39*, 819–832.

Cooper, L., Johnson, D. W., Johnson, R., and Wilderson, F. (1980). Effects of
cooperative, competitive, and individualistic experiences on interpersonal attraction among heterogeneous peers. *Journal of Social Psychologist, 111*, 243–252.

Deutsch, M. (1992). *The effects of training in cooperative learning and conflict resolution in an alternative high school.* New York: Columbia University,
Teachers College.

Devin-Sheehan, L., Feldman, R., and Allen, V. (1976). Research on children
tutoring children: A critical review. *Review of Educational Research,
46*(3), 355–385.

DeVries, D. L., and Edwards, K. J. (1974). Student teams and learning games:
Their effects on cross-race and cross-sex interaction. *Journal of Educational Psychology, 66*, 741–749.

DeVries, D. L., Edwards, K. J., and Slavin, R. E. (1978). Biracial learning teams
and race relations in the classroom: Four field experiments on Teams-
Games-Tournament. *Journal of Educational Psychology, 70*, 356–362.

Edwards, K. J., DeVries, D. L., and Snyder, J. P. (1972). Games and teams: A winning combination. *Simulation and Games, 3*, 247–269.

Gerard, H. B., and Miller, N. (1975). *School desegregation: A long-range study.* New
York: Plenum Press.

Gonzales, A. (1979). Classroom cooperation and ethnic balance. Paper presented
at the annual convention of the American Psychological Association,
New York.

Gonzales, A. (1981). An approach to independent-cooperative bilingual education and measures related to social motives. Unpublished manuscript,
California State University at Fresno.

Hallinan, M. T., and Teixeira, R. A. (1987). Students' interracial friendships:
Individual characteristics, structural effects, and racial differences.
*American Journal of Education, 95*, 563–583.

Hansell, S., and Slavin, R. E. (1981). Cooperative learning and the structure of
interracial friendships. *Sociology of Education, 54*, 98–106.

Hansell, S., Tackaberry, S. N., and Slavin, R. E. (1981). Cooperation, competition, and the structure of student peer groups. *Representative Research in
Social Psychology, 12*, 46–61.

Harrison, A. A. (1976). *Individuals and groups: Understanding social behavior.*
Monterey, Calif.: Brooks/Cole.

Hawley, W. D., and others. (1983). *Strategies for effective desegregation.* Lexington,
Mass.: D. C. Heath.

Hewstone, M., and Brown, R. (eds.). (1986). *Contact and conflict in intergroup
encounters.* Oxford, England: Basil Blackwell.

Johnson, D. W., and Johnson, R. T. (1981). Effects of cooperative and individualistic learning experiences on interethnic interaction. *Journal of Educational Psychology, 73*, 444–449.

Johnson, D. W., and Johnson, R. T. (1987). *Learning together and alone*, 2nd ed. Englewood Cliffs, N.J.: Prentice-Hall.

Jones, J. D., Erickson, E. L., and Crowell, R. (1972). Increasing the gap between whites and blacks: Tracking as a contributory source. *Education and Urban Society, 4*, 339–349.

Kagan, S. (1991). *Cooperative learning resources for teachers*, 4th ed. San Juan Capistrano, Calif.: Resources for Teachers.

Kagan, S., and others. (1985). Classroom structural bias: Impact of cooperative and competitive classroom structures on cooperative and competitive individuals and groups. In R. E. Slavin and others, (eds.), *Learning to cooperate, cooperating to learn* (pp. 277–312). New York: Plenum.

Lott, A. F., and Lott, B. E. (1965). Group cohesiveness as interpersonal attraction: A review of relationships with antecedent and consequent variables. *Psychological Bulletin, 64*, 259, 309.

Lucker, G. W., Rosenfield, D., Sikes, J., and Aronson, E. (1976). Performance in the interdependent classroom: A field study. *American Educational Research Journal, 13*, 115–123.

Miller, N., Brewer, M. B., and Edwards, K. (1985). Cooperative interaction in desegregated settings: A laboratory analogue. *Journal of Social Issues, 41*(3), 63–79.

Miller, N., and Harrington, H. J. (1992). Social categorization and intergroup acceptance: Principles for the design and development of cooperative learning teams. In R. Hertz-Lazarowitz and N. Miller (eds.), *Interaction in cooperative groups* (pp. 203–227). New York: Cambridge University Press.

Oakes, J. (1992). Can tracking research inform practice? Technical, normative, and political considerations. *Educational Researcher, 21*(4), 12–21.

Oishi, S. (1983). Effects of team assisted individualization in mathematics on cross-race interactions of elementary school children. Unpublished doctoral dissertation, University of Maryland.

Oishi, S., Slavin, R., and Madden, N. (1983). Effects of student teams and individualized instruction on cross-race and cross-sex friendships. Paper presented at the annual meeting of the American Educational Research Association, Montreal, Canada.

Patchen, M. (1982). *Black-white contact in schools: Its social and academic effects*. West Lafayette, Ind.: Purdue University Press.

Pettigrew, T. F. (1986). The intergroup contact hypothesis reconsidered. In M. Hewstone and R. Brown (eds.), *Contact and conflict in intergroup encounters*. Oxford, England: Basil Blackwell.

Rosenbaum, J. (1980). Social implications of educational grouping: *Review of Research in Education, 8*, 361–401.

Sarthory, J. A. (1968). The effects of ability grouping in multi-cultural school situations. *Dissertation Abstracts, 29,* 451A.

Schofield, J. W. (1991). School desegregation and intergroup relations: A review of the literature. In G. Grant (ed.), *Review of Research in Education,* Vol. 17 (pp. 335–409). Washington, D.C.: American Educational Research Association.

Scott, R., and McPartland, J. (1982). Desegregation as national policy: Correlates of racial attitudes. *American Educational Research Journal, 19,* 397–414.

Sharan, S., and others. (1984). *Cooperative learning in the classroom: Research in desegregated schools.* Hillsdale, N.J.: Erlbaum.

Sharan, S., and Shachar, H. (1988). *Language and learning in the cooperative classroom.* New York: Springer.

Sharan, Y., and Sharan, S. (1992). *Expanding cooperative learning through group investigation.* New York: Teachers College Press.

Showers, B., Joyce, B., and Bennett, B. (1987). Synthesis of research on staff development: A framework for future study and a state-of-the-art analysis. *Educational Leadership, 45*(3), 77–87.

Slavin, R. E. (1977). *Student learning team techniques: Narrowing the achievement gap between the races.* Report No. 228. Johns Hopkins University, Center for Social Organization of Schools.

Slavin, R. E. (1979). Effects of biracial learning teams on cross-racial friendships. *Journal of Educational Psychology, 71,* 381–387.

Slavin, R. E. (1985). Cooperative learning: Applying contact theory in desegregated schools. *Journal of Social Issues, 41,* 45–62.

Slavin, R. E. (1986). *Using student team learning: Third edition.* Baltimore, Md.: Johns Hopkins University, Center for Social Organization of Schools.

Slavin, R. E. (1987). Ability grouping and student achievement in elementary schools: A best-evidence synthesis. *Review of Educational Research, 57,* 347–350.

Slavin, R. E. (1990a). Ability grouping and student achievement in secondary schools: A best-evidence synthesis. *Review of Educational Research, 60,* 471–499.

Slavin, R. E. (1990b). *Cooperative learning: Theory, research, and practice.* Englewood Cliffs, N.J.: Prentice-Hall.

Slavin, R. E. (in press). Cooperative learning and intergroup relations. In J. Banks (ed.), *Handbook of research on multicultural education.* New York: Macmillan.

Slavin, R. E., and Karweit, N. (1984). Mastery learning and student teams: A factorial experiment in urban general mathematics classes. *American Educational Research Journal, 21,* 725–736.

Slavin, R. E., Leavey, M., and Madden, N. A. (1984). Combining cooperative learning and individualized instruction: Effects on student mathematics achievement, attitudes, and behaviors. *Elementary School Journal,* 84, 409–422.

Slavin, R. E., and Madden, N. A. (1979). School practices that improve race relations. *American Educational Research Journal,* 16(2), 169–180.

Slavin, R. E., and Oickle, E. (1981). Effects of cooperative learning teams on student achievement and race relations: Treatment by race interactions. *Sociology of Education,* 54, 174–180.

Stephan, W. G. (1978). School desegregation: An evaluation of predictions made in *Brown v. Board of Education. Psychological Bulletin,* 85, 217–238.

Weigel, R. H., Wiser, P. L., and Cook, S. W. (1975). Impact of cooperative learning experiences on cross-ethnic relations and attitudes. *Journal of Social Issues,* 31(1), 219–245.

Wenning, R. J. (1992). The characteristics of discriminatory ability grouping and evidence of its extent. Paper presented at the annual meeting of the American Educational Research Association, San Francisco.

Witte, P. H. (1972). The effects of group reward structure on interracial acceptance, peer tutoring, and academic performance. *Dissertation Abstracts International,* 32(9-A), 5367.

Ziegler, S. (1981). The effectiveness of cooperative learning teams for increasing cross-ethnic friendship: Additional evidence. *Human Organization,* 40, 264–268.

*Chapter Twelve*

# Multicultural Education and the Modification of Students' Racial Attitudes

## James A. Banks

The heated discourse on multicultural education, especially in the popular press and among nonspecialists (Gray, 1991; Leo, 1990; Schlesinger, 1991), often obscures the developing consensus among multicultural education specialists about the nature, aims, and scope of the field. Both Gay (1992) and Banks (1989) have noted the high level of consensus about aims and scope in the literature written by multicultural education theorists. Gay, however, points out that there is a tremendous gap between theory and practice in the field. (In her view, theory development has outpaced development in practice, and a wide gap exists between the two.)

A major goal of multicultural education, as stated by specialists in the field, is to reform schools, colleges, and universities so that students from diverse racial, ethnic, and social-class groups will expe-

This chapter is adapted with permission from two of the author's previous publications: Multicultural education for young children: Racial and ethnic attitudes and their modification. In B. Spodek (ed.), *Handbook of research on the education of young children* (pp. 236–250). New York: Macmillan, copyright 1993; and Multicultural education: Historical development, dimensions, and practice. In Linda Darling-Hammond (ed.), *Review of research in education* (Vol. 19) (pp. 3–49). Washington, D.C.: American Educational Research Association, copyright 1993.

rience educational equality. Another important goal of multicultural education is to give both male and female students an equal chance to experience educational success and mobility (Klein, 1985; Sadker and Sadker, 1982). Multicultural education theorists are increasingly interested in how the interaction of race, class, and gender influences education (Banks, 1989; Banks and Banks, 1995; Grant and Sleeter, 1986; Sleeter, 1991). However, the emphasis that different theorists give to each of these variables varies considerably.

Although there is an emerging consensus about the aims and scope of multicultural education (Banks, 1993a; Banks and Banks, 1995), the variety of typologies, conceptual schemes, and perspectives within the field reflects the fact that complete agreement about its aims and boundaries has not been attained (Baker, 1983; Banks, 1988; Bennett, 1990; Gollnick and Chinn, 1990; Garcia, 1991). The current, rather acrimonious debate about the extent to which the histories and cultures of women and people of color should be incorporated into the study of Western civilization in the nation's schools, colleges, and universities has complicated the quest for sound definitions and clear disciplinary boundaries within the field (Asante, 1991; Asante and Ravitch, 1991; Ravitch, 1990; Schlesinger, 1990).

## The Dimensions of Multicultural Education

There is general agreement among most scholars and researchers in multicultural education that, if it is to be implemented successfully, institutional changes must be made, including changes in the curriculum; the teaching materials; teaching and learning styles; the attitudes, perceptions, and behaviors of teachers and administrators; and the goals, norms, and culture of schools (Banks, 1992; Bennett, 1990; Sleeter and Grant, 1988). However, many school and university practitioners have a limited conception of multicultural education, and view it primarily in terms of curriculum reform that involves changing or restructuring the curriculum to include content about ethnic groups, women, and other cultural groups. This conception of multicultural education is widespread because curriculum reform was the main focus when the movement first emerged in the 1960s and 1970s (Blassingame, 1972; Ford, 1973), and because the multiculturalism discourse in the popular media has focused on curriculum reform and largely ignored other dimensions and components of multicultural education (Gray, 1991; Leo, 1990; Schlesinger, 1990, 1991).

If multicultural education is to become better understood and implemented in ways more consistent with theory, its various dimensions must be more clearly described and researched. Multi-cultural education is conceptualized in this chapter as a field that consists of the five dimensions formulated by Banks (1993a): con-tent integration, the knowledge construction process, prejudice reduction, an equity pedagogy, and an empowering school culture and social structure. Below, each of these dimensions is defined and illustrated. Their interrelationship is discussed later.

1. *Content Integration.* Content integration concerns the extent to which teachers use examples, data, and information from a vari-ety of cultures and groups to illustrate key concepts, principles, gen-eralizations, and theories in their subject area or discipline. In many school districts, as well as in popular writings, multicultural educa-tion is viewed only or primarily in terms of content integration. The widespread belief that content integration constitutes the whole of multicultural education might be an important factor that causes many teachers of subjects such as mathematics and science to view multicultural education as an endeavor primarily for social studies and language arts teachers.

2. *Knowledge Construction.* The knowledge construction process describes the procedures by which social, behavioral, and natural scientists create knowledge, as well as the ways in which implicit cultural assumptions, frames of reference, perspectives, and biases within a discipline influence the ways that knowledge is constructed within it (Berger and Luckman, 1966; Gould, 1981; Harding, 1991; Kuhn, 1970). When implemented in the classroom, the knowledge construction process helps students to understand how knowledge is created and how it is influenced by the racial, ethnic, and social-class positions of individuals and groups.

3. *Prejudice Reduction.* The prejudice reduction dimension of

multicultural education describes the characteristics of children's racial attitudes and strategies that can be used to help students develop more democratic attitudes and values. Researchers have been investigating the characteristics of children's racial attitudes since the 1920s (Lasker, 1929). Since the intergroup education movement of the 1940s and 1950s (Miel with Kiester, 1967; Trager and Yarrow, 1952), a number of investigators have designed interventions to help students to develop more positive racial attitudes and values.

4. *Equity Pedagogy*. An equity pedagogy exists when teachers use techniques and methods that facilitate the academic achievement of students from diverse racial, ethnic, and social-class groups. This dimension focuses on research studies, approaches, theories, and interventions that are designed to help both male and female students who are members of low-status population groups to increase their academic achievement (Delpit, 1988; Ogbu, 1990; Shade, 1989).

5. *Empowering School Culture and Social Structure*. This dimension concerns the process of restructuring the culture and organization of the school so that students from diverse racial, ethnic, and social-class groups will experience educational equality and cultural empowerment (Cummins, 1986). For students of color as well as low-income students, creation of an empowering school culture involves restructuring the culture and organization of the school. Toward this end, the variables that need to be examined are grouping practices (Braddock, 1990; Oakes, 1958), labeling practices (Mercer, 1989), the social climate of the school, and the expectations that the staff has for student achievement (Brookover and others, 1979; Darling-Hammond, 1995).

This dimensions typology is an ideal-type conception in the Weberian sense: it approximates but does not describe reality in its total complexity. Like all classification schema, it has both strengths and limitations. It is helpful as a conceptual tool because it provides a way to organize and make sense of the complex and disparate data and literature on diversity and education. However, its five dimensions are interrelated and overlapping, rather than mutually exclusive. Content integration, for example, describes any approach that is used to integrate content about racial and cultural groups into the curriculum. And the knowledge construction process describes a method in which teachers help students to understand how knowledge is created, reflecting the experiences of various ethnic and cultural groups.

Content integration is a necessary but not sufficient condition for the knowledge construction process; in other words, it can take place in the absence of the latter. For example, teachers can insert content into the curriculum about Mexican Americans without helping students to view the content from Mexican American perspectives. However, the knowledge construction process cannot be included in the curriculum if content integration has not first taken place.

## The Modification of Young Children's Racial Attitudes

In this chapter I discuss only one dimension of multicultural education—prejudice reduction—because of its limited scope. (Readers are referred to Banks [1993a] for a comprehensive discussion of each of the five dimensions. In two previous publications [Banks, 1991a; Banks, 1993b], I also discuss the nature of children's racial attitudes and intervention methods and strategies more extensively.)

The research that describes the racial awareness, attitudes, and self-identification of children (Milner, 1983; Phinney and Rotheram, 1987) is much richer than the research that describes ways in which their intergroup attitudes can be modified (Katz, 1976; Stephan, 1985; Banks, 1991a, 1993b). Clark and Clark (1939, 1940) make no reference to interventions designed to modify the racial preferences that children made in their famous doll studies in the 1930s and 1940s. Of the few intervention studies conducted in the 1940s (for example, Agnes, 1947; Jackson, 1944), most were conducted using adolescent youths as subjects. The number of intervention studies did not increase substantially until the intergroup education movement reached its peak in the 1950s (Cook and Cook, 1954). Most of the intervention studies conducted during the intergroup education movement of the 1940s and 1950s also used older children as subjects. One exception was the important study by Trager and Yarrow (1952), which was conducted using children between the ages of five and eight in kindergarten, first, and second grades. A cumulative body of research and theory on the modification of young children's racial attitudes did not develop until studies were conducted by Williams and his colleagues at Wake Forest University in the 1960s and 1970s (Best, Smith, Graves, and Williams, 1975; Williams and Edwards, 1969).

Several types of studies have been conducted to help children develop more democratic racial attitudes and behaviors. These include the *reinforcement studies* conducted by Williams and his colleagues (Best, Smith, Graves, and Williams, 1975; Williams and Edwards, 1969; Williams and Morland, 1976); the *perceptual differentiation studies* conducted by Katz and her colleagues (Katz, 1973, 1976, 1982; Katz and Zalk, 1978); the *curricular intervention studies* conducted by such researchers as Litcher and Johnson (1969), Trager and Yarrow (1952), and Yawkey and Blackwell (1974); and studies that use *cooperative activities* and *contact situations* to help children to develop more democratic attitudes and values (see, for example, Aronson and Bridgeman, 1979; DeVries, Edwards, and Slavin, 1978; Slavin, 1979, 1983, 1985). Most of the intervention studies conducted using preschool and primary-grade children as subjects have been reinforcement studies. Only a few perceptual differentiation studies have been reported. Most of the curriculum intervention studies have used older students as subjects (Banks, 1991a). All of the cooperative learning intervention studies reviewed by the present author used elementary-school and high school students as subjects; none used kindergarten and primary-grade children. Each of the four categories of studies identified here is discussed in the next section of this chapter.

## Reinforcement Studies

In the 1960s and 1970s, Williams and his colleagues (Williams and Edwards, 1969; Williams and Morland, 1976) conducted a series of laboratory reinforcement studies designed to modify preschool children's attitudes toward the colors black and white, and to determine whether a reduction of white bias toward objects and animals would generalize to white and black people. One of the first of a series of laboratory experiments was conducted by Williams and Edwards (1969). The sample consisted of 84 white preschool children in Winston Salem, North Carolina, who ranged in age from five to eleven years of age when the intervention began.

Two kinds of assessments were used to determine the children's color concepts and racial attitudes: (1) a picture-story procedure for assessing connotative meanings of black and white, and (2) a picture-story technique that measured attitudes toward black and white persons. The following is an example of the first procedure. The experimenter showed the child a white horse and a black horse and asked, "Which is the good horse? Which is the ugly horse? Which is the clean horse? Which is the stupid horse?" The next example is from the second procedure. A child was shown drawings of two identical human figures, one pinkish-tan with light yellow hair (white); the other medium-brown with black hair (African American). The experimenter said: "Here are two girls. Everyone says that one is pretty. Which is the pretty girl?"

In the experimental groups, the children received positive reinforcement either for choosing black animals in response to story sentences that contained positive adjectives or for choosing white animals when responding to story sentences that contained negative adjectives. The subjects were divided into three experimental groups and one control group. The three experimental groups were designated as follows: (1) positive reinforcement only, (2) negative reinforcement only, and (3) positive and negative reinforcement. The control group received no reinforcement.

The color-meaning procedure involving animals was administered twice at two-week intervals; the racial-attitude procedure using human figures was administered two weeks after the administration of the second session of the color-meaning procedure. During the administration of the color-meaning procedure, children who made a "correct" response were given candy in the positive reinforcement group, whereas those who made an "incorrect" response in the negative reinforcement group lost two of the thirty pennies they had been given. The children in the positive/negative reinforcement group also received candy when they gave a correct response and lost two pennies when they gave an incorrect response. In the control group, no mention was made of right and wrong answers and no reinforcement was given. Moreover, when the racial attitude procedure was administered, no reinforcement was given in any of the groups.

Williams and Edwards (1969) found that their reinforcement procedures reduced white bias in the children, and that children whose white bias had been weakened generalized their attitude to people. In other words, they showed a decreased tendency to describe African Americans negatively and whites positively. The investigators pointed out, however, that while the change in racial attitude was statistically significant, it was not substantial. Williams and Edwards also emphasized that even though the reinforcement procedure reduced white bias, it did not remove the children's color connotations for black and white. They wrote, "In the typical case, the procedure merely weakened the customary connotations of white as good and black as bad, and left the child with no consistent evaluative response to the colors" (p. 748).

These findings were confirmed in several later studies (Edwards and Williams, 1970; Hohn, 1973; Parish and Fleetwood, 1975; Parish, Shirazi, and Lambert, 1976), all of which concluded (1) that preschool children tend to evaluate the color black negatively and white positively, (2) that reinforcement procedures can reduce bias toward white, and (3) that children's reduced white bias can be generalized to African American people.

Spencer and Horowitz (1973), using procedures they adapted from Renninger and Williams (1966), examined the color perception of twenty-four African American and white children and designed a reinforcement procedure to modify both color connotations and racial attitudes. They found that the African American preschool children were as negative about the color black as were the white preschoolers, that the children generalized color concepts to racial concepts, that social and token reinforcement reduced white bias, and that the effects of the experiment were evident in all of the children over a two-week period and, in some, over as much as a four-week period.

### Perceptual Differentiation Studies

In a series of interesting and innovative studies, Katz (1973) and Katz and her colleagues (Katz, Sohn, and Zalk, 1974; Katz and Zalk, 1978) examined the perceptual concomitants of racial attitudes in young children. Katz (1973) predicted that preschool children would have more difficulty differentiating the faces of outgroup individuals than the faces of individuals who were members of their own racial groups. She tested this prediction using a sample of 192 African American and white preschool children who lived in New York City. Katz's prediction was confirmed; she concluded that "racial labels may increase the perceptual similarity of faces of another group" (1973, p. 298).

Katz reasoned that if children could be taught to perceptually differentiate among minority-group faces, racial prejudice would be reduced. She and Zalk (1978) investigated this possibility in an important study in which they also examined the effects of three other interventions: increased positive racial contact, vicarious interracial contact, and reinforcement of the color black. The researchers examined the effects of these interventions on second- and fifth-grade white students who exhibited high levels of prejudice. The children were randomly assigned to one of the four experimental treatment groups just described.

The experimental interventions were as follows. In the racial contact situation, two African American and two white children worked together to complete a jigsaw puzzle as fast as they could in order to win a prize. Each of the experimental interventions lasted for fifteen minutes in order to control for time. The children in the vicarious contact situation listened to a story, accompanied by slides, that described an African American boy (for the males) or girl (for the females) who was heroic. In one of the two experimental conditions for the stimulus predifferentiation groups, the children were shown four slides of the same model that varied along several dimensions. In the other condition, they observed African American faces. This intervention taught the children to differentiate among minority-group faces. The children participated in several tasks in the reinforcement condition. In one of them, they were shown ten pictures of black animals and ten pictures of white ones. When they chose a black animal, they were reinforced with marbles that could be exchanged for prizes.

The investigators found that each of the interventions resulted in a short-term reduction of prejudice on the combined attitude measures used in the study. The most effective interventions for reducing prejudice were the vicarious contact and the perceptual differentiation conditions. The children's racial attitudes were measured two weeks after the experiment and, again, four to six months later. Most of the experimental gains were reduced over time, but some were maintained. The vicarious contact and perceptual differentiation groups were found to be the most effective interventions for inducing long-term effects.

## Curriculum Interventions

Since the 1940s a number of curriculum intervention studies have been conducted to determine the effects of teaching units and lessons, multiethnic materials, role playing, and other kinds of simulated experiences on the racial attitudes and perceptions of students. One of the earliest of these, conducted by Trager and Yarrow (1952), examined the effects of a curriculum intervention on the racial attitudes of children in the first and second grades. In one experimental condition, the children experienced a democratic curriculum; in the other, nondemocratic values were taught and perpetuated. No experimental condition was created in the control group. The democratic curriculum was found to have a positive effect on the attitudes of both the students and the teachers.

White, second-grade children developed more positive racial attitudes after using multiethnic readers, in a study conducted by Litcher and Johnson (1969). However, when Litcher, Johnson, and Ryan (1973) replicated this study using photographs instead of readers, the children's racial attitudes were not significantly changed. According to the latter investigators, the shorter length of the second study (one month compared to four), and the different racial compositions of the two communities in which the studies were conducted, may help to explain why no significant effects were produced on the children's racial attitudes n the second study. The community in which the second study was conducted had a much higher percentage of African American residents than did the community in which the first was conducted.

A longitudinal evaluation of the television program *Sesame Street*, conducted by Bogatz and Ball (1971), supports the postulate that multiethnic simulated materials and interventions can have a positive effect on the racial attitudes of young children. These investigators found that children who had watched the program over long periods of time expresssed more positive racial attitudes toward outgroups than did children who had watched the show for shorter periods.

The effects of a simulation on the racial attitudes of third-grade children were examined by Weiner and Wright (1973). They divided a class into orange and green people. The children wore colored armbands that designated their group status. On one day of the intervention the students wearing orange armbands experienced discrimination. On the other day, the children wearing green armbands were the victims. On the third day, and again two weeks later, the children expressed lower levels of prejudiced beliefs and attitudes.

The effects of multiethnic social studies materials and related experiences on the racial attitudes of African American four-year-old children were examined by Yawkey and Blackwell (1974). The children were divided into three groups. The students in Group One read and discussed the materials. The Group Two students not only read and discussed the materials but also took a related field trip. The students in Group Three experienced the traditional preschool curriculum. The interventions in Groups One and Two were found to have a significant, positive effect on the students' racial attitudes toward African Americans and whites.

## Cooperative Learning and Interracial Contact

Since 1970 a group of investigators has accumulated an impressive body of research on the effects of cooperative-learning groups and activities on students' racial attitudes, friendship choices, and achievement. Much of this research has been conducted as well as reviewed by investigators such as Aronson and Bridgeman (1979), Aronson and Gonzalez (1988), Cohen (1972, 1986), Cohen and Roper (1972), Johnson and Johnson (1981, 1991), and Slavin (1979, 1983, 1985). Most of this research has used elementary school and high school students as subjects, rather than kindergarten and primary-grade students (Slavin, 1983, 1985).

This research is based on the theory of intergroup relations developed by Allport (1954), who stated that prejudice would be reduced if the intergroup situation was cooperative rather than competitive, if group members pursued common goals, if group members had equal status, if they got to know each other as individuals, and if the contact had institutional support and was sanctioned by authorities.

The research accumulated since 1970 lends considerable support to the postulate that cooperative interracial contact in schools has positive effects on both student interracial behavior and student academic achievement, if the conditions stated by Allport are present in the contact situations (Slavin, 1979, 1983). Similarly, in his review of nineteen studies of the effects of cooperative-learning methods, Slavin (1985) found that sixteen had positive effects on interracial friendships.

Most of this research supports the following postulates: (1) that students of color and white students show a greater tendency to make cross-racial friendship choices after they have participated in interracial learning teams involving the Jigsaw method (Aronson and Bridgeman, 1979) and the Student Teams-Achievement Divisions, or STAD (Slavin, 1979); (2) that the academic achievement of students of color, such as African Americans and Mexican Americans, is increased when cooperative-learning activities are used; and (3) that the academic achievement of white students remains about the same in both cooperative- and competitive-learning situations (Aronson and Gonzalez, 1988). Investigators have also found that cooperative-learning methods increase student motivation and self-esteem (Slavin, 1985),and have helped students to develop empathy (Aronson and Bridgeman, 1979).

An essential characteristic of effective cooperative-learning groups and methods is that the students experience equal-status contact (Allport, 1954). As Cohen (1972) has pointed out, both African American and white students expect that a higher status will be attributed to whites in initial interracial contact situations, thus possibly perpetuating white dominance. Cohen and Roper (1972) designed an intervention to change this expectation. They taught African American children to build transistor radios and to teach this skill to others. The African American children then taught the white children to build radios after all of the children watched a videotape showing the African American children building radios. When interracial work groups were structured, only those African American children who had taught the white students to build radios experienced equal status. The white children dominated in the other groups. This research indicates that equal status between groups in interracial situations needs to be constructed rather than assumed.

## The Positive Effects of Curriculum Interventions

The four types of intervention studies reviewed above lend considerable support to the postulate that the racial attitudes and interracial behavior of students can be changed through well-conceptualized and planned interventions. As Katz (1976) has pointed out, the intervention research involving children is much more hopeful than that dealing with adults. Indeed, adults' racial attitudes and behavior are more difficult to change because they are well crystallized and tenacious (Stephan, 1985). This research indicates that early childhood is the best time for educators to positively influence racial and ethnic attitudes. It becomes increasingly difficult to influence these attitudes of children as children grow older and move through the grades.

A variety of curricular interventions can be used to help students develop more positive racial attitudes and perceptions, including multicultural materials, vicarious experiences, role playing, and simulations. The most famous race-related curriculum intervention is the one undertaken by Jane Elliott, a third-grade teacher in Riceville, Iowa, who discriminated against brown-eyed children the first day and blue-eyed children the next. Elliot's intervention is described in a book (Peters, 1987) as well as in two video presentations, *The Eye of the Storm* and *A Class Divided*.

## Implications for Practice: The Need for Total School Reform

Research over the last six decades has established the fact that young children have accurate knowledge about racial differences and the evaluations that society makes of different racial and ethnic groups (Lasker, 1929; Clark and Clark, 1939; Milner, 1983; Abound, 1987). Research also indicates that many white children by the age of four have developed strong ingroup preferences and negative attitudes toward other racial groups (Abound, 1987; Milner, 1983), though it is less clear about the extent to which African American and Mexican American children form ingroup preferences. Many such children do, however, exhibit more outgroup than ingroup preferences, and others make biracial choices, because of the ways in which they have been socialized.

The research reviewed in this chapter indicates that educators can help students to develop more positive racial attitudes and behaviors (defined here as biracial choices) by implementing well-planned and well-conceptualized curricular interventions. The major goals of these interventions should be to help students of all racial, ethnic, and cultural groups (1) to develop more positive connotations for brown and other nonwhite colors; (2) to have positive vicarious experiences with people from a variety of racial and ethnic groups; (3) to learn to differentiate among the faces of individuals from different racial and ethnic groups; and (4), where possible, to have positive cross-racial interactions with children from different ethnic groups that are characterized by cooperation, equal status, and shared goals, and sanctioned by the teacher as well as by the school culture.

If these goals are to be reached, multicultural education must be implemented. *Multicultural education* is defined here as a restructuring and transformation of the total school environment so that it reflects the racial and cultural diversity that exists within U.S. society and helps children from diverse groups to experience educational equality (Banks, 1988, 1991b; Banks and Banks, 1989, 1995). To successfully implement multicultural education, each school as a whole must be conceptualized as a unit, (see Figure 12.1) and significant changes must be made in such variables as the values and attitudes of the school staff, the curriculum and teaching materials, assessment and testing procedures, teaching and motivational styles, and the values and norms sanctioned and perpetuated by the school. A number of useful resources are available to help practitioners to implement multicultural education; examples include Banks (1991b), Derman-Sparks and the A.B.C. Task Force (1989), Kendall (1983), Ramsey (1987), and Saracho and Spodek (1983).

## Approaches to Curriculum Reform

While all of the variables described in Figure 12.1 must be restructured in order to successfully implement multicultural education, it

# Figure 12.1. Multicultural School Reform

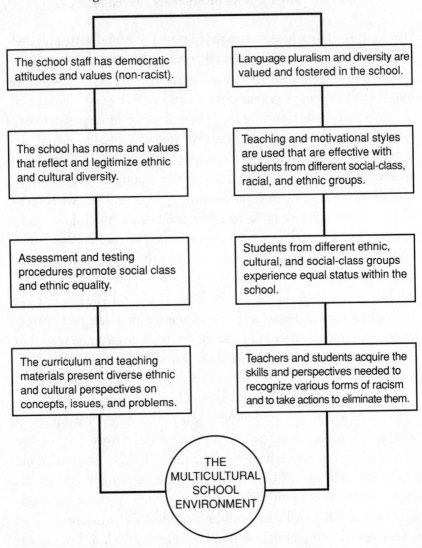

The school staff has democratic attitudes and values (non-racist).

Language pluralism and diversity are valued and fostered in the school.

The school has norms and values that reflect and legitimize ethnic and cultural diversity.

Teaching and motivational styles are used that are effective with students from different social-class, racial, and ethnic groups.

Assessment and testing procedures promote social class and ethnic equality.

Students from different ethnic, cultural, and social-class groups experience equal status within the school.

The curriculum and teaching materials present diverse ethnic and cultural perspectives on concepts, issues, and problems.

Teachers and students acquire the skills and perspectives needed to recognize various forms of racism and to take actions to eliminate them.

THE MULTICULTURAL SCHOOL ENVIRONMENT

*A reformed school environment based on a multifactor paradigm (holism).* This figure describes the characteristics of a multicultural school environment that has experienced reform based on a multifactor, holistic paradigm. The total school environment is conceptualized as a system which consists of a number of identifiable factors, such as the staff attitudes and values, assessment and testing procedures, and the curriculum and teaching materials. In the reformed, idealized multicultural school, each of these variables has been changed and reflects ethnic, cultural, and social-class equality. While any one of these factors may be the focus of initial school reform, changes must take place in each of them to create and sustain a school environment in which students from diverse groups experience equality.

*Source:* Banks, J. A. (1993). Multicultural education for young children: Racial and ethnic attitudes and their modification. In Bernard Spodek (ed.), *Handbook of research on the education of young children* (pp. 241–244, 246–248). New York: Macmillan. Copyright 1993. Adapted with permission.

is reasonable and practical to begin school reform by focusing on the curriculum. I have identified four major approaches to multi-cultural curriculum reform (Banks, 1991b): the contributions approach, the additive approach, the transformation approach, and the personal, social, and civic action approach. The *contributions approach* is frequently used by teachers to infuse ethnic content into the curriculum. This approach is characterized by the addition of ethnic heroes to the curriculum who are selected using criteria similar to those used to select mainstream heroes. The mainstream curriculum remains unchanged in terms of its basic assumptions, goals, and salient characteristics.

The heroes and holidays approach is a variant of the contributions approach. Here, ethnic content is limited primarily to special days, weeks, and months related to ethnic events and celebrations. Cinco de Mayo, Martin Luther King's birthday, and African American History month are examples of ethnic holidays that are celebrated in the schools. When this approach is used, the students study little or nothing about ethnic groups before or after the special event or occasion.

The contributions approach can readily be used by teachers attempting to integrate ethnic content into the curriculum. However, it has two serious limitations. First, it encourages students to view ethnic groups not as an integral part of U.S. society and culture but, rather, as an addition to the curriculum and thus as an appendage to the main story of the development of the nation. Second, this approach, especially when used in the early childhood curriculum, tends to focus on the material aspects of the cultures of ethnic groups, such as foods and dances, rather than on the cultural meanings of material objects and artifacts within an ethnic culture. In so doing, it encourages the stereotyping of ethnic groups as static and unchanging.

The *additive approach* is characterized by the addition of ethnic content, concepts, themes, and perspectives to the curriculum without changing its basic structure, purposes, and characteristics. It is often attained by the addition of a book or unit to the existing curriculum. The additive approach can be the first phase of a more substantial curriculum reform effort. However, it shares several problems with the contributions approach. Its most important shortcoming is that it usually results in the teaching of ethnic content from the perspectives of mainstream writers, artists, storytellers, and historians. When kindergarten children study Thanksgiving by viewing the Indians primarily from the point of view of the Pilgrims, the additive approach is being used. The Indians are "added" to the curriculum, but they are viewed through the eyes of the Pilgrims.

The *transformation approach* differs fundamentally from the contribution and additive approaches in that it changes the basic assumptions of the curriculum and enables students to view events, concepts, themes, issues, and problems from several ethnic perspectives and points of view. A teacher would be using the transformation approach if he or she presented the views of *both* the Indians and the Pilgrims. For instance, in addition to stories about Thanksgiving told from the perspective of the Pilgrims, the teacher might read documents describing how the Indians perceived the occupation of their lands by the British colonists. Thus, what was a "thanksgiving" for one group was in many ways a day of mourning for another. The teacher might also ask the students to assume the roles of both the Pilgrims and the Indians in role-play situations.

The *personal, social, and civic action approach* includes all of the elements of the transformation approach but adds components that require students to make decisions and to take actions related to the concept, issue, or problem they have studied in a lesson or unit. Elementary school students, though limited in the actions they can take related to racial and ethnic issues, can help create an ethnically more accepting school culture. For example, they can make a commitment to stop laughing at racist jokes, to stop using ethnic slurs, to read books that deal with children from other cultures and ethnic groups, and to make friends with children from other racial, ethnic, or religious groups. At the same time, the teacher can help students to become more sensitive to, and critical of, the images of people of color that are depicted on television.

To effectively implement multicultural education, educators should make infrequent use of the contributions approach to ethnic content integration and move gradually toward the full implementation of the transformation and social action approaches. These four approaches can readily be blended in actual classroom practice. For various reasons a teacher may wish to begin with the contributions approach. However, the goal should be to move toward a transformation and action-oriented curriculum so that students can understand the complex nature of ethnic groups in U.S. society and develop the knowledge, skills, and attitudes needed to become effective citizens in the pluralistic society of the next century.

## The Importance of the Teacher

Teachers play a key role in implementing multicultural education and in helping students to develop democratic racial attitudes and behaviors. Because they bring their own cultural perspectives, values, hopes, and dreams to the classroom, they are in a position to strongly influence the views, conceptions, and behaviors of students. Their values and perspectives also mediate what they teach and influence the ways in which their messages are communicated and perceived by students. Teachers who express strong ingroup preferences and believe that white is more beautiful than brown or that whites have been the main contributors to American culture and civilization will, whether they intend to or not, convey these attitudes and beliefs to students. Thus effective multicultural education depends on teacher education to counteract the Eurocentric values and attitudes that many teachers have internalized, as exemplified by the research reviewed in this chapter (Gay, 1986).

Teacher educators must help classroom teachers attain the knowledge, attitudes, and skills they need to function effectively in the multicultural classroom of the twenty-first century (Banks, 1988, 1991b; Gay, 1986; Ladson-Billings, 1995). Above all, we must create a more caring nation, especially given the demographic changes that are taking place in U.S. society. About 46 percent of the nation's school-age youth will be students of color by 2020

(Pallas, Natriello, and McDill, 1989). This increasing racial, ethnic, and cultural diversity presents new challenges as well as new opportunities. If the United States does not become a more culturally sensitive society in which citizens from different racial and cultural groups can live and work in harmony, its survival as a strong and democratic nation will be imperiled. The research described in this chapter is intended to provide educators with hope as well as with specific guidelines for the decisive action needed to transform the total school culture. Transformation of the total school is essential to the development of citizens who have the multicultural literacy, perspectives, and cross-cultural competencies needed to function effectively in the next century.

# References

Abound, F. E. (1987). The development of ethnic self-identification and attitudes. In J. S. Phinney and M. J. Rotheram (eds.), *Children's ethnic socialization: Pluralism and development* (pp. 32–55). Beverly Hills, Calif.: Sage.

Agnes, M. (1947). Influences of reading on the racial attitudes of adolescent girls. *Catholic Educational Review*, 45, 415–420.

Allport, G. W. (1954). *The nature of prejudice.* Cambridge, Mass.: Addison-Wesley.

Aronson, E., and Bridgeman, D. (1979). Jigsaw groups and the desegregated classroom: In pursuit of common goals. *Personality and Social Psychology Bulletin, 5,* 438–446.

Aronson, E., and Gonzalez, A. (1988). Desegregation, jigsaw, and the Mexican-American experience. In P. A. Katz and D. A. Taylor (eds.), *Eliminating racism: Profiles in controversy* (pp. 301–314). New York: Plenum Press.

Assante, M. K. (1991). The Afrocentric idea in education. *Journal of Negro Education, 60,* 170–180.

Asante, M. K., and Ravitch, D. (1991). Multiculturalism: An exchange. *The America Scholar, 60* (Spring), 267–276.

Baker, G. (1983). *Planning and organizing for multicultural instruction.* Menlo Park, Calif.: Addison-Wesley.

Banks, J. A. (1988). *Multiethnic education: Theory and practice,* 2nd ed. Boston: Allyn & Bacon.

Banks, J. A. (1989). Multicultural education: Characteristics and goals. In J. A. Banks and C.A.M. Banks (eds.), *Multicultural education: Issues and perspectives* (pp. 2–26). Boston: Allyn & Bacon.

Banks, J. A. (1991a). Multicultural education: Its effects on students' racial and gender role attitudes. In J. P. Shaver (ed.), *Handbook of research on social studies teaching and learning* (pp. 459–469). New York: Macmillan.

Banks, J. A. (1991b). *Teaching strategies for ethnic studies*, 5th ed. Boston: Allyn & Bacon.

Banks, J. A. (1992). The history of multicultural education. In M. C. Alkin and M. A. Linden (eds.), *Encyclopedia of educational research*, 6th ed. (pp. 83–94). New York: Macmillan.

Banks, J. A. (1993a). Multicultural education: Historical development, dimensions, and practice. In L. Darling-Hammond (ed.), *Review of research in education*, Vol. 19 (pp. 3–49). Washington, D.C.: American Educational Research Association.

Banks, J. A. (1993b). Multicultural education for young children: Racial and ethnic attitudes and their modification. In B. Spodek (ed.), *Handbook of research on the education of young children* (pp. 236–250). New York: Macmillan.

Banks, J. A., and Banks, C.A.M. (eds.). (1989). *Multicultural education: Issues and perspectives*. Boston: Allyn & Bacon.

Banks, J. A., and Banks, C.A.M. (eds.). (1995). *Handbook of research on multicultural education*. New York: Macmillan.

Bennett, C. I. (1990). *Comprehensive multicultural education*, 2nd ed. Boston: Allyn & Bacon.

Berger, P. L., and Luckman, T. (1966). *The social construction of knowledge: A treatise in the sociology of knowledge*. Garden City, N.Y.: Doubleday.

Best, D. L., Smith, S. C., Graves, D. J., and Williams, J. E. (1975). The modification of racial bias in preschool children. *Journal of Experimental Child Psychology, 20*, 193–205.

Blassingame, J. W. (1972). *The slave community: Plantation life in the ante-bellum South*. New York: Oxford University Press.

Bogatz, G. A., and Ball, S. (1971). *The second year of Sesame Street: A continuing evaluation*. Princeton, N.J.: Educational Testing Service.

Braddock II, J. H. (1990). Tracking the middle grades: National patterns of grouping for instruction. *Phi Delta Kappan, 71* (Feb.), 445–449.

Brookover, W. B., and others. (1979). *School social systems and student achievement: Schools can make a difference*. New York: Praeger.

Clark, K. B., and Clark, M. P. (1939). The development of consciousness of self and the emergence of racial identification in Negro preschool children. *Journal of Social Psychology, 10*, 591–599.

Clark, K. B., and Clark, M. P. (1940). Skin color as a factor in racial identification and preference in Negro children. *Journal of Negro Education, 19*, 341–358.

Cohen, E. (1972). Interracial interaction disability. *Human Relations, 25*, 9–24.

Cohen, E. G. (1986). *Designing groupwork: Strategies for the heterogeneous classroom*. New York: Teachers College Press.

336 Toward a Common Destiny

Cohen, E. G., and Roper, S. S. (1972). Modification of interracial interaction disability: An application of status characteristic theory. *American Sociological Review*, 37, 643–657.

Cook, L., and Cook, E. (1954). *Intergroup education*. New York: McGraw-Hill.

Cummings, J. (1986). Empowering minority students: A framework for intervention. *Harvard Educational Review*, 56, 18–36.

Darling-Hammond, L. (1995). Inequality and access to knowledge. In J. A. Banks and C.A.M. Banks (eds.), *Handbook of research on multicultural education* (pp. 465–482). New York: Macmillan.

Derman-Sparks, L., and the A.B.C. Task Force. (1989). *Anti-bias curriculum: Tools for empowering young children*. Washington, D.C.: National Association for the Education of Young Children.

Delpit, L. D. (1988). The silenced dialogue: Power and pedagogy in educating other people's children. *Harvard Educational Review*, 58, 280–298.

DeVries, D. L., Edwards, K. J., and Slavin, R. E. (1978). Biracial learning teams and race relations in the classroom: Four field experiments on Teams-Games-Tournament. *Journal of Educational Psychology*, 70, 356–362.

Edwards, C. D., and Williams, J. E. (1970). Generalization between evaluative words associated with racial figures in preschool children. *Journal of Experimental Research in Personality*, 4, 144–155.

Ford, N. A. (1973). *Black studies: Threat-or-challenge*. Port Washington, N.Y.: Kennikat Press.

Garcia, R. L. (1991). *Teaching in a pluralistic society: Concepts, models, strategies*, 2nd ed. New York: HarperCollins.

Gay, G. (1986). Multicultural teacher education. In J. A. Banks and J. Lynch (eds.), *Multicultural education in Western societies* (pp. 154–177). London: Holt, Rinehart & Winston.

Gay, G. (1992). The state of multicultural education in the United States. In K. Adam-Moodley (ed.), *Education in plural societies: International perspectives* (pp. 47–66). Calgary, Alberta: Detselig.

Gollnick, D. M., and Chinn, P. C. (1990). *Multicultural education in a pluralistic society*, 3rd ed. Columbus, Ohio: Merrill.

Gould, S. J. (1981). *The mismeasure of man*. New York: Norton.

Grant, C. A., and Sleeter, C. E. (1986). Race, class, and gender in education research: An argument for integrative analysis. *Review of Educational Research*, 56, 195–211.

Gray, P. (1991). Whose America? *Time* (July 8), pp. 12–17.

Harding, S. (1991). *Whose science? Whose knowledge? Thinking from women's lives*. Ithaca, N.Y.: Cornell University Press.

Hohn, R. L. (1973). Perceptual training and its effect on racial preference of kindergarten children. *Psychological Reports*, 32, 435–441.

Jackson, E. P. (1944). Effects of reading upon the attitudes toward the Negro race. *Library Quarterly*, 14, 47–54.

Johnson, D. W., and Johnson, R. T. (1981). Effects of cooperative and individualistic learning experiences on interethnic interaction. *Journal of Educational Psychology, 73*, 444–449.

Johnson, D. W., and Johnson, R. T. (1991). *Learning together and alone*, 3rd ed. Englewood Cliffs, N.J.: Prentice-Hall.

Katz, P. A. (1973). Perception of racial cues in preschool children: A new look. *Developmental Psychology, 8*, 295–299.

Katz, P. A. (1976). Attitude change in children: Can the twig be straightened? In P. A. Katz (ed.), *Towards the elimination of racism* (pp. 213–241). New York: Pergamon.

Katz, P. A. (1982). A review of recent research in children's attitude acquisition. In L. Katz (ed.), *Current topics in early childhood education*, Vol. 4 (pp. 17–54). Norwood, N.J.: Ablex.

Katz, P. A., Sohn, M., and Zalk, S. (1975). Perceptual concomitants of racial attitudes in urban grade-school children. *Developmental Psychology, 11*, 135–144.

Katz, P. A., and Zalk, S. R. (1978). Modification of children's racial attitudes. *Developmental Psychology, 14*, 447–461.

Kendall, F. E. (1983). *Diversity in the classroom: A multicultural approach to the education of young children*. New York: Teachers College Press.

Klein, S. S. (ed.). (1985). *Handbook for achieving sex equity through education*. Baltimore: Johns Hopkins University Press.

Kuhn, T. S. (1970). *The structure of scientific revolutions*, 2nd ed., enlarged. Chicago: University of Chicago Press.

Ladson-Billings, G. (1995). Multicultural teacher education. In J. A. Banks and C.A.M. Banks (eds.), *Handbook of research on multicultural education* (pp. 747–759). New York: Macmillan.

Lasker, B. (1929). *Race attitudes in children*. New York: Holt, Rinehart & Winston.

Leo, L. (1990). A fringe history of the world. *U.S. News and World Report* (November 12), pp. 25–26.

Litcher, J. H., and Johnson, D. W. (1969). Changes in attitudes toward Negroes of White elementary school students after use of multiethnic readers. *Journal of Educational Psychology, 60*, 148–152.

Litcher, J. H., Johnson, D. W., and Ryan, F. L. (1973). Use of pictures of multiethnic interaction to change attitudes of White elementary school students toward Blacks. *Psychological Reports, 33*, 367–372.

Mercer, J. R. (1989). Alternative paradigms for assessment in a pluralistic society. In J. A. Banks and C. A. M. Banks (eds.), *Multicultural education: Issues and perspectives* (pp. 289–304). Boston: Allyn & Bacon.

Miel, A., with Kiester, E., Jr. (1967). *The shortchanged children of suburbia: What schools don't teach about human differences and what can be done about it*. New York: American Jewish Committee.

Milner, D. (1983). *Children and race*. Beverly Hills, Calif.: Sage.

Oakes, J. (1985). *Keeping track: How schools structure inequality*. New Haven, Conn.: Yale University Press.

Ogbu, J. U. (1990). Overcoming racial barriers to equal access. In J. I. Goodlad and P. Keating (eds.), *Access to knowledge: An agenda for our nation's schools* (pp. 59–89). New York: College Board.

Pallas, A. M., Natriello, G., and McDill, E. L. (1989). The changing nature of the disadvantaged population: Current dimensions and future trends. *Educational Researcher, 18*, 16–22.

Parish, T. S., and Fleetwood, R. S. (1975). Amount of conditioning and subsequent change in racial attitudes of children. *Perceptual and Motor Skills, 40*, 79–86.

Parish, T. S., Shirazi, A., and Lambert, F. (1976). Conditioning away prejudicial attitudes in children. *Perceptual and Motor Skills, 43*, 907–912.

Peters, W. (1987). *A class divided: Then and now*, expanded ed. New Haven, Conn.: Yale University Press.

Phinney, J. S., and Rotheram, M. J. (1987). (eds.). *Children's ethnic socialization: Pluralism and development*. Beverly Hills, Calif.: Sage.

Ramsey, P. G. (1987). *Teaching and learning in a diverse world: Multicultural education for young children*. New York: Teachers College Press.

Ravitch, D. (1990). Diversity and democracy: Multicultural education in America. *American Educator* (Spring), pp. 16–48.

Renninger, C. A., and Williams, J. E. (1966). Black-white color connotations and race awareness in children. *Perceptual and Motor Skills, 22*, 771–785.

Sadker, M. P., and Sadker, D. M. (1982). *Sex equity handbook for schools*. New York: Longman.

Saracho, O. N., and Spodek, B. (eds.). (1983). *Understanding the multicultural experience in early childhood education*. Washington, D.C.: National Association for the Education of Young Children.

Schlesinger, A., Jr. (1990). When ethnic studies are un-American. *Social Studies Review* (Summer), pp. 11–13.

Schlesinger, A., Jr. (1991). *The disuniting of America: Reflections on a multicultural society*. Knoxville, Tenn.: Whittle Direct Books.

Shade, B. J. (ed.). (1989). *Culture, style, and the educative process*. Springfield, Ill.: Charles C. Thomas.

Slavin, R. E. (1979). Effects of biracial learning teams on cross-racial friendships. *Journal of Educational Psychology, 71*, 381–387.

Slavin, R. E. (1983). *Cooperative learning*. New York: Longman.

Slavin, R. E. (1985). Cooperative learning: Applying contact theory in desegregated schools. *Journal of Social Issues, 41*, 45–62.

Sleeter, C. E. (ed.). (1991). *Empowerment through multicultural education*. Albany: State University of New York Press.

Sleeter, C. E., and Grant, C. A. (1988). *Making choices for multicultural education: Five approaches to race, class and gender*. Columbus, Ohio: Merrill.

Spencer, M. B., and Horowitz, F. D. (1973). Effects of systematic social and token reinforcement on the modification of racial and color concept attitudes in Black and in White preschool children. *Developmental Psychology, 9,* 246–254.

Stephan, W. G. (1985). Intergroup relations. In G. Lindzey and E. Aronson (eds.), *The handbook of social psychology,* 3rd ed. (pp. 599–658). New York: Random House.

Trager, H. G., and Yarrow, M. R. (1952). *They learn what they live: Prejudice in young children.* New York: Harper & Brothers.

Weiner, M. J., and Wright, F. E. (1973). Effects of undergoing arbitrary discrimination upon subsequent attitudes toward a minority group. *Journal of Applied Social Psychology, 3,* 94–102.

Werner, N. E., and Evans, I. M. (1968). Perception of prejudice in Mexican-American preschool children. *Perceptual and Motor Skills, 27,* 1039–1046.

Williams, J. E., and Edwards, C. D. (1969). An exploratory study of the modification of color and racial concept attitudes in preschool children. *Child Development, 40,* 737–750.

Williams, J. E., and Morland, J. K. (1976). *Race, color and the young child.* Chapel Hill: University of North Carolina Press.

Yawkey, T. D., and Blackwell, J. (1974). Attitudes of 4-year-old urban Black children toward themselves and Whites based upon multi-ethnic social studies materials and experiences. *Journal of Educational Research, 67,* 373–377.

*Chapter Thirteen*

# Education in Multicultural Settings: Perspectives from Global and International Education Programs

## Judith Torney-Purta

Education to promote ethnic and racial diversity as a resource, a priority for many schools, has been defined in different ways over the past several decades. A recent review by Banks (1993) distinguishes among four models of multicultural education: intergroup education, prejudice reduction, equity pedagogy, and a restructuring of the culture and organization of the school so that students from diverse racial, ethnic, and social-class groups can experience educational equality. He argues that effective programs rely on the recognition of race, class, and gender as intersecting issues. In this chapter I build on that perspective, arguing that effective models of multicultural education for the next decade also require the intersecting of immigrant status and national identity with race, gender, and class. I also examine existing global or international education programs for suggestions applicable to these new models.

Since at least the mid-1970s, countries such as the U.K., the Netherlands, and Sweden have had multiethnic populations in many of their schools, resulting from waves of migration across their borders (see the reviews of educational policy and practice of several of these nations in Sigel and Hoskin, 1991). In both extent and meaning, diversity and multiculturalism in the United States are also becoming increasingly complex because of immigration. A decade ago these issues were of primary concern only for states such as Texas, California, New York, and Florida. And it is in those states that anti-immigrant feeling has been most prominent. But immigrant groups are now much more broadly spread, in suburban and rural as well as urban areas across the nation. Ogbu (1992) reports that in 1968–1970 in Stockton, California, only six ethnic groups were represented in his school sample. By 1986 this number had tripled. Differences between Vietnamese, Korean, and Chinese, between Puerto Ricans, Mexicans, and Peruvians, or between African Americans born in Haiti or Nigeria and those born in the United States are increasingly important.

Recent ethnographies of schools and community settings clearly illustrate the importance of national origin, national identity, and immigrant status as they influence peer interaction, family-school linkages, and cognitive performance in U.S. schools (Lamphere, 1992; Peshkin, 1991; Gibson and Ogbu, 1991). Among children from immigrant families (especially undocumented families) there is often a lack of trust in school-based and other authorities. Children who are themselves immigrant, or whose parents recently immigrated, grow up with a particular sense of national and linguistic identity. LaFramboise and her colleagues used many examples from Latin American and other immigrant groups, as well as from Native American and African American groups, in defining bicultural competence:

> [An] affective element of bicultural competence is the ability to develop and maintain positive attitudes toward one's culture of origin and the second culture in which he or she is attempting to acquire competence. . . . An individual will also need to acquire knowledge of both cultures in order to develop the belief that he or she can be biculturally competent, which we have labeled bicultural efficacy [LaFramboise, Coleman, and Gerton, 1993, p. 48].

A related issue is increasing complexity in the meaning and salience of identity as it relates to ethnic, racial, national, and linguistic groups. Heath and McLaughlin (1993), in their study of inner-city neighborhood organizations, note that adolescents do not define their identities primarily in terms of the ethnic and racial categories often used by adults or those outside their neighborhoods to define them. Rather, their identities are "embedded" in complex networks of the family and the local community that more often relate to subcultural groups than to American society as a whole. Adolescents often express differences with their elders in their sense of who they are and where they belong. As McLaughlin puts it, "There are powerful signals to youth about their value, social legitimacy, and future. Youth responded to these community-level attitudes by retreating to the confines of their cultural group and by distrusting the possibility or desirability of ever becoming part of broader society" (1993, p. 43).

In short, my argument in this chapter is that effective models of multicultural education for the next decade require concern for the intersection of immigrant status and national identity with race, gender, and class. Two conceptual frameworks dealing with cultural diversity, developed by Ogbu and Brislin respectively, are briefly reviewed, followed by a brief history of international or global education programs, brief summaries of four program approaches in which some of these complex intersections have been explored, and a summary of research and evaluation relating to programs incorporating international dimensions. Finally, issues such as authenticity of involvement, cross-cutting identities, the role of community as well as of in-school programs, and the implications of peer groups for practice, policy, and research are discussed.

## Two Approaches to Conceptualizing Ethnic and Racial Diversity

Ogbu's work (1992, 1993; Gibson and Ogbu, 1991) has had a formative effect on the understanding of contrasts between immigrant groups and ethnic groups such as African Americans, pointing up hitherto unrecognized distinctions. Brislin (1993) has noted similar issues relating to intercultural contact, regardless of whether the cultures are living across the street or across an ocean from one another. In this section I review the two frameworks in order to elaborate on the importance of national identity and immigrant status in multicultural education and to suggest ways of using programs of international and global education.

In a program of ethnographic research on the academic achievement of students from diverse groups, Ogbu (1992, 1993; Gibson and Ogbu) discusses the distinction between immigrant and non-immigrant minorities. He also focuses on the family's and community's models of social realities and competence, including the perceived value associated with education. His aim is to understand these meaning structures in order to assist minority groups that have traditionally not done well in school. He describes the paradoxical situation whereby some groups do better in school in various national settings, citing West Indian children, who are most successful academically in the continental United States, where they regard themselves as immigrants; less successful in Canada, where they identify themselves as part of the Commonwealth; and least successful in Britain, their former colonial power.

Ogbu's most significant distinction is between voluntary immigrant minorities, who have moved by choice to the United States to obtain opportunities, and involuntary minorities, who were brought against their will, through either slavery or colonization. This sense of coercion prevails even across generations, according to Ogbu. Both groups experience difficulties due to differences between the culture of the home and community and that of the school, but these difficulties are compounded when young people create "oppositional identities" in a secondary culture that rejects the value of educational achievement. Ogbu makes the point that these oppositional identities reflect perceptions common in the community about the lack of an open opportunity structure that ensures economic advancement via traditional credentialing. According to Ogbu, a student who decides to do well in school faces a conflict between the community or peer group, which provides a sense of worth and belonging, and the school, where a sense of worth may be achievable only by giving up these other valued identities.

African American children whose families have suffered discrimination over generations are the most likely to develop these oppositional identities; but, as Ogbu recognizes, it is also possible for certain recent immigrant groups to develop such beliefs, especially when opportunities to gain status are perceived to be limited and peer group influence is strong. For example, Vietnamese refugee youth in Southern California appear likely to devalue academic striving. The process Ogbu describes is much like the development of oppositional identities among working-class youth in England (Willis, 1977); it also resembles the development of identities stressing attractiveness and devaluing achievement among women college students (see Holland and Eisenhart, 1990).

Ogbu argues that interventions should be based on ethnographic research that describes different groups' cultural adaptations and recognizes the situations within peer groups and communities in which these oppositional identities or sets of meaning develop. Certain aspects and applications of Ogbu's formulation have been criticized, but his broader point is that race, class, gender, and immigrant status intersect in complex ways. These factors have powerful meanings constructed within the society, the community, and the peer group—meanings that influence the behavior of youth (see also Delgado-Gaitan and Trueba, 1991).

The impact of immigrant status upon youth is discussed by Brislin (1993), whose research has been used in preparing adults to move from their home country to other regions of the world. I have expanded his discussion, integrating recent material on situated cognition to provide an elaborated framework for examining the role of international dimensions within multicultural education.

First, according to Brislin, there are many dimensions along which sharp contrasts exist between cultures—for example, the treatment of time, the ways in which adults and children or males and females speak to each other, emotional expressiveness, and how individualism is balanced with loyalty to face-to-face groups such as the peer group or the family. Recognizing these contrasts has been the subject of many intercultural training programs for adults preparing to live abroad. Role playing and other techniques designed to help individuals consider alternative perspectives are frequently part of these programs and have potential for this enhanced view of multicultural education.

Second, by the time they enter school, children have been immersed for several years as involved observers or "peripheral participants" in the family and its activities, goals, and belief structures. The work of Lave and Wenger (1991), which points to the way cognition is "situated" within a cultural context and oriented toward specific goals, provides examples of learning through apprenticeship by tailors in Liberia, midwives in Latin America, and adults estimating costs in the supermarket in the United States. This analytic framework of situated cognition has not previously been comprehensively applied to an understanding of the ways that cognitions and relationships are situated within cultural contexts and related to superordinate goals for children growing up in multiethnic situations. Understanding how behavior is situated in the community, the family, and the peer group and how the child moves from peripheral participation as an involved observer to full participation in each setting has considerable potential for this new view of multicultural education. Indeed, ways of involving children from different cultural groups in common superordinate goals within the classroom, sometimes in peripheral roles and sometimes more fully, can be a powerful part of intercultural education.

Third, because passing on culture to the young and ensuring their identification with the family are important goals for parents and other relatives, the potential for misunderstandings between parents and children who are involved in intercultural situations outside the family is even greater than that for misunderstandings among adults crossing cultures (Brislin, 1993). Thus it is important to multicultural education that educators recognize the role of identification of the young person with groups at various levels, as reinforced by peers and community as well as by family.

Fourth, families who have recently immigrated, and those in "involuntary minorities," often find themselves occupying a low-status position within a society in terms of prestige, power, and influence. Because this position usually includes economic power, the stresses and strains experienced by a family will also be substantial. Thus, providing situations in which children from different cultures enjoy equality of status within classroom groups can be important in multicultural education.

In short, both Ogbu and Brislin point to the lack of clear boundaries between multicultural, intercultural, and international education and to the potential for cross-fertilization. Although there is a great deal of debate over the terminology in the field, this chapter refers to international education, global education, global perspectives in education, education for international understanding, international human rights education, and world studies as similar in content and focus. The next section briefly reviews the history of this field.

## A Brief History of International and Global Education

Efforts to use education to further harmonious relations between individuals from different countries and cultures have a long history. The period beginning about a hundred years ago and extending to the start of the First World War was one of especially great activity. Certain practices from this period—for example, textbook revisions to eliminate misconceptions—can still be recognized. Concern for immigrant populations, or for racial prejudice and discrimination, was not a priority among these efforts, however.

At several points along the way, there was undue optimism regarding how easily education or similar initiatives might bring about change. In 1910, in a letter to the Trustees at the Establishment of the Carnegie Endowment for International Peace, Andrew Carnegie envisioned a time when war would be "discarded as disgraceful to civilized men." He was concerned that the endowment not be misused, so, upon the elimination of war, the Trustees were to "consider what is the next most degrading evil or evils" and use the endowment's resources accordingly.

The establishment of UNESCO in 1945 was an important postwar event in international education. Its major early programs included the establishment of the UNESCO Associated Schools, a network that stretched across the world (with a few U.S. schools as members). Among the educational themes still pursued by the member-schools are human rights and the cultures of other countries. Actual projects frequently involve recognition of cultural diversity as a strength.

The late 1960s saw further activity when the U.S. Office of Education supported a proposal of the Foreign Policy Association to prepare "An Examination of Objectives, Needs, and Priorities in International Education in the United States," by James Becker and Lee Anderson. These authors argued against what was then the operative view of international education as committed to teaching about "strange lands and friendly people who are different from us" or as limited to a single school subject such as world history or geography. These definitions did not sufficiently emphasize the global nature of world reality and increasing interdependence, they argued. The topics on which education should focus included earth as a planet, humankind as one species of life, and the international system as a level of social organization. Phrases such as "a global perspective on education," as well as approaches that involve seeing international linkages within one's everyday life rather than only in the actions of national political leaders, can be traced to this report. Among the programs reviewed later in the present chapter, several have explicit ties to this vision of global education.

Another milestone occurred in 1974, when UNESCO at its General Conference passed a Recommendation on Education for International Understanding, Cooperation and Peace and Education relating to Human Rights and Fundamental Freedoms. For the first time, the issue of human rights as defined in the Universal Declaration of Human Rights became recognized as an essential theme of international education (Buergenthal and Torney, 1976). This UNESCO Recommendation predated Jimmy Carter's election and his subsequent stress on human rights in American foreign policy. Until about 1981 the United States was an active participant in international debates about global dimensions of education in schools and the ways in which education about internationally recognized human rights might be included. In many other countries, international education is still related to provisions of this

UNESCO recommendation. In the mid-1980s, the United States withdrew from membership in UNESCO, thus ending its official connection with these programs.

Nevertheless, international and global education, with its increasing recognition of multiculturalism, has continued to grow rapidly in the United States. And at present, nearly every state has some mandate in this area ranging from required world history courses to full curricula in global education (see Becker, 1991).

Problems of definition and the absence of a clear conceptual framework have continued to concern many educators (see Massialas's chapter [1991] in the recent *Handbook of Research on Social Studies Teaching and Learning*). Some, however, feel that by engaging students in those activities associated with global or international education, they are making a positive contribution to cross-cultural understanding, world peace, and understanding across racial and cultural groups. If this instruction is effective, they have relatively little concern about whether it is called global education or multicultural education or education for international or cross-cultural understanding.

In the next section I present brief reviews of four different programs that fall under the rubric of international or global education. The first is a professional network for which a set of objectives for international education has been laid out; the second is a statewide program; the third, a framework and set of programs of the Association for Supervision and Curriculum Development, is designed for elementary schools; and the fourth, a program based at the University of Maryland, links adolescents in other countries as well as across the United States using computer networking. Many other programs could have been included, such as CHART, the Collaboration for Humanities and Arts Teaching, sponsored by the Rockefeller Foundation (here I refer especially to the New York and World projects, see Jennings, 1993); efforts to use global education as a major component in school restructuring (Tye and Tye, 1992); a set of curriculum designs each based on a different disciplinary orientation (Woyach and Remy, 1989); and curricular change linked with a global focus on interdependence as districts plan schooling for the twenty-first century (Kniep and Martin-Kniep, 1995).

## Four Illustrations of Global Education Programming

### AEGIS: The Alliance for Education in Global and International Studies: A Coordinating Network

A national professional organization was established in the late 1980s to coordinate global and international education and provide opportunities for informed discussion of important cross-cutting issues. The Alliance for Education in Global and International Studies is a consortium of U.S. organizations working to improve the international dimensions of elementary and secondary education. The statement of purpose notes:

> We seek an education which develops in elementary and secondary students . . . :
>
> 1. A knowledge of the histories, languages, and institutions—political, economic, religious, artistic, humanistic—of other cultures, as well as their own;
>
> 2. A knowledge of the interconnections among world regions, events, and peoples . . . ;
>
> 3. An understanding that contemporary issues and world cultures have been shaped by a multiplicity of historical, religious, political, economic, and geographical factors;
>
> 4. An ability and willingness to consider historical and contemporary world events and issues from the perspectives of people whose culture, value orientations, or life experience—gender, age, opportunity, ethnic background—are different from their own and, in so doing, develop a deepened understanding of their own standards and goals;
>
> 5. An understanding of the nature of conflict and of approaches for managing it constructively;
>
> 6. An ability to think analytically about complex national and international issues . . . ; and

7. An ability to make informed personal and public policy decisions and to participate in local, national, and international
decision-making processes.

This list includes ideas that are familiar to individuals interested in
education with a multicultural focus, especially in topics dealing
with conflict resolution and an understanding of several perspectives on an issue.

Among AEGIS's current projects is an effort to assist the more
than one hundred federally funded Title VI Foreign Area and
International studies centers located at major universities throughout the country whose mandates include outreach to kindergarten
through grade twelve classes. Many of these universities have little
tradition of collaboration with other schools. In addition to conferences for Area studies centers' outreach directors, AEGIS works
to coordinate the efforts of centers with those of state departments
of education in three states. Several of the centers dealing with area
studies in Africa and Latin America involve education relating to
the African American identity; they are also concerned with issues
relevant to immigrant populations from Latin America.

## CISP: The California International Studies Project

In 1985 the California legislature and governor approved a legislative measure establishing the California International Studies
Project (CISP), designed to strengthen students' knowledge of
international issues, other cultures, and foreign languages. A network of resource centers representing collaborations among local
colleges or universities, school districts, and community world affairs
organizations was established. The project is managed through the
School of Education at Stanford University.

At first, CISP focused on the study of other countries and cultures using innovative methods and stressing ways of enhancing students' ability to see the world from several different perspectives. But
largely because of demographic change in California, leading to the
location of several of these centers in areas with large immigrant
populations, many of the projects now give special emphasis to help-

ing diverse children succeed in the educational system. Toward this end, CISP currently supports a project based at San Diego State University that emphasizes the educational needs of Mexican and Central American immigrant students who are pulled back and forth across the border and live in communities where the opportunity structures and meaning systems related to education are perceived to be negative. The project is intended to help teachers better understand and teach about the root culture, the immigrant experience, and intercultural contact, with the goal of aiding children in this transition process. In subsequent years the plan is to focus on Africa and on Asia. Meanwhile, connections with various community groups working on human relations issues are being incorporated.

A second CISP-funded project has brought Cohen's group work on the heterogeneous classroom into several school sites (Cohen and others, 1994). The Program on Complex Instruction, of which this is a part, addresses the needs of academically low-status students and recognizes that the child's status outside the school follows him or her into the classroom. In other words, a child more comfortable speaking Spanish or Chinese than English, or speaking with an accent, or unable to purchase the kinds of new clothes that others wear, or moving back and forth across the border and missing school will be given low status by other children. This may, in fact, be the first step in oppositional identity development.

Under the auspices of this project, teachers receive training in equalizing the status of children in the classroom—for example, by offering specific praise for the contributions of specific children to goals. Even more important is a type of cooperative learning whereby students participate in a project organized around a theme, such as challenging the authority of an institution (as in China's democracy movement) or solving the problems faced in forming a community of countries (such as the European Community). Toward this end, a class is divided into small groups and specific students (including the low-status students) are assigned roles, such as that of facilitator, recorder, or materials monitor. Then each small group approaches the problem from a different skill base. Some use their academic skills and read various texts about the period or problem; some take a graphic or spatial point of view by interpreting maps or diagrams; others use their artistic talents to draw and interpret political cartoons; and still others turn to dramatic role playing or use their skills in assembling multimedia presentations. The groups then rotate through those different skill or ability tasks and roles. Several studies, summarized in Cohen (1990) and in Cohen and others (1994), document the reduction in status imbalance that results from the sustained use of these programs.

The low-status students who are given opportunities to have their diverse skills recognized in the program are often the immigrant or limited-English-proficiency students. In this connection, note CISP's emphasis on teaching international content in order to help culturally diverse students achieve in all subject areas. The materials developed by the Stanford Project in International and Intercultural Education (SPICE) have also continued to be useful as resources for setting the group tasks because these materials were deliberately designed with the idea of representing multiple perspectives.

Group cooperation in pursuit of a shared superordinate goal that cannot be achieved without the participation of everyone is an important aspect of these projects. Indeed, CISP recognizes the "situated" nature of student identity formed in the community (including groups based on national origin) and reflects the context of the group of peers in the classroom, thus weaving together the intercultural, international, status-equalizing, and community-situated aspects of education.

### ASCD: The Association for Supervision and Curriculum Development, A Global Education Framework

In 1991 the ASCD, the largest nonunion organization of education professionals in the United States, convened a group of educators to formulate a framework for elementary and middle school global education. This group was formed in recognition of the importance of the early years of schooling and built upon the yearbook of the organization issued that year (Tye, 1991).

The Global Education Framework, discussed and modified by a consensus-building process, was piloted in fifteen schools in the

United States and one in the Netherlands (all were chosen from 125 applications to serve as pilot sites). The final steps in this process were as follows: first, the construction of thematic units based around the framework's big ideas or "messages to students" (including the message "You are a citizen of a multicultural society"), and second, suggestions for performance-assessment techniques to accompany the publication of the framework and units (Anderson, Nicklas, and Crawford, 1994).

One of the pilot schools that has chosen to work on an aspect of global education of special relevance to multicultural education is a school in Minneapolis designated as a "multicultural gender-fair laboratory demonstration site." This ASCD pilot school has incorporated wide-ranging evaluation, action research, and alternative assessments that teachers have been trained to administer in their program. They use what has been described as a "multisensory interdisciplinary curriculum," focus on at least five cultural groups, employ a diversity of learning styles, and stress continuous staff development.

This approach and a variety of others have effectively blended elements of multicultural, international, and intercultural education so as to make them viable for the early years of schooling.

### The ICONS Computer-Assisted International Simulation: A University-Centered Technology-Based Project

The International Communication and Negotiations Project (ICONS) is housed in the Department of Government and Politics at the University of Maryland, College Park. This computer-assisted simulation, in which students role-play diplomats from different countries and negotiate using a computer system, was developed in the early 1980s for university students studying international relations. Then, in the mid-1980s, the Maryland Summer Center for International Studies was established. About eighty twelve- to sixteen-year-olds from Maryland participate each summer; topics of negotiation using the computer network have included apartheid and economic development (see the evaluations in Torney-Purta,

1989, 1992). This program was followed in the late 1980s by simulation exercises that operate during the school year and include teams from schools throughout the United States as well as in other countries. One such site is the Academic Champions of Excellence Program at Maryland for African American early adolescents, who, in the process of being introduced to college opportunities, participated in a simulation exercise stressing international health and environmental issues. Finally, as part of the CISP project previously described, diverse average and low-achieving ninth and tenth graders in the Los Angeles area participated in 1993 and 1994 in ICONS simulations on health, immigration, and the environment.

The ICONS project uses a sophisticated computer-networking program (developed by Jon Wilkenfeld) to link students who are pretending to be diplomats from different countries. That is, teams of students in the summer programs or school classes in the semester program are assigned to role-play a diplomat from, say, Brazil or South Africa. Following introductory lessons or lectures, and after being given time to research and write a position paper on selected foreign policy issues in the assigned country, students begin negotiations centering on agendas of international issues such as human rights and the global environment.

The function of the computer and software is to provide a sophisticated communications network. All communication within the team about the messages to be sent takes place within the team or classroom face to face; but all communication between teams utilizes the network provided by the computer system, sometimes through electronic mail but primarily during scheduled on-line conferences in which students communicate simultaneously with teams representing other countries and see the text of messages both on screen and in printed records. Heated debate about the wording of such messages often takes place. This cognitive conflict among peers stimulates individuals to restructure their social and political concepts. Overall, the experience is a collaborative one, involving the co-construction of social and political knowledge, in which the peer group provides an important situation for cognition.

Research conducted on the Maryland Summer Center has used

several sources of data to identify the characteristics of this program that seem successful in promoting change in cognitive structures and in producing the high level of involvement observed. These characteristics are described in the following paragraphs. (Note that the average participant reported some kind of task-related behavior such as discussing messages or reading messages from other teams approximately 80 percent of the time during on-line conferences, as corroborated by raters of videotapes.)

First, the computer screen is an object of highly focused student attention because it is constantly changing and providing valued information in a way that the blackboard or textbook does not. One student enters a proposed message, which then becomes visible to all team members. The process of co-construction and group revision of the message on the screen provides a potent stimulus for students' discovery that what seems obvious to one about a situation is not obvious to another. Often participants suddenly see complications even in a simple proposal about border monitoring to slow immigration or about treating economic rights as equivalent in importance to civil and political rights.

Second, the participants are working toward a superordinate goal and are responding to the opinions of their peers and seeking status from them, not primarily from an adult leader or teacher. The participants are also pressed to arrive at an agreed-upon message to carry forward their goals, and they must search for their own judgment criteria to satisfy themselves and their peers. (A participating school in Miami included a number of Haitian and Cuban immigrant students; when some of the messages were sent over the computer system in Spanish and in French, it had a tremendous effect on their status in the classroom because they possessed a skill that none of the other students had.) Peer leadership in the teams shifts among equal participants and includes content (how to word a message), social guidance (helping the team feel good about progress), and metacognitive monitoring (suggesting what the team should consider next).

Third, the existence of the messages in a printed form, as well as repeated pressure on students to participate as if they were diplomats engaging in discourse on real global issues, gives a sense of authenticity much more closely connected to the real world than do most classes in social studies. The participants realize the importance of saying clearly what they mean when they craft a message for their team. (This outcome contrasts with that of programs like the Model UN, where between-team communication takes place orally and one person often makes statements for the entire country.) The printout also allows participants to refer back to a previous message, thus tracking their progress toward the agreed-upon goals of the team.

Fourth, the continual stating of positions in terms of "Nigeria believes" or "France concludes" provides a cross-cutting identity for diverse students and also transmits a sense of status. On the last day a participant said sadly, "It's really too bad; next week there won't be any messages for us as Nigerian diplomats. We'll have to go back to just being students." Eighty to 90 percent of the participants reported high or moderate levels of identification with the country they represented. (For a discussion of the difference between real and simulated national identity, see Dougherty, Eisenhart, and Webley, 1992.)

These four program approaches represent a small sample of international and global education dealing with issues important to diverse groups within the school. They share common dimensions that appear to contribute to their effectiveness—for example, opportunities for embedding and reflecting upon identities that cut across racial or ethnic lines, active participation with others toward superordinate goals that necessitate everyone's skills, awareness of and respect for diverse perspectives, and recognition of the classroom peer group as a situation for cognition in which students can gain a sense of status.

## Research on International Education

Much more investment has been made in program development than in research on international education. In the late 1970s and early 1980s, surveys were used on several occasions to establish base-line information on the level of knowledge of global issues and other cultures among American young people. For example, the International Association for the Evaluation of Educational Achievement (IEA), in a civic education survey in which more than 30,000 students (ten, fourteen, and seventeen to twenty years of age) participated, showed variations in the patterns of knowledge of domestic and international politics (Torney, Oppenheim, and Farnen, 1975). Fourteen-year-old students in the United States ranked seventh out of eight countries in their knowledge of international processes and institutions; in contrast, they ranked second out of eight countries in their knowledge of domestic politics (Torney, 1977). Although the phrase "situated or contextualized cognition" was not yet popular, the types of factors that appeared to account for this outcome included the lesser need for international knowledge and availability of international contact in daily life than in other countries.

Torney and Tesconi (1977) showed from an analysis of the attitude portion of the IEA study that the countries with the greatest ethnic tolerance were those containing relatively moderate numbers of immigrant and racial minority groups. They concluded that unless students "are provided with extensive educational experience to equip them to cope with high diversity, they will be overwhelmed by it and low intercultural tolerance will result" (Torney and Tesconi, 1977, p. 120).

A more general finding of the IEA survey was that participation in discussion of political issues in the classroom in a climate of the free exchange of opinion was a positive predictor in all countries of high achievement in civics. As several other authors in this volume have noted with respect to classroom discussions of intercultural issues, complex, long-term, and elaborated experiences are more likely to be effective than superficial approaches.

In the mid-1970s a large-scale survey of knowledge and attitudes regarding other countries was conducted by the Educational Testing Service (ETS) on a national probability sample of fourth-, eighth-, and twelfth-grade students in the United States (Pike and Barrows,

1979). This research, as well as the survey conducted by ETS about five years later among U.S. college students (Barrows, 1981) showed relatively low levels of knowledge about international issues.

Utilizing a modification of the ETS questionnaire, a study of different types of programs in nine U.S. states compared secondary students who had been enrolled in global education courses with others who had enrolled only in social studies courses with a domestic focus (Torney-Purta, 1984). Differences favoring students with a global education were observed only for those in a program combining curricular with extracurricular activities and for those in a program that had invested extensive resources in teacher training over a period of several years.

The section of the Stanford Study of the Schools focusing on international topics found in a regression analysis that important predictors of knowledge included the perception that one could discuss issues in the classroom and disagree with the teacher. Immigrant status was a strong predictor of concern and interest in international topics in this study (Torney-Purta and Landsdale, 1986). In both this study and the one mentioned previously, the complexity, duration, and stability of the programs was found to be important, as Janet Schofield indicates (in Chapter 10 of this volume) with respect to programs dealing more directly with racial tolerance.

In 1991 Massialas concluded from his *Handbook* review of research that it is essential to provide the student with more content, more opportunity for discussion, and higher expectations regarding performance on tests that measure knowledge (and, to some extent, attitudes) about people in other countries. Among Massialas's recommendations are the following: specifications of competencies and associated measures of outcomes are needed for evaluating programs; ethnographic and experimental studies must be integrated in order to broaden the understanding of programs; teachers need to focus on the implicit curriculum of the school and on the classroom climate; and mediating factors such as gender and age must be recognized. These are important factors, but the review does not integrate American multicultural issues with international and global education. In fact, a separate chapter by Banks (1991) on multicultural education appears in the *Handbook of Research on Social Studies Teaching and Learning*. And the frame in which research is considered by Massialas is the individual student confronting facts and generalizations about other countries and cultures in classrooms, usually set apart from everyday lives and often in the absence of concern about authentic interactions between individuals who are constructing meaning from their own experience of other cultures. Interaction with immigrants or other students with a bicultural identity makes the process of global and international education more complex, more difficult, and potentially more rewarding. (See Chapter 5 in this volume for a discussion of similar issues.)

Research by Merryfield (1992, 1994) brings together these concerns about curriculum as well as these issues of individual differences and ethnic status. Merryfield's methodology involved extensive observations of teachers of world studies or global education courses in twelve classrooms in Ohio. After transcribing and analyzing these observations, she interviewed each teacher about her transcripts. Special attention was paid to contextual influences on the teachers' decision-making processes, as well as to individual differences among the students.

Merryfield also presented profiles for each teacher that stress the guiding principles behind their instruction and the factors influencing it. Two such profiles appear at the end of this chapter. They show that no matter what the curriculum or text or state mandate, the teachers' backgrounds, beliefs, and students create enormous diversity in actual instruction. Of the teachers Merryfield observed, all endorsed the presentation of multiple perspectives and the encouragement of tolerance and respect. Further, all moderated their day-to-day decisions about curriculum according to their students' behavior and interest, and showed sensitivity to racial, ethnic, and religious differences in their classes. An anecdote told by one of the teachers illustrates the complexity of these issues, however: "I found my white and African American students talking about Asians in stereotypes right in front of them as though they weren't even in class. This was particularly ironic as these same students didn't want to participate in a unit on prejudice and discrimination because they said they were above all that" (Merryfield, 1994, p. 242). These teachers were socially constructing the meanings of ethnicity, race, and immigrant status for their students on a daily basis, within the social structure of the classroom and of current events. They were attempting to make instruction responsive to cross-cutting identities and to involve students in the cooperative pursuit of superordinate goals, as several chapters in this volume would endorse. However, conducting research on these attempts was a daunting process because of the many dimensions that influenced both the teachers' decision-making processes and the students' responses.

Another research strategy has been used in evaluating the ICONS project previously described. It involves the analysis of each individual's construction of knowledge and conceptual restructuring using think-aloud problem solving of international problems, studies of decision making, concept mapping, and other techniques derived from cognitive psychology to study conceptual change. In this project a continuum of expertise in international problem solving (ranging from pre-novice, novice, and post-novice to pre-expert and expert) has been conceptualized in order to clarify what constitutes expertise in thinking about international issues such as apartheid or underdevelopment and how experiences such as this project influence it (see Torney-Purta, 1992).

To summarize, there is considerable evidence that classroom climate—especially one in which students' goals are to make material about the world meaningful by discussing it with each other—has positive results on tests of content knowledge as well as attitudes. The role of peer groups in the classroom is not merely an adjunct or a distraction to the educational process. Discourse within the peer group is an essential context for the development of social and political knowledge because this is the community of practice and discourse that matters most to adolescents, and is one where ideas are tried. Semi-structured discussion groups and cooperative-learning programs sensitive to status contribute to the construction of meaningful understanding, as corroborated by the research and programs reviewed in Chapters 10 and 11 in this volume. Personal support networks are important, as LaFramboise and her colleagues (1993) note in their discussion of bicultural identity. And finally, environments of interaction outside the classroom, including the climate of understanding between cultures in the community and expectations about status and opportunity, provide the context for in-school learning.

## Implications of an Agenda for Practice, Research, and Policy

The primary message of this chapter is that effective multicultural programs should include concern for the intersection of issues of race, social class, gender, and immigrant status or national identity. In this connection I have noted the importance of factors such as experience in the everyday environment in dealing with individuals from other cultures and the embedding of negotiation about important issues of culture and identity both within the classroom and within peer, family, and community groups (including those based around national identity) outside of school.

There are several factors that need to be taken seriously. First, educators must recognize the diversity of programs and the way they are adapted in actual classrooms, a point raised by Merryfield (1992, 1994), by Banks (1993), and by the ASCD project. Second, they must consider the importance of embeddedness of identity in peer and community groups and the unique value of programs outside of as well as in schools, a point raised by Heath and McLaughlin (1993), Ogbu (1992, 1993), and the CISP project. Third, they must recognize the importance of superordinate and authentic goals in programs that create a community of discourse characterized by cross-cutting identities, as shown by the ICONS projects and the

IEA study. Fourth, they must understand the issues of status and power, a point raised by Cohen and others (1994), by the CISP and ICONS projects, by Ogbu (1992, 1993), and by Brislin (1993). And fifth, educators must acknowledge the value of multiple learning styles and in-depth programming, as illustrated by the CISP project and the ASCD Minnesota project as well as by the IEA study and ICONS.

Future research should address both the social and the individual construction of knowledge, using observational and interview studies of teachers such as those conducted by Merryfield, coupled with studies of student conceptual change. It will be important to include observations as well as various types of student performance measures, along with authentic assessment techniques such as concept mapping or problem solving.

High-quality graduate dissertations have a role to play in carrying forward a research agenda such as this. Willing and well-informed students, together with strong research advisers, can make a significant contribution. Indeed, many graduate students are attracted to the qualitative or case-study approach and have the perseverance to carry it through. Research by teachers or practitioners can make an important contribution as well, although such work would require advice from research specialists. Because many dissertations and practitioner research projects are not published, outlets for the dissemination of well-crafted short versions of such research through professional meetings and publications should be cultivated. A conference of young researchers, including those at the pre-dissertation level or those in small grants programs, might be vehicles for stimulating this work.

The work of more established researchers in the field whose interests may coincide with aspects of this research agenda should also be examined. Research undertaken in an alternative context may well have implications for international/multicultural education. For example, there are many researchers in both Europe and North America who study intergroup tolerance as experimental social psychologists. An invitational conference and associated book publication might be an appropriate incentive for these individuals as well as for ethnographic researchers to consider the issues involved in the intersection of race, social class, gender, and immigrant status discussed in this chapter. Here, special attention should be given to the related issues of situated or embedded cognition and oppositional identities.

Finally, there is the matter of policy. Certainly the designation of models and technical assistance provided by established programs are important. Targeted information should be provided to the many educational policy makers involved in what are often separate efforts in multicultural, gender-fair, and global or international education. Exploring how electronic technologies or networks might be used in the reform of instruction and school structure, international communication, and research should also be on the policy agenda.

## References

Anderson, C., Nicklas, S., and Crawford, A. (1994). *Global understandings: A framework for teaching and learning*. Alexandria, Va.: Association for Supervision and Curriculum Development.

Banks, J. (1993). Multicultural education: historical development, dimensions, and practice. In L. Darling-Hammond (ed.), *Review of research in education, 19*, 3–50.

Banks, J. (1991). Multicultural education: Its effects on students' racial and gender role attitudes. In J. Shaver (ed.), *Handbook of research in social studies teaching and learning*. New York: Macmillan.

Barrows, T. (ed.). (1981). *College students' knowledge and beliefs: A survey of global understanding*. New Rochelle, N.Y.: Change Magazine Press.

Becker, J. (1991). Curriculum considerations in global studies. In K. Tye (ed.), *Global education from thought to action* (pp. 67–85). Alexandria, Va.: ASCD.

Brislin, R. (1993). *Understanding culture's influence on behavior*. Fort Worth, Tex.: Harcourt Brace College Publishers.

Buergenthal, T., and Torney, J. (1976). *International human rights and international education*. Washington, D.C.: U.S. Government Printing Office.

Cohen, E. (1990). Teaching in multiculturally hetereogeneous classrooms. *McGill Journal of Education, 26*, 7–22.

Cohen, E., and others. (1994). Complex instruction: Higher order thinking in hetereogeneous classrooms. In S. Sharan (ed.), *Handbook of cooperative learning methods*. Westport, Conn.: Greenwood Press.

Delgado-Gaitan, C., and Trueba, H. (1991). *Crossing cultural borders: Education for immigrant families in America*. Bristol, Penn.: Falmer Press.

Dougherty, K. C., Eisenhart, M., and Webley, P. (1992). The role of social representation and national identities in the development of territorial knowledge. *American Educational Research Journal, 29*, 809–836.

Gibson, M., and Ogbu, J. (1991). *Minority status and schooling*. New York: Garland.

Heath, S. B., and McLaughlin, M. (1993). Ethnicity and gender in theory and practice. In S. B. Heath and M. McLaughlin (eds.), *Identity and inner city youth: Beyond ethnicity and gender* (pp. 13–35). New York: Teachers College Press.

Holland, D., and Eisenhart, M. (1990). *Educated in romance: Women, achievement, and college culture*. Chicago: University of Chicago Press.

Jennings, R. (ed.). (1993). *Fire in the eyes of youth: The humanities in American education*. St. Paul: Occasional Press.

Kniep, W., and Martin-Kniep, G. (1995). Schools and curriculum for the 21st century. In J. Beane (ed.), *Yearbook for Supervision and Curriculum Development*. Alexandria, Va.: Association for Supervision and Curriculum Development.

LaFramboise, T., Coleman, H., and Gerton, J. (1993). Psychological impact of biculturalism: Evidence and theory. *Psychological Bulletin, 114*, 395–412.

Lamphere, L. (1992). *Structuring diversity: Ethnographic perspectives on the new immigration*. Chicago: University of Chicago Press.

Lave, J., and Wenger, E. (1991). *Situated learning: Legitimate peripheral participation*. Cambridge, England: Cambridge University Press.

McLaughlin, M. (1993). Embedded identities: Enabling balance in urban contexts. In S. B. Heath and M. McLaughlin (eds.), *Identity and inner city youth: Beyond ethnicity and gender* (pp. 36–67). New York: Teachers College Press.

Massialas, B. (1991). Education for international understanding. In J. Shaver (ed.), *Handbook of research on social studies teaching and learning*. New York: Macmillan.

Merryfield, M. (1992). Teacher decision-making in global perspectives in education: The dynamism of guiding principles and contextual factors. Paper presented at the American Educational Research Association conference, San Francisco.

Merryfield, M. (1994). Shaping the curriculum in global education: The influence of student characteristics on teacher decision-making. *Journal of Curriculum and Supervision, 9*, 233–249.

Messick, D., and Mackie, D. (1989). Intergroup relations. In M. Rosenzweig and L. Porter (eds.), *Annual Review of Psychology, 40*, 82.

Ogbu, J. (1992). Understanding cultural diversity and learning. *Educational Researcher, 21*(8), pp. 5–14.

Ogbu, J. (1993). Differences in cultural frame of reference. *International Journal of Behavioral Development, 16*, 483–506.

Peshkin, A. (1991). *The color of strangers and the color of friends*. Chicago: University of Chicago Press.

Pike, L., and Barrows, T. (1979). *Other nations, other peoples*. Washington, D.C.: U.S. Government Printing Office.

Sigel, R. S., and Hoskin, M. (1991). *Education for democratic citizenship: A challenge for multi-ethnic societies.* Hillsdale, N.J.: Erlbaum.

Torney, J. (1977). The international knowledge and awareness of adolescents in nine countries. *International Journal of Political Education, 1,* 3–19.

Torney, J., Oppenheim, A. N., and Farnen, R. F. (1975). *Civic education in ten countries: An empirical study.* New York: Wiley.

Torney, J., and Tesconi, C. (1977). Political socialization research and respect for ethnic identity. In M. M. Tumin and W. Plotch (eds.), *Pluralism in democratic society* (pp. 95–132). New York: Praeger.

Torney-Purta, J. (1984). *Predictors of global awareness and global concern among secondary school students.* Columbus, Ohio: Ohio State University, Mershon Center.

Torney-Purta, J. (1989). Political cognition and its restructuring in young people. *Human Development, 32,* 14–23.

Torney-Purta, J. (1992). Cognitive representations of the political system in adolescents: The continuum from pre-novice to expert. In H. Haste and J. Torney-Purta (eds.), *The development of political understanding: A new perspective.* San Francisco: Jossey-Bass.

Torney-Purta, J., and Landsdale, D. (1986). Classroom climate and process in international studies: Data from the American Schools and the World Project. Paper presented at the American Educational Research Association conference, San Francisco.

Tye, K. (ed.). (1991). *Global education from thought to action.* Alexandria, Va.: Association for Supervision and Curriculum Development.

Tye, B., and Tye, K. (1992). *Global education: A study of school change.* Albany: State University of New York Press.

Willis, P. (1977). *Learning to labour: How working class kids get working class jobs.* New York: Columbia University Press.

Woyach, R., and Remy, R. (1989). *Approaches to world studies: A handbook for curriculum planners.* Boston: Allyn & Bacon.

# Teacher Profiles from Merryfield (1992)*

## *Robert and Carl's Profile*

Teaming with Carl, Robert taught fourth- and fifth-graders in an urban elementary international magnet school. Robert has certification in elementary education and a B.A. in history. At the time of this writing he was in his nineteenth year of teaching.

---

*Adapted and used with permission of the author.

1. Guiding principle. Integrate the students' cultural heritages with the interconnections of the world past and present:

Contextual factors:

- Robert's belief in building on students' experiences and interests.
- Robert's teaming with Carl and their joint decision making.
- The course of study.

Example: 10/17. In unit on migrations, students traced movement in their families' history and compared them with major global migrations.

2. Develop a sense of community through cooperation, participation, and tolerance.

- Robert's valuing of the class as a caring community.
- Robert's beliefs in actively dealing with prejudice and intolerance.
- Robert's concern that students have input into instructional/class decision making.
- Diversity in student backgrounds and abilities.
- Support from parents as helpers inside and outside the classroom.
- School's mission in building a community.

Example: 9/4. Students developed a bill of rights for the class.

3. Approach global education through interdisciplinary themes such as culture, conflict, migrations, and technology and through mandated skills in reading, writing, and comprehension.

- Robert's commitment to interdisciplinary instruction.
- Teaching in an international magnet school.
- Units are developed with Carl, his teaming partner.

Example: 10/3. Students examined the geography and economics of transporting petroleum and discussed how trade affects current conflicts in the Middle East.

4. Provide a wide range of perspectives, materials, hands-on experiences, and discovery activities.

- Robert's experiences in teaching.
- Interests of the students.
- Planning with his teammate.

Example: 2/8. Students experimented with different ways of cleaning up an oil spill as a follow-up activity to a discussion of the oil spill in the Persian Gulf.

5. Use literature (both fiction and nonfiction) to prompt questions that lead to student research about people and their worlds.

- Children's literature gets first priority. Robert values a literature-based approach to learning.
- School program is literature-based.
- Local library allows 2,000 books a year to be used by Robert and Carl's students.

Example: 12/6. The students selected and read books about people or families going through migration or immigration and then wrote poems about the travels described in the books.

### Carol's Profile

Carol taught ninth-grade "world area studies" and tenth-grade "global history" in an urban high school. She has certification in secondary social studies as well as a B.A. and an M.A. She has also done doctoral work in social studies education. At the time of this writing she was in her twenty-third year of teaching.

1. Guiding principle: Make connections between global content and the students' experiences and interests.

Contextual factors:

- Carol's commitment to global perspectives.

- Carol's belief in making content relevant to students.
- Students consist of ninth- and tenth-grade African Americans and whites, along with several new immigrants from Asia and the Middle East.
- School is an English as a Second Language (ESL) magnet school that draws new immigrants from the entire system.

Example: 2/11. Carol explained her decision to spend more time on Africa because of the interests of her African American students.

2. Enable students to see global interconnections, cultural diffusions, global systems, and global issues throughout history and in today's world.

- Carol's concern that students see the world as a system.
- The course of study, written by Carol, for tenth-grade global history and ninth-grade world area studies (geography).
- Student characteristics include a limited view of the world.

Example: 9/6. Carol divided students into regional groups (Africa, Asia, Europe, etc.) and then compared the world's peoples in terms of literacy, population, life expectancy, religion, wealth, and food in order to explain the concept of a global system.

3. Help students learn to appreciate other cultures and multiple perspectives in a comparative framework, with special attention to non-Western cultures.

- Carol's valuing of multiple perspectives.
- Students' knowledge/stereotyping of non-Western peoples.
- Students from other countries.
- The ethnocentrism of much of the media.
- Supplementary materials and resources including speakers, videos, simulations, decision-making scenarios.

Example: 1/28. After discussing the history of conflicts in the Middle East, the students simulated a Middle East Peace

Conference by role-playing diplomats from Syria, Iraq, the United States, Israel, Jordan, the United Nations, England, Turkey, and Palestine.

4. Have students collect, reflect on, and challenge, information and evidence, and ask them to make presentations evaluating what they are learning about the world and its peoples.

- Carol's valuing of student research and problem solving.

- Carol's valuing of active learning.

Example: 4/17. Students examined the geography and history of an island where two groups of people were fighting over borders, and they acted as a "UN" team of negotiators to settle the dispute by drawing permanent boundaries.

5. Provide opportunities for students to identify cause-and-effect relationships and turning points in both history and geography.

- Carol's interest in student analysis of information.

- The course of study.

- Carol's assessment that students respond well to such activities.

Example: 9/24. Students analyzed the relationships between events in the history of Latin America and the current demographics, culture, and political and economic circumstances of the area.

6. Teach through a variety of strategies, materials, and resources, using the textbook as just one source of information.

- Carol's evaluation of the textbook.

- Carol's research and collection of materials.

- Carol's participation in in-service education and curriculum development.

- Students respond well to a variety of strategies and materials.

Example: 1/23. Students read literature from Arabia, India, and Persia in order to understand and appreciate the cultures of these regions.

## Chapter Fourteen

# The Mediation of Interethnic Conflict in Schools

Peter T. Coleman
Morton Deutsch

## Introduction

In a recently published paper (Deutsch, 1993b), it was suggested that there are four key components to any comprehensive educational program intended to enable students to develop attitudes, knowledge, and skills for resolving their conflicts constructively rather than destructively. They are cooperative learning, conflict resolution training, the constructive use of controversy in teaching subject matters, and the creation of dispute resolution centers in the schools. A rationale for each of these components follows.

### Cooperative Learning

Cooperative learning fosters a sense of positive interdependence ("we sink or swim together") and helps students to acquire the social skills involved in working together effectively. It also provides students with opportunities to interact cooperatively with other students who are different in ability, race, gender, ethnicity, religion, disability, and so on. Since Deutsch's early theoretical and experimental work on cooperation-competition (Deutsch 1949a, 1949b), there has been much research on cooperative learning. As Slavin (1983) and Johnson and Johnson (1989) have indicated in their extensive summaries of the research literature, cooperative learning has many positive effects on students, including a reduction in their prejudices toward students who are typically categorized as "different."

We want to emphasize that successful and effective cooperation with individuals and groups of different ethnic backgrounds is a necessary component of any comprehensive educational program to improve ethnic relations, whether among youths or adults. However, it is not sufficient, by itself, since cooperation tends to deteriorate and fail under conditions of destructive conflict.

## Constructive Conflict Resolution

There is much to suggest that a two-way relation exists between effective cooperation and constructive conflict resolution. Good cooperative relations facilitate the constructive management of conflict; and the ability to handle constructively the inevitable conflicts that occur during cooperation facilitates the survival and deepening of cooperative relations.

In recent years, conflict resolution training programs have sprouted in a number of schools across the country. Although we believe these programs are very promising, little systematic research on their effectiveness has yet been done apart from "consumer satisfaction" studies (which generally indicate high levels of satisfaction). The International Center for Cooperation and Conflict Resolution at Teachers College, Columbia University, has recently completed a fairly extensive study in an inner-city alternative high school (Deutsch, 1993a), but its focus was not on ethnic relations. In brief, our data show that as students improved in managing their conflicts, they experienced increased social support and less victimization from others. This improvement in their relations with others led to increased self-esteem as well as to a decrease in feelings of anxiety and depression and more frequent feelings of positive well-being. The higher self-esteem, in turn, produced a greater sense of personal control over their own fates. Moreover, the increases in their sense of personal control and in their positive feelings of well-being led to higher academic performance.

Apart from the "victimization scale," which included items relating to whether the student was victimized in particular ways (robbed, assaulted, sexually harassed, insulted, etc.), we have no data specifically relevant to this conference. Nevertheless, we believe that a constructive conflict resolution training program in schools would be likely to have desirable effects in reducing destructive ethnic conflicts.

## The Constructive Use of Controversy in Teaching Subject Matters

Our limited experience with training in constructive conflict resolution suggests that a single course or workshop is not usually sufficient, by itself, to produce lasting effects in most students; they must have repeated opportunities and encouragement to practice their skills of constructive conflict resolution in a supportive atmosphere. Constructive conflict resolution can be infused into "teachable moments" in various courses and student activities. In addition, the active use of constructive controversy in teaching different subject matters (Johnson and Johnson, 1992) can provide repeated and diverse opportunities for students to learn the skills of lively controversy rather than those of deadly quarrel.

There are difficult conflicts that the disputing parties, even when well trained, may not be able to resolve constructively without the help of third parties such as mediators. Informal mediation is one of the oldest forms of conflict resolution, and formal mediation has been practiced in behalf of international and labor-management conflicts for many years. More recently, formal mediation has been increasingly applied in such areas as divorce, small-claims cases, neighborhood feuds, landlord-tenant relations, environmental and public-resource controversies, industrial disputes, school conflicts, and civil cases. Following this explosion of the practice of mediation (coupled with the proliferation of textbooks and "how-to-do-it" books on mediation), there has been modest but important growth in research and theorizing on the topic. Kressel and Pruitt's book, *Mediation Research* (1989), provides a definitive review of the research being done in this area. They indicate that there is considerable evidence of user satisfaction with mediation and some evidence that the agreements reached through mediation are both less costly to the conflicting parties and more robust than traditional adjudication. However, there is also strong evidence to suggest that mediation has dim prospects of being successful under adverse circumstances. As Kressel and Pruitt (1989) have succinctly expressed it: "Intensely conflicted disputes involving parties of widely disparate power, with low motivation to settle, fighting about matters of principle, suffering from discord or ambivalence within their own camps, and negotiating over scarce resources are likely to defeat even the most adroit mediators" (p. 405).

Third parties (mediators, conciliators, process consultants, therapists, counselors, etc.) who are called upon to provide assistance in a conflict require four kinds of skills if they are to have the flexibility required to deal with the diverse situations that mediators face.

In the *first* set of skills are those related to the third party's establishment of an effective working relationship with each of the conflicting parties so that they will trust the third party, communicate freely with the mediator, and be responsive to the mediator's suggestions regarding an orderly process for negotiations. In the *second* set are those skills related to establishing a cooperative problem-solving attitude among the conflicting parties toward their conflict. *Third* are the skills involved in developing a creative group decision-making process. This process clarifies the nature of the problems that the conflicting parties are confronting by reframing their conflicting positions into a joint problem to be solved. It also helps to expand the range of alternatives that are perceived to be available, facilitates realistic assessment of their feasibility as well as their desirability, and assists in the implementation of agreed-upon solutions. As for the *fourth* set of skills, it is often helpful for the third party to have considerable substantive knowledge about the issues around which the conflict is centered. Such knowledge can enable the mediator to see possible solutions that might not occur to the conflicting parties and thus permit the mediator to help them assess proposed solutions more realistically.

The mediation of interethnic conflict clearly calls for all four types of skills. In addition, it calls for an understanding of the specific social psychological processes involved in ethnic conflict. Since other authors in this volume have addressed this topic in detail, we simply want to note that a mediator of such conflict should be tuned into (1) the misunderstandings and miscommunications that often arise from cultural differences; (2) the ethnocentrism characteristic of most groups; (3) the stereotypes of one group that are frequently held by the other; (4) the importance of an individual's ethnic membership in defining his or her self-identity; (5) the emblems, symbols, personages, and historic events that are central to the group's definition of itself; and (6) the prior relations between the conflicting ethnic groups—their rewarding experiences as well as those that have led to grievances.

## Dispute Resolution Centers in Schools

We have searched the literature to see what research has been done on the mediation of interethnic conflict. And so far as we could determine, very little (if any) systematic research has been conducted. So we briefly discuss the existing research on school mediation instead. Only a few studies have assessed school-based dispute resolution or mediation programs in a systematic fashion (see Lam, 1989, for a review). Those studies that have explored their impact indicate that, in general, the participants are satisfied with the training and find it useful. Educators want conflict resolution and/or mediation programs in the schools for several reasons. The reason most frequently given has to do with the increase in violence among students and between students and teachers. Such violence ultimately affects the quality of education in schools.

More than thirty-five college and university campuses now have mediation programs. Many more elementary, middle, and high schools offer training in conflict resolution and mediation, according to *The Fourth R*, the newsletter of the National Association for Mediation in Education (NAME). Rationales and evaluative summaries of some of these programs are given in Wilson-Brewer, Cohen, O'Donnell, and Goodman (1991) and in Lam (1989). Following the conflict resolution and mediation movement initiated in the United States, some schools in Canada have incorporated conflict resolution skills training into their curricula.

If popularity is an indicator of value, there is ample evidence to show that conflict resolution and mediation training are considered to be successful by many educators. Several feature articles have reported the beneficial aspects of these programs as ascertained by both subjective and objective measures. Evaluations of student mediation programs further show that the student disputants have been satisfied with the mediation outcomes (Lam, 1989). Additionally, studies of peer mediators show that their self-image is enhanced (Lam, 1989). A profile of one student mediator showed improvements not only in her feelings about her relationships but also in her grades.

Keeney (in Lam, 1989) reports that the principals and teachers of the schools involved in the New Mexico Mediation in the Schools program have reacted positively to the program. They feel that the school atmosphere and student interpersonal relations have improved now that there is a constructive and legitimate channel for dealing with conflicts. One good indicator of program acceptance in the school is that about 60 percent of the upper elementary students wanted to be trained to become mediators. No negative effects of the program have been noted.

Clark and Mann (in Lam, 1989) report that the mediation program at Poughkeepsie Middle School has been successful in improving attendance, building self-esteem, and creating a sense of responsibility within the student body. Positive effects of conflict resolution/mediation training have also been noted by parents. For example, the parents of student conflict managers in the New Mexico Mediation in the Schools program have reported being pleased with their children's involvement and have described a carry-over into the family of the skills that were learned in their school. In one district, parental training has actually been initiated at the request of parents. As Keeney (1989) indicates, it is often the changes that parents see at home that arouse their interest. These reports are encouraging because they point to the beneficial aspects of conflict resolution training in areas outside of the school.

Parents have benefited from conflict resolution programs in other ways as well. In one study, the parents involved in disputes with the school were considerably more satisfied with conflict mediation after the school personnel had been trained in conflict resolution skills than they were prior to that training. The post-training ratings made by independent observers of the performance of the participants were also higher (Maher, in Lam, 1989). In addition, the observers commented that such a program would be beneficial to themselves.

In short, many reports note the enthusiasm of the parties involved with school mediation/conflict resolution training programs. Several researchers and practitioners, however, point out the caveat involved in uncritically lauding these programs. Although the idea of mediation/conflict resolution is being sold to schools extensively, only very few intensive efforts have been made to evaluate what is working and what is not, thus possibly limiting the potential of such programs (Lam, 1989). Clearly there is a need for more systematic assessments of these programs following their implementation, using rigorous data collection and analysis procedures.

## The Mediation of Interethnic Conflict

In light of the scarcity of research on the mediation of interethnic conflict, we decided to conduct an "experience survey" of a select group of expert mediators in the New York area who have served as mediators in interethnic conflicts. In the spring of 1992, co-author

Peter Coleman, who is a mediator and mediation trainer, interviewed eleven individuals who had mediated ethnic group conflicts themselves. The interviews followed a semi-structured format, using open-ended questions that focused on the conditions, processes, and effects of mediating ethnic group conflicts. A few follow-up interviews were also conducted with disputants who had been involved in the mediations and were willing to waive their right to confidentiality. A variety of ethnic groups were represented in the sample of disputants; among them were Hispanics, Asians, whites, African Americans, Africans, Hassidic Jews, Central Americans, American Indians, and Haitians. The disputants also ranged in years from high school age to adult, included both males and females, and came from a wide range of socioeconomic classes. The mediators represented a broad range of ethnic groups as well. The conflicts varied in level of severity from minor arguments and misunderstandings to organizational standstills, industrial sabotage, and acts of violence. Many of the conflicts had long histories. In a few of the cases, legal proceedings were pending over the issue of concern to the mediation. With one exception, all of the cases utilized a formal mediation process; however, many of the cases also utilized other conflict resolution strategies. The majority of the conflicts existed within some type of system, such as a school, government agency, or community.

What emerged from the interviews was a broad scope of information concerning ethnic group conflict mediation, which we have organized into five general categories of mediator activities. Kressel and Pruitt (1989), in describing what mediators do, have indicated that their diverse actions can be grouped under four major headings: (1) establishing a working alliance with the parties; (2) improving the climate between them; (3) addressing the issues; and (4) applying pressure for settlement. To these we have added a fifth: (5) ensuring implementation of the agreement.

In focusing our discussion on these five points we hope to articulate more specifically some of the "do's and don'ts" of effective ethnic group mediation, so as to broaden both our practical and our theoretical understanding of the processes involved.

## Establishing a Working Alliance with the Parties

### Initial Contact Between the Disputing Parties and the Mediators.

The mediator (or mediation center) may be approached by one or more of the disputing parties, or the mediation may occur as the result of third parties—for example, through the outreach of the mediator, through that of a school's mediation center, or at the insistence of teachers, administrators, parents, or the courts. Almost all mediators believe that mediation is more successful when the disputing parties participate in it on a voluntary basis. However, successes have been reported even when initial participation in mediation was not truly voluntary—particularly when the mediator is able to convince the conflicting parties that they *need* mediation. In any case, as a school's mediation center becomes well known and well respected, more and more students will bring their conflicts to it.

The mere existence of a conflict resolution curriculum in a school setting can provide a basic language for and familiarity with the process, thus facilitating the willingness of disputants to participate. Often the students involved in this curriculum become the "eyes and ears" of the mediation centers in the school, referring conflicts to mediation and encouraging their peers to use the service. Many of Coleman's interviews revealed that the involvement of these students, their own personal transformations, and the diffusion of their enthusiasm for mediation throughout the school were crucial to the success of the centers, forming the core of an actual culture change with regard to handling conflicts.

Some mediators believe that mediation should begin at an early phase of a dispute, before positions have hardened; others feel that the issues are clearer at a later stage, when polarization has occurred. We think the earlier, the better.

### Establishing Trust.

Of course, all mediators emphasize the importance of a trusting relationship between the mediator and the disputing parties. There are three interrelated bases of such trust: the personal credibility of the mediator, the credibility of the institution with which the mediator is affiliated, and the credibility of the procedures that the mediator employs. In interethnic conflict, the possible ethnic bias of the mediator or institution is sometimes an issue. To overcome such doubts, some mediators believe that the professional role of the mediator and its ethical code requiring impartiality should be stressed. Others emphasize that the mediator is only a facilitator, with all decisions being made by the disputing parties. Still others believe that it is helpful to have a team of mediators, so that each of the disputing ethnic groups is represented on the mediation team.

Personal credibility is often established through mediator contacts with each of the disputing parties prior to mediation. At such meetings, the mediator—in terms of appearance, manner, and behavior—must impress the party with whom he or she is meeting that he or she is impartial, fair, professional, and understanding of both the substance and the feeling of what is being said. The use of students who have been trained as mediators, rather than adults, has been recommended for student-student conflicts because of their greater ability to understand and speak the language of their fellow students.

### Improving the Climate Between the Parties

This initial aspect of the mediation process can be particularly difficult in interethnic conflicts, but successful mediation can provide an experience that will ultimately foster better relations between the ethnic groups. Improved climate between the parties can be approached in several ways.

*Setting the Stage.* One such way is illustrated in this quote from a mediator who was working on a conflict between faculty members at a school:

> So I did a lot of behind-the-scenes talking to everybody. I ran a multi-cultural sensitivity training for 1/2 day. Taught something

about culture. Taught how culture could influence conflict. In the interim, The Black Teachers Caucus put on an evening [presentation] of a Black event which was spectacular! The Site Based Management negotiating team went. It was a first class event. Black spirituals and food and it was fabulous. This was the first time that the African American teachers had put on an evening. In this school people get status by putting on activities. So by the time mediation had evolved the multicultural thing had happened, and they had the Black cultural event [from Coleman's interviews].

*Providing a Procedural Heuristic.* Mediation can provide a cognitive framework that encourages the safe and constructive resolution of conflict. It provides disputants access to the other party, establishes ground rules to ensure civil discourse and safety, offers a forum on which to understand the other party's predicaments and concerns, and, most important, focuses the parties on future solutions rather than on past blame. This procedural heuristic is particularly important in cross-cultural mediation because it provides a common context within which differing cultures can communicate.

*Allowing and Moving Beyond Emotions.* Allowing the appropriate ventilation of anger, frustration, and resentment of the parties enables disputants to "let out" and get beyond the intense feelings of hurt, loss, and fear that may be clouding their perceptions of the issues. Indeed, once such feelings have been expressed (within the limits of ground rules set by the mediator), the disputants may be better able to identify the real issues in the conflict.

Of course, there are considerable differences in cultural beliefs about what is an appropriate level of acknowledgment and expression of emotion. In interethnic conflicts, these differences should be identified by the mediator and openly stated.

*Identifying and Clarifying Ethnic Assumptions.* Culture can influence one's view of what conflict is, the appropriate way to respond to it, where responsibility lies in reaching an agreement, the role of the mediator, and what is possible under an agreement. Moreover, differing assumptions, beliefs, actions, and perceptions can polarize the groups, stirring ethnocentrism and stereotyping. Many of these assumptions are so subtle that they demand a considerable amount of patience from the mediator, who must listen carefully to the exchange, identify and confirm assumptions, and then share them with both sides. In short, mediators can facilitate the process by which different ethnic groups are made aware of how each group's background is affecting the conflict and its mediation.

**Intervening in Ethnocentrism.** In his book *Folkways*, Sumner (1906) defined *ethnocentrism* as "the technical name for the view of things in which one's own group is the center of everything. . . . Each group nourishes its own pride and vanity, boasts itself superior . . . and looks with contempt on the outsider" (pp. 12–13). This can be an issue even for conflicting groups that are not culturally different. Ethnic differences almost guarantee ethnocentrism.

The formula for intervening is as follows: (1) identify and clarify existing ethnic assumptions, misperceptions, and so on; (2) move on to the substantive issues (if they still exist); and (3) reframe the issues by focusing on the cooperative pursuit of resolving the reoccurrence of the problem in the future. This process is illustrated in the following example:

> What happened at the multi-cultural event was that I realized that many came from the "melting pot" approach. Whites came from old generation Italian, Jewish, and Irish, and had bought into the "melting pot" theory of race relations. Blacks were into the "salad bowl" theory. So in my head I thought how could this be solved. So I reframed it as a mediator that we need both soup and salad. I then asked them to brainstorm on the issue based on the reframing of how do you develop a governing structure that's fair and equitable and also includes representation of all the constituency groups. . . . The solution was that there would be a Multi-Cultural Task Force made up of seven people appointed by the principal each year. The seven

would be appointed based on the student demographics of the year, with proportional representation. So it seemed like a rational proposal that they all contributed to and felt very happy that they agreed to it. There exists a better understanding between members of the team. It provided for the development of cohesion and team building. They are better friends. In this situation the main concern was a recognition of the fact that there were needs on both sides. The opposition dissolved after this was agreed. The results are very strong to date [ from Coleman's interviews].

*Avoiding Stereotypes.* Stereotyping, as Walter Lippman once pointed out, is a natural process aimed at simplifying the complex set of data that impinge upon our perceptual and cognitive apparatuses. Negative stereotypes often develop to justify and explain hostilities that began with ethnocentrism and unresolved conflicts of interest. But once formed, they hamper the mediation process and constructive conflict resolution. Other chapters in this volume address the issues involved in reducing prejudice and avoiding stereotypes—issues that must also be confronted by mediators themselves. Indeed, they must, first of all, be aware of their own prejudices and curb them. Second, they must foster diverse, extended, informal interactions between members of different ethnic groups at meals, during coffee breaks, in recreational situations, in problem-solving subgroups, and so on. These informal interactions should be structured in such a way as to individuate the members of the different ethnic groups; to allow for the recognition of individual aspirations, hurts, and needs; and to enable the understanding of others' views in the context of the mediators' own life experiences.

## Addressing the Issues

Before the issues can be addressed, they must be identified. But this task is often difficult in interethnic conflicts because the opposing groups may have been frozen into antagonistic positions that are not good representations of their underlying interests. In some conflicts, a group's interests may be hidden out of the group's fear of being exploited or because of a desire to exploit the other; but, in many instances, the members of a group do not have a clear picture of their own needs and interests. Often the emotional turmoil associated with interethnic conflict beclouds the true issues. In such cases, it is only after the emotional heat has been reduced and a working relationship has been established between the conflicting groups that these issues can be recognized and addressed.

There are several approaches that a mediator can take to help the conflicting groups identify and address the issues between them. When the hostility between the groups is so great that face-to-face discussions are unfeasible or unlikely to be productive, the mediator may work with each group separately to probe for the members' underlying interests and realistic aspirations, to identify a range of options for satisfying these interests, and to appraise the options in terms of their desirability, feasibility, and timeliness as well as in terms of objective criteria of fairness. The mediator may shuttle back and forth between the groups in an attempt to broaden the areas of agreement and narrow the differences between them. If this is successfully accomplished, the groups may be brought together to work out the details of a full agreement. If not, the mediator may draw up what he or she considers to be a fair agreement that addresses the interests of both. The mediator will then ask the two groups to use this text as the basis for negotiating a mutually acceptable agreement.

A second approach is to have the mediator facilitate a direct problem-solving interaction between the two parties. The basic steps involve identifying the problems between the two groups; analyzing their causes; developing suggestions for solving the problems; evaluating these suggestions in terms of their desirability, feasibility, and timeliness; selecting the preferred options and developing a plan for implementing them; and, finally, developing methods of checking how well they are being implemented and establishing a future time for assessing the progress in the two parties' relations. The typical rules of interaction during a mediation, to which the mediator continuously adheres, help to establish a civilized discourse during the process of cooperative problem solving.

A third approach to intergroup problem-solving starts with ideals rather than problems. It involves several different steps. First, the mediator has the members of each group meet in separate parts of a room, where each group identifies what it thinks an ideal relationship between the two groups would be. Then, the two groups meet together to see if they can agree on the characteristics of such a relationship—and, with the help of the mediator, they often can. Next, the groups meet separately to discuss the nature of their present relationships. Again, they are brought together to see if, with the help of the mediator, they can agree on their present relationship. At this point, the mediator helps in identifying the various discrepancies between their ideal and the existing relationship. The two groups together or in mixed subgroups then develop specific suggestions for moving toward an improved relationship. Finally, these suggestions are evaluated in terms of their desirability, feasibility, timeliness, and fairness. And so on.

A practical recommendation for dealing with these issues has also been outlined by Pruitt and Olczak (in press) in a paper addressing intractable conflicts. After pointing to the impracticality of expecting to be able to confront and resolve every issue to a conflict through a win-win framework, these authors encourage a combination of problem solving and conflict avoidance. They note that parties to a conflict are frequently unable to distinguish between long-term idealistic objectives and those objectives that might be attainable within a realistic time frame. Thus the parties need to be helped to tone down their aspirations for the agreement so as to address only what is currently possible, and to avoid or tolerate their remaining differences, at least temporarily.

### Applying Pressure for Settlement

Although mediators of interethnic conflicts cannot impose a settlement, they have an interest in obtaining an agreement that is responsive not only to the interests of the conflicting parties but also to those of the broader community of which they are a part: an agreement that is both fair and likely to endure. To obtain such an agreement, they may have to use pressure on one or both sides at various stages of the mediating process. There are various sorts of influence tactics that a mediator can employ, such as statements about the realistic consequences of no agreement or of the use of a given strategy or tactic; reliance on his or her own authority as an expert; expressions of approval or disapproval; the involvement of higher authorities than the local representatives of the conflicting ethnic groups (for example, the mediator can bring in national leaders of the conflicting ethnic groups); threats to withdraw as the mediator; provision of incentives for an agreement; and so on. It is evident that the use of pressure from the mediator can sometimes help a stalled negotiating process to get moving. Yet such pressure may also backfire or fail to have a lasting desirable effect if it is not viewed as a legitimate influence attempt.

### Ensuring Implementation of the Agreement

The mediator's role does not end with the achievement of an agreement between the conflicting parties. There are several other functions he or she can perform: providing advice and help in "selling" the agreement to the members of each ethnic group so that they will also support the agreement; identifying the steps involved in operationalizing the agreement, including, when necessary, access to the resources necessary to its implementation; establishing criteria and procedures for monitoring and evaluating compliance with the agreement; and creating procedures for appropriate responses to either intentional or unwitting noncompliance.

Another important function the mediator can perform to help ensure implementation of the agreement is to anticipate the conflicts and responses they may arise *within* each ethnic group as a result of the mediation process and agreement. Indeed, there may be extremists within a group who are committed to maintaining the struggle and who will intensify their opposition as progress is made toward an agreement. Consider, for example, the recent upsurge of militant violence in the West Bank of Israel that occurred just after the peace agreement between Israel and the PLO had been signed. This potentiality for increased resistance and/or violence needs to be identified and communicated to both parties in advance so that, in the event that the conflict does escalate, the parties responsible and not the peace process itself will be held accountable. Anticipation of these responses can inoculate the parties and act to partially nullify their effects.

## Summary and Conclusions

In this chapter, we have tried to provide an overview both of the current state of research on mediation in the schools and of the procedures involved in the mediation of interethnic conflict. The research suggests that school mediation programs have such positive effects as reduction of violence and enhancement of the self-esteem and social skills of the mediator. Yet we must also note that this research is sparse, poorly funded, and of less than high quality.

The research on the mediation of interethnic conflict is almost nonexistent. It mainly consists of a few case descriptions written by mediators themselves. As noted, Peter Coleman supplemented these case studies by conducting interviews with eleven expert mediators who have worked on interethnic conflicts in schools and elsewhere. Combining our own knowledge and experience with insights garnered from these experts, we have discussed here some of the issues involved in mediating interethnic conflict. Many of these issues are the same as those involved in the mediation of any conflict. But the issues unique to interethnic conflict emerge from cultural misunderstandings, ethnocentrism, long-held stereotypes, and the importance of ethnic identity to self-identity. Although interethnic conflicts are not easy to mediate, our experts indicated many successful outcomes of such mediation.

In conclusion we now provide a brief outline of some suggestions for education and research in this area. Our model for the education of professionals in conflict resolution and mediation is based on a program of Graduate Studies in Conflict Resolution and Mediation that was recently instituted at Teachers College, Columbia University. And our suggestions for research are illustrated in relation to a systemwide conflict resolution intervention that was recently implemented by the New York City Board of Education.

## Education

The recently established Teachers College program of Graduate Studies in Conflict Resolution and Mediation offers a set of core courses and practical as well as supplementary associated courses. The core courses provide students with knowledge of the theoretical and research basis for professional practice in the areas of cooperative learning, constructive conflict resolution, and mediation. They also provide students with supervised practice of the skills involved in these areas so that they can use these skills effectively in their personal lives as well as in their work. Advanced practica training enable them to train others in these skills. Additionally, as part of their education, students engage in continuous reflection on what they are learning; toward this end they are required to formulate significant researchable questions and to keep personal diaries related to their education and practice.

One set of associated, supplementary courses is directed toward providing students with the knowledge and skills to work effectively as facilitators, change agents, or administrators in an organization. Most conflict resolution specialists will work in organizational settings such as a school, industry, or community. To be influential and effective in such settings, students also need to be knowledgeable about consultation in organizations.

A second cluster of associated courses revolves around social and cultural diversity, dealing with the characteristics of different ethnic groups, cultural conflict, racism, sexism, ageism, and so on.

In a multicultural society, conflict resolution specialists need to have knowledge of and skill in working with different cultural groups and in helping people from various backgrounds to work together cooperatively in resolving their mutual problems.

A third group of courses focuses on psychological development and personality and cultural differences. It is evident that conflict resolution and mediation must be taught in such a way as to remain responsive to the cognitive, emotional, moral, and social development of individual students. Being aware of the nature and stages of psychological development throughout the life span as it is influenced by the sociocultural context enables the mediator to formulate developmentally appropriate training. Similarly, recognition of the nature of individual differences in personality is helpful in individualizing training and in deciding whether or not a given person can benefit from it.

By itself, the Teachers College program of Graduate Studies in Conflict Resolution and Mediation does not yet lead to a degree. Its core courses can, however, be taken as components in any of several degree programs in various departments. Conflict resolution and mediation are inherently interdisciplinary and thus relevant to many different institutional contexts, whether interpersonal, family, intergroup, school, work, community, or international in orientation. In our own experience, it has been valuable to mix students from these different contexts in our program. They broaden their perspectives as they learn from one another in useful and unexpected ways.

To sum up, we favor the professional model of the "reflective practitioner." In this rapidly developing field, the cumulating experience of practitioners and, we hope, the increasing research will require professionals to be continuously reflective about their own work if they are to remain up to date.

## Evaluation and Research

It is typical of practitioners in this field to support interventions around issues such as violence prevention and multicultural understanding, and yet not to support research and evaluation of the interventions that we implement. Due to the diverse nature of the types of interventions utilized, the differing levels of intensity with which they are introduced, the idiosyncratic differences among the trainers, and the vastly different environments into which they are introduced, research on the effects of the interventions is badly needed—indeed, essential to their refinement and level of efficacy. There is also a need for more general theoretical research on interethnic conflict mediation. Support from field studies and qualitative research such as the interview data presented earlier can begin to shed light on these issues, but such data have to be supplemented by more systematic, controlled studies of the phenomena. We now briefly describe an actual intervention in a school system and suggest some of the ingredients of a program of research to investigate it.

### New York City Board of Education Conflict Resolution Project

Beginning in April 1992 and ending in June 1993, the International Center for Cooperation and Conflict Resolution (ICCCR) at Teachers College, Columbia University, undertook a project for the New York City Board of Education in conflict resolution in all of the city's high schools. The training project had two strands: one focused on starting a pilot program in conflict resolution in curricular areas; the other focused on establishing a peer mediation program within the schools. Two professionals from each school received ten days of training/support in one of the two strands over a period of several months. The aim of the program was for the two professionals to return to their schools and, with the support of their principal, a district conflict resolution specialist, and the ICCCR staff, to design a program of conflict resolution specifically tailored to the needs and limitations of their individual schools. Furthermore, these professionals received instruction enabling them to train both students and other school professionals in negotiation and mediation skills. Our overall objective was to begin to replicate and spread these skills and cooperative attitudes through the school system and, over time, to transform its predominantly competitive, violent culture into a safer, more cooperative one.

Unfortunately, we were unable to obtain funding for a research component to help monitor and evaluate the effectiveness of the interventions. We therefore outline a general program of research that we feel would be valuable in the way of assessing the effects of this intervention or any other systems-level intervention of conflict resolution.

We recommend that research in this area address the following three general questions:

1. Was the initial training with the high school professionals successful?
2. Were the high school professionals successful in getting a program started in their school?
3. What were the short-term and long-term effects of the interventions on the students?

These general questions provide an overview of the most important issues at this stage in the development of and research on systems-level conflict resolution interventions. A more specific discussion of each of the areas follows.

Our first question concerns the effectiveness of the initial training and should address the issues of training integration and transfer of skills. Specifically, were the professionals able to actually integrate the attitudes and skills from the training and begin to use them in their own personal lives? The assumption here is that the trainers who are most effective with young people are those who use and can model the skills from the training, not only during the training but in other aspects of their personal and professional lives as well. In short, the repeated exposure of the students to the professional allows for the modeling and transfer of skills over time.

If the initial training was effective, we then ask whether the professionals can effectively train others. In other words, do they have the intelligence, energy, enthusiasm, creativity, and interpersonal style to help others learn, and can they effectively transfer their skills to other adults and young people? Again, our assumption is that young people will be most profoundly affected by trainers who both can train effectively and are seen to be living by their word. Although little research has been conducted on the integration of training or transfer of skills, both of these issues could be investigated through interviews with the professionals and students, through self-report questionnaires, and/or through behavioral-rating measurements of the work of the professionals.

Our second general question addresses issues of organizational change, support, and resource acquisition. As a corollary we must also ask, "What are the conditions necessary to enable the program to get started in a school and be most effective?" The answer requires that the following issues be addressed: Were the professionals successful as "change agents" in their system? Were they able to obtain "buy-in" early on from the sources of power (principal, deans, local youth officer, etc.) in their school and district? Were they able to obtain the necessary resources (time, space, students, etc.) to sustain the program? Did they network effectively through their peers and through the student body to promote the program and gain the needed support and "voice" for the program? Were they able to correctly identify and address areas of resistance to the project? Did they establish a mechanism to help monitor and fine-tune the interventions on an ongoing basis? And, finally, did the professionals receive the necessary training and/or assistance with these aspects of the intervention? There is a large body of research on organizational change and development that could be used to facilitate the investigation of these issues. It is usually best, however, to work with outside consultants for these types of inquiries because of the politically sensitive nature of the questions.

Our final question—concerning the effects of the interventions on students—is the most important and deserves the most thorough study. Deutsch (1992), with others, addressed this question by researching the effects of conflict resolution training and cooperative learning on students in an alternative high school in New York City. The study demonstrated that training in these areas led to an improvement in the students' social skills and ability to constructively resolve conflict and work together, which in turn led to more positive student relations (that is, to greater social support and less victimization), greater self-esteem, more frequent positive mental states, less frequent negative mental states, a greater sense of control, and greater achievement in terms of academic and vocational performance.

We strongly recommend the replication of this study, but we encourage the investigation of other issues as well. Particularly relevant to our discussion would be a more thorough exploration of the effects of these interventions on interethnic, intergroup categorizations and perceptions. It would be useful to obtain pre- and post-intervention measures of individual-level cognitive categorization and recategorization of ingroup/outgroup distinctions for ethnic group members to see if the interventions have short-term cognitive effects. It would similarly be useful to collect pre- and post-intervention measures of perceptions of positive or negative interdependence between members of different ethnic groups to look for mediating effects here. Furthermore we might simply check for post-intervention increases in cross-cultural awareness and acceptance. This type of research could build on past research dealing with Allport's contact theory (1954), Deutsch's theory of cooperation and conflict resolution (1949a), and Tajfel and Turner's social identity theory (Tajfel, 1982), as well as on recent advances in the area of social cognition.

We would also recommend an investigation into the specific conditions that enhance the effectiveness of the programs with young people. We might ask, for example, whether certain variables—such as the students' level of intelligence, communication skills, or ability to remain nonviolent—are necessary to ensure success in the program. And is the design of the program (in terms of teaching materials, examples, etc.) culturally sensitive enough to be effective with a multicultural population? Furthermore, it would be important to determine whether the effects of the training spread to the students' family, community, and work environments. And do the effects last? This question would entail a follow-up study of the young people past high school and into their college years or work life.

At a more general level, more valid and reliable instruments would have to be developed for the assessment of the individual, group, organizational, and larger system-level effects of mediation and other conflict resolution interventions. As previously indicated, research in this area is sparse, and the instruments utilized are mostly ad hoc combinations of components of older instruments. It would also be useful to develop (through surveys, interviews, and observations) a typology of formal and informal conflict resolution interventions that may exist at the disciplinary, curriculum, peda-gogical, and cultural levels of schools, so as to begin to assess the relative effects of the mediation programs in these schools. Fur-thermore, some method of assessing the degree of exposure of each of the above conflict resolution interventions at each of the school campuses should be developed so that the unique and/or combined contribution of each intervention could be weighed. The develop-ment of these instruments could better facilitate the measurement of the comparative effectiveness of the various different training approaches that exist for mediation and negotiation.

The current trend of research in this area appears to be oriented toward assessing the average effectiveness of these programs of inter-vention in general. What we encourage instead is specific research to identity the processes and conditions that determine whether or not a given type of intervention will be effective. It is through the answers to these questions that the field will truly move forward.

Clearly, then, there is a need to support both more education and more research in this area. It is our impression that only very few schools with educational programs would qualify their gradu-ates to be experts in this field—experts with sufficient knowledge to be able to train other experts. Such educational programs are necessary if school mediation programs are to be developed in an effective and responsible manner. And given the insufficient research in this specialty of professional practice, there is an obvious need for the development of research institutes to develop the knowledge to guide professional practice and the procedures to evaluate and improve it.

# References

Allport, G. W. (1954). *The nature of prejudice*. Cambridge, Mass.: Addison-Wesley.

Deutsch, M. (1949a). A theory of cooperation and competition. *Human Relations, 2*, 129–151.

Deutsch, M. (1949b). An experimental study of the effects of cooperation and competition upon group processes. *Human Relations, 2*, 199–231.

Deutsch, M. (1992). *The effects of training in cooperative learning and conflict resolution in an alternative high school: A summary report*. New York: International Center for Cooperation and Conflict Resolution, Teachers College, Columbia University.

Deutsch, M. (1993a). Cooperative learning and conflict resolution in an alternative high school. *Cooperative Learning, 13*(4), 2–5.

Deutsch, M. (1993b). Educating for a peaceful world. *American Psychologist, 48*, 1–8.

Johnson, D. W., and Johnson, R. T. (1989). *Cooperation and competition: Theory and research*. Edina, Minn.: Interaction Book Company.

Johnson, D. W., and Johnson, R. T. (1992). *Structuring academic controversies: Creating conflict in the classroom*. Edina, Minn.: Interaction Book Company.

Kressel, K., and Pruitt, D. G. (1989). *Mediation research*. San Francisco: Jossey-Bass.

Lam, J. A. (1989). *The impact of conflict resolution programs on schools: A review and synthesis of the evidence*. Amherst, Mass.: NAME.

Pruitt, D. G., and Olczak, P. V. (in press). A multimodal approach to seemingly intractable conflict. In J. Z. Rubin and B. B. Bunker (eds.), *Cooperation, conflict, and justice: Essays reflecting on the work of Morton Deutsch*. New York: Sage.

Slavin, R. E. (1983). *Cooperative learning*. New York: Longman.

Sumner, W. G. (1906). *Folkways*. New York: Ginn.

Tajfel, H. (ed.). (1982). *Social Identity and intergroup relations*. Cambridge, England: Cambridge University Press.

Wilson-Brewer, R., Cohen, S., O'Donnell, L., and Goodman, I. F. (1991). *Violence prevention for young adolescents: A survey of the state of the art.* Revised version of working paper prepared for the conference "Violence Prevention for Young Teens," held in Washington, D.C., July 12–13, 1990.

*Chapter Fifteen*

# Preparing Educators for Cross-Cultural Teaching

## Kenneth M. Zeichner

Between 1990 and 1995 I have co-directed a research project for the National Center for Research on Teacher Learning, entitled "Educating Teachers for Cultural Diversity." (Susan Melnick, of Michigan State University, and I are co-principal investigators for this project.) In this project, we conducted case studies of several preservice teacher education programs across the country that have had some success in preparing typical teacher education students (that is, white, monolingual students with little intercultural experience) to teach poor students of color.[1] The purpose of this project is to make the practices of these teacher educators more visible and to direct more substantive attention to issues of diversity in preservice teacher education programs.[2]

Although there is some good work going on in this area in both preservice and inservice teacher education, the U.S. teacher education enterprise as a whole has done little to address the problem of preparing teachers to work with culturally and linguistically diverse students since the alarm that was sounded in 1969 by B. O. Smith in the widely read book *Teachers for the Real World*. In this book, Smith charged that individual and institutional racism was pervasive in American teacher education and that teacher education programs needed to be fundamentally reconstructed to more adequately prepare teachers to educate poor students of color. There is plenty of evidence that things have not changed all that much in programs of teacher education since 1969, despite all of the rhetoric and hype surrounding multicultural education and diversity in recent years and the attempts of accreditation bodies to force teacher educators to pay more serious attention to the issue (Garcia and Pugh, 1992). Graduates of the 1,200 or so teacher education institutions across the United States are not exactly fighting with each other over who can get to teach in places like Los Angeles, Chicago, Detroit, and the American Indian reservations of the Southwest, and most teacher education students and teachers still say that they feel unprepared to teach students of color (see, for example, Trent, 1990).

In our research, Susan Melnick and I are also investigating a variety of institutional issues such as various ways in which teacher education programs can overcome the limitations of their own faculties in addressing issues of cultural diversity. Teacher education for diversity is not just a matter of curriculum and instruction; it also requires significant changes in the staffing patterns, reward structures, and moral commitments of teacher education institutions.

We have been out in the field now since 1991 and have focused our attention on three preservice teacher education programs: (1) The Teachers for Alaska program at the University of Alaska at Fairbanks, (2) The Urban Education Program of the Associated Colleges of the Midwest in Chicago, and (3) The Native American Cultural Immersion Project sponsored by Indiana University's School of Education.[3]

We began our project with a review of the literature in the area, which focused on three major questions: (1) What do teachers need to be like, to know, and to be able to do to teach poor ethnic and language minority students successfully? (2) What strategies have been used in U.S. teacher education programs to try and prepare prospective teachers to work with these students? (3) What do we know about the success of different approaches to teacher education for diversity (Zeichner, 1993)?

The purpose of the present chapter is to summarize the key points—both from the literature review and from initial analyses of our case-study data—that relate to questions (2) and (3). I will also share some of my general impressions from the recent extension of our analysis into teacher education for diversity at the inservice level. Much of the literature on teacher education for diversity (at both the preservice and inservice levels) is fugitive and hard to get hold of, and some of the good work going on is proceeding without much public attention beyond program sites. Efforts have been made in our project to reach out beyond traditional data sources in identifying program strategies and to include the voices of teacher educators whose good work has received little notice in the literature.

## Preservice Teacher Education for Diversity

When we began our review of different approaches to educating teachers for cross-cultural teaching, we focused only on the identification of different curricular and instructional approaches to the problem. Then, soon after becoming immersed in the literature, we broadened our focus and defined the problem of teacher education for diversity as (1) a problem of selection; (2) a problem of socialization (having to do with curriculum and instruction, for example); and (3) an institutional problem. Following is a summary of our initial findings related to each of these three aspects of the task of preparing teachers for cross-cultural teaching.

### Teacher Education for Diversity as a Problem of Selection

Almost every paper written in the last decade on teacher education and diversity has a section in it about the growing disparity between teachers and teacher educators on the one hand and public school students on the other, and about the continually growing crisis of inequality in our schools and in our nation. Like almost everyone else who has looked at this issue, we concluded that teacher education students, who are predominantly white and monolingual, come to their teacher education programs with very little direct intercultural and interracial experience—even in states with a lot of cultural diversity, such as California. Indeed, recent research has clearly shown that many teacher education students view diversity as a problem rather than as a resource, and that they generally have very little knowledge about different ethnic and racial groups in the United States, their cultures, their histories, and their contributions to the making of our nation. According to recent national studies of teacher education students, most such students want to teach pupils who are like themselves in communities that are familiar to them (Paine, 1989; Zimpher and Ashburn, 1992). As Goodlad (1990) concluded, many teacher education students are not even convinced that all pupils are capable of learning: "The idea of moral imperatives for teachers was virtually foreign in concept and strange in language for most of the future teachers we interviewed. Many were less than convinced that all students can learn; they voiced the view that they should be kind and considerate to all, but they simply accepted as fact the theory that some simply can't learn" (p. 264).

While it is possible for these and other similar factors to be remedied by preservice teacher education programs, the likelihood is that they are not adequately addressed by programs as currently organized, and that they cannot be remedied in the future, even with program modifications. The literature on teacher learning overwhelmingly supports a view of teacher education programs as weak interventions, even under the best of circumstances (Zeichner and Gore, 1990). One cannot be too optimistic about the power of changes in curriculum and instruction alone to overcome the negative effects of anticipatory socialization. Some screening of teacher education candidates on the basis of criteria related to their potential ability to be successful cross-cultural teachers is definitely needed. The work of Martin Haberman (1987) at the University of Wisconsin, Milwaukee in developing an interview for the purpose of screening teachers for employment in urban schools is an example of some of the research currently being done in the area of teacher education for diversity and selection. Most preservice teacher education programs continue to select their students solely on the basis of academic criteria such as grade point averages and test scores, despite what we know about the limited power of teacher education programs to overcome the effects of prior socialization and later socialization in the workplace.

Some researchers, like Haberman (1993), have argued that typical teacher education students—who are very young in addition to being white, monolingual, and interculturally inexperienced—are developmentally not ready to make the kinds of adjustments needed for successful cross-cultural teaching. Haberman recommends that we focus on "picking the right people rather than on changing the wrong ones" and is very pessimistic about the likelihood that university-based preservice teacher education programs can become powerful enough interventions to do more than simply reinforce the dispositions and attitudes that students bring to teacher education: "Teacher education can be most readily improved by making teacher training more available to experienced, older constituencies. This is a most vital need as we consider the needs of urban schools and the competencies required of teachers to work with low income children and children who represent racial and language minorities. It takes somebodys to make somebodys; nobodys don't make somebodys" (Haberman, 1993, p. 284).

## Teacher Education for Diversity as a Problem of Socialization

Much of our work has focused on the identification of curricular and instructional strategies with which teacher educators have sought to prepare teachers for cross-cultural work and for teaching in a multicultural society. Despite the marginalization of this issue by the teacher education research community (Grant and Secada, 1990), several different strategies were evident in the teacher education literature and in our study of the three programs.

There are two ways in which these curricular and instructional strategies could conceivably be employed. One possibility, the infusion approach, is for teacher education for diversity to be integrated throughout the various courses and field experiences in a teacher education program, including courses outside of schools, colleges, and departments of education. Another possibility, the segregated approach, is for teacher educators to deal with this issue as a topic or add-on to a teacher education program in one or a few courses and field experiences, while other courses remain untouched by issues of diversity.

Despite a clear preference for the integrated approach on the part of scholars who have assessed the impact of teacher education programs (for example, Gay, 1986), the segregated approach is clearly dominant (Grant and Sleeter, 1985). There are very few teacher education programs of a permanent nature that have integrated attention to issues of diversity throughout the curriculum.[4] It is also very common for any course work related to cultural diversity, beyond basic survey courses, to be optional rather than compulsory (Gay, 1986).

There is good reason for scholars to prefer the integrated approach to issues of cultural diversity in preservice teacher education: research studies have clearly demonstrated the limited impact of the segregated approach on the attitudes, beliefs, and teaching practices of teacher education students (see, for example, Grant and Koskella, 1986; Haberman and Post, 1992). Following is a summary of the different curricular and instructional approaches we have identified.

*Biography.* According to Hollins (1990), "Part of the teacher education curriculum should be aimed at resocializing preservice teachers in ways that help them view themselves within a culturally diverse society. This could entail restructuring self-perceptions and world views. Part of designing appropriate experiences for preservice teachers is making meaningful connections between students' personal/family history and the social context of life as experienced by different groups within a culturally diverse society" (pp. 202–203).

Preservice teacher education for diversity often begins with helping teacher education students to better understand their own cultural experience and to develop more clarified cultural identities. There is a consensus in the literature that the development of one's own cultural identity is a necessary precursor to cross-cultural understanding (see, for example, Banks, 1991). In my literature review (Zeichner, 1993), I discuss several examples of the work of teacher educators using case studies and autobiographical/life history methods to help prospective teachers locate themselves culturally in a multicultural society (see also Gomez, 1991).

**Attitude Change.** A next step, according to some teacher educators, is to help prospective teachers learn more about and reexamine their attitudes, assumptions, and beliefs about ethnic, racial, and language groups other than their own. This includes knowledge about prejudice and about specific strategies that can help reduce prejudice and racism among students (Banks, 1993).

Some teacher educators who have written about their efforts to help their students reexamine their attitudes and beliefs about various ethnic and racial groups have stressed the importance of both the intellectual challenge and the social support that comes from a group of students (Gomez and Tabachnick, 1991; King and Ladson-Billings, 1990). The existence of cohesive cohort groups, in which teacher education students stay in close contact with each other over a period of time, is often cited as a critical ingredient for successful teacher education interventions that lead to attitude change (Nelson-Barber and Mitchell, 1992). Even with the existence of these collaborative learning environments, however, the process of helping student teachers confront their attitudes about other ethnic, racial, and language groups can be a very difficult one in which students resist and rebel against the efforts of teacher educators to effect attitude change (Ahlquist, 1991). There is substantial evidence that more than conventional university classes (whether field- or campus-based) are needed to avoid simply reinforcing the prejudices and misconceptions that students bring to teacher education programs (see for example, Cross, 1993).

*Countering Low Expectations for Pupils.* One of the most common elements addressed in preservice teacher education for diversity is the typically low expectations that teacher education students hold for poor ethnic and language minority pupils. There are several ways in which teacher educators have attempted to deal with the problem of low expectations that Goodlad (1990) found to be widespread among teacher education students in the United States. One way is to expose teacher education students, through readings or direct contact, to examples of successful teaching for poor students of color (see, for example, Moll, 1988; Ladson-Billings, 1991). This attention to cases of success is often supplemented by helping students examine the ways in which schools help structure inequality through various practices in curriculum, instruction, grouping, and assessment.

Another way in which teacher educators have attempted to counter low expectations and give teachers a framework for organizing classroom learning environments is to give attention in the teacher education curriculum to research on the relationships among language, culture, and learning. This body of research has convincingly demonstrated the superiority of a situational as opposed to a stable-trait view of intelligence and competence. It is "situational" in that it sees behavior as a function of the context of which it is a part (Cazden and Mehan, 1990). This research also provides numerous examples of how learning environments have been created through adaptations in schools and classrooms that facilitate the success of students who in many cases have not been successful in school (see, for example, Tharp and Gallimore, 1988).[5] As Bowers and Flinders (1990) argue, there are two things that teachers often realize after being exposed to this sociocultural knowledge base: "[The first has to do with] the need to view students' behavior, in part, as the expression of patterns learned through membership within their primary culture. The second has to do with the belief that teachers' professional judgment should include a knowledge of how their own cultural patterns may both obstruct students' ability to learn and influence their own judgments about students' performance" (p. 72).

**Cultural Knowledge.** Yet another strategy used by teacher educators is to try to overcome the lack of knowledge among teacher education students about the histories of different cultural groups and their participation in and contributions to the making of our nation and world. As Ellwood (1990) has argued, an ethnic studies component in teacher education programs can potentially do a great deal to prevent mistakes by teachers that are rooted in cultural ignorance. Often, efforts by teacher educators to address cultural ignorance are focused on the specific groups that prospective teachers are being prepared to teach. For example, in our research we observed an orientation workshop for the Native American Cultural Immersion Project, sponsored by Indiana University, where students were being prepared to do their student teaching on the Navajo reservation. A great deal of time was spent during this workshop informing the students about the history and culture of the Navajos through film, poetry, artwork, and discussions with Navajo people. The focus here was both on the common elements in the Navajo culture and on the rich diversity within the culture. The same kind of cultural education is also evident in the other two programs we have studied although in Chicago the focus is on the many different ethnocultural communities in the city rather than on a single group. The role of noncertified ethnic minority adults as teacher educators in providing this cultural education to prospective teachers seems to be a critical element in the success of these efforts (Mahan, 1993). All of the programs we have studied put teacher education students out into communities to experience firsthand the cultures that they are learning about. All of these programs also provide carefully structured activities for students while they are in the community and closely monitor both the experiences and the later analysis of the experiences.

Another part of this strategy is to provide students with information about some of the unique characteristics and learning styles of students from different groups. However, because these are general characteristics, not limited to specific cultural groups or necessarily applicable to individual learners in specific classrooms, we need to be careful to avoid stereotypic responses to students as members of groups that ignore individual characteristics (McDiarmid and Price, 1990). A necessary supplement to giving information about general group characteristics is teaching teacher education students how to gather, and then how to incorporate into their instruction, information about their own students, their families, and communities. This involves an examination of the cultures of the home and community as well as an assessment of the degree of congruence between these cultures and the cultures of the classroom and school. Indeed, teachers must learn how to incorporate home and community cultures into their classrooms as the starting point for curriculum and instruction (Villegas, 1991).[6]

One example of a teacher education program that attempts to teach prospective teachers to do research about their own students, their families, and communities, in the tradition of Heath's seminal work in Appalachia (1983), is the Teachers for Alaska program (Noordhoff and Kleinfeld, 1993). This program supplements the giving of cultural information about particular groups of people with a focus on developing prospective teachers' dispositions to find out about the context, helping them learn experientially about their own students and their communities, and then helping them learn how to use that information to tailor their instruction to particular cultural contexts. One way in which Teachers for Alaska (TFA) faculty help prospective teachers learn how to tailor their instruction to particular contexts is to provide them with examples of such adaptations that have been preserved in case studies written by local teachers (see, for example, Kleinfeld, 1992).

There is also much discussion in the literature about how to take general knowledge about particular ethnic, racial, and language groups and to make use of it in developing multicultural curriculum materials and culturally responsive instructional strategies and classroom organizational structures. Much of this work focuses on the integration of a multicultural perspective into all that a teacher does in the classroom (see, for example, Bennett, 1990). With regard to curriculum, the emphasis is often on two things: (1) developing teachers' skills in analyzing existing curriculum materials for bias and in adapting them to correct for these biases, and (2) developing teachers' capabilities in designing multicultural curriculum materials on their own.

With regard to instruction, prospective teachers are often taught various instructional strategies and classroom organizational schemes that are sensitive to cultural and linguistic differences and enable them to build upon the cultural resources that pupils bring to school (see, for example, Tharp and Gallimore, 1988). Prospective teachers are also taught a variety of curriculum-based and potentially culturally sensitive methods of assessment such as portfolio development.

*Field Experiences.* As Hilliard (1974) has pointed out, "If teachers are to work successfully with students from cultures different from their own, it is imperative that the training program provide for more than intellectualization about cross-cultural issues. Teacher growth in this area is possible only to the extent that the teacher's own behavior in a cross-cultural setting is the subject of examination and experimentation" (pp. 49–50).

Probably the most frequent topic of discussion in the teacher education for diversity literature is the provision of some type of field experience to help sensitize prospective teachers to cultural differences and/or to help them become more capable cross-cultural teachers. Included in this category are relatively brief community field experiences with poor children and adults of color that are part of university courses and include reflective seminars in which students analyze their experiences. These community experiences are often used as a basis for helping prospective teachers learn how to interact in more authentic ways with parents and other adults from different racial and ethnic backgrounds.

Other field experiences discussed in the literature entail the required completion of a minimum number of practicum and student teaching experiences in schools serving ethnic and language minority students, and intensive cultural immersions of varying lengths of time in which students live and teach in a minority community and often do extensive community service work. Another possibility would be to combine elements of both of these strategies into one program component and to require practicum and student teaching experiences in schools serving students of color that include a community component as part of the field experience. Linking a community field experience to a course in which students serve in the role of student teacher seems to help develop teaching capabilities beyond what is gained in the way of increased sensitivity in community experiences alone. For several years now, Jim Mahan (1982), at Indiana University, has provided examples of how to structure cross-cultural field experiences in such a way as to prompt a reexamination of values and beliefs rather than their reaffirmation. In any case, we need to be very careful about the cross-cultural field experiences that we provide for prospective teachers because of the clear evidence that, under some conditions, they strengthen and legitimate the very stereotypes and prejudices that they were designed to correct (see, for example, Haberman, 1991; Haberman and Post, 1992).

In all three of the programs we are studying, community immersion experiences are a key program component and non-certified adults play key roles as teacher educators in these experiences. Merely requiring that teacher education students complete field experiences in settings that require cross-cultural teaching is not sufficient for developing the cultural sensitivity and intercultural competence needed, because many of the schools in which students are placed are isolated from their communities (Zeichner,

1992). In short, the connectedness of the teacher education program to the community is an important part of preservice teacher education for diversity.

*Research About the Effectiveness of Different Strategies.* In general, the empirical evidence regarding the success of these various strategies of teacher education for diversity is very weak. At best, some teacher educators such as Etta Hollins (1990), Gloria Ladson-Billings (1991), and Lanny Beyer (1991) have been able to demonstrate some immediate influence of one or more of these strategies through the presentation of student-teacher self-reports. In no case, however, have we been able to find convincing evidence related to the long-term impact of these strategies on teachers and their teaching practices. One reason for this lack of evidence may be the narrow definition of teacher education for diversity that has been adopted by many institutions. Much of the literature and many institutions have defined this problem as one of socialization (as noted, having to do with curriculum and instruction, for example) and have ignored the selection and institutional aspects of the situation. Until teacher educators begin to adopt a broader perspective on teacher education for diversity and to focus on both institutional and individual change, the demonstrated impact of preservice teacher education programs in this area is likely to remain minimal.

Much of our knowledge about preservice teacher education for diversity comes from very brief and often vague self-reports about the use of particular teacher education curricula and instructional strategies. With very few exceptions there are no detailed descriptions available that illuminate either the nature of these programs or their consequences over the long-term for the prospective teachers who participate in them. A much closer look at the various approaches to teacher education for diversity is thus critical. We need to learn more about the particular community and school experiences, as well as college and university courses, that facilitate the kind of personal and professional transformations that many white, monolingual student teachers must undergo to become successful cross-cultural teachers.

## Teacher Education for Diversity as an Institutional Problem

In addition to considering the problems of selection and socialization in the preservice preparation of teachers for cultural diversity, our research has addressed some of the institutional dimensions of the issue. Specifically, we have been concerned with how the culturally insular nature of the education professoriate and the general lack of multicultural learning communities in teacher education programs act as impediments to reform. So many faculty say that they are trying to deal with the issue of diversity in their teacher education programs, but it appears that, in most institutions, teacher education faculty are just as white and culturally encapsulated as their students (Howey and Zimpher, 1990).

Teacher education for diversity clearly entails much more than the transfer of information from teacher educators to their students. What is involved if we are to succeed in preparing more culturally sensitive people and more capable cross-cultural teachers is the transformation of people and many of the worldviews and assumptions that they have carried with them for their entire lives. An important part of becoming a multicultural teacher is becoming a multicultural person (Nieto, 1992). This task is beyond the current capabilities of most faculties of teacher education.[7]

Our work has uncovered four different approaches to dealing with the limitations of most teacher education faculties. The first involves the active recruitment of faculty of color into teacher education through the establishment of new institutional policies and programs such as the "Madison Plan" established by Donna Shalala at the University of Wisconsin, Madison several years ago. This program provides special incentives to departments to hire qualified faculty of color. The second involves the idea of a consortium whereby a group of institutions gets together and hires staff with expertise in teacher education for diversity to handle a portion of the teacher education program, usually student teaching and a few courses and seminars related to multicultural education. We have located three such consortia so far: the Urban Education Program of the Associated Colleges of the Midwest in Chicago, the Cooperative Urban Education Program in Kansas City, Kansas, and the Urban Education semester of the Venture Consortium in New York City. The third approach involves systematic staff development for teacher education faculty in teacher education for diversity, similar to that currently being conducted by the Multicultural Infusion Center at San Diego State University. Finally, there is the idea of partnership agreements between predominantly white teacher education institutions and either teacher education institutions with significant numbers of faculty and students of color or schools and school districts in areas with large numbers of students of color (see, for example, Mills, 1984). Whatever approach is used, it is clear that teacher education for diversity has to include some significant effort to change the environment in which the teacher education program is delivered. Merely focusing on the adoption of particular strategies of curriculum and instruction is insufficient.

## Inservice Teacher Education for Diversity

Although our research project has focused primarily on preservice teacher education, we have just begun to explore the literature on inservice teacher education for diversity. Most scholars who have examined this literature, including our research team, have found the literature on inservice teacher education for diversity to be so sparse as to be almost nonexistent (see, for example, Grant and Secada, 1990; Sleeter, 1992; Gay, 1993). Here the situation is similar to the one in preservice teacher education. While a few studies have been able to demonstrate the limited impact of some staff development activity on the attitudes and behaviors of teachers (for example, Baty, 1972; Sleeter, 1992), there is little empirical evidence of any kind regarding the long-term impact of staff development for diversity or the impact of these efforts on the way people teach.

In the general literature on staff development, there is much discussion of different purposes for staff development and of effective practices of staff development for the different types (see, for example, Sparks and Loucks-Horsley, 1990). Staff development for the development of teaching skills has received much of the attention of those who have tried to identify effective staff development practices (see, for example, Joyce and Showers, 1988). The literature includes such recommendations as involving teachers as planners of staff development activities; placing an emphasis on self-instruction with differentiated activities; emphasizing demonstration, supervised trials, and ongoing feedback and support; and linking staff development to schoolwide school-improvement efforts (Sparks and Loucks-Horsley, 1990).

Because of the complex and demanding nature of the personal and professional changes needed to enable teachers to become more effective cross-cultural teachers, these recommendations are insufficient by themselves for guiding staff development for diversity. Haberman (1993) has identified five levels of change that can serve as goals for staff development of diversity. These levels begin with the recognition of differences and tolerance of diversity and end with active efforts to combat racism and discrimination. Our initial examination of staff development for diversity has uncovered two university-based programs that appear to result in changes beyond the initial levels in Haberman's typology.[8] Both of these programs involve a substantial cultural immersion experience in which teachers live and work in a minority community and make friends from another culture (Pfisterer and Barnhardt, 1992; Mahan and Rains, 1990). These immersion experiences are carefully structured and are complemented by university course work. Here, as in successful examples of preservice teacher education for diversity, noncertified ethnic minority adults play key roles as teacher educators and the community-based nature of the programs seems to be a key element in their success.

# Conclusion

In this chapter we have attempted to summarize some of the preliminary findings from an ongoing investigation of successful efforts to educate teachers and prospective teachers for cross-cultural work. While all teachers need to be educated to teach all students, our research has focused on the education of white, monolingual teachers to teach poor students of color. Although we were able to identify a variety of strategies of curriculum and instruction that are used by teacher educators to promote greater cultural sensitivity and intercultural teaching competence, the empirical evidence for the long-term impact of these strategies on teachers and their teaching practices is weak. One reason for the lack of evidence may be the fact that many teacher educators have defined teacher education for diversity as merely a problem of curriculum and instruction. It is important for teacher educators to recognize the limits of teacher education programs, even under the best of conditions, to transform teacher education students. Teacher education programs need to begin to broaden the criteria that are used to admit students into such programs, so as to take into account a commitment and potential to teach all children. It is also important that teacher educators begin to address the institutional dimensions of the problem, such as the culturally encapsulated nature of most teacher education faculties and the norms and reward structures that encourage this insularity and discourage faculty from expending effort on building the high-quality teacher education programs that are needed to address issues of diversity.

The literature on staff development for diversity offers a variety of typologies of different types of staff development and several comprehensive lists of what are claimed to be research-based effective staff development strategies. There is very little evidence, however, that any of the staff development for diversity reported in this literature has been effective over the long term in producing anything more than surface-level changes in teachers or their teaching practices. Here, as in preservice teacher education for diversity, what little success has been demonstrated seems to be closely linked with cultural immersion experiences in which noncertified adults from the community play key roles as teacher educators. And again, here, as in preservice teacher education for diversity, institutional change needs to complement efforts to bring about change in teachers. While it is too early for us to draw any firm conclusions from our work, we feel confident in stating that some of the most common recommendations in the literature, such as requiring field experiences in culturally diverse schools and providing an ethnic studies component that gives teachers general information about different racial and ethnic groups, are inadequate by themselves for effecting the needed changes. In fact, as noted, these recommendations may lead, under some conditions, to the strengthening of the very prejudices and stereotypes that they are designed to confront. Developing the disposition and capability in teachers to find out about their own students, their families, and communities, and teaching them how to use the cultural resources that students bring to school as the starting place for instruction, seems to offer far more potential than the common advice offered to teacher educators in the literature. Unless the institutional and selection aspects of teacher education for diversity are addressed, however, none of these more promising directions will prove to be very fruitful.

## Notes

1. In limiting our focus to the preparation of white teachers to teach poor students of color, we are not assuming that teachers who are members of a minority group can necessarily translate their cultural knowledge into culturally relevant pedagogy (Montecinos, in press). We are also not saying that it is unimportant to continue to try and recruit more people of color into teaching. On the contrary, these efforts are extremely important; but even under the most optimistic scenario for their success, the problem of educating teachers for diversity will largely continue to be one of educating culturally insular and mono-

lingual white teachers to teach poor students of color. Finally, we are not saying that multicultural education is important only for schools attended by poor students of color. Multicultural education, and the intercultural competence of teachers, is an important issue in all schools and for all teachers. In short, we are focusing on a small aspect of a much larger issue.

2. We use the phrase "teacher education for diversity" to describe efforts to prepare teachers for cultural diversity. While diversity includes many factors such as social class, gender, race, ethnicity, language, age, religion, exceptionalities, sexual preference, and so on, our work focuses primarily on social class, race, ethnicity, and language differences.

3. Data collected by others about a fourth program, Teachers for Diversity at the University of Wisconsin, Madison, are also included in the final report from our project (Gomez and Tabachnick, 1991; Tabachnick and Zeichner, in press).

4. The desire to integrate a concern for diversity throughout an entire teacher education program is a specific case of the more general position that curriculum designs in teacher education should represent an outgrowth of shared conceptions of teaching, learning, and schooling among faculty (Barnes, 1987). Indeed, the lack of integration with regard to issues of diversity is a part of a general problem of fragmentation in the curriculum of teacher education programs (Liston and Zeichner, 1991).

5. Some states, such as California, have begun to require all prospective teachers to complete course work related to language acquisition and second-language learning.

6. Garcia (1993) identifies three different ways in which this has been done by successful teachers of culturally and linguistically diverse students: (a) using cultural referents in both verbal and nonverbal forms to communicate instructional and institutional demands, (b) organizing instruction to build on rules of discourse from the home and community cultures, and (c) respecting equally the values and norms of the home and community cultures and the school culture.

7. In addition to the culturally insular nature of most teacher education faculties, the norms and reward systems in many institutions make it difficult to sustain the kind of programmatic effort needed to enable the personal and professional transformation of teacher education students that is needed (Liston and Zeichner, 1991).
8. We have not yet begun to examine school-based staff development efforts in this area.

# References

Ahlquist, R. (1991). Position and imposition: Power relations in a multicultural foundations class. *Journal of Negro Education*, 60(2), 158–169.

Banks, J. (1991). Teaching multicultural literacy to teachers. *Teaching Education*, 4(1), 135–144.

Banks, J. (1993). Multicultural education: Historical development, dimensions, and practice. In L. Darling-Hammond (ed.), *Review of research in education*, 19, 3–50. Washington, D.C.: American Educational Research Association.

Barnes, H. (1987). The conceptual basis for thematic teacher education programs. *Journal of Teacher Education*, 38(4), 13–18.

Baty, R. (1972). *Reeducating teachers for cultural awareness*. New York: Praeger.

Bennett, C. (1990). *Comprehensive multicultural education: Theory and practice*. Boston: Allyn & Bacon.

Beyer, L. (1991). Teacher education, reflective inquiry and moral action. In B. R. Tabachnick and K. Zeichner (eds.), *Issues and practices in inquiry-oriented teacher education* (pp. 113–129). Bristol, Pa.: Falmer Press.

Bowers, C. A., and Flinders, D. (1990). *Responsive teaching: An ecological approach to classroom patterns of language, culture, and thought*. New York: Teachers College Press.

Cazden, C., and Mehan, H. (1990). Principles from sociology and anthropology: Context, code, classroom, and culture. In M. Reynolds, (ed.), *Knowledge base for the beginning teacher* (pp. 47–57). Washington, D.C.: American Association of Colleges for Teacher Education.

Cross, B. (1993). How do we prepare teachers to improve race relations? *Educational Leadership*, 50(8), 64–65.

Ellwood, C. (1990). The moral imperative of ethnic studies in urban teacher education programs. In M. Diez (ed.), *Proceedings of the fourth national forum of the Association of Independent Liberal Arts Colleges for Teacher Education* (pp. 1–6). Milwaukee, Wis.: Alverno College.

Garcia, E. (1993). Language, culture, and education. In L. Darling-Hammond (ed.), *Review of research in education* (vol. 19) (pp. 51–100). Washington, D.C.: American Educational Research Association.

Garcia, J., and Pugh, S. L. (1992). Multicultural education in teacher preparation programs: A political or an educational concept? *Phi Delta Kappan*, pp. 214–219.

Gay, G. (1986). Multicultural teacher education. In J. Banks and J. Lynch (eds.), *Multicultural education in Western societies* (pp. 154–177). New York: Praeger.

Gay, G. (1993). *Effective strategies for multicultural professional development.* Paper presented at the annual meeting of the American Educational Research Association, Atlanta.

Gomez, M. (1991). Teaching a language of opportunity in a language arts methods class: Teaching for David, Albert and Darlene. In B. R. Tabachnick and K. Zeichner (eds.), *Issues and practices in inquiry-oriented teacher education* (pp. 91–112). Bristol, Pa.: Falmer Press.

Gomez, M., and Tabachnick, B. R. (1991). Preparing preservice teachers to teach diverse learners. Paper presented at the annual meeting of the American Educational Research Association, Chicago.

Goodlad, J. (1990). *Teachers for our nation's schools.* San Francisco: Jossey-Bass.

Grant, C., and Koskella, R. (1986). Education that is multicultural and the relationship between preservice campus learning and field experiences. *Journal of Educational Research, 79,* 197–203.

Grant, C., and Secada, W. (1990). Preparing teachers for diversity. In W. R. Houston (ed.), *Handbook of research on teacher education* (pp. 403–422). New York: Macmillan.

Grant, C., and Sleeter, C. (1985). The literature on multicultural education: Review and analysis. *Educational Review, 37,* 97–118.

Haberman, M. (1987). *Recruiting and selecting teachers for urban schools.* New York: ERIC Clearing House on Urban Education, Institute for Urban & Minority Education.

Haberman, M. (1991). Can culture awareness be taught in teacher education programs? *Teaching Education, 4*(1), 25–31.

Haberman, M. (1993). Teaching in multicultural schools: Implications for teacher selection and training. In L. Kremer-Hayon, H. Vonk, and R. Fessler (eds.), *Teacher professional development* (pp. 267–294). Amsterdam: Swets & Zeitlinger B.V.

Haberman, M., and Post, L. (1992). Does direct experience change education students' perceptions of low-income minority children? *Midwestern Educational Researcher, 5*(2), 29–31.

Heath, S. B. (1983). *Ways with words: Language, life and work in communities and classrooms.* New York: Cambridge University Press.

Hilliard, A. (1974). Restructuring teacher education for multicultural imperatives. In W. A. Hunter (ed.), *Multicultural education through Competency-*

*Based Teacher Education* (pp. 40–55). Washington, D.C.: American Association of Colleges for Teacher Education.

Hollins, E. (1990). Debunking the myth of a monolithic white American culture; or moving toward cultural inclusion. *American Behavioral Scientist, 34*(2), 201–209.

Howey, K., and Zimpher, N. (1990). Professors and deans of education. In W. R. Houston (ed.), *Handbook of research on teacher education* (pp. 349–370). New York: Macmillan.

Joyce, B., and Showers, B. (1988). *Student achievement through staff development.* New York: Longman.

King, J., and Ladson-Billings, G. (1990). The teacher education challenge in elite university settings: Developing critical perspectives for teaching in a democratic and multicultural society. *European Journal of Intercultural Studies, 1*(2), 15–30.

Kleinfeld, J. (1992). Learning to think like a teacher: The study of cases. In J. Shulman (ed.), *Case methods in teacher education* (pp. 33–49). New York: Teachers College Press.

Ladson-Billings, G. (1991). Like lightning in a bottle: Attempting to capture the pedagogical excellence of successful teachers of black students. *International Journal of Qualitative Studies in Education, 3,* 335–344.

Liston, D., and Zeichner, K. (1991). *Teacher education and the social conditions of schooling.* New York: Routledge.

McDiarmid, G. W., and Price, J. (1990). *Prospective teachers' views of diverse learners: A study of the participants in the ABCD project* (Research Report 90-6). East Lansing: Michigan State University, National Center for Research on Teacher Education.

Mahan, J. (1982). Native Americans as teacher trainers: Anatomy and outcomes of a cultural immersion project. *Journal of Educational Equity and Leadership, 2*(2), 100–110.

Mahan, J. (1993). *Native Americans as non-traditional, usually unrecognized, influential teacher educators.* Paper presented at the annual meeting of the Association of Teacher Educators, Los Angeles.

Mahan, J., and Rains, F. (1990). Inservice teachers expand their cultural knowledge and approaches through practica of American Indian communities. *Journal of American Indian Education, 29,* 2, 9.

Mills, J. (1984). Addressing the separate but equal predicament in teacher preparation. *Journal of Teacher Education, 35*(6), 18–23.

Moll, L. (1988). Some key issues in teaching Latino students. *Language Arts, 65*(5), 465–472.

Montecinos, C. (in press). Multicultural teacher education for a culturally diverse society. In R. Martin (ed.), *Practicing what we preach: Confronting diversity in teacher education.* Albany, N.Y.: SUNY Press.

Nelson-Barber, S., and Mitchell, J. (1992). Contributions of research on teacher assessment to culturally appropriate teacher education. In M. Dillworth (ed.), *Diversity in teacher education* (pp. 229–262). San Francisco: Jossey-Bass.

Nieto, S. (1992). *Affirming diversity: The sociopolitical context of multicultural education*. New York: Longman.

Noordhoff, K., and Kleinfeld, J. (1993). Preparing teachers for multicultural classrooms. *Teaching and Teacher Education, 9*(1), 27–40.

Paine, L. (1989). *Orientation towards diversity: What do prospective teachers bring?* (Research report 89-9). East Lansing, Mich.: National Center for Research on Teacher Learning.

Pfisterer, B., and Barnhardt, R. (1992). Cross-cultural orientation at Old Minto camp. *College of Rural Alaska Newsletter* (Spring–Summer), p. 9.

Sleeter, C. (1992). *Keepers of the American dream: A study of staff development and multicultural education*. London: Falmer Press.

Smith, B. O. (1969). *Teachers for the real world*. Washington, D.C.: American Association of Colleges for Teacher Education.

Sparks, D., and Loucks-Horsley, S. (1990). Models of staff development. In W. R. Houston (ed.), *Handbook of research on teacher education* (pp. 234–250). New York: Macmillan.

Tabachnick, B. R., and Zeichner, K. (1993). Preparing teachers for cultural diversity. In M. Smith and P. Gilroy (eds.), *International perspectives in teacher education* (pp. 113–124). Abingdon, United Kingdom: Carfax.

Tharp, R., and Gallimore, R. (1988). *Rousing minds to life: Teaching, learning and schooling in social context*. New York: Cambridge University Press.

Trent, W. (1990). Race and ethnicity in the teacher education curriculum. *Teachers College Record, 91*, 361–369.

Villegas, A. M. (1991). *Culturally responsive pedagogy for the 1990's and beyond*. Princeton, N.J.: Educational Testing Service.

Zeichner, K. (1992). Rethinking the practicum in the professional development school partnership. *Journal of Teacher Education, 43*(4), 296–307.

Zeichner, K. (1993). *Educating teachers for cultural diversity*. East Lansing, Mich.: National Center for Research on Teacher Learning.

Zeichner, K., and Gore, J. (1990). Teacher socialization. In W. R. Houston (ed.), *Handbook of research on teacher education* (pp. 329–348). New York: Macmillan.

Zimpher, N., and Ashburn, E. (1992). Countering parochialism among teacher candidates. In M. Dillworth (ed.), *Diversity in teacher education* (pp. 40–62). San Francisco: Jossey-Bass.

Part Four

---

*Prospects for the Future*

*Chapter Sixteen*

# Strategies for Reducing Racial and Ethnic Prejudice: Essential Principles for Program Design

Willis D. Hawley
James A. Banks
Amado M. Padilla
Donald B. Pope-Davis
Janet Ward Schofield

## Overview

The United States is among the most racially and ethnically diverse societies in the world. While virtually all Americans take pride in this reality when it is described in general terms, racial and ethnic discrimination has been and remains a major constraint on the opportunities for people of color and a major limitation on the quality of life for most Americans, regardless of the color of their skin or their racial or ethnic background.

The nation's obsession with race and ethnic difference is not likely to yield to exhortation about justice or moral responsibility. We will eliminate racial and ethnic discrimination as a major force in our society only if we better understand the *sources* of prejudice and discrimination and use this knowledge to develop and implement theoretically grounded strategies for changing beliefs and behavior, and altering the institutions and structures within which people function.

Few strategies now employed to reduce racial and ethnic prejudice and discrimination have been carefully evaluated. Given that there are numerous programs and activities meant to improve inter-

424 Toward a Common Destiny

group relations, how does one decide which alternatives have the greatest chances of success? In order to give some guidance to educators and others interested in adopting or developing strategies to improve intergroup relations, we have developed, under the auspices of the Common Destiny Alliance (CODA), a set of "design principles." These principles can serve as criteria for assessing programs or as guidelines for formulating programs appropriate to particular circumstances.

The design principles were developed on the basis of a five-step process. First, nationally prominent scholars were commissioned to conduct reviews of relevant research. Second, these reviews were evaluated at a meeting where several scholars were involved in preparing syntheses and subsequent revisions. (They now appear as several chapters in the present volume.) Third, a summary of the research related to program effectiveness was prepared. Fourth, the research summary was evaluated by a "consensus panel" for accuracy and completeness. Fifth, the panel determined the wording of the thirteen design principles outlined below. The members of the CODA Consensus Panel on Race Relations were James A. Banks, Amado M. Padilla, Willis D. Hawley, Donald B. Pope-Davis, and Janet Ward Schofield.

It is important to emphasize that while the design principles presented here are derived from research, they go beyond the available evidence and reflect the "wisdom of practice"—the understandings, experiences, and observations—of the panel members. In any case, as implied above, the available research is not sufficiently robust that one could use it to definitively identify the characteristics of effective strategies to improve intergroup relations. The role of the consensus panel was to provide policy makers and practitioners with sensible and productive guidelines for action.

Strategies for improving intergroup relations can take many different forms, including instructional methods, curricula, extracurricular activities, workshops, and simulations. But regardless of their form, the CODA panel believes that the effectiveness of strategies for improving intergroup relations will be enhanced to the extent that they embody the following principles.

No effort has been made to summarize the research that supports these principles in the brief discussion that follows each of them. Those readers who are seeking related research will find much of what they are looking for in the present volume.

*Principle 1: Strategies should address both institutional and individual sources of prejudice and discrimination in the contexts and situations in which the participants in the program or activity learn, work, and live.*

Sources of prejudice and discrimination are often rooted in particular historical and social contexts, and are shaped by institutional structures and practices. Seeking to change individuals without dealing with these influences, or without engaging the specific issues that shape intergroup relations, is often futile.

Institutional and contextual forces that might be considered in the development and implementation of a strategy for improving intergroup relations include structures and practices—such as tracking, assessment practices, or selection processes—and beliefs, stereotypes, and stories that have become part of the local lore. However, a key point to keep in mind in designing programs and practices is that power differences, real or imagined, are often at the heart of intergroup tensions and have to be dealt with if behaviors are to change in significant ways.

*Principle 2: Strategies should seek to influence the behavior of individuals, including their motivation and capability to influence others, and not be limited to efforts to increase knowledge and awareness.*

There are two separable but related points embedded in this principle. First, when strategies meant to improve intergroup relations do not specifically include lessons about how to act in accordance with new awareness and knowledge, they are likely to be ineffective in changing relationships. Most of us are not as competent as we need to be in our interactions with people we perceive to be culturally different. Even people with good intentions sometimes do the wrong thing. Second, prejudice and discrimination are socially influenced. Thus, altering our own behavior may require that we enlist the support of others. Moreover, changing the experience of those who are the victims of prejudice and discrimination may require that we contribute to a climate of tolerance and goodwill by seeking to change the behavior of others whose words and actions reflect racial or ethnic prejudice.

*Principle 3: Strategies should deal with the dispositions and behavior of all racial and ethnic groups involved.*

Often, race relations programs and activities focus on awareness and knowledge about, and behavior toward, persons of color. And some of these programs focus on the treatment of and attitude toward a single racial or ethnic group. Where racial and ethnic diversity exists, diversity provides an opportunity for learning and for comparison that can help avoid oversimplification or stereotyping. Moreover, whites have varying cultures and identities. Raising awareness of this reality may serve to increase the sophistication of the lesson being taught and learned.

*Principle 4: Strategies should include participants who reflect the racial, ethnic, and linguistic diversity of the context and should be structured in such a way as to ensure cooperative, equal-status roles for persons from different groups.*

The best-documented strategy for improving racial and ethnic relations involves the creation of opportunities for positive equal-status interaction among people from different groups. These strategies are most effective when they organize cooperative activities so as to ensure that people from different backgrounds can contribute equally to the task involved.

People involved in intergroup activities bring to those experiences assumptions about the roles they should play that are based on expectations shaped by preexisting attributions of power, by stereotypes, and by habits of behavior of groups. These assumptions may lead to very unequal participation by different racial and ethnic groups, which, in turn, may affect what is learned and the value that participants assign to the experience. Thus, strategies involving cooperative interdependence among persons of different races and ethnic groups should be carefully structured to ensure that all participants are encouraged to make useful and valued contributions to the group. Note, however, that when strategies involving competition among groups are used to encourage cooperation, situations should be avoided in which racially or ethnically identifiable groups compete against one another.

*Principle 5: Strategies should have the support and participation of those with authority and power in any given setting.*

People with power and authority send messages more by their deeds than by their words. Those who are asked to engage in learning activities meant to improve intergroup relations will usually want to know what those who have put them into the situation have done and are doing about the lessons they are being asked to learn. When those in positions of authority are too busy too participate in race relations programs, the impact of the program will be undermined unless the leaders' record on the issue of discrimination is clear.

People in organizations where better intergroup relations and equity are being advocated will ask whether those in authority are modeling appropriate behaviors and "walking the talk." They will also want to know whether qualified persons of color are being aggressively recruited for high offices, whether those who pursue equity with enthusiasm are being supported and rewarded, and whether those who engage in discriminatory behavior are being negatively sanctioned.

*Principle 6: Strategies should involve children at an early age, and new entrants to organizations should be continually encouraged and reinforced.*

There are good reasons to start teaching the importance of and strategies for positive intergroup relations when children are young. But "early intervention" is not enough. As children mature, they become more conscious of racial and ethnic differences, and the many sources of prejudice and discrimination they experience can influence them in negative ways. Lessons learned at an early age or at the time a person becomes a member of an organization may not stick even though they do make later lessons related to prejudice and discrimination easier to teach and learn.

In many organizations, new participants are told of the organizations' commitment to positive intergroup relations. This introduction may include workshops on "diversity" or other activities aimed at facilitating racial and ethnic harmony in the organizations. As people experience racial and ethnic tension, or perceive that the commitment to equity and positive intergroup relations is not complete, they need to have opportunities to learn how to deal with these problems.

People cannot be inoculated against prejudice. Given the differences in living conditions of various racial and ethnic groups, as well as the existence of discrimination throughout our society, improving intergroup relations is a challenge that requires ongoing work.

*Principle 7: Strategies should be part of a continuing set of learning activities that are valued and incorporated throughout the school, college, or other organization.*

In many settings, improved intergroup relations are the responsibility of a given officer or instructor, and the most common strategy is the episodic workshop or the "introductory" course—short or long. But there is little evidence that this strategy, in and of itself, is adequate. In some cases, the one-time workshop, course, or learning module that focuses on sources of conflict or on racial or ethnic differences can even reinforce negative predispositions.

The conventional wisdom among advocates of strategies to

improve intergroup relations is that opportunities to learn should be infused throughout the curriculum or the tasks that make up the work of the organization involved. However, while this practice is desirable, it is difficult to achieve for at least two reasons. First, the level of commitment to the goal will vary within the school, program, or organization. Second, the expertise needed to adequately integrate experiences that promote positive intergroup relations is scarce. Thus, strategies to improve race relations need to include both highly focused activities and efforts to ensure that positive intergroup relations are pursued throughout the organization involved.

*Principle 8: Strategies should examine similarities and differences across and within racial and ethnic groups, including differences related to social class, gender, and language.*

Efforts to improve intergroup relations often overstate differences among and within racial and ethnic groups, and neglect beliefs and values that are shared across racial and ethnic "lines." The search for generalizations that would promote sensitivity to differences and encourage positive responses to those differences often leads to oversimplification. An example can be found in data suggesting that some groups of Latinos are more likely than Anglos to prefer cooperative tasks. Here, of course, we cannot conclude that all Latinos are more cooperatively oriented than all Anglos. Indeed, there are big differences in the cultures of groups that are encompassed by terms such as Latino and Anglo.

It is understandable if strategies to improve intergroup relations do not deal with the full complexity of intraracial and intraethnic differences, but to ignore this complexity is to encourage another form of stereotyping. The focus on differences between racial and ethnic groups, and the failure to deal with differences within these groups, has the consequence of understating common human characteristics and directing attention away from the influence of gender, language, and social class on interpersonal relations.

In short, it is important to make clear that while racial and ethnic groups may have differences, they often have a lot in common. Making "the other" seem less different, strange, or exotic can encourage positive interactions and avoid stereotyping.

*Principle 9: Strategies should recognize the value of bicultural and multicultural identities of individuals and groups, as well as the difficulties confronted by those who live in two or more cultures.*

The concept of the "melting pot" is highly valued by many Americans, especially those of European descent. Persons of color and immigrants are often expected to assimilate into the "dominant white culture" and are resented when they hold on to cultural traditions or language. The effort to identify English as the official language of the United States is a manifestation of the value that many whites place on assimilation, as is the recent concern that multicultural education will lead to a breakdown of our national identity. In fact, the expectation of assimilation is a repudiation of the value that can be derived from the nation's diversity and is actively resisted by many groups.

While some people insist that persons of color and certain ethnic backgrounds should abandon their racial and ethnic identities, others insist that individuals should choose a single cultural identity. Strategies to improve intergroup relations and to ensure policies and practices that require people to identify with one racial or ethnic group inadvertently communicate a lack of respect for persons with bicultural and multicultural identities. Similarly, when racial and ethnic groups put pressure on persons with complex identities to be "one or the other," they discriminate against such individuals. Some would argue that persons who are bicultural or multicultural are a *bridge* to improved intergroup relations.

*Principle 10: Strategies should expose the inaccuracies of myths that sustain stereotypes and prejudices.*

Many stereotypes and sources of conflict are based on myths and misinformation. It is by confronting these myths directly that we undermine the justifications for prejudice. For example, assumptions many whites hold about the proportion of black males who commit violent crimes, the percentage of black college students who receive race-based scholarships, and the rates of alcohol and drug abuse among Latinos and African Americans are invariably wrong, and substantially so. Learning what people believe about persons of other races and ethnic groups, and being prepared to correct misconceptions, should be the responsibility of those who work to improve intergroup relations. At the same time, we cannot assume that correcting misconceptions, in and of itself, will be enough to change behavior.

*Principle 11: Strategies should include the careful and thorough preparation of those who will implement the learning activities and provide opportunities for adapting methods to the particular setting.*

It is obvious that the better trained a person is to foster learning that improves intergroup relations, the more effective that person will be. Preparation is especially important when the particular strategies focus on sources of conflict or involve confrontation—as in activities where participants are asked to express their "true feelings," to play the role of prejudiced persons, or to "get all of their frustrations on the table."

Principle 1 emphasized the importance of relating strategies to the particular context in which the participants are involved on a continuing basis. The value of this principle depends on the abilities of those implementing the strategy to adapt the approach to fit the situation. Moreover, in some cases, those responsible for implementing a strategy are not fully committed and communicate that lack of commitment to participants. Consider, for example, those teachers who do not see the relationship between efforts to improve intergroup relations and the responsibility they have to teach students about a given subject. Such teachers would tend to view intergroup relations strategies as marginal, if not downright distracting. Engaging those who must implement a strategy in program development, and identifying and addressing the sources of their lack of commitment, can contribute significantly to the effectiveness of the effort.

*Principle 12: Strategies should be based on thorough analyses of the learning needs of participants and on continuing evaluation of outcomes, especially effects on behavior.*

Discovering what people need to learn about intergroup relations is not an easy task, especially when the strategies are being implemented by an "expert" from outside the organizational unit involved. Many strategies to improve intergroup relations fail to make an adequate investment in diagnosing the problems that are particular to the setting involved. Not surprisingly, some will miss the mark, leading participants to view the strategies as superficial.

Evaluation is an invaluable source of program improvement. But many evaluation efforts are limited to post-event questionnaires about levels of satisfaction. Many programs receive positive evaluations, or so their advocates claim. But the real meaning of positive responses to satisfaction questions is unclear, given that negative responses might be seen as a lack of commitment to the goal of better intergroup relations and that responses may not reflect careful consideration. One consequence of such cursory evaluations is that the strategies used remain superficial and episodic, often relying on outside experts who have mastered techniques of presentation. What is needed are follow-up studies of individual and organizational change, even if such studies involve low-cost self-reports of changes in behavior and policies.

*Principle 13: Strategies should recognize that lessons related to prejudice and its consequences for any particular racial or ethnic group may not transfer to other races or groups.*

Prejudice is often specific to particular groups of people, even though an individual may be prejudiced against many different groups. Thus, teaching lessons focused on relations between any given two groups may not affect the prejudices being held against the people of a third group. Since most people recognize that racism is inconsistent with democratic values, it is often the case that prejudiced persons have developed what they think are reasonable justifications for prejudices and discriminatory behavior that are specific to particular groups.

## Final Comments

These principles for designing and implementing effective strategies for improving intergroup relations and reducing discrimination are not guarantees. Weak implementation can undermine the best-designed strategies. Moreover, every strategy need not incorporate every principle in order to be effective. The CODA Consensus Panel examined numerous strategies it felt were worthy of implementation that incorporated only two or three of those principles. None of the programs reviewed met the criteria of all the principles.

The design principles developed by the CODA panel are meant to provide guidelines for action to those selecting or developing strategies to improve intergroup relations. They are also meant to focus discussion and research on the characteristics of program effectiveness. The panel invites critical analyses of its conclusions. Comments can be sent to CODA, The College of Education, University of Maryland, College Park, MD 20742.

## Chapter Seventeen

# Toward a Common Destiny:
# An Agenda for Further Research

Anthony W. Jackson

As we look to the future, the idea of a common destiny for our nation's children is an appealing one. It conjures up a vision of a society where equality of educational and economic opportunity are the rule rather than the exception, and where relations between groups, if not universally positive, are at least relatively free from conflict. Somehow, the deep historical schisms that now divide racial and ethnic groups within our country will be healed, and Martin Luther King Jr.'s compelling dream of children of all colors learning and playing together in America's schools will be realized.

A less appealing vision of a common destiny is one of increasing inequality between groups and escalating conflict and violence. The dream becomes a nightmare; and schools, a focal point of prejudice, distrust, and intergroup hostility.

These conflicting images of American society have long defined the polar opposites of possible futures for American youth. What is perhaps different now, as compared to the past, is the troubling sense that *it could go either way.* As racial and ethnic diversity has increased in recent years, there has also been a profound change in the structure of economic opportunities for both high- and low-skill workers, bringing intensely increased competition for what many

Park/Burg.
conflict
theory

see as diminishing shares of a secure future. As expectations for upward social and economic mobility decline, tensions between adults and children of "competing" groups increase—a situation that, when combined with easy access to lethal weaponry as a means of settling differences, sets the stage for deadly conflict. In the face of these socially debilitating forces, continued progress toward positive intergroup relations cannot be assumed as it was in the past, at least since the end of the Second World War.

Relations between children of different racial and ethnic groups could get worse, but they do not have to. What will be required to achieve a common destiny worth striving for, rather than one to be feared? And as long-term changes in the economy play themselves out, what can be done in the near term to prevent or reduce intergroup tensions and promote positive intergroup contact?

In May 1993 the Carnegie Corporation of New York convened a group of scholars from a range of academic disciplines to review existing research on relations between racial and ethnic groups in American schools. The intent of the meeting was to provide the corporation, and the scholarly community more generally, a broad base of knowledge upon which new efforts to promote positive intergroup relations among diverse groups of children and youth could be established. The papers commissioned for the meeting appearing in this volume, along with chapters commissioned specifically for the book, respond to one or both of these basic questions: (1) What is known about the causes of positive or negative intergroup relations? And (2) what are effective ways of promoting positive relations between diverse groups of children and youth?

This review affirms that there is, indeed, a significant body of factual information and unifying theory that addresses both the causes and potential solutions for poor intergroup relations. Equally apparent, however, is the need to build on the rich tradition of research in intergroup relations to address the rapidly changing demographic characteristics of our society. Most of the research on youth intergroup relations, for example, involves only African

American and white children. Relatively few studies address the dynamics of multicultural and multilingual settings, yet more and more schools and communities encompass a very wide variety of racial, ethnic, and linguistic backgrounds.

It is to be hoped that increased diversity in American schools and communities, structural changes in the economy, and the proliferation of violence will add a greater sense of urgency to the identification of promising lines of inquiry in intergroup relations in the 1990s than appears to have existed in the 1980s, at least among institutions that support such research. Included in that group of institutions are foundations and the federal government, both of which have been key supporters of such research in the past. One of the primary intentions in publishing this volume is to stimulate a renewal of interest in research on the causes and consequences of prejudice, the prevention of intergroup conflict, and the promotion of positive intergroup relations.

This chapter outlines several important potential lines of research emanating from the previous chapters. It makes no attempt to be comprehensive but, rather, suggests directions for research that will contribute to a new base of knowledge on intergroup relations for the 1990s and beyond. As in previous chapters, this concluding chapter focuses especially on the opportunities and challenges in schools for fostering positive relations. In particular, it suggests an agenda for research on intergroup relations that addresses three broad areas: (1) historical and contemporary patterns of contact, (2) developmental and contextual influences on intergroup relations, and (3) strategies for promoting positive relations in schools, especially in the context of the current education reform movement.

## Historical and Contemporary Patterns of Contact

The history of poor relations between racial and ethnic groups in our country is well known to all of us. Yet as we search for ways to prevent or resolve tensions today, David Tyack's analysis (in Chapter One) reminds us that so many of our current problems in fostering harmonious relations in schools are grounded in past prejudices and inequitable educational practices. Tyack shows that the images and stereotypes that groups hold for each other, exaggerated over time, exert tremendous influence on current intergroup attitudes and behavior.

To better understand the power of the past on the present, we need to more fully investigate how historical events and prevailing worldviews have influenced the images and expectations that racial and ethnic groups hold for each other (and about themselves) and how these understandings are conveyed to children. How and by whom are prejudiced images created to justify unequal treatment of devalued groups? Are such images consciously created to excuse inequities, or do they stem from "habits of mind" deeply rooted in the human species for purposes of protection and survival? How are past prejudices legitimated in their retelling to children?

Relations between groups throughout American history have also been profoundly affected by demographic factors, including immigration and emigration trends, and by patterns of movement and habitation. We need to examine further when these trends have resulted in conflict between groups and when instead they have fostered cooperation and mutual support. What factors appear to account for the different outcomes? How applicable are historical patterns of racial and ethnic interaction to contemporary circumstances?

A historical view of demographic shifts leads naturally to a fine-grained analysis of contemporary demographic patterns, possibly allowing us to predict where the greatest risks and opportunities for positive intergroup relations exist. What is the current racial and ethnic composition of the United States, and what can we expect for the future? Shirley Heath (in Chapter Two) and Jomills Braddock, Marvin Dawkins, and George Wilson (in Chapter Nine) provide important windows on these critical questions and suggest numerous additional avenues for research. In schools, for example, what is the true extent of integration, and what are the "normal" patterns of contact and interaction between students of different racial and ethnic groups? How do patterns of interaction compare inside and outside the school? Across settings, what inhibits or facilitates positive intergroup relations, and how do experiences in one setting influence those in another? How do demographic and economic changes interact with characteristics of housing, schools, and other social institutions to facilitate or limit intergroup contact and influence the quality of relations?

Heath's chapter accentuates our need to know more about how youths experience intergroup relations today and what meaning they construct from their interactions. What are the prevailing norms regarding prejudice among youth, what level of hostility or friendliness now prevails, and how do these dimensions influence the nature of such interactions? To what extent do young people's experience and interpretation of intergroup relations differ depending on their own racial and ethnic backgrounds and those of the other groups involved? Perhaps most intriguing, under what circumstances do race and ethnicity really matter to young people, and when do other factors such as school of attendance, neighborhood residency, and gang or organizational membership become more salient?

## Developmental and Contextual Influences on Intergroup Relations

A new agenda for research on intergroup relations will need to look carefully at what we know about the developmental origins of intergroup attitudes, beliefs, and behavior. The analyses by Cynthia García Coll and Heidie Vásquez García (Chapter Four), Nancy Gonzales and Ana Cauce (Chapter Five), Eugene Garcia and Aída Hurtado (Chapter Six), William Cross (Chapter Seven), and Kenyon Chan and Shirley Hune (Chapter Eight) each contribute to our knowledge of how children's understanding of themselves and others evolves over time and is constructed through a complex interaction between "internal" cognitive and emotional stages and "external" family, community, and social influences.

## Developmental Processes and the
## Formation of Ethnic Identity

At great risk of oversimplification, key questions for research in this domain involve the place of race and ethnicity within the negotiation that developing children experiences between forces that pull them toward affiliation with others and forces that push them away. We know a great deal, for example, about the developmental pathways of empathy, altruism, prosocial skills, and cooperative behavior—the emotional and cognitive processes that have the potential to bind human beings to each other—but relatively little about how these processes specifically contribute to attitudes and behaviors that members of different races and ethnic groups have toward each other. So too are there well-developed traditions of research on the origins of in- and outgroup categorization, stereotyping, and prejudice leading to conflict and violence—the roots of separatism and hatred—but their implications for intergroup relations require much greater exploration.

We need also to examine how developmental processes cluster together and reinforce one another toward the development of specific beliefs. For example, do children develop general tendencies toward affiliation or disaffiliation with individuals or groups that they perceive as different, or do children more often have internal benchmarks for the "degree of difference" of one group versus another that governs their behavior toward them? If the latter, how do children learn their repertoire of responses to different groups? Perceived differences in the intelligence, competence, and moral development of others are especially fertile ground for racial and ethnic prejudice. How do children acquire these perceptions, and what are the most effective ways of countering misconceptions and resulting stereotypes?

Heath describes a multiethnic group of youths who, at considerable risk, defy group norms regarding interpersonal and group affiliation in order to join together to write and act out a play based on their own experiences. What drives these young people to step outside the lines? Why are some youth more resistant to the "hardening" of prejudice in the face of social, peer, or family pressures? More generally, is outgroup stereotyping necessary if children are to be socialized toward positive within-group affiliation? If not, what is required in order to build on within-group affiliation and thereby form a basis for positive intergroup relations?

The development of a secure identity is critically important to every child's maturation and to his or her relations with others. But how critical is ethnic and racial identity? As several of this book's authors have observed, a healthy ethnic identity can be viewed as an important aspect of a multicomponent identity that involves one's race, ethnicity, gender, religion, and myriad other characteristics. New research on identity development will need to examine how children form "multicomponent identities" and why some children are more successful in developing a complex, integrated identity than others. Specifically regarding the ethnic and racial components of identity, how important is it to children's self-esteem—that of both white children and children of color—to value these aspects of themselves highly? Is a relatively malleable identity structure always more beneficial to children's healthy development? Or, as Gonzales and Cauce speculate, are there "psychic costs" associated with traversing identity boundaries?

## Contextual Influences on Attitudes and Behavior

It is certainly true, as Coll and Garcia state, that current developmental theories find virtually every developmental outcome to be a function of individual developmental processes in transaction with environmental influences. Their separation here is for heuristic purposes only. Future research on family, peer, community, and societal influences on children's intergroup attitudes and behaviors should parallel and in many instances intersect with research on stages of cognitive processing and children's constructions of self-identity.

For most children, the family is clearly the most salient contextual influence on the development of attitudes and behaviors toward members of their own and other racial and ethnic groups. Given the growing diversity within the United States, the potential for research on how family interactions influence the quality of intergroup relations is virtually limitless. For example, how do family influences on the development of children's intergroup attitudes vary between and within ethnic and racial groups? What influences the content and endurance of images and stereotypes that groups have for each other, and how are children socialized within families to accept these views or to form their own opinions?

An intriguing related line of research would look at differences in self-identification and intergroup relations across generations *within* individual families. How do different generations within a family experience intergroup relations differently, and what impact can these differences have on the nature of interactions within that family? As Heath asks, Is there a gap in the way race and ethnicity are understood between generations?

Further research is also warranted in the important area of peer-group influences on intergroup relations. In this volume, Janet Schofield (Chapter Ten) and others note important studies that link peer influence to both the reduction and the increase of intergroup prejudice. Clearly the psychological processes at work here need further explication, and we should expect them to be rather complicated given the myriad settings in which peer influence is important and the wide mix of races and ethnicities that may be involved.

Children's intergroup relations are also undoubtedly affected by images conveyed in various media. A recurring concern in contemporary discussions about intergroup relations is the belief that national leaders' unofficial sanction of intolerance for racial and ethnic minorities, conveyed in the media during the 1980s, may have exacerbated intergroup tensions. The question of whether national figures can have such negative influence on young people's attitudes—and if so, how—clearly warrants additional research, as does that of the potential for positive influence by leaders who support efforts to end prejudice. As James Lynch suggests (in

Chapter Three), a partial answer to the latter question may be forthcoming from longitudinal research on Canadian youths' attitudes toward intergroup relations, given that nation's official policy of support for multiculturalism.

Media images of individuals from various racial and ethnic backgrounds and of relations between them are conveyed both in the content of news and entertainment shows and in the method of their presentation. Like the influence of media-depicted violence, the effect of media images of various racial and ethnic groups on children's intergroup attitudes and behaviors is controversial and greatly in need of sophisticated research and analysis. A possible starting point would be to assess the current content of racial and ethnic group images in electronic and print media. Are there distinctive patterns in the manner in which groups are portrayed? What are the conditions that appear to lead to conflict between groups, and what conditions lead to cooperation instead? Regarding the effect of media images on youth, does repeated stereotyping of certain racial and ethnic groups cause young people to "lump them all together" and disregard intragroup variation? Conversely, does depiction of minorities in a variety of roles lead to greater recognition of intragroup differences by young media consumers?

## Strategies for Promoting Positive
## Intergroup Relations in Schools

Ultimately, the goal of research on intergroup relations is to provide a base of knowledge for efforts designed to prevent or reduce conflict between groups and to promote positive interaction. As several authors in this volume note, a useful method for evaluating the potential value of an intervention is to assess the degree to which it meets several conditions first described by Allport in 1954 and later affirmed in numerous research studies. Robert Slavin (in Chapter Eleven) summarizes these conditions as follows: equal role status for students of different races, cooperation across racial and ethnic lines, contact across racial lines that permits students to learn about one another as individuals, and support from authorities for intergroup contact.

How can schools and other educational institutions serving children promote intergroup interaction that satisfies Allport's conditions? James Banks (in Chapter Twelve) as well as Schofield, Slavin, and others report numerous successful attempts to achieve this goal, targeted primarily on curriculum, pedagogy, and student grouping. As these authors acknowledge, however, existing barriers and potential opportunities to promote positive intergroup relations can be found not only in these three areas but in virtually all aspects of the educational system. Thus a comprehensive set of reforms to address intergroup relations is required.

A holistic examination of educational policies and practices in view of their potential to promote intergroup affiliation is especially timely, given the current, far-reaching movement to reform American education. Driving this movement is the recognition that, with continuing advances in technology, higher intellectual development for all students, including racial and ethnic minority children, is necessary if an internationally competitive workforce is to be achieved in the next century. However, the "thinking work" of the future will also routinely require communication and collaboration between workers, so the extent to which proposed reforms promote understanding and tolerance within an increasingly pluralistic population of children is arguably just as critical as their value in producing higher academic achievement.

In the following pages, many of the components of educational reform that appear to hold significant currency among experts and practitioners alike are examined for their potential to promote positive intergroup relations. These include proposed reforms in curriculum, student assessment, instructional methods, school organization and student grouping, school governance, teacher professional development, and the involvement of parents and influential community members. Possible lines of future research are drawn from the analysis of each reform component. Allport's conditions for successful intergroup contact are used throughout to frame the discussion.

## Curriculum

The development of curriculum standards that describe what students at various grade levels should know and be able to do is a pivotal element of the current reform movement. Curriculum standards are intended to make clear to educators, parents, and students alike what the outcomes of education are supposed to be. These standards are also intended to be the basis for establishing acceptable levels of student performance—performance standards—that determine grade promotion and graduation. In some reform schemes, the number or percentage of students reaching the appropriate performance standards would serve as a benchmark for determining rewards and sanctions for educators.

The definition of curriculum standards has definite implications for intergroup relations. If the standards define curricula that engage students of all races and ethnicities equally in learning, one would expect greater equality in students' performance. This, in turn, should promote greater equality in students' status, the first of Allport's criteria for successful interventions. However, as Banks and Heath forcefully argue, merely infusing or adding multicultural material to curricula is unlikely to scratch beyond the surface of students' interests, particularly in middle and high school. Attention needs to be paid to the capacity of the curriculum to help all groups understand the meaning and impact of racial and ethnic status and to equip them with skills to address inequities. Obviously the extent to which curriculum standards explicitly define mutual respect and understanding between groups as important tools will also directly affect the quality of intergroup relations.

Research on the potential of new curriculum standards to promote intergroup relations would need to focus first on their actual content. How are the experiences, circumstances, and contributions of racial and ethnic minorities addressed? As the standards are implemented, the focus will naturally shift toward their impact—specifically, in terms of whether and how these new standards stimulate education that engages all students, leading to the acquisition of knowledge across racial and ethnic lines that helps them know each other as individuals.

Curriculum standards are also intended to establish equally high expectations for all students and, in turn, equal demands for high performance from teachers. To the extent that students are aware of and accept the standards, their expectations for themselves should also be equally high. Both of these outcomes should contribute to the leveling of status differences between students. In practice, the question of whether or not curriculum standards translate into higher teacher and student expectations will require careful examination. If standards alone are not sufficient to raise expectations, further study will be needed to determine the additional knowledge or training required for standards to have their intended effects.

## Student Assessment

As Schofield describes, student assessment has historically differentiated students along racial and ethnic lines in their perceived ability levels because of the persistent relationship among measures of academic achievement, the extent and nature of learning opportunities afforded by social and economic status, and students' race or ethnicity. Today, the hope is for new forms of student assessment that will provide opportunities to equalize students' status and contribute to better intergroup relations.

A consensus is emerging that these new forms of assessment should be "authentic"; that is, they should test students' ability to use knowledge to solve real (or realistically simulated) problems rather than to address abstract problems that have marginal intrinsic value. Authentic assessment seems to offer the prospect of tailoring the content and context of "test problems" to students' individual interests and cultural background. There is also agreement that the new forms of assessment should be performance based, and that they should provide students numerous opportunities and forms of expression to exhibit their strengths. In short, authentic performance-based tests should provide opportunities to individualize assessment in such a way as to reduce bias that may operate along racial and ethnic lines and, in theory, produce more equitable outcomes. Schofield notes a third facet of assessment that could help equalize students' status across racial and ethnic lines: basing students' evaluation on improvement relative to curriculum goals as well as to their absolute attainment.

Research on the extent to which new forms of assessment promote greater student equity should first determine if these new assessments actually provide greater and more authentic opportunities than current testing practices for students from all backgrounds to show what they know and are able to do. If so, additional studies could help determine whether these new assessments help foster positive intergroup relations by showing, for example, that students from all backgrounds are more alike than different in their ability to excel intellectually.

## Instructional Methods

The chapters by Schofield and Slavin describe a number of instructional techniques that promote good intergroup relations. Cooperative learning is the best researched among these techniques. Both authors note, however, that despite the solid body of evidence on the effectiveness of cooperative learning for intergroup contact and academic achievement, more research is needed to understand *how* it achieves its effects. Also unclear is the question as to why cooperative learning appears to have somewhat different effects depending upon the race and ethnicity of the students involved.

In addition to cooperative learning, reformers are calling for more project-based work to engage students in real-world problems and give them the opportunity to use knowledge in context. There is a clear link in this recommendation to the new ways of thinking about assessment addressed earlier, so one would expect project-based instruction to help reduce students' status differences in much the same manner as performance-based assessment is expected to have this effect. Project-based instruction should also provide opportunities for students to cooperate across racial and ethnic boundaries as equals *if the situations are structured appropriately*. If, on the other hand, social hierarchies related to race and ethnicity are replicated in project-based work, there is significant potential for creating or reaffirming negative attitudes that students hold for each other.

Community service as a mode of instruction, or "service learning," is now viewed by many as a necessary component of comprehensive school reform. Service learning is a form of project-based learning that has the explicit intent of addressing an important issue or remedying a significant problem that exists in the school or larger community. As a form of project-based instruction, service learning should provide opportunities for students to work cooperatively and learn about each other across racial and ethnic lines, so its potential to foster positive intergroup relations is substantial.

As service learning and other forms of project-based learning become more entrenched in schools, many opportunities will arise for educators to examine not only the impact these instructional methods have on intergroup relations but also the conditions that inhibit or facilitate their effect. We may find that the *nature* of a service learning activity has an impact on the quality of students' interactions beyond the effect of their working cooperatively together. When the service learning project itself addresses racial and ethnic prejudice, for example, peer condemnation of prejudice, it may add to the implicit push toward positive intergroup relations provided by the service learning experience alone.

## Student Grouping and School Organization

Establishing schools that are richly diverse communities of learners is the basis upon which all specific strategies to promote positive intergroup relations rely. Racial and ethnic diversification is occurring in many American schools today in the wake of massive demographic shifts in cities and in many regions of the country. Legal mandates to desegregate also account for some of the increasing pluralism in our nation's schools, but the pace of desegregation has slowed significantly in recent years. (The need for research to determine contemporary patterns of intergroup contact in multicultural settings was noted earlier in this chapter.) In addition to these demographic studies focused on children, there is a pressing need to understand contemporary attitudes of adults toward pluralism and intergroup contact in schools generally and desegregation policy specifically. Such studies should perhaps start with government officials sworn to enforce desegregation and other mandates against discrimination. Is there, today, unequivocal support for interracial contact, one of Allport's prerequisites? And how well aligned are the views of authorities with the general public?

Reformers have been largely silent on the subject of desegregation as a tool for educational change. Yet there has been a consistent call for the elimination of the primary means by which *resegregation* occurs in already diverse schools—namely, through tracking. Slavin describes the potential for improved intergroup relations that "untracking" may afford. He also notes the potential hazards for intergroup relations and student achievement if students from lower tracks, often minority children, are placed in classrooms in which teachers have neither the education nor the resources to teach heterogeneous groups of students. Careful, longitudinal research on the impact of untracking on intergroup dynamics is clearly warranted.

The creation of smaller schools, and the division of existing schools into schools-within-schools or houses, is another tenet of the reform movement that bears examination for its intergroup potential. Underlying the "small is better" recommendation is a belief that learning should be a constructive process relying heavily both on collaboration between students-as-colleagues and on "coaching" by teachers. Small or subdivided schools are thought to provide the intimacy and consistency in contact necessary for students to routinely work cooperatively and to engage in other forms of constructivist learning. Do smaller school units, in practice, fulfill Allport's conditions for cooperative contact and cross-group learning? If so, is there a demonstrable effect on intergroup relations? And if not, why not? In other words, what are the barriers that inhibit small schools' potential to foster positive intergroup relations?

### School Governance

Schofield draws attention to the critical role that principals and teachers can play in creating a school climate conducive to positive intergroup relations. Administrators and faculty will have an even greater opportunity to influence the culture of the school within decentralized management systems characteristic of most current reform plans. At the extremes, school staffs may create and run new schools that are loosely coupled to district or state bureaucracies, as in the charter school movement. More often, school-based management teams will be increasingly invested with decision-making authority over key aspects of school policies.

School-based governance is theoretically a means not only of bringing educational decision making closer to the processes of teaching and learning but also of democratizing decision making— that is, of investing authority in a broader range of individuals within the school. As such, it increases the potential for faculty members of diverse racial and ethnic backgrounds to participate in important school matters on an equal-status basis with their colleagues and, in doing so, to model such behavior for students. Perhaps even more important to the intergroup climate in the school will be the *policies* that school governance bodies create. The question is whether or not such policies will explicitly and forcefully address discrimination and prejudice, on the one hand, and the promotion of positive contact across racial and ethnic lines, on the other.

The policies of school governance committees regarding intergroup relations and their effect constitute a ripe area for research, particularly with respect to schools that are designed to provide a choice to parents and students based on the nature of the school program. How often do schools choose to emphasize positive intergroup relations as an "attraction," and what is the response from parents and students? Casting the same question in the negative, we might ask, Under what conditions does catering to choice result in a de-emphasis on positive intergroup relations?

## Professional Development

There is perhaps no issue on which education reformers agree more than the need for vastly improved pre- and inservice professional development for teachers. Virtually all other recommendations for change require better-trained teachers. The potential of these recommendations to promote positive intergroup relations is likewise dependent on the development of better, very different forms of teacher preparation than currently exist. Without reforms in professional development, neither academic achievement nor intergroup relations is likely to improve.

Kenneth Zeichner (in Chapter Fifteen) argues persuasively that current efforts to prepare teachers for work in pluralistic school settings are generally very weak. The need for research leading to effective programs is enormous. According to Zeichner, such research would need to focus on the characteristics of institutions dedicated to preparing teachers, the kinds of training experiences within and outside these institutions that have to be developed to help prepare teachers to work in pluralistic settings, and the processes of recruitment, selection, induction, and mentoring necessary to ensure a diverse, well-prepared teacher work force.

Two strategic methods for improving professional development systems would be to reform the way that teachers are certified and licensed to teach, and to change the manner by which teacher education programs are accredited. For example, standards for initial and advanced teacher certification established in each state could require teachers to demonstrate competency in teaching diverse groups of children. Toward this end, states could follow the lead of the National Board for Professional Teaching Standards, which, in its assessments for advanced, nationally recognized teacher certification, addresses teachers' abilities to work well in multicultural settings. Accreditation of teacher education programs could depend, in part, on whether prospective teachers are provided high-quality training for teaching in multicultural classrooms, including methods that foster good intergroup relations.

Mandates of this kind will be empty gestures, however, if a knowledge base on how to teach children from diverse cultures is not created. The hope is that new teacher-training requirements could act as a stimulus to the creation of such knowledge. Changes in certification, licensure, and accreditation will therefore need to be carefully evaluated to document any changes in the content of training that result from new standards. More important, research will be needed to examine whether changes in the content of teachers' training improve the quality of teaching in multiracial, multiethnic schools.

New professional development opportunities for practicing teachers are equally critical to the reform of inservice teacher education. There is wide agreement that one-shot workshops offered or required by the district office are of marginal value and that school staffs themselves must be deeply involved in designing their own inservice training. In the process of designing school-based programs of professional development, teachers would be provided the opportunity to reflect on the requirements of effective teaching in the context of their own students' needs. If teachers win the right to design their own programs, it will be very interesting to study how they approach their own needs for training to teach children from diverse backgrounds and to promote positive relations between them. In short, we must ask, What methods will be most effective, and how can promising new models of inservice professional development be shared broadly with other groups of teachers who may be interested in learning from their colleagues' experiences?

## Parent and Community Involvement

As with reform movements of the past, the current call for change champions greater and more meaningful school involvement of parents and members of the community. Schofield describes several ways that parents and other key authority figures can influence the climate within a school by encouraging positive intergroup contact and by modeling respectful relations themselves.

As recommendations for decentralized management of schools are enacted across the country, particular attention should be paid to parents' involvement in school-based governance committees and to the impact they have on policies for addressing the needs of diverse groups of children and for promoting positive intergroup relations. In multiethnic schools, are parents from different backgrounds equally active on school committees? More important, what impact do parents and community members have on the school climate and on school policies related to intergroup relations?

## Conclusion

The study of relations between children and youth of different racial and ethnic backgrounds has always been important, but never more so than today. In fact, because ethnic and racial diversity is now so characteristic of our society, any research on the dynamics of childhood development in and outside of schools that does not consider intergroup relations would seem seriously flawed from the outset.

As stated earlier, the lines of research outlined in this chapter are in no way exhaustive of the possibilities for scholarly contributions to a new knowledge base on intergroup relations. The broad agenda laid out here is intended to stimulate thinking about the importance of such research and to illuminate only a few of the areas in which it is badly needed. The hope is that this volume will help catalyze a resurgence in support for such research, along with a new era of scholarship on ethnic and racial relations.

# Appendix

# Common Destiny Alliance

CODA, which was founded in 1991, is the only national coalition whose primary concern is interethnic and interracial relationships. It is also unique in its commitment and potential to link research to effective practice, a virtue that is particularly important with respect to the emotional content of the issues it engages. CODA has twenty-eight organizational partners and thirty-nine research partners, as follows.

## Organizational Partners

American Association for Higher Education
American Association of School Administrators
American Council on Education
American Federation of Teachers
ASPIRA
Association of Teacher Educators
Children's Defense Fund
The College Board

Council of Chief State School Officers

Council of the Great City Schools

Institute for Educational Leadership

Intercultural Development Research Associates

Lawyer's Committee for Civil Rights Under the Law

Multicultural Education, Training and Advocacy, Inc. (META)

National Association for Asian and Pacific American Education

National Association for Gifted Children

National Association for the Advancement of Colored People

National Association of Human Rights Workers

National Conference of Christians and Jews

National Council of La Raza

National Education Association

National Fair Housing Alliance

National Parent Teacher Association

National Urban League

National Urban Alliance for Educational Excellence

Parents for Public Schools

Southern Education Foundation

Teaching Tolerance

## Research Partners

Kathryn H. Au, Kamehameha Public Schools

James Banks, University of Washington, Seattle

Jomills H. Braddock, University of Miami

Center for Bilingual and Bicultural Education and Research—Arizona State University

Kenyon Chan, University of California, Northridge

Reginald Clark, California State University, Fullerton

Elizabeth G. Cohen, Stanford University

Robert L. Crain, Columbia University

National Center for Restructuring Education, Schools and
   Teaching, Columbia University

Lisa D. Delpit, Morgan State University

Center for the Applied Study of Ethnoviolence

Edgar Epps, University of Chicago

Ricardo R. Fernandez, City University of New York

Doug Fuchs, Peabody College

Lynn Fuchs, Peabody University

Adam Gamoran, University of Wisconsin, Madison

Geneva Gay, University of Washington, Seattle

Carl Grant, University of Wisconsin, Madison

Jennifer L. Hochchild, Princeton University

Jacqueline Jordan Irvine, Emory University

Geoffrey Maruyama, University of Minnesota

Milbrey McLaughlin, Stanford University

Richard J. Murname, Harvard University

National Center for Research on Cultural Diversity and
   Second Language Learning

M. Susana Navarro, University of Texas, El Paso

Michael T. Nettles, University of Michigan, Ann Arbor

Jeannie Oakes, University of California, Los Angeles

John Ogbu, University of California, Berkeley

Gary Orfield, Harvard University

Amado Padilla, Stanford University

Thomas F. Pettigrew, University of California, Santa Cruz

Vanderbilt Institute for Public Policy Studies

Janet W. Schofield, University of Pittsburgh

Center for Research on Effective Schooling for the Disadvantaged, Johns Hopkins University

Mark A. Smylie, University of Illinois, Chicago

William Trent, University of Illinois, Urbana/Champaign

Anne Wheelock, Center for Improvement in Urban Education, Northeastern University

John F. Witte, University of Wisconsin, Madison

Kenneth Zeichner, University of Wisconsin, Madison

CODA seeks to mobilize action around four general concerns related to improving interracial and interethnic relations. The first concern is to identify barriers to positive interracial and interethnic interaction and ways to overcome them. The second is to search for effective ways to take advantage of the special opportunities for learning and collaboration that interaction among persons of different races and ethnicities afford. These two concerns reflect a priority to seek ways to promote quality learning experiences in racially and ethnically integrated environments.

However, the opportunities that people, especially young people, have to engage in productive interracial and interethnic relationships are limited by racial and ethnic isolation in residential areas and schools. Thus, a third general concern of CODA is to find ways that the students and parents in racially isolated schools and communities can develop the understanding and skills that will facilitate positive interracial and interethnic relationships when such opportunities do arise.

Prejudice and discrimination undermine interracial and interethnic relations in numerous ways. Therefore, a fourth concern that CODA addresses is to identify public policies and practices that limit access by persons of color to quality learning opportunities, wherever these constraints occur.

CODA has been funded by The Lilly Endowment, the George Gund Foundation, the Carnegie Corporation, the Ford Foundation, and other donors. CODA's coordinating activities are based at the University of Maryland at College Park. For further information, write to CODA, College of Education, University of Maryland, College Park, MD 20742, or call (301) 405-2341.

Carnegie Corporation of New York is a philanthropic foundation created by Andrew Carnegie in 1911 "to promote the advancement and diffusion of knowledge and understanding among the people of the United States." Subsequently, its charter was amended to include the use of funds for the same purposes in certain countries that are or have been members of the British overseas Commonwealth. Its basic endowment in 1911 was $135 million; the market value of its assets was approximately $1.11 billion as of July 31, 1994.

# The Editors

Willis D. Hawley is dean of the College of Education and professor of education and of public affairs at the University of Maryland, College Park. From 1980 to 1993 he was professor of education and political science at Vanderbilt University. He served as dean of Peabody College at Vanderbilt until 1989 and then as director of the Center for Education and Human Development Policy at Vanderbilt Institute for Public Policy Studies. He received his Ph.D. in political science, with distinction, from the University of California, Berkeley, in 1970. He taught at Yale and Duke Universities before going to Vanderbilt.

He is the author or coauthor of *Nonpartisan Elections and the Case for Party Politics* (1976), *Theoretical Perspectives on Urban Politics* (1976), *Strategies for Effective School Desegregation: Lessons from Research* (1983), *Good Schools* (1984), and *The Politics of Government Reorganization* (1988). He is finishing a book entitled *Revisioning the Education of Teachers*, to be published by Jossey-Bass.

Hawley has published numerous articles and book chapters dealing with teacher education, school reform, urban politics, political learning, organizational change, and educational policy. His most recent research deals with family influences on the academic performance of Southeast Asian children in the United States, the education of teachers, school restructuring, and race relations. He has edited or coedited several volumes, including the present one, *The Search for Community Power* (1974), *Improving the Quality of Urban Management* (1974), *The Consequences of School Desegregation* (1983), and *Japanese Teacher Education* (1993).

Hawley has served as consultant to numerous public agencies including the U.S. Office of Management and Budget, the U.S. Department of Health, Education and Welfare, the U.S. Senate Committee on Labor and Human Resources, and the U.S. Department of Education, as well as many state and local governments and foundations. In 1977–78 he served as director of Education Studies, President's Reorganization Project, Executive Office of the President of the United States. He is currently working as an adviser to the U.S. Department of Education, to Family Communications, Inc. (producer of the television series *Mr. Roger's Neighborhood*), to *Education Week*, and to the Maryland State Department of Education.

Hawley also directs the Common Destiny Alliance (CODA), a coalition of national organizations and scholars interested in improving intergroup relations.

**Anthony W. Jackson** is a program officer of Carnegie Corporation of New York. He joined the Carnegie staff in October 1989 to develop a grant-making program—the Middle Grade School State Policy Initiative (MGSSPI)—in the area of early adolescent education. Prior to becoming a program officer he was the director of education of adolescents for the Carnegie Council on Adolescent Development. In that capacity he served as the project director and principal writer for the Council's Task Force on Education of Young Adolescents, which issued a major report on restructuring the education of students in middle and junior high schools entitled *Turning Points: Preparing American Youth for the 21st Century.*

Earlier in his career, Jackson was a senior professional staff member of the House Select Committee on Children, Youth and Families. He also served as a legislative aide for representative Ted

Weiss (D–NY). While in graduate school, Jackson served as project director for the National Conference on Black Families and the Medium of Television for the Bush Program in Child Development and Social Policy at the University of Michigan. He received a B.A. degree from the University of California and M.A. and Ph.D. degrees from the University of Michigan. He recently received the Career Achievement Award in Mental Health Policy from the Minority Fellowship Program of the American Psychological Association.

# The Contributors

**James A. Banks** is professor of education and director of the Center for Multicultural Education at the University of Washington, Seattle. He has written or edited fourteen books on multicultural education and on social studies of education. His books include *An Introduction to Multicultural Education: Teaching Strategies for Ethnic Studies*, 5th edition; *Multicultural Education: Issues and Perspectives*, 2nd edition (with Cherry A. McGee Banks); *Multiethnic Education: Theory and Practice*, 2nd edition; and *Teaching Strategies for the Social Studies*, 4th edition. Banks has also written more than a hundred articles, contributions to books, and book reviews for professional publications. He is also coeditor (with Cherry A. McGee Banks) of the *Handbook of Research on Multicultural Education*. Banks received an honorary Doctorate of Humane Letter (L.H.D.) from the Banks Street College of Education in 1993.

**Jomills Henry Braddock II** received his Ph.D. from Florida State University (1973). Prior to joining the University of Miami as professor and chair of sociology, he served as director of the Center of Research on Effective Schooling for Disadvantaged Students at Johns Hopkins University. He has also held faculty/research appointments in the Department of Sociology at the University of Maryland, College Park, and at Johns Hopkins University's Center for Social Organization of Schools/Department of Sociology. His broad research interests in issues of inequality and social justice have been supported by public and private grants and contracts addressing equality of opportunities in education, employment, and sports. His work on these topics typically involves secondary analyses of large-scale national longitudinal data and addresses public policy issues.

**Ana Mari Cauce** is an associate professor in the Department of Psychology, University of Washington, where she is currently director of clinical training. She received her Ph.D. in clinical/community psychology at Yale University (1984) under the mentorship of Edmund W. Gordon.

Cauce's research has primarily focused on factors that influence the socioemotional and adaptive functioning of ethnic minority adolescents and "at-risk" adolescents, such as runaway and homeless youth. At present, Cauce is completing a study, funded by the National Institute of Child Health and Human Development, that employs an ecological model of development to explore familial and extrafamilial factors contributing to competence in African and Asian American young adolescents. She is also in the final year of a longitudinal study, funded by the National Institute of Mental Health/Center for Mental Health Services, investigating the effectiveness of a case management intervention with homeless youth. This latter project reflects her emergent interest in services research.

Cauce also has interests in social policy affecting children and families, and has provided service to various local and national panels and advisory boards. This service includes work with the Alliance for Children, Youth, and Families of Washington; the Washington Council for the Prevention of Child Abuse and Neglect; the CONSEJO Counseling and Referral Service; the National Institute of Mental Health; the American Psychological

Association; the Florida Mental Health Institute; and the National Academy of Sciences.

**Kenyon S. Chan** is professor and chair of the Asian American Studies Department at the California State University, Northridge. He also serves as president of the Association for Asian American Studies. He received his Ph.D. in educational psychology from the University of California, Los Angeles, in 1974.

**Cynthia T. García Coll** is director of The Stone Center for Developmental Services and Studies at Wellesley College, research psychologist at Women and Infants Hospital of Rhode Island, associate professor of pediatrics for the Brown University Program in Medicine, and adjunct assistant professor of psychology at Brown University. She has authored more than forty-five published articles focusing on multiculturalism, early childhood development, and teenage pregnancy. She has also coauthored a book entitled *The Psychosocial Development of Puerto Rican Women* and is currently coeditor of a special issue of *Child Development* highlighting children and poverty, coinvestigator of a Maternal and Child Health (MCH)-sponsored grant entitled "Longitudinal Study of the Growth and Development of African American and Puerto Rican Children," and consultant at Better Homes Foundation for a population-based study on homelessness.

**Peter T. Coleman,** an advanced doctoral student in social/ organizational psychology at Teachers College, Columbia University, works as a mediation and negotiation trainer for the International Center for Cooperation and Conflict Resolution and as a community mediator for the Queens Mediation Center in New York City. He also teaches organizational psychology at Barnard College, Columbia University.

**William E. Cross, Jr.,** received his doctorate in psychology from Princeton University (1976) and is currently an associate professor of African American Studies and Psychology at the Africana Studies and Research Center, Cornell University. He is considered one of the leading experts on the study of African American identity, and his long-awaited scholarly text on this topic was published in 1991: *Shades of Black: Diversity in African-American Identity*. His model of African American identity development has been the focus of countless essays and numerous empirical studies, and the distinction he makes between personal identity and group identity in the dynamics of African American identity is the focus of a great deal of scholarly debate within the fields of psychology and African American Studies. At Cornell, Cross teaches two very popular courses—one on the family and African American identity development, and the other on the history of African American education.

**Marvin P. Dawkins** is associate professor of sociology and director of the Caribbean, African and Afro-American Studies Program at the University of Miami. He received a B.S. degree in social sciences from Edward Waters College and a Ph.D. in sociology from Florida State University. In the latter field of study he specialized in race and ethnic relations and the interdisciplinary study of urban minority problems. Dawkins's most recent research has focused on the impact of school desegregation on long-term life consequences, on substance abuse and its prevention among African Americans, and on economic boycotts in racial disputes.

**Morton Deutsch** is E. L. Thorndike Professor Emeritus and director of the International Center for Cooperation and Conflict Resolution at Teachers College, Columbia University. He has received many honors and awards for his research and scholarly writings on cooperation and competition, conflict resolution and social justice.

**Eugene E. Garcia** is director of the Office of Bilingual Education and Minority Languages Affairs at the U.S. Department of Education in Washington, D.C. Dr. Garcia is on leave from his post as dean of the Division of Social Sciences and as professor of education and psychology at the University of California, Santa Cruz. He earned his B.A. in psychology from the University of Utah and his Ph.D. in human development from the University of Kansas.

**Heidie A. Vázquez García** is a research assistant at The Stone Center for Developmental Services and Studies at Wellesley College. Currently she is working on a number of research projects, including one entitled "The Normative Development of Puerto Rican Adolescents and the Boston After School Experiences Study," and is a consultant for other Center programs. She has coauthored an article on Hispanic children and poverty, and is now working on several other manuscripts as well. She received her B.A. degree in psychology from Brown University in 1993.

**Nancy A. Gonzales** received her Ph.D. in clinical psychology from the University of Washington in 1992. Upon graduating she received the "Jeffrey S. Tanaka, Ph.D., Memorial Dissertation Award" for her dissertation work entitled "Family Influences on Adolescent Adjustment Within African-American Families." She has since taken a position as assistant professor of psychology at Arizona State University, where she is affiliated with the Prevention Intervention Research Center and the Hispanic Research Center. Her research interests include ethnic minority mental health, family influences on adolescent development, and prevention research.

**Shirley Brice Heath** is a linguistic anthropologist whose primary interests are language acquisition, sociocultural contexts of learning, and relations between oral/written language and acting/thinking across cultures and institutional settings. She began her career teaching bilingual students and maintains an active involvement with language minority students and their teachers, working with them in collaborative inquiry and classroom interventions. Her primary research since 1989 has been conducted in inner-city youth organizations and in the workplaces of young people, where she has documented the organizational structures and communication that surround everyday learning and progression in complex task achievement. At Stanford University she is a professor in the English and Linguistics Departments, with courtesy appointments in anthropology and the School of Education.

**Shirley Hune** is professor of urban planning and associate dean in the graduate division for graduate programs at the University of California, Los Angeles. She served as president of the Association for Asian American Studies from 1987 to 1989 and received her Ph.D. in American civilization from George Washington University in 1979.

**Aída Hurtado** is associate professor of psychology at the University of California, Santa Cruz. Her research focuses on the effects of subordination on social identity. She is especially interested in group memberships, such as ethnicity, race, class, and gender, that are used to legitimize unequal distribution of power between groups. Hurtado has expertise in survey methods with bilingual/bicultural populations. She has published extensively on issues of language and social identity for the Mexican-origin population in the United States. Hurtado received her B.A. in psychology and sociology from Pan American University in Edinburg, Texas, and her M.A. and Ph.D. in social psychology from the University of Michigan.

**James Lynch** is an education expert with the World Bank in Washington, D.C. He is a former elementary school teacher, professor, and dean of education in the United Kingdom. He has also been visiting professor at the universities of Frankfurt, Germany, Washington, Seattle, and Graz, Austria. He is currently working on projects in China and francophone Africa, and is task manager of a major regional study of children with special educational needs. He has published many books and papers on issues of cultural diversity and has acted as an adviser to governments and international agencies in both developed and developing countries. His most recent publications are *Cultural Diversity and the Schools* (1993), coedited by Sohan and Celia Modgil; *Education for Citizenship in a Multicultural Society* (1992); *Multicultural Education in a Global Society* (1991); and *Prejudice Reduction and the Schools* (1987).

**Amado M. Padilla** received his Ph.D. in experimental psychology from the University of New Mexico. He is professor of Psychological Studies in Education and chair of the Language, Literacy, and Culture Program in the School of Education at Stanford University. Previously, he directed two national research centers, the Center for Language Education and Research and the Spanish-speaking Mental Health Research Center at the University of California at Los Angeles, where he served as professor of psychology from 1974 to 1988. His current research interests include the social adaptation of immigrants and their children to American society and the acquisition and teaching of second languages to adolescents and adults. He was founding editor of the *Hispanic Journal of Behavioral Sciences*, which is currently in its sixteenth year of publication. He has published extensively in numerous areas, including bilingualism and Hispanic mental health. His books include *Latino Mental Health* (1973), *Crossing Cultures in Therapy* (1980), *Acculturation* (1980), *Chicano Ethnicity* (1987), *Introduction to Psychology* (1989), *Bilingual Education* (1991), and *Foreign Language Education* (1991).

**Donald B. Pope-Davis** is an associate professor in the Department of Counseling and Personnel Services at the University of Maryland, College Park. He received his doctorate in counseling psychology from Stanford University. His area of research and interest is in multicultural education, counseling, and training for cultural competence.

**Janet Ward Schofield** is a professor of psychology and a senior scientist in the Learning Research and Development Center at the

University of Pittsburgh. She has also served as a faculty member at Spelman College and in policy research positions at the National Institute of Education and the Office of Economic Opportunity. She received a B.A. magma cum laude from Radcliffe College, where she was elected to Phi Beta Kappa. She received her Ph.D. from Harvard University in 1972. Schofield is a social psychologist whose major research interest for more than two decades has been social processes in desegregated schools. She has authored or coauthored more than two dozen papers in this area as well as two books. One of these—*Black and White in School: Trust, Tension or Tolerance?*—was awarded the Society for the Psychological Study of Social Issues' Gordon Allport Intergroup Relations Prize.

**Robert E. Slavin** is currently director of the Early and Elementary School Program at the Center for Research on Effective Schooling for Disadvantaged Students at Johns Hopkins University. He received his B.A. in psychology from Reed College in 1972 and his Ph.D. in social relations from Johns Hopkins University in 1975. Slavin has authored or coauthored more than 140 articles and 14 books, including *Educational Psychology: Theory into Practice* (1986, 1988, 1991, 1994), *School and Classroom Organization* (1989), *Effective Programs for Students at Risk* (1989), *Cooperative Learning: Theory, Research, and Practice* (1990, 1995), and *Preventing Early School Failure* (1994). He received the American Educational Research Association's Raymond B. Cattell Early Career Award for Programmatic Research in 1986, and the Palmer O. Johnson award for the best article in an AERA journal in 1988.

**Judith Torney-Purta** is professor of human development in the College of Education at the University of Maryland, College Park. She received an B.A. in psychology from Stanford University in 1959 and an M.A. and Ph.D. in Human Development from the University of Chicago in 1962 and 1965, respectively. She has authored three books and many articles, chapters, and conference papers on education and developmental psychology in the United States and

Western Europe. She is currently a member of the Board on International Comparative Studies in Education, organized under the Commission on Behavioral and Social Sciences of the National Research Council (National Academy of Sciences), and previously served as a member of the Task on Youth Development and Community Programs of the Carnegie Council on Adolescent Development. She is also a fellow of the American Psychological Association and of the American Psychological Society.

**David Tyack** is Vida Jacks Professor of Education and professor of history at Stanford University. Since writing a study of Cape Verdean immigration to the United States in 1952, he has sought to relate the history of racial and ethnic diversity to the social history of public schooling.

**George Wilson** is an assistant professor of sociology at the University of Miami. His current research interests focus on the institutional production of racial and ethnic inequality in the workplace and the social structural determinants of beliefs about the causes of economic and racial inequality.

**Kenneth M. Zeichner** is Hoefs-Bascom Professor of Teacher Education in the Department of Curriculum and Instruction at the University of Wisconsin, Madison, and a senior researcher in the National Center for Research on Teacher Learning at Michigan State University. He received a B.B.A. in pre-law from Temple University in 1969, an M.A. in urban education from Syracuse University in 1970, and a Ph.D. in school organizational behavior and change/teacher education from Syracuse University in 1976. Zeichner's areas of expertise include clinical teacher education, teacher supervision, and preparation of teachers for cultural diversity, particularly in urban schools. His recent publications include *Teacher Education and the Social Conditions of Schooling*, with Dan Liston; *Issues and Practices in Inquiry-Oriented Teacher Education*, with Bob Tabachnick; *Educating Teachers for Cultural Diversity* (National Center for Research on Teacher Learning); and "Traditions of Practice in U.S. Teacher Education" in *Teaching and Teacher Education*. Zeichner serves on the editorial boards of several major journals in teacher education and has published his work not only in North America but in Europe, Asia, and Australia as well.

# Index